Non-Marxian Historical Materialism: Reconstructions and Comparisons

Poznań Studies in the Philosophy of the Sciences and the Humanities

Founding Editor
Leszek Nowak (1943–2009)

Editor-in-Chief
Katarzyna Paprzycka-Hausman (*University of Warsaw*)

Editors
Tomasz Bigaj (*University of Warsaw*) – Krzysztof Brzechczyn
(*Adam Mickiewicz University*) – Jerzy Brzeziński (*Adam Mickiewicz
University*) – Krzysztof Łastowski (*Adam Mickiewicz University*) –
Joanna Odrowąż-Sypniewska (*University of Warsaw*) – Piotr Przybysz
(*Adam Mickiewicz University*) – Mieszko Tałasiewicz (*University of Warsaw*) –
Krzysztof Wójtowicz (*University of Warsaw*)

Advisory Committee

Joseph Agassi (*Tel-Aviv*) – Wolfgang Balzer (*Munchen*) – Mario Bunge
(*Montreal*) – Robert S. Cohen†(*Boston*) – Francesco Coniglione (*Catania*) –
Dagfinn Follesdal (*Oslo, Stanford*) – Jacek J. Jadacki (*Warszawa*) – Andrzej
Klawiter (*Poznań*) – Theo A.F. Kuipers (*Groningen*) – Witold Marciszewski
(*Warszawa*) – Thomas Müller (*Konstanz*) – Ilkka Niiniluoto (*Helsinki*) – Jacek
Paśniczek (*Lublin*) – David Pearce (*Madrid*) – Jan Such (*Poznań*) – Max Urchs
(*Wiesbaden*) – Jan Woleński (*Krakow*) – Ryszard Wójcicki (*Warszawa*)

VOLUME 120

The titles published in this series are listed at *brill.com/ps*

Non-Marxian Historical Materialism: Reconstructions and Comparisons

Edited by

Krzysztof Brzechczyn

BRILL

LEIDEN | BOSTON

Cover illustration: photograph by Kirk Lai, published in 2019 via unsplash.com.

This publication was financially supported by the previous Institute of Philosophy and Faculty of Social Sciences and the present Faculty of Philosophy, Adam Mickiewicz University in Poznań, Poland.

The Library of Congress Cataloging-in-Publication Data is available online at https://catalog.loc.gov

Typeface for the Latin, Greek, and Cyrillic scripts: "Brill". See and download: brill.com/brill-typeface.

ISSN 0303-8157
ISBN 978-90-04-50726-5 (hardback)
ISBN 978-90-04-50729-6 (e-book)

Copyright 2022 by Krzysztof Brzechczyn. Published by Koninklijke Brill NV, Leiden, The Netherlands.
Koninklijke Brill NV incorporates the imprints Brill, Brill Nijhoff, Brill Hotei, Brill Schöningh, Brill Fink, Brill mentis, Vandenhoeck & Ruprecht, Böhlau and V&R unipress.
Koninklijke Brill NV reserves the right to protect this publication against unauthorized use. Requests for re-use and/or translations must be addressed to Koninklijke Brill NV via brill.com or copyright.com.

This book is printed on acid-free paper and produced in a sustainable manner.

Contents

Preface   VII
  Krzysztof Brzechczyn
List of Tables and Figures   XV
Notes on Contributors   XVI

PART 1
On Methodology of Non-Marxian Historical Materialism

1 Reflections on the Historiosophical System of Non-Marxian Historical
   Materialism   3
     Jerzy Topolski

2 Leszek Nowak's Historiosophy from Historical and Systematical
   Perspectives   16
     Waldemar Czajkowski

3 Modeling the Dynamics of the Social Process in the Philosophy of
   Liberalism: Leszek Nowak's Critique of Liberal Historiosophy   40
     Piotr Przybysz

4 An Analysis of the Methodology of Leszek Nowak's Non-Marxian
   Historical Materialism   57
     Krzysztof Kiedrowski

5 The Paraphrase Method in Leszek Nowak's Interhuman Model of
   Man   84
     Aleksandra Gomułczak

PART 2
Non-Marxian Historical Materialism: Paraphrases and Comparisons

6 The Class Structure of Hydraulic Societies: An Attempt at a Paraphrase
   of Karl August Witttfogel's Theory in the Conceptual Framework of
   Non-Marxian Historical Materialism   111
     Tomasz Zarębski

7 The Image of a Social Structure in *Manusmṛti:* An Attempt at a
   Theoretical Analysis   127
     Marta Bręgiel-Pant

8 A Victorious Revolution and a Lost Modernization: An Attempt
   to Paraphrase Theda Skocpol's Theory of Social Revolution in the
   Conceptual Apparatus of Non-Marxian Historical Materialism   161
     Krzysztof Brzechczyn

9 The Elitarian versus Class Theory of Democracy: An Attempt to
   Paraphrase the Mechanism of the Absorption of the Elites from Eva
   Etzioni-Halevy's Theory in the Conceptual Apparatus of Non-Marxian
   Historical Materialism   195
     Karolina Rutkowska

10 Leszek Nowak's non-Marxian Historical Materialism and Pareto's Elite
    Theory: Similarities and Differences   216
      Giacomo Borbone

11 The Iron Law of Oligarchy versus the Rule of Political Competition: An
    Attempt at a Comparison between Robert Michels' and Leszek Nowak's
    Approaches to Power   238
      Regina Menke

12 The Social Role of the Ceremonial: Andrzej Falkiewicz's Conception of
    Culture and the Theory of the Spiritual Momentum in Non-Marxian
    Historical Materialism   258
      Iwo Greczko

    Index of Names   277
    Subject Index   280

Preface

The indication of the autonomous conflict between political (and spiritual) classes, being one of the principal factors of the historical process in non-Marxian historical materialism, broadens the set of main factors assumed in Marxian materialism. According to Leszek Nowak, the mechanism of political class struggle (between the class of rulers and the class of citizens) modifies Marxian historical materialism (in the slavery, feudal and capitalist formations) where the mechanism of economic class struggle was recognized the most important factor. However, in the case of supra-class societies (late capitalism and socialism) social divisions accumulated and the mechanism of political class struggle is becoming the principal factor of the historical process. The conceptualization of the development of such societies leads to the non-Marxian theory of historical process. Therefore, according to Nowak: "Marxian historical materialism is a dialectically retarded theory" (Nowak 1985a, p. 82, see also: Nowak 1985b, pp. 145–147), when viewed from the perspective of non-Marxian historical materialism.

In my foreword, I would like to compare these two theories, with an emphasis not on their methodological connection but on their meta-theoretical assumptions: holism, antagonicity, and materiality.[1]

Holism is one of the characteristic features of Marx's historical materialism. Like any other theory of such a broad scope, Marx's theory presents a holistic vision of the past, from the original community, through slavery, feudalism, and capitalism, to socialism and communism. Thus, historical materialism can function as a simplified map of the historical process and social structures, and provide initial guidance for the participants of social life.

Another characteristic of Marxism is a conflict-based vision of society, which makes it possible to explain, among other things, social change. In the original Marxian theory, the existence of one actual axis of conflict – which runs through the economy – is assumed. Cultural wars, inter-civilizational conflicts, and democratic revolutions will be explained when those phenomena are successfully reduced to the economic sphere and the social interests of economically understood social classes.

The third feature of Marxism is the search for the material foundations of social life. Marx only looked for them in the economic sphere and interests.

---

1 An example of another meta-theoretical analysis of non-Marxian historical materialism, see: Ciesielski 2016. It is worth noting that materialist understanding of history was not only present of European philosophy of history in modern times. For a discussion of ancient materialism in Chinese social thought, see: Rogacz 2021.

Contemporary social scientists search for them by *deepening* and/or *broadening* the initial theory. For example, in sociology, materiality is *deepened* by exploring the biological foundations of social life. In comparative historical sociology, Marxian intuitions are *broadened* by associating them with Max Weber's concepts. Within the framework of that scientific subdiscipline, the mutual autonomy and independence of the economy, politics, and culture is assumed (Brzechczyn 2007b).

The generalization of the concept of class divisions leads to radicalization (in comparison with historical materialism), and thus deepens its *antagonicity*. In n-Mhm, it is assumed that politics, culture, and the economy have similar internal structures (Nowak 1983; 1991). In each of them, there are certain material social means: the means of production in the economy, the means of indoctrination in culture, and the means of coercion in politics. It is also assumed that in each domain it is possible to distinguish two social groups. The basis of this division is the relation to the material means, with one group being a minority which has at its disposal the respective material social means, and which decides as to how they will be used, and with one being a majority without such influence. In each area of human activity, there is a conflict of interest between the minority group and the majority group (priests and the indoctrinated in culture, the owners and direct producers in economy, and the rulers and citizens in politics). It is in the priests' interest to increase their spiritual authority at the cost of the followers' spiritual autonomy, in the owners' interest – to increase surplus product at the cost of the variable capital available to direct producers, and in the rulers' interest – to increase power regulation at the cost of citizens' political autonomy. Political conflict is autonomous and cannot be reduced to the social conflicts present in other areas of social life. The abovementioned social divisions may accumulate, and one social class can have at its disposal the means of coercion, production, and indoctrination, at the same time. One example of such a system in which power has been accumulated is real socialism, where a class of triple-lords (the party-state apparatus) controls the means of coercion, production, and mass communication.

Both concepts are historiosophical theories of a broad scope. In principle, the development scheme assumed in historical materialism (slave formation – feudalism – capitalism – socialism) describes the lines of development of societies from the European civilization. The peculiarities of the development of societies outside of Europe are to be explained in the so-called Asian social formation.

Non-Marxian historical materialism is capable of interpreting over 2,500 years of the history of European societies. In contrast to classic historical materialism, n-Mhm is not a universalistic or dualistic concept – but a pluralistic one (Brzechczyn 2006). In its conceptual apparatus, one can generate eighteen types of societies and separate lines of developments (Brzechczyn 2004; 2007a).

The basic distinguishing feature of Western European societies was the separation of social classes – the rulers, owners, and priests – and the preservation of balance among them. That balance was significantly disturbed in the history of Russia. The political and economic powers were accumulated there twice, during the reigns of Ivan the Terrible and Peter the Great.

The accumulation of various class divisions did occur in the history of non-European societies, over longer periods of time and to a greater degree. Still, Western European societies are not somehow immune to processes leading to the accumulation of political, economic, and spiritual class divsions (Nowak 1989; Ciesielski 2013, 2022; Zarębski 2003; 2022). The differences between European and non-European societies in that regard are quantitative and not qualitative in nature. That is why it seems that non-Marxian historical materialism can avoid the charge of Eurocentrism (Rogacz 2019, pp. 45–69). First, that theory is not a universalistic historiosophy which would indiscriminately apply the European development model to the history of non-European societies. Second, n-Mhm is not even a dualistic historiosophy which would assume a constant, immutable division into the West and the rest – it is a pluralistic theory which postulates a multiplicity of development lines. Third, class divisions have been accumulated in the history of Western and Central European societies as well (Brzechczyn 1993; 2020).

Let us add that non-Marxian historical materialism was partially used for interpreting the history of the Mexican (Brzechczyn 2004), Ottoman (Karczyńska 2013; 2022), and Chinese (Rogacz 2016; 2022) societies, and even of the social divisions presented in the Hindu religious treaty *Manusmriti* (Bręgiel-Benedyk 2013; Bręgiel-Pant 2022).

It follows that the generalization of the concept of class divisions can be an example of the *strengthening* of the approach based on social antagonicity, and of the *broadening* of the material foundations of the historical process. The *deepening* of the theory of the historical process would be the creation of the anthropological foundations of non-Marxian historical materialism, by disclosing the limitations of the rationalistic concept of the individual. Nowak distinguishes three areas of interpersonal relations: The normal realm is ruled by the principle of mutuality. An individual responds with hostility to hostility from the partner of the interaction, and repays kindness with kindness. However, the more evil that the person has experienced, the weaker the tendency to respond in kind becomes. In the final stage of this process – the enslavement phase – the individual gives up his or her own preferences for the sake of the oppressors' ones. On the other hand, when an individual experiences more and more good, his or her proclivity to respond in the same way diminishes. In the final stage of that process – the depravation phase – the individual likewise relinquishes the realization of their preferences; instead, the counter-preferences of the partner of the interaction are followed.

This volume *Non-Marxian Historical Materialism: Reconstructions and Comparisons* can be considered to be a continuation of the book *New Developments in Theory of Historical Process. Polish Contributions to non-Marxian Historical Materialism* published as volume 119 of *Poznań Studies in the Philosophy of the Sciences and the Humanities.* This book is divided into two parts. In the first part "On methodology of non-Marxian historical materialism," the meta-theoretical and methodological assumptions of non-Marxian historical materialism are analyzed. In the second part, "Non-Marxian historical materialism: Paraphrases and Comparisons" the content of this theory is discussed in the context of other social theories, by way of a paraphrase or comparison.

In "Reflections on the Historiosophical System of non-Marxian Historical Materialism," Jerzy Topolski emphasizes the openness and anti-finalism of n-Mhm. In Nowak's theory, there is no final point of history toward which it would head. In Topolski's approach, that is an advantage of this theoretical framework. Waldemar Czajkowski ("Leszek Nowak's Historiosophy from Historical and Systematical Perspectives") considers non-Marxian historical materialism from two points of view. In the historical perspective, n-Mhm is a continuation of the analytical branch of Polish philosophy, begun by the Lwów–Warsaw School. From the systematic point of view, Nowak's theory can be compared with the theories of Immanuel Wallerstein and André Gunder Frank. In the article "Modeling the Dynamics of the Social Process in the Philosophy of Liberalism: Leszek Nowak's Critique of Liberal Historiosophy," Piotr Przybysz reconstructs Leszek Nowak's views on the historiosophy of liberalism. In the first part of his paper, the author reconstructs Nowak's interpretation of the anthropological and social assumptions of liberal historiosophy. In the second part, Przybysz reconstructs the libertarian model of the evolution of state institutions from anarchy to the minimal state presented by Robert Nozick. In the third part of the paper, Przybysz compares Nozick and Nowak's approach to modeling the historical process and analyzes the relation between normative and descriptive levels in both approaches.

The authors of the two subsequent articles in that part analyze the methodology of non-Marxian historical materialism. In his article "An Analysis of the Methodology of Leszek Nowak's Non-Marxian Historical Materialism," Krzysztof Kiedrowski presents the methodological structure of the theory of

PREFACE

power, ownership, and spiritual supremacy. In Kiedrowski's view, Nowak made use of not only idealization and concretization but also of similar procedures of abstraction, stabilization and destabilization. Aleksandra Gomułczak, in the article "The Paraphrase Method in Leszek Nowak's Interhuman Model of Man," discusses the peculiarities of the paraphrase method as one of the ways of developing non-Marxian historical materialism.

In the second part of the book, the authors make use of the methods of interpretation, paraphrase, and comparison to test the explanatory power of non-Marxian historical materialism. Those methods lead to either a broadened application of n-Mhm or such a development of the conceptual apparatus of non-Marxian historical materialism as allows the interpretation of the selected point of reference. A comparison of non-Marxian historical materialism with other theories and concepts makes it possible to indicate the differences between them and subsequent ways in which non-Marxian historical materialism may be developed.

The first strategy was used by Tomasz Zarębski and Marta Bręgiel-Pant. In his article "The Class Structure of Hydraulic Societies: an Attempt at a Paraphrase of Karl August Wittfogel's Theory in the Conceptual Framework of Non-Marxian Historical Materialism," Zarębski paraphrases various variants simple of hydraulic societies: semicomplex, complex, theocratic and quasi-hierocratic. In the article "The Image of a Social Structure in *Manusmriti*. An Attempt at a Theoretical Analysis" Marta Bręgiel-Pant interprets class divisions in the Indian normative text *Manusmriti*.

Krzysztof Brzechczyn ("A Victorious Revolution and a Lost Modernization: An Attempt to Paraphrase Theda Skocpol's Theory of Social Revolution in the Conceptual Apparatus of Non-Marxian Historical Materialism") and Karolina Rutkowska ("The Elitarian versus Class Theory of Democracy: an Attempt to Paraphrase the Mechanism of the Absorption of the Elites from Eva Etzioni-Halevy's Theory in the Conceptual Apparatus of Non-Marxian Historical Materialism") develop the framework of this theory (with, respectively, the concept of class symbiosis and of elite absorption) in a way that makes it possible to paraphrase the Theda Skocpol's concept of agrarian bureaucracies and Eva Etzioni-Halevy's concept of the co-optation of social elites.

In next two articles, Nowak's theory is compared to the concepts of two classical thinkers of the theory of elites: Robert Michels and Vilfredo Pareto. Giacomo Borbone, in the article "Leszek Nowak's non-Marxian Historical Materialism and Pareto's Élite-Theory: Similarities and Differences," compares Nowak's theory with the thought of Pareto, who created the theory of elites, and he points to the similarity between Pareto's concept of circulation and

Nowak's concept of cyclical revolutions. As regards the differences between them, Borbone notes their explanations of the political phenomena mentioned above: Nowak refers to political mechanisms, and Pareto – to psychological and cultural ones.

In the article "The Iron Law of Oligarchy versus the Rule of Political Competition: an Attempt at a Comparison between Robert Michels's and Leszek Nowak's Approaches to Power," Regina Menke demonstrates the relation between Robert Michels's concept of social and political processes, with its emphasis on the constant trend toward the oligarchization of politics in contemporary democracy, and Nowak's theory of power. The differences lie in the explanations of the said social and political processes. Michels ascribes oligarchization to, among other things, insufficient education, while Nowak explains it with the mechanism of political competition.

The last article in the volume is Iwo Greczko's "The Social Role of the Ceremonial: Andrzej Falkiewicz's Conception of Culture and the Theory of Spiritual Momentum in Non-Marxian Historical Materialism." Its author compares the two theories of culture authored by Falkiewicz and Nowak. Falkiewicz viewed culture in solidaristic way as the main domain of social life and the base of other social practices. For Nowak, the cultural momentum, conceptualized in an antagonistic way, was one of the three momentums of social life.

Krzysztof Brzechczyn

References

Bręgiel-Benedyk, M. (2013). Obraz struktury społecznej w *Manusmryti*. Próba analizy teoretycznej In: K. Brzechczyn, M. Ciesielski, E. Karczyńska (eds.). *Jednostka w układzie społecznym. Próba teoretycznej konceptualizacji*, pp. 291–319. Poznań: Wyd. Naukowe WNS UAM.

Bręgiel-Pant, M. (2022). The Image of a Social Structure in *Manusmṛti*: An Attempt at a Theoretical Analysis. In: K. Brzechczyn (ed.) *Non-Marxian Historical Materialism: Reconstructions and Comparisons*. Poznań Studies in the Philosophy of the Sciences and the Humanities, vol. 120, pp. 127–160. Leiden/Boston: Brill.

Brzechczyn, K. (1993). The State of the Teutonic Order as Socialist Society. In: L. Nowak, M. Paprzycki (eds.) *Social System, Rationality and Revolution. Poznań Studies in the Philosophy of the Sciences and the Humanities*, vol. 33, pp. 397–417. Amsterdam – Atlanta, GA: Rodopi.

Brzechczyn (2004). *O wielości linii rozwojowych w procesie historycznym. Próba interpretacji ewolucji społeczeństwa meksykańskiego* [On the Multitude of the Lines of

PREFACE

Developments in the Historical Process: An Attempt at Interpretation of Evolution of Mexican Society]. Poznań: Wydawnictwo Naukowe UAM.

Brzechczyn (2006). Obrazy przeszłości a filozoficzne wizje historii [The Pictures of the Past and the Philosophical Visions of History]. In: K. Łastowski, P. Zeidler (eds.) Filozofia wobec nauki, człowieka i społeczeństwa, pp. 55–75. Poznań: WN IF UAM.

Brzechczyn, K. (2007a). On the Application of Non-Marxian Historical Materialism to the Development of Non-European Societies. In: J. Brzeziński, A. Klawiter, T.A.F. Kuipers, K. Łastowski, K. Paprzycka, P. Przybysz (eds.), *The Courage of Doing Philosophy. Essays Presented to Leszek Nowak*, pp. 235–254. Amsterdam-Atlanta: Rodopi.

Brzechczyn, K. (2007b). Rozwój teorii rewolucji w socjologii historyczno-porównaw-czej. Próba analizy metodologicznej [Development of the Theory of Revolution in Historical-Comparative Sociology: An Attempt at Methodological Analysis]. In: K. Brzechczyn, M. Nowak (eds.), *O rewolucji. Obrazy radykalnej zmiany społecznej* , pp. 37–64. Poznan: WN IF UAM.

Brzechczyn, K. (2020). *The Historical Distinctiveness of Central Europe: A Study in Philosophy of History*, Berlin: Peter Lang.

Ciesielski, M. (2013). Problem kumulacji podziałów klasowych we współczesnym kap-italizmie. Próba interpretacji teoretycznej [The Problem of the Accumulation of Class Divisions in Modern Capitalism. An Attempt at a Theoretical Interpretation]. In: K. Brzechczyn, M. Ciesielski, E. Karczyńska (eds.). *Jednostka w układzie społec-znym. Próba teoretycznej konceptualizacji,* pp. 131–152. Poznań: Wyd. Naukowe WNS UAM.

Ciesielski, M. (2016). O integracji opozycyjnych paradygmatów nauk społecznych. Próba rewizji założeń nie-Marksowskiego materializmu historycznego [Towards a Theory Integrating Contradictory Paradigms of Social Sciences. An Attempt at a Revision of Assumptions of non-Marxian Historical Materialism]. *Człowiek i Społeczeństwo* (special issue: Modelowanie świata społecznego. Założenia – rekon-strukcje – analizy, ed. by K. Brzechczyn), 42, 73–91.

Ciesielski, M. (2022). The Problem of the Accumulation of Class Divisions in Contemporary Capitalism: An Attempt at a Theoretical Analysis. In: K. Brzechczyn (ed.) *New Developments in the Theory of the Historical Process. Polish Contributions to Non-Marxian Historical Materialism*. Poznań Studies in the Philosophy of the Sciences and the Humanities, vol. 119, pp. 217–238. Leiden/Boston: Brill.

Karczyńska, E. (2013). Struktura społeczna Imperium Osmańskiego. Próba analizy teo-retycznej [The Social Structure of the Ottoman Empire. An Attempt at Theoretical Analysis]. In: K. Brzechczyn, M. Ciesielski, E. Karczyńska (eds.). *Jednostka w układzie społecznym. Próba teoretycznej konceptualizacji,* pp. 273–290. Poznań: Wyd. Naukowe WNS UAM.

Karczyńska, E. (2022). The Social Structure of the Ottoman Society: An Attempt at a Theoretical Analysis. In: K. Brzechczyn (ed.) *New Developments in the Theory of the Historical Process. Polish Contributions to Non-Marxian Historical Materialism.* Poznań Studies in the Philosophy of the Sciences and the Humanities, vol. 119, pp. 294–313. Leiden/Boston: Brill.

Nowak, L. (1983). *Property and Power. Towards a non-Marxian Historical Materialism.* Dordrecht: Reidel.

Nowak, L. (1985a). Marxian Historical Materialism: The Case of Dialectical Retardation. In: B. Chavance (ed.). *Marx en Perspective,* pp. 77–95. Paris: Éditions de l'École des Hautes Études en Sciences Sociales.

Nowak, L. (1985b). O konieczności socjalizmu i jego zaniku [On Necessity of Socialism and its Disappearance]. *Przyjaciel Nauk. Studia z Teorii i Krytyki Społecznej* , 1–2, 105–150.

Nowak L. (1989). An Idealizational Model of Capitalist Society. In: L. Nowak (ed.), *Dimensions of the Historical Process. Poznań Studies in the Philosophy of the Sciences and the Humanities,* vol. 13, pp. 217–258. Amsterdam: Rodopi.

Nowak L. (1991). *Power and Civil Society. Toward a Dynamic Theory of Real Socialism.* New York: Greenwood Press.

Rogacz, D. (2016). Dynamika władzy w powojennych Chinach. Próba analizy teoretycznej [Dynamics of Power in Post-War China. An Attempt at Theoretical Analysis]. *Człowiek i Społeczeństwo* (special issue: Modelowanie świata społecznego. Założenia – rekonstrukcje – analizy, ed. by K. Brzechczyn), 42, 161–181.

Rogacz, D. (2019). *Chińska filozofia historii. Od początków do końca XVIII wieku* [Chinese Philosophy of History. From the Beginnings to the End of the Eighteenth Century]. Poznań: Wydawnictwo Naukowe UAM.

Rogacz, D. (2021). Historical Materialism in Medieval China: The Cases of Liu Zongyuan (773–819) and Li Gou (1009–1059). *Asian Philosophy,* /doi.org/10.1080/09552367.2021.1924437.

Rogacz, D. (2022). The Dynamics of Power in Postwar China: An Attempt at a Theoretical Analysis. In: K. Brzechczyn (ed.) *New Developments in the Theory of the Historical Process. Polish Contributions to Non-Marxian Historical Materialism.* Poznań Studies in the Philosophy of the Sciences and the Humanities, vol. 119, pp. 314–334. Leiden/Boston: Brill.

Zarębski, T. (2003). Problem totalitaryzacji kapitalizmu [The Problem of Totalitarization of Capitalism]. In: K. Brzechczyn (ed.) *Ścieżki transformacji. Ujęcia teoretyczne i opisy empiryczne,* pp. 229–260. Poznań: Zysk i S-ka.

Zarębski, T. (2022), The Problem of Totalitarization of the Capitalist Society. In: K. Brzechczyn (ed.), *New Developments in the Theory of the Historical Process. Polish Contributions to Non-Marxian Historical Materialism.* Poznań Studies in the Philosophy of the Sciences and the Humanities, vol. 120, pp. 127–160. Leiden/Boston: Brill.

Tables and Figures

Tables

4.1 The realistic and idealizing assumptions in the subsequent models of the theory of property 62

4.2 The variants of model III of the theory of property 64

4.3 The realistic and idealizing assumptions in the subsequent models of the theory of power 69

7.1 Basic determinants of ideological and utopian thinking 134

9.1 A comparison of Nowak's and Etzioni-Halevy's theories 208

12.1 A comparison of Falkiewicz's conception of culture and the theory of the spiritual momentum in Non-Marxian historical materialism 273

Figures

4.1 The structure of the theory of property within the framework of non-Marxian historical materialism 66

4.2 The structure of the theory of power within the framework of non-Marxian historical materialism 71

4.3 The methodological architecture of the core of non-Marxian historical materialism 79

6.1 The classification of hydraulic societies in terms of the presence of private ownership 118

6.2 The classification of hydraulic societies in terms of the relations between politics and religion 118

8 1 The social structure of an agrarian bureaucracy. Abbreviations used: ↔ common social interests; → conflict of social interests 168

8.2 A model of social revolution 174

10.1 The structure of economical momentum 219

Notes on Contributors

Giacomo Borbone
is a research fellow at the Department of Human Sciences, Catania University, Italy. giacomoborbone@yahoo.it

Marta Bręgiel-Pant
graduated philosophy from the Institute of Philosophy, Adam Mickiewicz University, Poznań, Poland

Krzysztof Brzechczyn
is full Professor at the Faculty of Philosophy, Adam Mickiewicz University, Poznań, Poland; the head of Epistemology and Cognitive Science Research Unit. He has recently authored The Historical Distinctiveness of Central Europe: A Study in the Philosophy of History (Berlin 2020), brzech@amu.edu.pl

Waldemar Czajkowski
Associate Professor at Silesian University of Technology (Gliwice, Poland), Department of Applied Social Sciences. Philosopher and mathematician. Areas of research interests: social philosophy, philosophical anthropology, metaphilosophy. Main work: *Images of Man. A Study On/In a Meta(-)Anthropology* (Gliwice, 2001).

Aleksandra Gomułczak
is a Ph.D. student at the Faculty of Philosophy, Adam Mickiewicz University in Poznań, Poland; gomulczak.a@gmail.com

Iwo Greczko
is a Ph. D. student at the Faculty of Philosophy, Adam Mickiewicz University, Poznań, Poland, iwo.greczko@amu.edu.pl

Krzysztof Kiedrowski
is a research fellow at the Institute of Philosophy, Adam Mickiewicz University in Poznań, Poland. krzysztof.kiedrowski@gmail.com

Przybysz Piotr
is a philosopher and cognitivist; Associate Professor at the Faculty of Philosophy, Adam Mickiewicz University, Poznań, Poland; przybysz@amu.edu.pl

NOTES ON CONTRIBUTORS

Karolina Rutkowska
graduated philosophy from the Institute of Philosophy, Adam Mickiewicz University, Poznań, Poland

Jerzy Topolski (1928–1998)
historian and methodologist of history; co-founder the Poznań School of Methodology. His three most important monographs are *Metodologia historii* (English edition: Methodology of History, 1976), *Teoria wiedzy historycznej* [Theory of Historical Knowlegde, Poznań 1983] and *Jak się pisze i rozumie historię. Tajemnice narracji historycznej* [How to Write and Understand History; Secrets of Historical Narrative, Warsaw 1996].

Tomasz Zarębski
graduated philosophy from the Institute of Philosophy, Adam Mickiewicz University, Poznań, Poland. He lectures at Gniezno College Milenium.

PART 1

On Methodology of Non-Marxian Historical Materialism

∵

CHAPTER 1

Reflections on the Historiosophical System of Non-Marxian Historical Materialism

Jerzy Topolski

Abstract[1]

The aim of the paper is to characterize Nowak's non-Marxian historical materialism at the methodological and theoretical level. According to the author, the main features of Nowak's theory is its openness and lack of a final stage in the historical process. In the second part of this paper, non-Marxian historical materialism is compared with analytical Marxism and the applicability of Nowak's theory to the history of Poland is discussed (specifically, the period of early feudalism).

Keywords

analytical Marxism – early feudalism – Leszek Nowak – non-Marxian historical materialism – philosophy of history

1

When learning about Leszek Nowak's historiosophical system, presented in his three-volume work titled *U podstaw teorii socjalizmu* (*The Foundations of Theory of Socialism,* Nowak 1991b, an English version: Nowak 1983; 1991a [editorial note]), every philosopher or historian will admire and recognize the scope of the philosopher's endeavor. Nowak is a prolific writer whose works were published in many forms – official, undergound, abroad – but all his readers will be aware he has created a very far-reaching theory, a proposal for the

---

1 The paper appears in English translation for the first time. The Polish original „Refleksje o systemie historiozoficznym nie-Marksowskiego materializmu historycznego" was published in: K. Brzechczyn (ed.), Ścieżki transformacji. Ujęcia teoretyczne i opisy empiryczne (Poznań: Zysk i S-ka, 2003), pp. 279–294. The abstract and key words have been added by the editor.

© JERZY TOPOLSKI, 2022 | DOI:10.1163/9789004507296_002

explanation of the course of the historical process on at least the European scale (as can be estimated on the basis of the materials he referred to) or, with regard to some aspects, such as the feudal system, on at least the Western-European scale. At the beginning, I would like to note that it is not clear to me what historical scope Nowak intended for his theory, because his declarations on that matter are contradictory. However, we may suppose that the purpose of the cited historical materials (as regards feudalism, they are basically restricted to a part of Western Europe) was only to illustrate particular theses of his general theory. Nowak's main aim is to construct a general theory, and he refers to those historical materials in order to confirm it – he interprets them in the light of that theory. A historian may be shocked by much of Nowak's writing (related to history) – for example, by his understanding of Russian history. Nowak's interpretations, though, are highly inspiring even if it is hard to agree with them. Still, the most important thing is the content and internal logic of Nowak's theoretical conception, which make his non-Marxian historical materialism a great achievement. For many researchers, perhaps even more in the West than in Poland, historical materialism – Marxian or Marxist, or, for many, Marxist-Leninist – has been a general theory of that kind: particular historical materials have been not so much compared with that theory as identified with it, and specific studies have always been interpreted within that predetermined framework. Thus, the development of that research was stalled, and if the theoretical framework was also treated as an ideology, in the sense of a justification of power, then history or another social science which referred to Marxism became primarily a confession of faith. Meanwhile, Nowak's theory, which undermines Marxian historical materialism, is much more general and is intended as a source of theoretical inspiration and not a dogmatic framework for particular inquiries. Unlike Marxism, which is focused on one main factor – the economic, Nowak introduces three factors: political (power), economic (satisfying material needs), and ideological (relating to consciousness). Power is assigned the greatest priority in this triad.

The great attractiveness of Nowak's historiosophical system – as opposed to many other systems of this kind – lies in the fact that there is no finalism built into it. In most general terms, Nowak's merit is that he provided a theory which, in contrast to historical materialism, is devoid of the eschatological aspect, that is, which does not presuppose or predict that the end of history of history will be reached, that some ideal state will be attained.

So far, many eschatological attempts have been made in theories of this kind (and new ones continue to appear). For example, Arnold Toynbee, in his analysis of various past civilizations which developed according to challenge and response dialectics, saw everything as leading toward Christian civilization at the end of history. As regards the newer ideas, Richard Rorty, one of the apostles of philosophical postmodernism, comes to the conclusion that the best thing in history, the things which is worth striving for and strengthening, is actually Western liberalism. Let us add that such a conclusion, made in *Contingency, Irony and Solidarity* (Rorty 1989), automatically made the author less popular among thinkers who were critical of contemporary capitalism in America. Francis Fukuyama (1992) comes to a similar conclusion, as if repeating Hegel's reflections. He argues that history has reached a safe (or last) harbor – which is also a model for all countries – namely, Western democracy.

In Nowak's theory, there is no such end point of history. For Nowak, socialism was – or is – but a stage in historical development, with an in-built mechanism of its own demise. There is no finalism in this conceptual framework, but there are 'forces' (just like in other historiosophical systems) which propel the system and prepare its fall. In non-Marxian historical materialism, the main 'force' which moves history is the constant striving of a social group (or even an individual, like a dictator who – as strongly emphasized by Nowak – always represent someone's interests) for power, that is, for subjugating their society – and the resistance of that society. The striving for power is, so to speak, an axiom of the whole concept. The author believes it to have been proven by history (in which we can observe attempts at gaining power and expanding its scope). Rulers and the ruled fight, and history goes through subsequent stages which can have diverse variants.

However, such unwavering striving for power could not continue ceaselessly in this model because then the model would not explain much, and it would require the completely unrealistic assumption of an entirely passive society subjected only to the influence of the state. In reality, societies rebel, and there are various kinds of class struggle. Nowak appropriately expands the concepts of power and class struggle. Power is only complete when rulers obtain a triple kind of domination over the ruled, that is, when they accumulate economic, political, and doctrinal power and become 'triple lords'. It follows that opposition to such domination must take place on those three levels.

The highest form of this resistance – which is decisive for the dialectics of the development of further formations, such as those described by Marx – is revolution. With regard to striving for power, revolution is the basic mechanism of history. The most important force is the pursuit of power, and the mechanism which determines the main course of history only appears when striving for power is met with social opposition. The question arises of whether one should not, in such a situation, introduce another developmental axiom to the model (of a 'force' accepted a priori), namely, that society (the ruled) strives for freedom.

On this occasion, we can note that as early as Stalinist times, Boris Porshnev, an author whose works were translated and well-known to his contemporaries in the West (he was seen as a representative of Marxist historiography), created a concept which explained changes in the models of forms of government in the history of the Russian state by referring to changes of the forms and intensity of class conflict. It is easy to see that in this way obliging authors developed the Stalinist theory of the supposed intensification of class struggle during the construction of the socialist society, and the resulting need for greater repressions. Class conflict, however, was only treated here as a 'people's' struggle in the strictest sense of the word, that is, as a struggle of the lowest layers of the enslaved. Porshnev's theory was so schematic that it was not taken seriously even in Stalinist times.

In Nowak's theory, the historical process is open. A victorious revolution does not really solve anything (actually, a defeat brings about greater benefits for a society since it is usually followed by concessions on the part of the authorities) because it does not eliminate the pursuit of power which pervades history. After a time, the hated system is recreated: there are new rulers and their subjects, new people's resistance, etc. That openness of Nowak's system is, in my view, its great advantage. As has been mentioned, in the existing great systems, some end points had always been assumed. Even the 'anti-metaphysical' Max Weber, who was so pessimistic about the expanding 'bureaucratization' of the historical process, does not discard his idea of the ever greater rationalization of that process.

At this point, naturally, we could ask how the creator of non-Marxian historical materialism knows that there is that desire for power in man. We could perhaps explain it in the same way as the 'economic factor': in order to live, a person must first eat, get dressed, etc., so it is a kind of a basic desire. However, the 'economic factor', the issue of power does not have an existential foundation. In other systems, the situation is the same. Sigmund Freud's assumptions about what forces motivated people differed from Marx's. Actually, he kept changing and developing his views on this issue throughout his whole life. At this point, another thing comes to mind. Marxian economic forces and Freudian compulsive mechanisms are distributed among people in a universal – although obviously individually differentiated – manner, but the pursuit of power is, in my view, problematic in that respect because it is only characteristic of certain individuals or groups, so it is less universal than striving to meet material or sexual needs. I believe that to be a sort of a puzzle in Nowak's system which can exist and inspire further research – with stronger or weaker foundations in factual material – even if the puzzle is not solved. Perhaps, though, my doubts are unjustified, perhaps I have not analyzed Nowak's model

HISTORIOSOPHICAL SYSTEM OF NON-MARXIAN HISTORICAL MATERIALISM   7

closely enough, especially his construct of the "Christian model of man" (who reacts in a "normal" way, for example, returns good for good) and the "non-Christian model of man" (who reacts in a different way due to his having been enslaved or "satanized"). Does that not lead to the conclusion that the main motivating 'force' which moves people, that is, defines the historical process, is fear? Be that as it may, several questions remain unanswered for me. Are some 'forces' which drive the model of the historical process accepted by way of arbitrary decisions (as quasi-axioms)? If that is not the case, does the author realize the threat of tautology: first, a factor is assumed to be the 'driving force' which moves the historical process, and then that 'force' is declared to be generated by that process? Perhaps I am wrong about that.

2

As he constructed non-Marxian historical materialism, Nowak used – as a starting point to be later critically rejected – a version (interpretation) of Marxism in which Marx's theory is accused of inconsistency; that version, by the way, was the most common in communist countries (the communist world had not fallen apart yet at the time when Nowak was writing his book). Thus, according to Nowak, Marx have claimed that productive forces were the decisive factors of history, and at other times, he have maintained that this role was played by class conflict. We can find many inconsistencies of this kind in his writing. However, there are also interpretations not taken into account by Nowak, which do not emphasize that supposed crack in Marx's theory. I have always been one of such interpreters of Marx. In my view, in the whole of Marx's theory, that contradiction – which Nowak wants to overcome in his model, together with other inconsistencies – is actually superficial. It was magnified by the fact that Marx never offered a holistic explication of either his early or his late views on the theory of historical materialism. We do not even know if he treated that concept more as a theory or as a kind of a summary of the knowledge about the historical process. When we read Marx's strictly historical works, however (such as *The Eighteenth Brumaire of Louis Napoleon*, Marx [1852] 1963), one can find here the most general layer of his views on history, one which is barely noticed in the literature on the subject, but which could be called a truly historical layer. In that most general layer, there is – this is another possible interpretation of Marx's theory – a relation between the objective factor (productive forces) and the subjective factor (class conflict); factors which, by the way, are understood much more broadly than just as productive forces and class conflict. At that highest level of Marx's theory, a deterministic interpretation also becomes impossible. Of course, the issue is disputable, just like any interpretation of Marx's writings, including Nowak's interpretation.

In his historiosophical system, Nowak overcomes the contradiction or inconsistency which, according to his interpretation, is present in Marx's theory. He builds a unitarian conception in which individual actions are guided by the agents' consciousness (motivations), and collective actions – by collective interest. In Nowak's system, the category of interest plays a very important and inspiring role. We are dealing here with an expansion – disputable as well, of course, but very innovative – of the field of historical explanation. I might add that the problem of collective actions has not been properly solved yet in the vast literature on historical explanation or in social science in general. The numerous concepts pertaining to that topic, with one conspicuous example being Mancur Olson's views expressed in, among other works, *The Logic of Collective Action* (Olson 1971) or *The Rise and Decline of Nations* (Olson 1982), are not sufficient for a discussion of, for instance, collective actions in unstable times, revolutionary actions, etc. Of course, Nowak could have constructed his system just as well on the basis of a different interpretation of Marx's writings, such as the one I have mentioned above. In my opinion, his system is original enough not to have to be founded on a negation of a previous theory. In his system, Nowak utilizes the earlier idea of developmental stages of a society; however, as has already been noticed, he has a different view on the mechanisms of historical changes, and in his eyes they are devoid of determinism (or fatalism) and finalism.

As a historian, I may add that I personally become more and more convinced that it is unjustified to construct a conception which would determine some stages of historical development, not in the sense of summarizing the development thus far, but rather as imposing a formation network (even if it is devoid of finalism) on the historical process. Once more, I would like to underline that to state that a given society or more societies have undergone particular stages of development and to explain those transitions is a different matter than to construct, on the basis – to a greater or smaller degree – of actual knowledge, a theory which can be applied generally to history, and which would also function as a theory of changes and development. Historical reality is so diverse and unpredictable (which is taken into account in, for example, theories of chaos, which are currently fashionable in political economy and are sometimes used in historical research) that it is hardly justified or fruitful to divide it, by any means, into developmental stages (even regionally delimited ones). The direction of the development of historical research is rather toward freeing historical narration from such limitations. One of those restrictions is the myth of evolution to which I have pointed in some of my works, and which consists largely in historians' unconscious conviction that what used to be must have been worse, less developed, and less perfect, and that reality must somehow be constantly modernized. Nowak's model is an effective weapon against such a way of thinking. Although it operates on the concept of developmental stages (formations), it is devoid of the myth of evolution. Personally, I believe that it is only worth constructing a theory if it is at a level more general than that of stages – not a theory on developmental phases but one which explains how the changes occur. Such an approach admittedly impoverishes the model, but it also protects it against possible criticism concerning its applicability to particular courses of historical events.

3

I understand that depriving the model of the whole structure of developmental research would change, to a degree, its nature, but not – in my opinion – its essence. The changed model would still take into account the pursuit of power and the opposition of various social groups to that pursuit, which would lead to various solutions of varying durability. The only missing thing would be the names of particular formations, the essence of which for Nowak is, by the way, different than for most other thinkers, especially those who remain under the influence of Marxism. The reflections above are not intended as a criticism of the model – rather, I would like my proposal to stimulate a different way of thinking about Nowak's theory. As I have already mentioned, one of its great advantages it is that it is very inspiring and does not leave readers indifferent to the presented content. In order to avoid misunderstandings, I will repeat that I am not in any way opposed to the construction of developmental stages as research tools for historical *ex post* ordering of factual material. Nowak's model, even interpreted as indicating the necessary developmental stages in history, can be very helpful for such a historical conceptualization. It provides a conceptual apparatus which does not depend on whether a given society (state, nation, etc.) has gone through the stages predicted by the model, toward the triple rule. Accordingly, it is my belief that Nowak's model can be very useful for understanding the history of Poland, especially the most recent events, even though I think that Polish history differs very much from Nowak's model. It is for that reason – the Polish case is not the only one – that I am against the construction of a line of development which would be ideal from the point of view of the stages; instead, I would prefer such an ideal line to be drawn at a higher level of the system.

As regards the history of Poland, the situation predicted in Nowak's model, that is, evolution in socialism toward the rule of triple lords (one group, perhaps headed by an individual) wielding all power (after 1939, Nowak believed that socialism had been brought to Poland by Germans who dispossessed Poles and overtook, as a state, great industrial and agricultural property, as well as minor peasant property in the territories incorporated into Germany). The development did not proceed from single rule to triple rule. The first Piasts, in the system of the so-called ducal law, owned the whole land of the state. At the same time, they had at their disposal the means of coercion in the form of armed forces. Moreover, at that time, the Catholic Church was so tightly interrelated with the state that its highest hierarchy – limited in number – constituted the ruling elite, together with the people closest to the duke. The elite, then, had all the power, which was not separate from ownership at that time. It was only with the disintegration of the ducal law system – in which the state managed the economy (very well described by Karol Modzelewski, 1975) – that the process of the privatization of land ownership took place. The privatization was made possible by ducal immunities, which meant that a duke passed his economic and judicial power onto the increasingly numerous lords and knights in the territories with immunities, that is, territories exempted from the duke's power. The Catholic Church became increasingly independent from the lay authorities as well, as is clearly proven by the election of the Cracow bishop in 1202, known as the double election in the literature on the subject. Those, however, are details which I cannot delve into in this short article. Therefore, I will only mention two more facts from the history of Poland here which do not quite fit the discussed model. The first one is the period with no peasant revolts, bigger rebellions, or insurrections in feudal Poland. They were possible in Russia where many peasants were not subdued within the framework the corvée system. That is why Ivan Bolotnikov's or Yemelyan Pugachev's revolts had such a great scope. In Pugachev's rebellion, armed Cossacks were a great force (of course, not the Kuban ones or those from Sich, but Yaik Cossacks). The rebels did not want a change of power per se, but rather access to the good tzar who, they believed, was being deceived by his milieu. The nature of the famous small, local diversion led by Aleksander Kostka-Napierski in 1651, just like Cossack movements in Ukraine, headed by Bohdan Khmelnytsky (1648 and the following years), was different. The former event was political diversion organized by Swedes who capitalized on the dissatisfaction of Podhale peasants. The latter was strongly nationalistic. We can hardly say, then, that there was a wave of peasant revolts in Poland during the feudal formation which were evidence of significant changes in the structure of feudalism. There exist, naturally, various concepts which explain this situation – namely, the lack of large scale peasant opposition (Brenner 1976) – but there still remains the problem of why the nobility was able to increase its power over peasants without causing their resistance, while similar actions of the German nobility caused a peasant war in 1525, which had the meaning described by Nowak. The literature on the topic is so rich and encompasses so many conceptual frameworks that it would not be judicious to discuss it in greater detail in this article.

The second fact pertains to the newest history, that is, the period of socialism characterized, according to Nowak, by the appearance (for example, in Poland) of the system of triple rule. The political and economic power in Poland, though, has never managed to gain a monopoly on the priests' function. That function remained, for the most part, a domain of the Catholic Church, especially after 1956. Before 1956, though, there was no ideological uniformity in Poland, either. After 1956, Marxism ceased to be the only intellectual or ideological direction accepted by party authorities, although it was still preferred by them. The efforts made to unify the society in a Marxist fashion came to naught. The thing left behind by the party (and state) is control (especially by means of censorship) of all that concerned the relations between Poland and USSR, the history of the party, and the current history of Poland (the evaluation of that history). That is why there were so-called blank pages in our history. That was not, however, power over people's minds. In that regard, the Catholic Church was more dominant. Therefore, there were no triple lords but only double lords (who may have believed themselves to be triple lords). Of course, the example given here does not devalue the model – understood as a kind of a 'measure' of the real historical process.

4

At this point, I am getting to the problem of a methodological (and not theoretical or historical) interpretation of Nowak's conceptualization, namely, the question whether that system is to be understood as a theory in a realistic sense, that is, as a simplified approach to reality – in the case of Nowak's system, the movement of the socio-economic formation, which means the movement in its 'pure' form (only subjected to the activity of the main factors, as stated by the author himself) – or whether it should be understood as a kind of a Weberian ideal type with which we compare reality, and which, at the same time, allows us to explain that reality and, consequently, to understand it better. Although it might be at odds with Nowak's own words, I would be willing to interpret the non-Marxian theory of the socio-economic formation as a complex ideal type – with various degrees of preciseness – rather than a theory in the sense of a simplified image of reality – also concretized to various degrees. An ideal type is also constructed on the basis of knowledge about reality, but it does not aspire to as close a relationship with reality as a theory which is understood in a realistic and not an instrumental manner. Such a theory presupposes a rather simple relation between itself and reality: after the idealizing assumptions have been gradually eliminated, the vision of reality gradually loses the deforming and caricaturizing characteristics which have been ascribed to it, and it becomes closer to the actual state of things, that is, of course, to the reality assumed in the theory because we do not know what the actual reality is like. We always learn about reality through our senses, language, conventions, etc. Non-Marxian historical materialism, understood as a theory with various idealizing conditions, remains undisturbed after we have assumed the truth accepted by Nowak (that is, the concept of essential truth).

If, however, we confront that system and its understanding of truth with other concepts of truth which function in philosophy, then difficulties arise. At this point, I am thinking about various coherence theories (for example, Hilary Putnam's – where the point of reference, of coherence, is the *consensus* of a society, for example, an academic society, or about such concepts popular in historical science where the reference system is the *corpus* of accepted knowledge, which, of course, has a lot in common with Putnam's internal realism). In such cases, there is no possibility of carrying out a concretization (within the meaning given to this term by Nowak) because there is no category of reality corresponding to the theory. If, on the other hand, we assume that Nowak's system is of the ideal type, then a comparison of our knowledge about what we believe to be reality with the ideal (more or less detailed) type can only be heuristic in nature and function as an inspiration – a pluralistic concept which does not impose a strict framework on us. In such a case, only a confrontation of many visions of reality (for example, of the so-called real socialism) with the model which has been proposed to us (the ideal type) can offer a closer approximation of reality or, more strictly speaking, can yield descriptions of reality with the greatest explanatory power or the greatest convincing power, that is, the power to make it possible to understand what has been, etc. At the same time, such an understanding of the theory immunizes the author against possible accusations that with regard to this or that fragment of the past, he does not align with reality. The possibility of understanding Nowak's historiosophical conception, both as a classical theory of the socio-economic formation and as a theory in the form of an ideal type, with the assumption of the correspondence theory of truth and of various versions of the theory of coherence, is also, in my opinion, a great advantage of that system, regardless of whether the author himself assumed such interpretations. As I am primarily a historian, Nowak's system is very inspiring to me. It allows a better understanding of many issues from the distant and recent past, although I am not convinced that historical development does indeed take place in the manner assumed in that theory – that is, that Nowak's non-Marxian historical materialism accurately describes the mechanisms of historical development – which, let me repeat, does not contradict my positive evaluation of it. Nowak does not describe history – he extracts its hidden mechanisms.

5

At the end of my reflection on Nowak's novel approach, I would like to place it within the panorama of contemporary humanistic thought. It is common knowledge that one very strong driving force for changes in philosophy in the last half of a century was the desire for liberation – in this case, intellectual liberation – from various kinds of pressure exerted by traditional opinions and concepts, for example, traditional epistemology – that is, realistic epistemology (in the sense of learning about objectively existing reality). A part of that emancipatory program, which gradually encompassed ever new fields of knowledge, was the creation of concepts in which various kinds of power were criticized, while an individual or society (social groups, speech communities, etc.) earned their proper (as was emphasized) places. All that led to the creation of the philosophical atmosphere which is now called postmodernism, and which is a mixture of the extremes of hermeneutic ideas, post-Saussurean linguistics, textual literary studies (related to Jacques Derrida), Ludwig Wittgenstein's theory of language games, and a selection of Friedrich Nietzsche's ideas.

Obviously, I do not want to associate Nowak's idea with postmodernism, because not all manifestations of the critique of power and enslavement (even enslavement by assigning particular meanings to words) led to postmodernism. This applies to concepts related in some way to Marxism, although it must be noted that Marxism, with its critique of the capitalist society and state, was, to an extent, absorbed – as a related theory – by Derridean deconstructionists (cf., among other authors, Michael Ryan [1982]). Leftists in the United States of America have contributed greatly to the popularization of deconstruction in literary studies and to its introduction to other areas of the humanities. Generally speaking, though, Marxism remained a different stream of the critique of power – of course, I mean modified Marxism here, such as Nowak's system. In the 1980s, that issue was widely discussed.

Apart from the so-called Japanese Marxism, new works were published by Perry Anderson (1974a; 1974b; 1976) and such authors as John Roemer (1982),

Eugene Lunn (1984), Paul Hirst (1985), Martin Jay (1985), Steven Lukes (1985), Jukka Gronov (1986), Kevin M. Brien (1987), Roger S. Gottlieb (1987), Jeffrey C. Isaak (1987) and Richard E. Appelbaum (1988). Each of them interprets and modifies Marx's theory in some way; nevertheless, Nowak's work was not only earlier – it was also more comprehensive than the other works.

Obviously, there were predecessors of Nowak's theory, primarily, I believe, in the Frankfurt School which fought – from its beginnings to its late theorists, including Jürgen Habermas – for the liberation of societies from various bonds (which was a projection of the experience of totalitarianism), but did not embrace the nihilism of postmodernism, as evidenced by Habermas's well-known debates (with Hans-Georg Gadamer, Rorty, and – in the more strictly historical field – Ernst Nolte's relativist evaluation of German Nazism in relation to Stalinism, which appeared to mitigate the evil nature of Nazism and somehow distribute it between Nazism and communism).

We also observe historians' greater interest in power-related issues. Let me mention two different examples. A few years ago, Antoni Mączak's book entitled *Rządzący i rządzeni* (Mączak 1986) was published. It mainly concerned European absolutism and presented power as a kind of an enterprise, a profit-generating economic business. At some point in his work, Nowak refers to Guy Bois, a researcher of French feudalism. In his book on the early Middle Ages, Bois criticized older approaches (although his approach is also subjected to critique) and recreated the structures of state power in that period, claiming it was more significant than had been assumed. Of course, there are more works which point to that direction. I can only say that Professor Nowak's historiosophical reflection is very much in tune with social needs.

References

Anderson, P. (1974a). *Lineages of the Absolute State*. London: NLB.

Anderson, P. (1974b). *Passages from Antiquity to Feudalism*. London: NLB.

Anderson, P. (1976). *Consideration on the Western Marxism*. London: NLB.

Appelbaum, R. P. (1988). *Karl Marx*. London: Sage.

Brenner, R. (1976). Agrarian Class Structure and Economic Development in Pro-Industrial Europe. *Past and Present* 70: 30–75.

Brien, K. M. (1987). *Marx, Reason, and the Art of Freedom*. Philadelphia: Temple University Press.

Fukuyama, F. (1992). *The End of History and the Last Man*. New York: The Free Press.

Gottlieb, R. S. (1987). *History and Subjectivity. The Transformation of Marxist Theory*. Philadelphia: Temple University Press.

HISTORIOSOPHICAL SYSTEM OF NON-MARXIAN HISTORICAL MATERIALISM   15

Gronov, J. (1986). *On the Formation of Marxism; Karl Kautsky's Theory of Capitalism. The Marxism of the Second International and Karl Marx s Critique of Political Economy.* Helsinki: Societas Scientiarum Fennica.

Hirst, P.Q. (1985). *Marxism and Historical Writing.* London: Routledge.

Isaak, J.C. (1987). *Power and Marxist Theory. A Realist View.* Ithaca: Cornell University Press.

Jay, M. (1985). *Permanent Exiles. Essays on the Intellectual Migration from Germany to America.* New York: Columbia University Press.

Lukes, St. (1985). *Marxism and Morality.* Oxford: Clarendon.

Lunn, E. (1984). *Marxism and Modernism. An Historical Study of Lukács, Brecht, Benjamin and Adorno.* Berkeley: University of California Press.

Marx, K. ([1852] 1963). *The Eighteenth Brumaire of Louis Bonaparte.* New York: International Publishers.

Mączak, A. (1986). *Rządzący i rządzeni. Władza i społeczeństwo w Europie nowożytnej* [Rulers and the Ruled; The Authorities and Society in Modern Europe]. Warsaw: PIW.

Modzelewski, K. (1975). *Organizacja gospodarcza państwa piastowskiego (X–XI w.)* [The Economic Organization of the Piast State]. Wrocław: Ossolineum.

Nowak, L. (1983). *Property and Power. Towards a non-Marxian Historical Materialism* (Theory and Decision Library, t. 27). Dordrecht/Boston/Lancaster: Reidel.

Nowak, L. (1991a). *Power and Civil Society. Towards a Dynamic Theory of Real Socialism.* New York/London: Greenwood Press.

Nowak, L. (1991b). *U podstaw teorii* socjalizmu [The Foundations of the Theory of Socialism]; vol. 1: *Własność i władza. O konieczności socjalizmu* [Property and Power. On the Necessity of Socialism]; vol. 2: *Droga do socjalizmu. O konieczności socjalizmu w Rosji* [The Road to Socialism. On the Necessity of Socialism in Russia]; vol. 3: *Dynamika władzy. O strukturze i konieczności zaniku socjalizmu* [The Dynamics of Power. On the Structure and Necessity of the Disappearance of Socialism]. Poznań: Nakom.

Olson, M. (1971). *The Logic of Collective Action: Public Goods and the Theory of Groups* Cambrigde, Mass.: Harvard University Press.

Olson, M. (1982). *The Rise and Decline of Nations: The Rise and Decline of Nations: Economic Growth, Stagflation, and Social Rigidities.* Yale Yale University Press.

Roemer, J. (1982). *A General Theory of Exploitation and Class.* Cambrigde, Mass.: Harvard University Press.

Rorty, R. (1989). *Contingency, Irony and Solidarity.* Cambridge: Cambridge University Press.

Ryan, M. (1982). *Marxism and Deconstruction. A Critical Articulation.* Baltimore: John Hopkins Univeristy Press.

CHAPTER 2

Leszek Nowak's Historiosophy from Historical and Systematical Perspectives

Waldemar Czajkowski

Abstract

This essay presents some remarks on Leszek Nowak's historiosophy, otherwise known as non-Marxian historical materialism. In the first part a very brief history of Polish analytical philosophy (inaugurated by Kazimierz Twardowski in 1895) is outlined, and the important place Nowak occupies in this tradition is highlighted. A very brief picture of the development of (post-)Marxian currents in the Western post-war philosophy is also presented; there are many interesting similarities and differences between these currents and Nowak's ideas. The second part contains some critical remarks on Nowakian historiosophy. It should be stressed that this criticism assumes Nowak's basic ideas as a paradigm of historiosophy. These critical remarks should thus be thus regarded as suggestions on how non-Marxian historical materialism could be developed further. These suggestions mainly concern the problem of the spatial dimension of historical process and some anthropological issues.

Keywords:

Historiosophy – Leszek Nowak – philosophy of history – Poznań School of Methodology

1 Introduction

Leszek Nowak (1943–2009) was a prominent philosopher but also an original and interesting personality (Klawiter, Łastowski 2007). As a thinker, he explored areas of metaphysics that are rather rarely "visited" by other philosophers (e.g. nothingness) and at the same time also presented his own interpretation of the history of Russia. He wrote huge books and concise feuilletons. He was a scholarly philosopher who was also politically active for ten years (1980–1990). He was open to the world and the people of various nations, to *Welatanschaungen* etc. – while being, at the same time, strongly attached to his

© WALDEMAR CZAJKOWSKI, 2022 | DOI:10.1163/9789004507296_003

own – Polish – traditions. And just for this reason I want to look first at Nowak's philosophy of history (= historiosophy) from a particular historical perspective – that of the history of Polish philosophy (see Coniglione 2010). This overview will be supplemented with a few brief remarks on those currents of world philosophy of the second-half of the 20th century in which some ideas similar to Nowakian ones can be found.

The second part of my paper will be devoted to the tasks which – in my opinion – are to be accomplished by those who would like to continue the ideas of non-Marxian historical materialism. Ideas which, I am deeply convinced, deserve continuation. And not only by this or that researcher but by a whole team realizing a long-term research program.

2 Non-Marxian Historical Materialism from a Historical Perspective

At the beginning, let's look at Nowak's historiosophy from the perspective of the history of Polish philosophy. Analytical philosophy has been one of its most important currents in the 20th and 21st centuries (Woleński 1989). One of its very characteristic traits has been *Weltanschauung* pluralism: Tadeusz Kotarbiński (reist) and Józef Maria Bocheński (tomist), Kazimierz Ajdukiewicz (conventionalist) and Stanisław Ossowski (close to Marxism) ... – Polish analytical philosophy has demonstrated that "obedience" to the rules of the profession – of the "philosophical craft", to the principles of "good philosophical work", is not incompatible with freedom of metaphysical or ideological choices.

And interestingly, the development of Polish analytical philosophy was – in the period 1918–1939, at least – not only parallel but in some way connected with the development of Polish mathematics. Due to the program (a phenomenon interesting from the viewpoint of sociology/the history of knowledge) created by the outstanding Polish mathematician, Zygmunt Janiszewski (1888–1920), Polish mathematicians focused their research on such branches of mathematics as topology and set theory. It is sufficient to invoke three important names: Stefan Banach (1892–1945), Wacław Sierpiński (1882–1969) and Alfred Tarski (1901–1983). The latter was mainly a logician (according to the widely accepted view, he was, alongside Kurt Goedel, one of the two greatest logicians of the 20th century, and one of the four greatest – adding Aristotle and Gottlob Frege – of all times), but he was also a mathematician (a disciple of Sierpiński; he had important achievements in algebra and geometry, but the most famous is the set-theoretical Banach-Tarski theorem, sometimes called a "paradox") and a philosopher (particularly renowned as the author of a definition of truth); he also influenced the development of the Stanford school of philosophy of science (cf. Garcia de la Sienra 2019). And it was logic that came to play the role of a vital link between mathematics and philosophy.

It should be stressed that the inter-war period was the time of particularly dynamic development in Polish logic. The achievements of at least four logicians should be mentioned: Apart from already mentioned Tarski, one should mention Jan Łukasiewicz (1878–1956) – the creator of multi-valued logics (unlike E. Post's ideas, Łukasiewicz's conception of many-valuedness has profound philosophical roots), Stanisław Leśniewski (1886–1939) – the author of original an original theory of sets (different from the standard Zermelo–Fraenkel theory) theory of sets, and Alfred Lindenbaum (1904–1941) – "Lindenbaum's algebra" and "Lindenbaum's lemma" are present in virtually all logic textbooks.

It should be noted, referring to the last sentence of the first passage of this chapter (on pluralism), that Polish logic was connected with various philosophical stances. On the one hand, Leśniewski's logic was adopted by Kotarbiński (see below) to his – radically materialist – reism; on the other – Rev. Jan Salamucha (1903–1944) tried to apply logic to the analysis of some parts of Thomas Aquinas' philosophy. It might be added that in the post-war period – to be more precise, in 1964 – the Polish philosopher Leonard S. Rogowski presented a logical reconstruction of a part of Hegel's philosophy (rather forgotten today). And yet one more name deserves mention here. I have in mind Oskar Lange (1904–1965) – one of the outstanding economists of the 20th century. In 1962 he published the book "Całość i rozwój w świetle cybernetyki" (*Whole and development in the light of cybernetics*) in which he tried to formulate the basic ideas of materialist dialectics in mathematical language (incidentally, having much more in common with probabilistic theory than with logic).

Let us return to the Polish analytical philosophy. As the date of birth of Polish analytical philosophy we can accept the day of 15th November 1885, when Kazimierz Twardowski (1866–1938), the single-handed creator of the Lvov-Warsaw School, arrived in Lvov. Almost all Polish analytical philosophers were direct or indirect disciples of Twardowski. Tadeusz Kotarbiński (1886–1981) and Kazimierz Ajdukiewicz (1890–1962) belong to the most outstanding. Janina Kotarbińska (1901–1997) – the supervisor of Nowak's MA dissertation, was a disciple of Kotarbiński. Among Ajdukiewicz's disciples one should mention Jerzy Giedymin (1925–1993), though his PhD dissertation was supervised by Adam Wiegner (1889–1967). Initially, Giedymin had been the supervisor of Jerzy Kmita's (1931–2012) PhD dissertation, though finally it was Wiegner who supervised it. One should mention one more of Ajdukiewicz's doctoral students – Andrzej Malewski (1929–1963). Jerzy Topolski (1928–1998) – a historian and methodologist (Topolski 1976) – was his close collaborator. This tradition is still alive, as is demonstrated by the research activity of Krzysztof Brzechczyn (born 1963) – the disciple of both Nowak and Topolski. Brzechczyn's book (Brzechczyn 2013) demonstrates the very possibility and importance of applying analytical philosophical methods to discussion of current and emotionally-laden political issues.

As the results from this short historical sketch show, along with the analysis of their philosophical output (to be presented below, though only partially), Jerzy Kmita, Leszek Nowak and Jerzy Topolski – the creators of the Poznań School of Methodology – are important representatives of the tradition initiated in Poland by Twardowski. In their (and their disciples') work one can easily see the aforementioned fundamental trait of this tradition: the combination of theoretical pluralism with respecting the norms of "good philosophical work."

I would like to end this part of my paper with two general remarks on Nowak's philosophical output. Its variety is striking: unitarian metaphysics and an interpretation of Russian history, the idealizational theory of science (Nowak 1980, also see Borbone 2016; 2021; Halas 2016) and an analysis of Leśmian's poetry. But this variety not only reflects the versatility of his interests and intellectual skills. Closer look at his works proves that between his early works devoted to the methodology of jurisprudence and his late works devoted to Leśmian there is subtle but continuous line connecting the beginning and the end of his creative itinerary.

And now a few remarks on world philosophy. Some twenty years after World War II, a few intellectual currents appeared that can be both classified as belonging to the Marxist tradition and acknowledged as original theoretical proposals. Let's start with this very short presentation with the so-called "structural Marxism" which came into existence in the 1960s. Louis Althusser (1918–1990), Etienne Balibar (1942-), Maurice Godelier (1934-), and Nikos Poulantzas (1936–1979) were its main representatives. The most important work, representative for this current, was *La lire de 'Capital'* written by Althusser and a few of his collaborators (Althusser et. al 1965).

The important works of Jurgen Habermas (born 1929) were published more or less at the same time. From the point of view of the history of the Marxist tradition, the book *Zur Rekonstruktion des Historischen Materialismus* (Habermas 1976) plays crucial role. However, as regards his magnum opus, *Theorie des kommunikativen Handels* (Habermas 1981), it is debatable to what extent this work can be included in the Marxist tradition. Personally, I would accept the label "Habermasian non-Marxian historical materialism" for this theory. But a solid justification for this opinion would require great deal of effort and time.

It is noteworthy that – in spite of many important differences – there is an element common to Althusser and Habermas: They try to elaborate in a systematical and theoretical way the idea of the "autonomy" of politics and culture – an idea that played a role in the origins of the Nowakian non-Marxian historical materialism. It also should be noted that both Althusser's and Habermas's philosophies are "continental philosophies", meaning they are very different in style from analytical philosophy.

But in 1970s an analytical version of Marxism ("analytical Marxism") also came into existence. Its most well-known representative was Gerald A. Cohen (1941–2009), the author of *Karl Marx's Theory of History* (1978). In contrast to Althusser and Habermas, Cohen did not offer any substantially new interpretation of historical materialism. Instead, he gave to it a new logical form – a form in line with the standards of Frege, Moore and others.

If viewed from this perspective, Nowakian historical materialism turns out to be a very original theoretical proposal: developing the idea of the autonomy of politics and economy (similarly to Althusser's and Habermas' endeavors), but doing this (similarly to Cohen) with the help of analytical tools.

To conclude this historical overview, I would like to mention some theories that were developed rather by social scientists than by philosophers – theories of "dependency" or of world system(s). Among the most important representatives of this current (which belong, without any doubt, to the Marxist tradition) the names of Samir Amin (1931–2018), Giovanni Arrighi (1937–2009), Andre Gunder Frank (1929–2005) and Immanuel Wallerstein (1930–2019) should be mentioned. The latter's work *The Modern World-System* (1974 – first volume) is the most comprehensive presentation of the ideas being developed in this current.

3 Non-Marxian Historical Materialism from a Systematic Perspective

As I have already declared, I think that Nowak's non-Marxian historical materialism is a theory that should be further developed. Firstly, I am deeply convinced that (in contrast to the opinions of Karl Raimund Popper, Isaiah Berlin, Jean-François Lyotard and others) historiosophy (the theory of historical process) is not only possible (logically, epistemologically ...) but is – in our times (in the epoch in which humankind might be responsible for its very existence) – badly needed. Secondly, it is a matter of very elementary, uncontroversial rationality to reconstruct an already existing theory instead of starting from scratch. And there are quite a few reasons why we should commence with Nowakian historiosophy (Nowak 1983; 1991, his summary, see Brzechczyn 2017).

First: it is consciously constructed as an idealizational theory (to my knowledge, it is the only historiosophy of this kind.) This might be its greatest merit:

Historiosophy needs the consistent application of idealization much more than many other theories: it is (supposed to be) a theory of the global historical process, which is an extremely complex object. It is very likely that in such a case not only the basic (initial) model has to be 'distant' from empirical reality, but so do the first derivative models (being concretizations of the initial one). The construction of a model being 'sufficiently close' to empirical reality needs much more time and effort than does relatively simple objects.

Second: Nowak's philosophy of history is based on a clearly defined philosophical anthropology. Again, I do not know of any other historiosophy which is similarly constructed. And this is its other great virtue: History – whatever else it should be – is a set of individual human actions; even Hegel would not seriously reject this thesis. Therefore, while developing historiosophy, one should first assume something about the nature of actions and of acting individuals (i.e. assume a philosophical anthropology). There are a great many possibilities (Czajkowski 2001): we can assume that human nature is 'fixed,' or in contrast – 'flexible'; 'good' or 'evil'; we can assume that individuals differ from each other only 'superficially' or 'essentially.' It is important to define what philosophical anthropology is assumed in the given historiosophy. And still better (as is the case in Nowak's non-Marxian historical materialism) – to demonstrate how anthropology 'works' inside historiosophy (Paprzycka, Paprzycki 1993).

Third: Nowak's historiosophy is based upon an original social ontology (Klawiter 1978; 1989). On the one hand it is monist, on the other it respects the specificity and autonomy of various 'momentums' of social reality: of economy, politics and culture. These 'momentums' are regarded as autonomous, but also structurally analogous (material instruments – of production, coercion and indoctrination, and relations of disposing/non-disposing these instruments, i.e. class relations are constitutive for the respective "momentums"). In contrast with Marxian historical materialism, the economy is not regarded as the 'base' of the social formation, and politics and culture as its 'superstructure'; consequently, neither politics nor culture is regarded as a "reflection" of the economy; they are neither 'functionally subordinated' to it nor instrumental to its reproduction. Nowakian social ontology, combined with the conflict/class vision of social relations results in an interesting image: we obtain three basic class divisions (owners–producers, rulers–citizens, priests–laymen) which can overlap in various ways.

Fourth: Nowak's theory contains a considerable number of subtle dynamic models. And only in their context is the role of anthropological assumptions clearly visible. They also demonstrate (irrespective of their empirical truthfulness/falsity) that it is possible to construct models that demonstrate the very existence of both some trends and some "chaotic fluctuations," and also – their interactions.

Fifth: It would be rather impossible to be speaking about a systematic confrontation of non-Marxian historical materialism with empirical knowledge about the past, but we can say that Nowakian historiosophy allowed us to look in an original, fresh way on the history of Russia, on the history of the USSR and other "real-socialist" states, and also on the history of Mexico (Brzechczyn 2004).

I think that the list of virtues of Nowak's theory of history could be made longer. But, in my opinion, the five remarks presented above, should sufficiently justify the opinion formulated at the beginning of this chapter.

I do not think that Leszek Nowak was a Popperist at any point on his creative road. It is, however, beyond any doubt that he shared with the author of *Open Society* the conviction concerning the fundamental role played by critique/criticism in the development of knowledge. Incidentally, in applying the rules of criticism to his own conceptions he was much more consistent than their most renowned advocate ... Thus, a critique of Nowak's theories is, I am deeply convinced, the best way to manifest faithfulness to his intellectual ethos.

Nowak's historiosophy is a large, much elaborated conception. And if one takes into account the complexity of the historical process, one should not be surprised that quite a few critical comments – some rather minor, some other of more fundamental character – could be addressed to this conception. For various reasons, I cannot debate here all the questions that would merit consideration. A selection is necessary. In the search of a 'key' with which I could do this, I have decided that it will be convenient to apply the method Nowak used while starting the construction of non-Marxian historical materialism. Almost certainly, the desire to understand 'real socialism' was the main motive behind his efforts to re-construct historical materialism. From my perspective, the desire to understand the complex of processes labelled 'globalization' is the main motive behind my thinking on (Marxian and Nowakian) historical materialism. To say this is but the first step in defining the direction of my critical reflections: This word has great many meanings and detailed discussion of them falls beyond the scope of the present work. Thus, I only say that globalization comprises a profound transformation of the 'social space of the world,' and of the 'relations between Man and Nature.' This transformation can be regarded as process of forming one eco-techno-cultural-social world system. It is this interpretation of globalization that influenced my choice of the Nowakian historiosophical concepts that I am going to discuss critically.

To analyze the transformation of the social space of the world, you should have a theory of social space. Unfortunately, neither Marxian nor Nowakian historical material possesses such a theory. (Why not? – This is an interesting question for the historical sociology of knowledge.) Happily, also in this case we do not have to start from scratch. We can, and in my opinion should, commence from the works of Amin, Arrighi, Frank and Wallerstein. This entails there is a huge amount of work to be done. Huge and complicated: Their works can by no means be regarded as complementary parts of a single theory. In fact, the set of their works contains various theoretical ideas and historical interpretations. Neither should we forget that their intellectual roots are very diverse. Of course, the Marxist tradition (in particular Rosa Luxemburg's *Accumulation of Capital*) plays an important a role. A similar role is played by ideas connected with the rise of the Third World, in particular: various forms of 'dependency theory' (e.g. Fernando Cardoso, Celso Furtado). And not to be forgotten is the tradition of the French *Annales* School, particularly that of Fernand Braudel). This variety of traditions, though in sense very inspiring, can be a source of difficulties which the interpretation of world-system theory in non-Marxian historical materialism may face. But all in all, this is a minor difficulty. A far more serious problem is not of a 'substantial' character; it is rather epistemological. The world-system theorists regard (any) theory as an instrument for the interpretation of historical processes. The idea of constructing idealized models of social reality seems to be completely foreign to them. But, on the other hand, we do not have to accept their epistemological convictions. We are fully entitled to try to extract from their analyses the general ideas which underlie them, and to transform them into a theory satisfying our own epistemological standards – in the present case: those defined by the theory of idealization.

Let's try to enumerate the basic ideas of what might be called 'Wallersteinian non-Marxian historical materialism' (Wallerstein 1974; 1999). Its most important theses include the following:

(1)   In the entire history of mankind only two great watersheds have taken place: the Neolithic (agrarian) revolution and the rise of the modern capitalist world-system.

(2)   At the turn of the 15th and 16th centuries, the European world-economy came into existence. Geographical discoveries made important contributions to this process.

(3)   The European world-economy is not an empire, though it is as large as a great empire and has some traits characteristic for empires. Nevertheless, it is something different and new. It appeared as a social system of new type, one which never existed before, and not it is typical for the modern world-system.

(4)   The modern world-system is an economic entity, but not a political one; unlike empires, city-states and nation-states, but it contains all these political forms.

(5)   This system is not a world system, but not because it should encompass the whole world, rather because it is larger than any legally defined political entity. This system is a "world economy," since the basic connections between its parts are of an economic character, even if they are strengthened by culture and political institutions.

(6)   Empire is a political unit. For the last 5000 years empires have been a permanent feature of the political 'world stage.' Political centralization has been a source both of its strength and of its weakness.

(7)   The strength of empire lay in the fact that it safeguarded, due to economic power (tributes, taxes) and monopolistic profits from trade, economic transfers from the peripheries to the center.

(8)   The weakness of empire lay in the fact that bureaucracy (necessary in this political system) tended to maximize exploitation, then exploitation resulted in revolts, and revolts caused the growth of military expenditures. In short: empires are primitive forms of economic domination.

(9)   The modern world created technology, which made possible the transfer of surplus from peripheries to the center without the waste caused by political bureaucracy.

(10)   Before the rise of the European world economy, other world economies had existed, but they had always undergone transformation into empires (China, Persia, Rome).

(11)   The modern world economy might have developed in the same direction

(12)   The world-system is composed of the core, semi-peripheries and peripheries.

(13)   This division is based upon the spatial division of (productive) labor.

(14)   The spatial division of labor generates an unequal exchange of commodities, thus the accumulation of capital in the core of the system takes place at the cost of the peripheries.

Some of these theses are shared by other world-system theorists, but not all of them. Without debating the differences between them, let me exemplify them with the most controversial issue at stake between Immanuel Wallerstein and Andre G. Frank: according to Wallerstein, the world-system has existed for ca.500 years, and according to Frank – for ca. 5000 years. Obviously, the issue is not purely a matter of numbers. The point is that according to Frank the basic social (economic etc.) mechanisms existed for thousands of years and their most fundamental essence has remained unchanged; while according to Wallerstein, fundamentally new mechanisms came into existence in the 'long 16th century.'

The task of transforming Wallerstein's (and/or Frank's) theory into a theory that can satisfy the rules of idealizational methodology is a difficult task, and one that cannot be undertaken here (Czajkowski 1993). Nevertheless, I will try to consider the question of the possible consequences of introducing a world-systemic dimension into the models constructed in the framework of non-Marxian historical materialism.

There is no doubt that Nowakian historical materialism is above all a theoretical account of class struggle(s). This interpretation calls for many corrections if we want to take into account the fact that humankind (living in the 'Old World') has for centuries (at least fifty, according to Frank) not constituted a set of even only relatively isolated societies.

First, we should take into account the possibility that a change of class relations (characteristic for a society) could result from external influences. I guess that the Napoleonic wars and their social (class) consequences for some European societies can be analyzed in this light. More or less the same can be said about the Soviet post-war political/military activity in Poland, Hungary etc. or USA & Co's intervention in Iraq.

Second, the 'demonstration effect' should be considered, especially if the 20th and 21st centuries are analyzed: The collapse of 'real socialism' in the Central-Eastern European countries (it resulted in transformations of class structures, though their nature is controversial). Without taking into account the changes in Poland in 1989 (symbolically: the election of 4th June and Mazowiecki's government appointment) we would have difficulties with explaining the changes in Czechoslovakia, Romania etc. Less obvious is impact of these changes on the transformations in distant parts of the world. However, the temporal coincidence between them (e.g. the de Klerk–Mandela agreement signed on 17 November 1993) does not seem incidental. The importance of the 'demonstration effect' has been much greater during the last hundred years or so than in the previous epochs: 'live images' exert a much stronger influence than words. (Marx wrote about the role the railway played in the development of the workers' movement. Today, TV and the Internet play a similar role).

Third, in recent years we have experienced some new phenomena that might be classified somewhere in-between direct external influence and the 'demonstration effect.' I mean here the Georgian 'Revolution of Roses' (2003), the Ukrainian 'Orange Revolution' (2004), or the Kyrgyz 'Tulip Revolution'

(2005). There are some dates suggesting the important role played in all these events by foreign (especially Serbian) activists.

Fourth. Among the forms of class struggle (in the broadest sense) we should include the 'exit' from a given system of class relations. This type of class struggle encompasses a broad spectrum of actions: from the change of place of work (of church, of university) to the emigration to other continents. It should be noted that this form of class struggle can sometimes be applied not only by the members of oppressed classes but also by those of oppressing classes (as in the case of capitalists transferring machines to other countries). The historically changing levels (determined by technologies of transportation and communication, by knowledge etc.) of the mobility of the labor force, of financial and 'real' capital etc. – determine the degree of the practical accessibility of these forms of class struggle.

Fifth. Geographical differentiation of the occurrence of various practices which are complementary to each other has been a factor co-determining the reproduction of various class structures. To give only two – interesting and historically important – examples. This first one is based on the modern history of sugar. It was produced in the plantations of West India. They were commodity-oriented (though, in a sense, capitalist) but based upon a slave labor force. They generated a permanent demand for slaves which were supplied by a specific sector of 'hunting for people' (managed by Africans). And finally: the British sector of sea transportation and trade which complemented this American-African-British triangle. The second example refers to the system of the production and distribution of narcotics. We face here a tangle of interests of peasants, local mafias, USA mafias etc. If we take into account the role that the (illegal) profits generated by the narcotics trade happens to play in supporting various political/military activities, wé obtain a still more complicated image (see Brzechczyn 2020).

As was mentioned, the introduction of the problem of (world) social space has to result in some corrections being made to non-Marxian historical materialism. However, the world-system theory should also be modified. And in my opinion, this should be done at the start – on the intuitive level and before methodological elaboration. Wallerstein's theory (modifying or rejecting some theses of Mhm) is in accordance with classical Marxism in one important point. This theory preserves what can be called Marx's 'economism.' But Nowak rejected 'economism.' Thus, we have to reject Wallerstein's theory in its original version. If we agree with Nowak that the economy, politics and culture are autonomous domains of social reality, but we want also to preserve important elements/ideas of Wallerstein's theory, then we will have to introduce the notions of economic, political and cultural world-systems. Of course, as in Nowak's theory, it should be assumed that the respective systems can connect themselves into three double systems and one triple system. I would like to stress that it is by no means a verbal problem: If you wish, you can preserve the notion of the world-system – an (economic and political and cultural) world-system, and speak about its autonomous sub-systems. But in any case you should reject one of the central ideas of Wallerstein's theory: the idea of functional interrelations between the world economy, the system of national states, and world culture. But this formulation requires some qualification: A 'dialectical' and not 'simple' rejection is necessary here. Accepting 'simple' rejection contradicts the thesis on the role which the 'reconstructed' world-system theory should play in the subsequent development of historical materialism. Thus: what is to be preserved from Wallerstein's theory? Certainly, the idea of the social differentiation of (physical, geographical) space: some areas of the globe are 'central,' some others – 'peripheral,' and still others – 'semi-peripheral.' The respective notions reflect fundamental asymmetries in the interactions between activities being performed in these areas. Also: the idea of the differentiation of social structures characteristic for various areas (say: 'more capitalist' relations in the center of world economy, 'more feudal' in the peripheries), and the differentiation of (mechanisms) of social processes (say: the 'limited' role of violence in the center, and the 'fundamental' role of violence in the peripheries). And last but not least: the fundamental role of the spatial division of labor in determining the structure of world social space (see Czajkowski 2008).

This would seem to be an opportune moment to introduce a new motive: I want to speak about an element common to the theories of Nowak and Wallerstein. Though they view the relations between the economy, politics and culture in different ways, they both share – and also with Marx – the idea that social reality can be divided into these three 'momentums' ('domains'...). Whether any of them, e.g. the economy, is regarded as 'basic' or is not –is an important question, but merely to ask it, one has regard the tripartite division as correct/given. And I will now make some critical comments about this very division. But before I begin, I would like to make a preliminary remark: I suppose that at a certain phase of the investigations, this division was probably unavoidable. It was a 'technical' (though not idealizational) simplification. But, I believe, its time is over. Simply put: we need a much more sophisticated image of social reality, and, in consequence – of social space.

Considering all the positive and negative aspects of the tripartite division would be a very large task, not to be undertaken here. Thus, instead a number of short observations will be provided.

First. In contrast to what was explicitly maintained by Nowak (and implicitly by Wallerstein), this division is by no means 'obvious.' For example: Althusser speaks about four types of social practice (distinguishing science and ideology), Michael Mann (Mann 1986) – about four type of organization of power (distinguishing political and military power), the Polish sociologist Edmund Wnuk-Lipiński – about four areas of globalization (regarding criminality as separate "social domain"). Since each of them in his own way characterizes the fourth domain, then by putting their taxonomies together we would obtain six domains. However, to evaluate these proposals in detail, behind each of them are arguments deserving some attention.

Second. Some logical-methodological arguments are also levelled against 'trinitarianism,' including: arbitrariness (lack of criteria) for distinguishing just (the aforementioned) three domains.

Third. The internal cohesion of these domains is very problematic. Do journalists and maths teachers, priests and rock-stars, make up a compact group to be contrasted with another compact (?) group composed of coalminers and computer experts, of farmers and bank clerks? – I doubt it. The list of such doubts could be made longer and longer. These doubts could be regarded (not without some justification) as a manifestation of logical pedantry. But there are some types of activity which, in my opinion, cannot be located in this taxonomy, and which are so important that cannot be theoretically neglected. Let us refer to Wnuk-Lipiński who distinguished 'organized criminality' (Wnuk-Lipiński 2004) as one of four areas of globalization (!). Let's consider Al-Qaeda and its activity. Its leaders have been 'something like' triple-rulers. But who exactly have been they? – Surely not triple-rulers in the standard sense of the name. It is difficult to say. And the bosses of the Medellin Cartel were 'something like' owners-rulers. But should they be included in the same group in which, for instance, medieval princesses belonged? I doubt it. – We can have some hope that in the future such phenomena as terrorism or mafia will disappear. But to counteract them effectively we should understand them. A proper theoretical conceptualization of them is above all a real-life, practical interest for all of us. And, of course, these interests are also cognitive and philosophical.

If we can hope that terrorist practices will be eliminated from our life, we know that in the coming decades medicine will develop and become increasingly complex. And, in result, medicine (doctors, managers of hospitals ...) will come to have a 'triple power' (spiritual, economic, and 'physical') over biological reproduction, inheritance and the nervous system – to mention but the most important elements of our biology. I am very skeptical as to the possibility of locating it in the trinitarian model: it is not a 'standard' part of the economy (even if we take into account the service sector: linking it with, say, the tourist or entertainment industry, would give very little, if any, information about its mechanisms). Including it in broadly understood science (and – indirectly – culture) has some justification: some mechanism determining its development may be identical with those governing the development of physics or archeology. Nevertheless, the relations between physicians and their patients are different from those linking physicists or archeologists with students or the audiences of popular lectures. On the other hand, when referred to a physician the word 'power' suggests analogies with, for example, policemen. But analogies seem to be no greater than differences.

Another important domain which cannot really be correctly described in the trinitarian framework is the sector of advertising. At first sight it is a part of the economy. But if we take into account its role in forming human desires or even 'philosophies of life' (e.g. consumerism) it should be regarded as a part of culture, though rather a specific part.

Each of these domains of social reality (organized criminality, medicine, advertising) could be an object of analyses looking for the 'sociological peculiarities' of each of them. I suppose that still quite a few similar domains could be indicated. But making this list longer serves no purpose. Today we know very well that no theoretical concept is 'congruent' with any part of material world. If the remarks presented above were but a repetition of this epistemological banality, they would not merit formulation. The trouble with 'trinitarinism' is, in my opinion, much more serious. Let's try to analyze this trouble.

They are some (not numerous) theses about social reality which are almost certainly true. Among them, we can include the following: In the historical process we can distinguish two interrelated yet clearly distinct sub-processes: on the one hand, the process of reproducing social structures, the network of all social relations; on the other hand, the process of reproducing the system of social practices (including all the 'material' and 'ideal' instruments/products of these practices). A possibly complete theory of history should study both processes. And the question of the nature of their interrelations might be regarded as one of the most important, belonging to historiosophy.

Having adopted this assumption, I can give the most fundamental (in my opinion) argument for rejecting 'triniatarianism': The division of social reality into the economy, politics and culture is not to be rejected because a dichotomic division into civilization and culture or Mann's fourfold division would be better. All such divisions can be the target of critical comments of the same sort as those addressed at 'trinitarianism.' Their common flaw is the fact that they accept as a 'starting point' what should be the 'arrival point': the structure of social practices should not be assumed, but theoretically inferred. Moreover, even very cursory analysis suggests that this structure is historically changing.

Analysis of these changes, of their mechanism, causes and effects, is as much an important task of historiosophy as the analysis of the changes in the network of social (class) relations.

As I have tried to demonstrate, the rejection of 'trinitarianism' is important for adequate description of the temporal dimension of social reality. It is no less important for adequate description of its spatial dimension. I am going to demonstrate briefly what consequences this rejection could have for the theory of social space.

Let's assume that at a given moment of time the set of autonomous social practices is well defined. To make the following reasoning more intuitive (visible) let's assume that the production of cars or practicing Buddhism are such practices. In addition, let's assume that to each of these social practices is ascribed a network of relations between actions (realized at any place on the Earth) belonging to a social practice. For instance, a network of relations between the production of cars in Japan, Spain, Brazil, or between practicing Buddhism in Thailand, California or Nepal. Such networks can be disconnected, thus in fact constituting a set of two or more connected networks. The interactions are more or less asymmetrical: some points (areas) are more often recipients of 'incoming' influences, some other are more often senders of 'outgoing' influences. The latter points (areas) make up the core of the given network, the former – its peripheries.

Since there are many networks (and their number increases since the number of various types of social practices also increases), there are many centers and many peripheries. It is most easy to find examples from the domain of culture (to be understood in a common, pre-theoretical sense of this word). For the sake of illustration, I would risk the hypothesis saying that Polish mathematics in the years 1919–1939, and Polish (classical) music in the 1970s and 1980s belonged to the centers, respectively, of the 'world of mathematics' and of the 'world of (classical) music.' Somewhat similarly, at the turn of 19th and 20th centuries Paris was the very center of painting, and Hollywood is the center of film industry. The Vatican is the center of Catholicism, and Teheran is part of the center of Islam.

It happens that at a certain place, a number of centers are located. It is possible that such a situation increases the probability that another center will be located at the same place. However, there is no automatism here. The problem needs both theoretical and empirical analysis.

Having sketched a (more general) version of world-system theory, as a part of theory of social space, I would like to draw the reader's attention to some important relations between the theory of social space and philosophical anthropology. You may remember that the fact that Nowak's historiosophy is based on clearly defined and original philosophical anthropology is in my view one of its most positive values. But some corrections and modifications of this anthropology seem to be desirable. Among them, are those related to the 'border area' between anthropology and space theory.

Nowak's anthropology belongs, together with anthropologies of Marx or Gombrowicz, to a class of anthropologies that might be named 'interactionist.' This term characterizes two aspect of these anthropologies: Firstly, their central point of interest. They are (mainly) interested in man's attitudes (behavior ...) toward others (and only secondarily towards God, Nature or art ...) Secondly, these attitudes are shaped in the process of inter-human interactions. So much for the whole group of anthropologies. As regards Nowak's anthropology, a tacit assumption seems to play a crucial role. I will call it the 'independence assumption.' According to this assumption, the course of interactions between two individuals is independent from the interactions between them and other people. (Nowak was aware of this problem: while writing about social atomization he discussed the role it plays in determining the individual's ability to resist oppression.) The 'independence assumption' is obviously a simplifying one: Each of us interacts with many individuals, and our experience demonstrates that the dynamics of 'dyadic' interactions are not independent: interactions between a person and his/her boss in an organization, his/her spouse, children, parents etc. influence each other interactions (for instance, the 'aggression transfer' from a boss to his/her own child). The way in which the 'dyadic' interactions influence each other depends on several factors, of which two seem to be most important: the number of people with whom the given individual interacts over a given period of time, and the time of the respective interactions. These two 'microsociological' factors seem to be dependent on a number of 'macrosoiological' factors. In particular, many structural factors (e.g. urbanization, spatial population density) determine the statistical distribution of the magnitude of 'individual social neighborhoods' (the group of people with whom the given individual interacts) and the degree of their temporal stability. In 'traditional' societies, these 'neighborhoods' are most often small and stable, while in 'modern' ones they tend to be rather large and less stable. To summarize, interpersonal interactions are structurally determined, and social structures/processes are the result of an immense number of 'dyadic' inter-human interactions.

To end the considerations on Nowak's anthropology, a few short remarks are necessary (see more: Czajkowski 1993; 2001). First, Nowak tacitly assumes that the partners of interactions mutually know their 'hierarchies of values.' This assumption seems to be approximately true in some (traditional, 'simple') societies. If applied to modern, 'complex' societies, it should be regarded as an idealizing one. One might guess that some cognitive errors (imprecise or even false recognition of the Other's hierarchy of values) can contribute to the chaotic character of some social processes (among other factors). Second, Nowak's anthropology is 'metaphysical' (in the sense made precise by Nowak in his categorial dialectics): it assumes (tacitly) the stability of 'human nature.' Of course, this is an acceptable philosophical stance. However, just in the context of Nowak's own ontology and historiosophy, some doubts should be formulated. Nowakian 'human nature' is mainly of a social character, and its biological, natural components seem to be of secondary importance. And the social character of 'human nature' should suggest considering the idea of its changeability, especially if social reality is viewed as changing itself 'deeply' and not only 'superficially.' Third (a concretization of the previous remark), any (applications in historiosophy oriented) anthropology should consider the problem of the 'flexibility' of 'human nature.' The experiences we have collected for the last few centuries, say, from the 16th century, (the development of propaganda, education, advertisement etc.) seem to demonstrate that it is possible to make 'human nature' an object of manipulations. Unfortunately, there is no reason to believe that we have reached the limits of our capabilities in this domain. Not to say that we should take into account the (intentional?/ unintentional?) effects that electronic media exert on our brains (and, thus, on our minds) Four, if a historiosophy has ambition to predict the future (and non-Marxian historical materialism surely has such ambitions), it should take into account the possibilities of transformations of the material (biological, e.g. genetic) foundations of human nature and analyze the possible consequences of such (hypothetical) actions. There is a possibility (danger!!!) that social divisions will be transformed into natural ones. In other words, putting aside the problem of small/great probability, the danger does exist that a *New Brave World* (the world of Alphas, Gammas and Deltas), as described by Aldous Huxley, will one day come into existence. Fifth, Nowak accepts some assumptions of a 'statistical' character in his anthropology. The very presence of such assumptions in an anthropology being developed as the basis for historiosophy is natural: One cannot seriously doubt that people are different. And not only physically ('black'/'white,' 'tall'/'small') but also as to their character/ personality, there are among us saints and sinners, great artists and 'simple' craftsmen ... Having assumed that any statistical distribution of 'types of personality' is possible (from 'society of saints' to 'society of sinners'), we would obtain a rather 'weak' (= excluding very few logically possible histories) historiosophy. Quite rightly, Nowak was looking for other assumptions. He assumes (though not quite explicitly) that the statistical distribution of 'types of personality' is approximately of a 'Gaussian' ('normal') sort. This is, in my opinion, a correct intuition. However, if we formulate it in this quasi-mathematical form, we will be able to formulate it more precisely and to correct it. It should be remembered that all empirical distributions are 'Gaussian' to a degree of approximation; in particular, they need not to be (perfectly) symmetrical. It might happen, due to purely stochastic mechanisms, that in one population the number of 'extremely good' will be greater than that of 'extremely bad,' and in another – conversely. If the difference were 'sufficiently great,' it could have some important consequences for the histories of these populations.\

At this moment I would like to make an additional remark on a hidden (and not yet discussed) assumption of Nowak's anthropology. Nowak seems to assume that an individual's character is (at least at a given moment in time) 'well defined' ('fixed'). But it does not have to be the case: characters can be more or less 'fuzzy,' and the process of their 'crystallization' may depend on the statistical distribution of characters in their population: those of average and 'fuzzy' character may become slightly 'better' persons in a population in which the number of 'saints' is greater than the number of 'sinners,' and slightly 'worse' persons in a population in which the 'sinners' outnumber the 'saints.'

To round off these considerations, note that migrations (thus specific changes of social space) may result in changes in the distribution of personalities in both societies: here 'exporting' people, and there 'importing' them.

The impossibility of the effective application of classical historical materialism to the analysis of the history of the Soviet Union and other 'real-socialist' countries and the conviction that 'Marx's fundamental error' (consisting in false theory of the polity/state as being a part of the 'superstructure' determined genetically and functionally by economic 'base') was the main motive behind Nowak's investigations, which resulted in his creating non-Marxian historical materialism. It is not surprising that a new materialist theory of politics also suggested that the sphere of culture can be modelled in a similar way.

As I have already declared, I regard Nowak's critique of Marx as basically correct. Nevertheless, I think that his critique of what could be called Marxian 'economism' is – in some points – going 'too far.' Before I try to be more precise and justify this contention, I would like to make a methodological (psychological) remark: It is almost obvious that someone who formulates a new conception focuses on what distinguishes it from the older conceptions – on what justifies the criticism which motivated its formulation. But four decades or so have passed since the basic ideas of non-Marxian historical materialism were formulated; thus it is time to critically discuss the Nowakian critique of Marx.

I would like to begin the discussion from the point at which the issue of 'economism' is interlinked with some problems of anthropology. It seems to me that Nowak (for rather obvious reasons – if we remember that his intellectual passions as philosopher were strongly interwoven with his political commitments as a citizen) passed over the important problem – for anthropology and historiosophy – of anthropogenesis: of emerging Man (humankind) out of the natural/animal world. Having rejected creationism, one has to agree that this process was more or less continuous: the 'purely animal' traits were incrementally supplemented with 'typically human' ones.

It is obvious that at least two (or three) basic attributes are shared by humans with our 'animal relatives.' First, we have, like all other organisms, to exchange matter/energy with the world (to obtain and assimilate food). Second, like all other species, we have to produce new individuals. I have to stress, even if very briefly, that is from a 'purely philosophical' perspective some works of Jolanta Burbelka (Burbelka 1975; 1980; 1982), Nowak's PhD student – devoted to 'familial historical materialism' can be regarded as the first manifestation of non-Marxian historical materialism. Third, individuals have to cooperate, and thus to communicate each other.

Having accepted these three points, we can say that any complete (relative to a given degree of detail/precision) anthropology/historiosophy should contain models presenting the process of emerging, out of 'elementary' (related with 'pre-human' elements of human nature) needs/actions, 'specifically human' needs/actions. I think that just for this reason any (whether Marxian or non-Marxian) historical materialism should assume some ideas known as 'Maslow's pyramid.' This conception is neither theoretically sophisticated nor based on large empirical investigations; nevertheless it expresses an important intuition concerning biological limits to social-historical (cultural) modifications of the structure (the ways of experiencing) of human needs: one can be more or rather less accustomed to hunger, one can experience it as something 'natural,' or instead as 'outrageous,' but it is not possible to get away from it and its consequences; the same could be said about physical pain. And so on. To put it somewhat differently: The degree of satisfying of 'subjectively experienced' (co-determined by history or culture) needs and 'objective' (determined by biology or evolution) needs is a factor of importance for modelling historical processes.

I would like to add some further comments on the relevance of the philosophy of Nature (and not of the natural sciences) for historiosophy. But first a remark on relations between Nowak's and Marx's historical materialism. I think that the Nowakian critique of Marx goes 'too far' – as regards some issues. But as regards other ones, it's not sufficiently radical. In particular, Nowak's models – very similar to those of Marx – focus on 'internal' social relations, on conflicts between social groups (classes). Nowak's models are more subtle and 'close to reality' than Marx's ones. But again a further step seems to be necessary today

(50 years after the Stockholm Conference): Humankind's history is not only a history of class (national, civilizational ...) struggles, however conceived of and accounted for: it is – also! – a history of the game(s) played by our species with Nature. (Some decades ago, we would have said: 'struggle with Nature'; the term 'game' seems to better render our contemporary view of Man-Nature relations.) At the time of Marx, we could still abstract from this dimension of history; today no serious historiosophy should/could neglect this dimension of history. And the point is not to attach 'mechanically' a 'summary' of ecology to historiosophy. (One could note at this moment that just the necessity of 'combining' the perspectives of both the social sciences/humanities and the natural sciences is one of the reasons why we should discuss the philosophy of history – with emphasis on "philosophy"). We need theories that account for the relations between our species and the world 'around us.' We need theories that account for the relations between these relations and those between various segments of humanity. (I have to add that Nowak noticed this problem, as it confirms his paper, published in this volume, devoted to an analysis of the pacifist, ecological and feminist movements. Unfortunately, he had no time to elaborate on these ideas and include them in his historiosophy. Let's add that from the perspective generated by the dialectical tradition (in the sense of 'categorial dialectics') one should expect that models of Man-Nature relations should demonstrate the changeability of these relations and the mechanisms of these changes.

Constructing such models might also have some (positive!) side-effects: it might suggest (or even necessitate) profound investigations of some problems pertaining to the border area between social ontology and historiosophy. Here I have two issues in mind. First, the problem of relations between conflict and cooperation: Most (or even virtually all) inter-human relations (from 'face-to-face' to relations between 'blocs of states') contain some elements of cooperation and some – of conflict (rivalry). The analysis of their interactions seems to be one of the historiosphical issues still waiting to be tackled. Second, this analysis, having importance in its own right, should also deliver the theoretical foundations for a theory of 'levels of integration' of social groups. Everyday observations supplemented with factual historical knowledge suggest that some groups being in conflict with others (and, to a degree, integrated by this conflict) are divided internally into conflicted (and struggling) sub-groups Such a situation may repeat itself many times: conflicted nations, each divided into conflicting social classes, social classes divided into territorial and/or professional groups. We could also try to go in the opposite direction and try to analyze the hypothesis that humankind – however internally conflicted – is in the process of transformation from a biological and/or statistical group into a social group. The relevance of this question for understanding globalization seems to be obvious.

I would like to say some words about the relevance of the philosophy of Nature for historiosophy, but viewed from a somewhat different perspective than that assumed above. Three points are to be made. First, non-Marxian historical materialism is a materialist theory: the notion of material instruments of production (coercion, indoctrination) or, simply put, of some material things/physical objects (like hammers, lathes, swords, cannons, papyruses, printing machines ...) is of central importance for this theory. Its further development needs a well elaborated theory of the material instruments of human actions. I am rather skeptical as to the meaningfulness of introducing to such a theory (at least to its initial models) the division of material instruments into tools of production, of coercion, and of indoctrination. What is made of steel – whether ploughs (surgical instruments ...) or swords (guns ...) – depends on many 'purely social' factors. But before such a decision is to be made, one has to know how to produce steel. And to produce steel one has to know how to produce and control great temperatures. And to produce great temperatures, one has to extract great amounts of coal ... It seems to me that the initial model of the development of the material tools of human actions should be 'naturalist' in its content, based on an ontology of the material world, and only in some phases of its concretization should social factors be introduced.

It is worthwhile to note the links between the issue discussed in the previous passage and the theory of social space. However we would like to define social space, one point is beyond any doubt: it is 'based' on our planet – Earth is its fundament. And it is extremely differentiated. Also (or, above all) it is a complex of objects of human actions. The particular natural features of this or that area of the planet co-determine the 'shape' which the basic (biological) human needs assume. For instance, climatic conditions decide whether warm clothing is needed, or 'light' clothing is sufficient. The particular traits of this or that co-determine (decide whether) satisfying basic needs demands hard work, or is relatively easy. For instance, the quantity of human labor necessary for the production of the given amount of food depends, *inter alia*, on the quality of soil (chernozem or rendzina).

It is also beyond any doubt that social space is co-determined by the (physical) movement of people and the objects of their actions. This movement is determined by a complex of social factors. But obviously it has its physical foundations. First, in some physical conditions moving is relatively difficult (big mountains), while in some others, it is relatively easy (large plains). Second: to what extent geographical conditions make moving difficult or easy depends on the means of transportation: one's own legs, or horses, or cars ...

Third, the evolution of the means of transportation (from horses to jets) is a central element of the evolution of social space. A similar role is played by the evolution of transport infrastructure (roads, bridges, train networks ...) and of communication infrastructure (radio, the Internet)

4   Final Remark

A lot of work is to be done. And this is a measure of the greatness of Nowak's historiosophy – that it can be developed in further and different directions.

And last but not least: if you think (as I do) that the prospects for us – for humanity – are not necessarily better and better (which does not necessarily imply that they are worse and worse), and that we are responsible for our future, for the future of our children, and their children ... we should try to understand our responsibility better. We should know what can be done and what cannot. And thus we need historiosophy.

References

Althusser, L. et al. (1965). *Lire Le Capital*. Paris: Francois Maspero.

Borbone, G. (2016). Question di Metoda. Leszek Nowak e la scienza come idealizzazione. Roma: Acireale.

Borbone, G. (2021). *The Relevance of Models. Idealization and Concretization in Leszek Nowak*. Műnchen: Grin Verlag.

Brzechczyn, K. (2004). *O wielości linii rozwojowych społeczeństwa meksykańskiego. Próba interpretacji ewolucji społeczeństwa meksykańskiego* [On the Multitude of the Lines of Development in the Historical Process. An Attempt at Interpretation of Evolution of the Mexican Society] Poznań: Wyd. UAM.

Brzechczyn, K. (2013). *O ewolucji solidarnościowej myśli społeczno-politycznej w latach 1980–1981. Studium z filozofii społecznej* [On the Evolution of the Socio-Political Thought of the Solidarity' in the Years 1980–1981. A Study in Social Philosophy]. Poznań: Wyd. UAM.

Brzechczyn, K. (2017). From Interpretation to Refutation of Marxism. On Leszek Nowak's non-Marxian Historical Materialism. *Hybris. Internetowy Magazyn Filozoficzny*, 37, 141–178.

Brzechczyn, K. (2020). *The Historical Distinctiveness of Central Europe: A Study in the Philosophy of History*. Berlin: Peter Lang.

Burbelka, J. (1975). Historical Materialism: Its Essence and Forms. In: *Poznań Studies in the Philosophy of the Sciences and the Humanities*. Amsterdam: Rodopi.

Burbelka, J. (1980). On Family Development Theory in Engels: Towards a Reconstruction. In: E. D'angeles (ed.), *Contemporary East-European Marxism,* vol. 1, pp. 51–64. Amsterdam: John Benjamin Publishing Company.

Burbelka, J. (1982). Historical Materialism: General Theory and Forms. In: L. Nowak (ed.), *Social Classes, Action & Historical Materialism,* pp. 211–235. Amsterdam: Rodopi.

Cohen, G. A. (1978). *Karl Marx's Theory of History. A Defense.* Princeton: Princeton University Press.

Cognilione, F. (2010). *Realta e astazione. Scuola polacca ed epistemologia post-positivista* . Roma: Bonanno.

Czajkowski, W. (1993). Social Being and Its Reproduction. In: L. Nowak & M. Paprzycki (eds.), *Social System, Rationality and Revolution. Poznań Studies in the Philosophy of the Sciences and the Humanities,* vol. 33. pp.153–176. Amsterdam: Rodopi.

Czajkowski, W. (2001). *Images of Man. A Study On/In Meta(-)Anthropology.* Gliwice: Wydawnictwo Politechniki Śląskiej.

Czajkowski, W. (2008). Od fenomenologii autostrady do teorii systemu światowego. Uwagi o ontologii/socjologii społecznej (czaso-)przestrzeni [From Phenomenology of Highways to World-System Theory. Remarks on Ontology/Sociology of Social (Time-) Space]. In: J. Mikołajec & I. Sobieraj (eds.), *Fenomenologia autostrady. Aspekt filozoficzny,* pp. 25–51. Zabrze: Oficyna Stowarzyszenia Na Rzecz Nauki Polskiej.

Garcia de la Sierra, A. (2019). *A Structuralist Theory of Economics.* London: Routledge.

Habermas, J. (1976). *Zur Rekonstruktion des Historischen Materialismus.* Frankfurt an Main: Suhrkamp.

Habermas, J. (1981). *Theorie des kommunikativen Handelns.* Frankfurt am Main: Suhrkamp.

Halas, J. (2016). Weber's Ideal Types and Idealization. *Filozofia Nauki,* 1, 5–26.

Klawiter, A. (1978). *Problem metodologicznego statusu materializmu historycznego* [The Problem of Methodological Status of Historical Materialism]. Warszawa: PWN.

Klawiter, A. (1989). Historical Materialism and the Visions of Social Development. In: L. Nowak (ed.), *Dimensions of the Historical Process. Poznań Studies in the Philosophy of the Sciences and the Humanities,* vol. 13, pp. 9–38. Amsterdam: Rodopi.

Mann, M. (1986). *The Sources of Power. Vol. 1: A history of power from the beginning to A.D. 1760.* Cambridge: Cambridge University Press.

Nowak, L. (1980). *Structure of Idealization. Towards a Systematic Interpretation of the Marxian Idea of Science.* Dordrecht: Reidel.

Nowak, L. (1983). *Property and Power. Towards a non-Marxian Historical Materialism.* Dordrecht: Reidel.

Nowak, L. (1991). *Power And Civil Society. Toward a Dynamic Theory of Real Socialism.* New York: Greenwood.

Paprzycka, K. & Paprzycki, M. (1993). How Do Enslaved People Make Revolutions? In: L. Nowak & M. Paprzycki (eds.), *Social System, Rationality and Revolution*, pp. 251–263. Amsterdam: Rodopi.

Przybysz, P. (2007). What Does *to be* Mean in Leszek Nowak's Concept of Unitarian Metaphysic? In: J. Brzeziński, A. Klawiter, T.A.F. Kuipers, K. Łastowski, K. Paprzycka, P. Przybysz (ed.), *The Courage of Doing Philosophy. Essays Presented to Leszek Nowak*, pp. 315–332. Amsterdam – New York, NY: Rodopi.

Topolski, J. (1976). *Methodology of History*. Dordrecht: Reidel.

Wallerstein, I. (1974). *The Modern World-System*, vol. 1: *Capitalist Agriculture and the Origins of the European World-Economy*. New York: Academic Press.

Wallerstein, I. (1999). *The End of the World as We Know It: Social Sciences for the Twenty-Fist Century*. Minneapolis: University of Minnesota Press.

Wnuk-Lipiński, E. (2004). *Świat międzyepoki. Globalizacja, demokracja, państwo narodowe*. (The World of the Inter-Epoch. Globalization, Democracy, Nation-State). Kraków: Znak.

Woleński, J. (1989). *Logic and Philosophy in the Lvov-Warsaw School*, Dordrecht: Kluwer.

CHAPTER 3

Modeling the Dynamics of the Social Process in the Philosophy of Liberalism: Leszek Nowak's Critique of Liberal Historiosophy

Piotr Przybysz

Abstract

The aim of this paper is to reconstruct Leszek Nowak's views on the historiosophy of liberalism. While Nowak did not deal more broadly with liberalism, liberal philosophy was an important point of reference for his own historiosophical research. In the first part of the paper, I reconstruct the basic anthropological assumptions and those concerning the nature of society with which Leszek Nowak characterizes liberal historiosophy. In the second part, I reconstruct the libertarian model of the evolution of state institutions from anarchy to a minimal state by Robert Nozick – one of the main representatives of philosophical and social libertarianism. In the third and last part of the paper, I compare Nozick and Nowak's approach to modeling the historical process and draw conclusions about the similarities and differences between liberal historiosophy and its counterparts derived from the Marxist tradition.

Keywords:

Liberal anthropology – liberal historiosophy – evolution of the state – Marxism

1 Introduction

Leszek Nowak did not devote too much attention to the philosophy of liberalism. Whenever he refers to liberalism in his works, he presents it as a theoretical orientation in historiosophical research (see Nowak 1985[1]; Nowak 1997a) or as a theory of political power which is an alternative to Marxism (Nowak 1991b,

---

1   Nowak compares alternative theories of the historical process, that is, 'historiosophies' – Marxian, liberal, and Christian (see Nowak 1985, pp. 105–106).

© PIOTR PRZYBYSZ, 2022 | DOI:10.1163/9789004507296_004

MODELING THE DYNAMICS OF THE SOCIAL PROCESS · 41

pp. 12–13). Thus, in Nowak's works, liberalism is primarily a point of reference for the construction of his own concept of historiosophy and theory of power. Nowak does not undertake a systematic and precise reconstruction of the assumptions of liberal doctrine. Instead, he sometimes polemicizes with representatives of liberalism, though – for example, with Karl Popper and Isaiah Berlin, questioning their methodologies of social research, and discussing theoretical differences between them (cf. Nowak 1973; Nowak 1991a, Nowak 1991b; Borbone 2021, pp. 134–148; Nowak 2022b).

Nowak expressed more interest in the theoretical status of liberalism at the end of the 1980s and beginning of the 1990s, that is, when Poland and other countries of the Soviet Bloc were undergoing a change of the form of government. After the fall of communism and the rise of the liberal democratic, capitalist rule, questions arose about the reasons for that fall and about the potential longevity of liberalism. Apart from referring to liberalism in his political publicism,[2] Nowak reconstructed the liberal model of historiosophy in a more systematic manner at the time, and he attempted to compare liberalism with Marxism on that basis. He also evaluated the theoretical and practical potential of both doctrines. He concluded, among other things, that Marxism is superior to liberalism with respect to theory, while liberalism surpasses Marxism program-wise and as regards practicality (see Nowak 1994, p. 118; 1997, pp. 11–16; 2022a; 2022b).

In this paper, my goal is to reconstruct Nowak's views on liberal historiosophy and to compare them with the position of Robert Nozick, one of the leading representatives of liberal philosophy of the 1970s. My choice of Nozick's theory for that comparison is not accidental. First of all, he was one of the few theoreticians of liberalism of that period who proposed a theory of social dynamism, which described the transition from the state of nature to the minimal state and which could be treated as an embryonic version of 'liberal historiosophy.' Second, Nozick's theory is an abstract model and, as we will see, is reminiscent of the idealizational modeling used by Nowak in his theory of non-Marxian historical materialism (see Nowak 1980; 1983; Brzechczyn 2007), and it could be interesting to set those two approaches, both based on the procedures of idealization, together.

This paper consists of three parts. In the first part, I reconstruct Nowak's views on liberal historiosophy. In the second part, I present the methodological assumptions of Nozick's theory and reconstruct his model of social dynamics. In the last part, I compare Nozick's and Nowak's approaches to the modeling

---

2 See the collection of Nowak's political writings (2011); in particular, part 4, *The Myths of Liberalism*.

of the historical process and make conclusions about the similarities and differences between liberal historiosophy and its counterparts from the Marxian tradition.

2 Leszek Nowak's Approach to Liberal Historiosophy

In Eastern Europe, the end of the 1980s and the beginning 1990s was the time of long-term geo- and sociopolitical changes – a turning away from the socialist state and economy. They were followed by changes of the ideology and dominant political worldviews which resulted in the rejection of Marxism by the then Eastern European cultural and intellectual elite and in changing its ideological colors from communist-leftist to mainly liberal.

However, for Leszek Nowak, those changes should not have triggered an automatic assessment of the theoretical status and truthfulness of the two competing paradigms of social philosophy, namely Marxism and liberalism (see Nowak 1994; 1997; 2022a; 2022b). For him the failure of the system based on the principles of institutional Marxism does not necessarily indicate that Karl Marx's philosophical thought itself is worthless, nor is the historical triumph of the system of liberal democracy a sufficient proof of the truthfulness of the principles of liberalism. Rather, the respective values of those theories should be measured by the degree to which their concepts can adequately describe social phenomena and by the explanatory power of their hypotheses. For this reason, Nowak believed that theories inspired by Marx's philosophy could still accurately explain the economic and political aspects of social phenomena, despite the historic collapse of institutional Marxism.

An example of that is, in his view, the quite good explanatory condition of theories originating from so-called analytical Marxism (see, for example, Gerald Allan Cohen's, Jon Elster's, Michio Morishima's, or Allen Wood's works). They draw on Marx's basic intuitions, but, at the same time, they reject the dogmatism of 'official Marxism', and they form their theses in the modern language of economics and analytic philosophy.[3] By introducing the concept of rationality, the language of rational choice theory, the category of technological progress and the concept of "rights to self-ownership" into social and economic analyzes, analytical Marxists were able to respond more adequately than traditional Marxism to the complex problems of contemporary societies.

---

3 Nowak's concept of non-Marxian historical materialism also fits into that stream of research inspired by Marx's work, and it is a Polish version of analytical Marxism (see: Nowak 1997; Brzechczyn 2017).

Therefore, according to Nowak, "we cannot simply assume that Marxism is an outdated theory and that there is no doubt as to the truthfulness of liberalism" (Nowak 1997, p. 11).

Nowak also pointed out the contradiction between the methodological declarations and philosophical concepts of liberalism. For example, in Berlin's, Popper's, or Leszek Kołakowski's versions of liberalism, the methodology adopted excludes the possibility of formulating laws of history and of constructing a theory of the historical process (see Nowak 1994, p. 119, 2022b cf. also Popper 1957). In spite of that, liberals sometimes referring to historical regularities, one example of which is Francis Fukuyama's "end of history" historiosophy (1992). According to Nowak, the declared anti-historicist methodology of liberals is at odds with the concepts they propose. Why is that the case? We could surmise that the purported anti-historicism of liberalism was initially motivated by the desire to criticize Marxism for its own historicism. But when neoliberalism won the confrontation with communism and became the dominant doctrine, liberals – now without any anti-historicist inhibitions – began to openly claim that capitalism with liberal democracy is the necessary end point of the journey of all societies (see Nowak 1994, p. 120; 2022b). Thus, they revealed their own tendency to speculation about historical regularities, for example, about the liberal-democratic society as the final product of the development of history – the kind of conjecture they used to accuse Marx and Marxist philosophers of making.

Nowak, then, appears to be suggesting that as regards the philosophy of history, liberalism and Marxism have a similar theoretical structure. Both doctrines (i) are based on specific anthropological assumptions, (ii) formulate rules concerning the reasons for the emergence of a state organization, and (iii) aspire to explain the regularities of social evolution.

According to Nowak, the basic assumptions of liberal historiosophy are:

I^{LN}: Human nature is, in principle, egoistic (*anthropological assumption*).

II^{LN}: Egoism is a destructive force. In order to harness it for the public good, society establishes certain institutions: parliamentary democracy and the free market based on private property (*the assumption about the functional role of social institutions*).

IIa^{LN}: Those institutions constitute a social system – liberal capitalism – which is a natural state of a society within the meaning given below:

(L) every society spontaneously tends to orient itself toward liberal capitalism; that trend can be stopped by force, but the result will only be a delay of that drive toward that natural state (*the assumption about the basic social tendency*).

III^{LN}: When a society reaches the state of liberal capitalism, it simply remains in it; parliamentary democracy respects the rights of humans and citizens, a free market based on private property ensures the welfare not only of elites but also of the middle class, that is, the whole – if we omit the margins – society. So, liberal capitalism is the end point of social history (see Nowak 1997, pp. 11–12; 2022a; and Nowak 1994, pp. 117–118; 2022b – *the assumption about the stabilization of social-political development within the framework of liberal democracy and the end of the historical process*).

Therefore, liberal historiosophy has its roots in particular anthropological assumptions and indicates a basic kind of social instinct which prompts people to secure their positions and create a state for that purpose. At the same time, it asserts that there exists a fundamental historical tendency toward a transformation of various forms of government into an organization resembling the liberal-democratic state. Finally, liberals believe that such a form of government is historically stable and constitutes the last stage of the development of history.

I agree with Nowak's claim that contrary to the anti-historicist methodology present in liberalism, which requires the rejection of "the formulation of general historical laws," we can find such a general scheme of the historical process in liberalism. Unfortunately, Nowak does not name the liberal philosophers – apart from Fukuyama, the author of the "end of history" thesis – whose works would contain a similar historiosophical model or scheme. In my opinion, such a model, expressed directly and presented in the form of a specific historiosophical utopia, is discernible in Nozick's *Anarchy, State, and Utopia*. That is why in subsequent sections of this article, I will reconstruct the appropriate fragments of this theory, and at the end, I will try to answer the question whether it is consistent with the scheme proposed by Nowak.

First, however, I would like to briefly discuss one more issue, namely, the possibility of classifying liberal historiosophy in the above version as a particular type of social theory. In this regard Nowak distinguishes three different criteria for distinguishing various types of social theories (see Nowak 1985, pp. 105–106).

The first one is: (1) which areas of social practice are considered to be the most important? – it could be the level of productive forces (materialist theories), of institutions and forms of government (institutionalist theories), or of binding social norms (idealist theories).

The second one is: (2) which factors, relations and social phenomena are treated as fundamental? – these can be economic relations (economist theories), political dependencies (political theories), or cultural phenomena (cultural theories).

MODELING THE DYNAMICS OF THE SOCIAL PROCESS 45

The third one is: (3) what is the main determinant of social development? – theories may either emphasize the antagonism and conflict between classes/layers/social unites (antagonicist theories) or the consensus and compromise, as a source of social balance (solidaristic theories).

Taking into account this conceptual framework, with the elementary distinctions concerning social theories, and criss-crossing the (1)–(3) divisions, Nowak concludes that:

IV^{LN}:   Liberal historiosophy, in the form of theses $I–III^{LN}$ (see above), is an example of *political, solidaristic and institutionalist theory* (see Nowak 1985, p. 106).

Liberalism is a political theory because it emphasizes the role of the dynamics of political life. It is an institutionalist theory as well because it underlines the search for institutional solutions for stability and social peace. Also, it is a solidaristic theory because it stresses the importance of understanding and compromise for reaching social goals. In the last part of my paper, I attempt a critique of that assignment and try to demonstrate that thesis IV^{LN} omits certain significant features of liberal historiosophy.

Nowak juxtaposes liberalism understood as a theory of political institutionalism with Marxist historiosophy. The latter one, unlike liberalism, can be classified as *economist, antagonicist and materialist theory*.[4] The nature of Marx's historiosophy is economist – because the basic social divisions in it concern ownership and economic property; materialist – because it shows that social development is determined by the division of the productive forces of the given society; and antagonicist – because it assumes that the conflict between economic classes is the actual 'driving force' of history.

From the methodological point of view – at least in Nowak's original interpretation – Marxist historiosophy is based on the idealization method (see Nowak 1980) which postulates that a theory should be built as a sequence of models differing with respect to the degree of idealization. The initial model of such a theory is assumed with the greatest possible number of simplifying and idealizing assumptions, while the subsequent models are constructed as increasingly concretized and closer to reality.

That is the idealizing structure of Marx's theory of the historical process (see Nowak 1994, pp. 127–128; also see Nowak 1980). The initial model of that theory comprises formulas for the adaptation of the relations of production and of social relations to the achieved material level of the means of production

---

4   Apart from the two social theories, liberalism and Marxism, Nowak's typology includes theories originating from the Christian social science. In Nowak's approach, such theories are classified as belonging to *cultural solidaristic idealism* (see Nowak 1984/1985, p. 106).

and of technology which apply to a closed-off, isolated society consisting of antagonicist social classes (see, for example, Marx 1967 or, for a broader discussion, Nowak 1983). According to the idealization method, the influence of such factors as technical progress or political power are only taken into account in further, more realistic and concretized models.

In Nowak's view, Marx's idealizational, economistic, materialist, and antagonicist historiosophical theory, thus understood, has an advantage over the political-institutionalist solidarism of liberal historiosophy, primarily because it can explain social phenomena in the broad historical context encompassing not only the period of the development of capitalist societies but also the development of societies in their earlier phases of development, like feudalism or slavery, as well as the development of non-European societies. The scope of liberal historiosophy, on the other hand, is limited because it "refers to the societies of the Western civilization in their latest form – capitalism" and because it cannot say much about, for example, the structure of the feudal society (Nowak 1997, p. 13).

It is worth noting – as an aside – that within the framework of his non-Marxian historical materialism, Nowak proposed an original correction of Marx's historiosophy, in the form of a critique of Marx's economism, and a correction of the initial model of Marx's social model, so as to take into account not only economic but also political and cultural social class antagonisms (see Nowak 1983, pp. 32–62; also see Brzechczyn 2004; 2007).

In the next section of the article, I will analyze Nozick's libertarian model of social dynamics, in an attempt to answer the question of whether and to what degree it is in line with points I–IV^{LN} (see above) which describe the assumptions of liberal historiosophy. Hopefully, that reconstruction will allow me to draw a few interesting conclusions about the similarities and differences between liberal and Marxian theories of social dynamics.

3 Toward the Liberal Historiosophy: Robert Nozick's Model of Social Dynamics

As we have seen above, Nowak accuses liberals – quite rightly, it would seems – of inconsistently claiming their approach is anti-historicist while actually referring to historical regularities. I assume that another contradiction in the liberal doctrine is its attitude to "abstraction,, "idealization" and theoretical "utopia." Contrary to their own anti-utopian and anti-abstract statements, liberals often refer to abstract constructs – such as individualist concepts of the decision-making subject, autonomous person, or utilitarian individual – in their social philosophy more often than they would care to admit. They propose idealized models of the state of nature, decision making in the original position, or the model of contractual society, and so on (see Rawls 1971; Buchanan 1976; Harsanyi 1976; also Przybysz 2009; 2016).

Those abstract and utopian models do not always assume the form of static representations. Sometimes they become quasi-historical constructs which illustrate social dynamics. That is the type of a model of transforming social relations presented by Nozick in his book titled *Anarchy, State, and Utopia* (1974), where the author characterizes the evolution of social relations from the natural state to the minimal state, which is close to the heart of neoliberals and libertarians (see Nozick 1974, chapters 2 and 3). I will maintain that Nozick's theory is an "embryonic historiosophy" which describes the transition from the natural state to the minimal state and which is worth comparing with Nowak's views on liberal historiosophy.

3.1 Between Anarchy and the State: the Philosophical Assumptions of Nozick's Theory

One of the main themes of Nozick's book is finding a way of transitioning from the original state of nature to the most desirable, optimal model of the state. That motif is introduced effectively with the following words:

> I argue that a state would arise from anarchy (as represented by Locke's state of nature) even though no one intended this or tried to bring it about, by a process which need not violate anyone's rights.
>
> NOZICK 1974, p. xi

That sentence is a very concise summary of Nozick's main thought. Nozick's aim is to justify the possibility of the existence of a state which would (a) emerge directly from the state of anarchy, (b) do so spontaneously, and (c) respect individual rights.

The endeavor, then, consists of three parts. The first problem is that of the *possible genesis* of the state, an explanation of how it could arise out of the state of anarchy. Nozick's argumentation is subservient to the task of political philosophy, that is, to finding the answer to the question of whether the state is needed at all and, if it is, what shape it should assume. Nozick asks "why not anarchy?," and he considers that question to be the fundamental question of political philosophy (Nozick 1974, p. 4). Contrary to anarchism, he claims that the state is not the complete opposite of the original anarchy but can be derived from the original anarchy, as its natural continuation. Not only is the state necessary, but its emergence is an indispensable stage of the process of social evolution.

The second problem of interest to Nozick is the possibility of the *naturally occurring evolution* of social relations. Nozick assumes a gradual, multi-step, unintentional process of transitioning from the anarchy to the state, from the natural state to the political society. As more and more people decide to seek the legal protection of the state, it is hard to indicate the precise point at which the anarchy ends and the state begins. Importantly, people do not leave the natural state behind as a result of a conscious decision or a social contract. Nozick writes: "No express agreement and no social contract fixing a medium of exchange is necessary" (Nozick 1974, p. 18). Exiting the state of nature is an unintentional effect of many actions. Nozick argues convincingly that the phenomena which emerge during a social evolution should be explained in a special way, by means of the "invisible-hand explanation" (see Nozick 1974, pp. 18–22), that is, by explaining phenomena which appear to be the product of someone's intentions as not caused by anyone's plans or aims.

Nozick's third interest is the *moral aspect* of the functioning of the state and the question of whether individual rights may remain unaffected by the process of the creation of the state. One of the main reasons why anarchists attack the idea of the state is the conviction that it is an oppressive institution. In turn, Nozick designs the minimal state with the assumption that such a spontaneously organizing state would not violate the rights of individuals to the possession of goods and that it would protect those rights (Nozick 1974, pp. 51–53 and chapter 5). In all other forms of the state, those rights are infringed upon as the state expands its competences beyond the minimum scope necessary to protect citizens against crime and violence (Nozick 1974, p. 51 and chapters 7–9). In such a situation, the state institution which tries to achieve a higher, 'socially justified' goal – for example, citizens' welfare, social security, or good fortune for future generations etc. – usually makes, at its discretion or by means of democratic voting, a plan for the redistribution of goods, and it violates individual rights in that way because people are forced to surrender the rights to their goods.

3.2 *Potential Fundamental Explanations in Social Science*

From our point of view, however, it is interesting that the evolution from the state of anarchy to the minimal state, as described by Nozick, is clearly counterfactual and somewhat reminiscent of idealizing modeling. Nozick attempts to reconstruct the possible and not actual genesis of the state, and the processes he outlines do not have direct counterparts in the history of actual societies.

MODELING THE DYNAMICS OF THE SOCIAL PROCESS   49

In this context, Nozick distinguishes so-called "fundamental potential explanations" (Nozick 1974, p. 8). They are explanations of politics with the use of non-political categories, for example, political choices are characterized in terms of the rational choice theory, which allows him to provide a significant explanation of a phenomenon "even if it is not the correct explanation. To see how, in principle, a whole realm could fundamentally be explained greatly increases our understanding of the realm" (Nozick 1974, p. 8).

In respect of political philosophy, a fundamental potential explanation will explain political phenomena in terms of more elementary categories of what is non-political. The point is to find reasons outside of politics – for example, among the more elementary anthropological concepts, concepts of action, theory of decision, etc. – for specifically political phenomena, such as power, authority, violence, or freedom, to search for the sources of politics outside of current politics, in the sphere of more basic laws, rules, and principles governing human life, political thinking, social decision making, and so on. Even if such explanations are wrong in that they point to an action or process as a possible cause of a phenomenon, while in reality that action or process did not have an effect on that phenomenon, the explanations fulfill their role by systematizing our knowledge about politics, economy, or morality.

As regards the central issue of the emergence of the state, we could say that a potential explanation of how the state could emerge from the state of nature will fulfill its explanatory role even if in reality no state emerged in that way:

> State-of-nature explanations of the political realm are fundamental potential explanations of this realm and pack explanatory punch and illumination, even if incorrect. We learn much by seeing how the state could have arisen, even if it didn't arise that way. If it didn't arise that way, we also would learn much by determining why it didn't; by trying to explain why the particular bit of the real world that diverges from the state-of-nature model is as it is.
>
> NOZICK 1974, p. 7

All in all, Nozick proposes that political philosophy should provide potential and fundamental explanations of political phenomena, and his concept of the emergence of the minimal state from the state of nature assumes such a form – of a potential and fundamental explanation.

3.3   *Modeling the Process of the Emergence of the Minimal State*

Nozick's political philosophy exemplifies the libertarian individualism approach, that is, it assumes that the basic social beings are individuals and that all social and state structures are only justified by being derived from individuals' aims and interests. As I have mentioned above, Nozick is interested in the possible and and not actual genesis of the liberal state, and the processes he outlines do not have counterparts in the history of actual societies. His model of the process of social evolution – which results in the emergence of the state – has, then, the form of philosophical fiction, which is, nevertheless, very instructive and inspiring. Below, I will try to characterize his assumptions about human nature, social relations and the trajectory of social evolution in a bit more detail.

As a libertarian, Nozick makes a number of individualist assumptions which characterize the individuals participating in the process of the emergence of the state. I propose to formulate them as follows:

I[RN]:   Individuals own themselves, they want to increase their own pool of goods, and they make autonomous decisions (*anthropological assumptions*).

Each of those individuals has some goods and protects them against intruders and competitors, either independently or by contracting specialist 'protective service agencies.' The decision whether the goods should be protected on one's own or with the assistance of a protective agency is made rationally by sovereign individuals who take into account economic considerations (Nozick 1974, pp. 12–17). Consequently, Nozick models a *quasi*-historical process of the emergence of the institution of the state, in which the basic driving force is to provide the best possible protection for private property. This can be summarized as follows: .

II[RN]:   The main function of social institutions, including the state, is to protect private property and prevent the inconveniences of the natural state (*the assumption about the functional role of social institutions*).

Nozick divides that process into several key stages. During the first stage of the evolution of a social system, individuals are in the (1) *natural state* – there is no state yet and no traditional institutions, and all people have the absolute rights to self-preservation, to protect their property, and to punish intruders and criminals on their own (Nozick 1974, 10–12). During the next stage of social development, called (2) *the state with associations for mutual protection*, rational individuals associate with others in order to protect themselves more effectively: "They may join with him to repulse an attacker or to go after an aggressor because they are public spirited, or because they are his friends, or because he has helped them in the past, or because they wish him to help them in the future, or in exchange for something" (Nozick 1974, p. 12). During the next stage of the evolution of a social system, there arises (3) *the state with private protection agencies*. The main feature of this stage is that there appear specialist private agencies which provide professional protection services to their members. In order to be able to fight the

MODELING THE DYNAMICS OF THE SOCIAL PROCESS

intruders who are the clients of other agencies, the given agency must simply be stronger than its competitors. Since such protection services are costly, the agency must charge fees for them. The competition between the agencies ultimately leads to a monopoly of one of them, and the creation of (4) *the state with a dominant protection agency* (see Nozick 1974, pp. 16–17). The logic of the action to which individuals are subjected in that abstract situation – the selection of the way in which they and their goods are to be protected – leads to the creation, in the next stage (4), as a consequence of spontaneous actions aimed at finding protection for one's goods and oneself in the case of a potential event of an attack by aggressors, of (5) the *ultraminimal state* which protects its citizens and which deprives those who do not want to become subjects of the right to self-defense (Nozick 1974, pp. 22–30 and pp. 102–110). During the last stage of the evolution of this idealized social system, there (6) *the minimal state* (Nozick 1974, pp. 110–117) appears, which also protects the individuals who had been independent until that time.

Thus, according to Nozick:

III[RN]: There exists a natural tendency to transitioning from the state of anarchy to the minimal state. That transition is rational and morally justified: "the first transition, from a system of private protective agencies to an ultraminimal state, will occur by an invisible-hand process in a morally permissible way that violates no one's rights" (Nozick 1974, p. 52). The emergence of the ultraminimal state is, then, morally admissible, and "the transition from an ultraminimal state to a minimal state morally must occur" (Nozick 1974, p. 52). The minimal state has the monopoly on the use of violence on the given territory, and it protects individuals' private property. "We argue that no state more powerful or extensive than the minimal state is legitimate or justifiable" (Nozick 1974, p. 53) (*the assumption about the emergence of the liberal minimal state from the natural state and on its moral legitimisation*).

This paper is not the right place for a critique of the particular steps of Nozick's argumentation. My only goal was to sketch, following the author of *Anarchy, State, and Utopia*, a model of social dynamics which would show how rational actions of individuals aimed at self-preservation and at protecting their own property could lead to the creation of a state which would be obligated to protect its citizens. Despite being counterfactual and not representing the actual historical process, that model is very interesting as it shows that liberal philosophy avails itself of quasi-historical reasoning to put in order the principles of social dynamics by recognizing the basic tendency to gradually transition from the initial, anarchical state of nature to the liberal (in this case – libertarian) state.

In the next section, I will try to assess if and to what degree Nozick's abstract and idealized model fulfills Nowak's criteria of liberal historiosophy. I also focus on the specificity of such modeling of social dynamics in liberalism.

4 Is Leszek Nowak's Model of Liberal Historiosophy Accurate? The Specificity of Modeling Social Processes in Liberalism

A closer look at my reconstruction of Nozick's arguments concerning the emergence of the liberal state shows that they are quite consistent with Nowak's scheme of "liberal historiosophy" (see points I–III[LN] from the first section of this text). To be more precise, Nozick's theory appears to be a clear exemplification of points I[LN] and II[LN] of Nowak's scheme. Obviously, Nozick constructs his model based on the assumption that people are driven by their egoism which manifests itself by, for example, striving to acquire more goods and to protect them. That desire, though, gives rise to conflicts between people, which are often destructive – unless the egoistic and rational individuals decide to create a state in order to protect their interests and private property (see point I[LN] of Nowak's scheme). Nozick also assumes that such a minimal state is, in a sense, an extension of the natural state – with the most troubling and dangerous aspects having been eliminated. That is also the sense in which liberals want the state to respect private property and interpersonal competition (viewed as the source of innovation and the driving force of development). According to liberals, members of every society spontaneously desire private property and compete with one another, and those tendencies should be values protected by the state. In conducive circumstances, the state – in Nozick's view – should arise as a natural consequence of those desires and trends inscribed in human nature (see point II[LN] of Nowak's scheme).

Therefore, I believe that Nowak's scheme of liberal historiosophy is an accurate account of the historiosophical intuitions of liberal thought and that Nozick's concept exemplifies them well. I have certain doubts about whether the model presented in *Anarchy, State and Utopia* is consistent with the content of point III[LN] of Nowak's scheme, that is, with the assumption about the stable continuation of liberal capitalism and of the liberal-democratic state, and about the so-called end of history. Nozick might not have wanted to make this assumption because of his libertarianism and lack of trust in any form of the redistributive and welfare state – and that is the popular form of contemporary liberal democracies in the West.[5]

The libertarian nature of Nozick's conception also invites reflection on the accuracy of Nowak's proposal that liberal historiosophy be classified as "political institutional solidarism" (see point IV[LN]). Seemingly, this classification is justified: liberalism attempts to construct – by means of politics – a strong (if limited) state which would contribute to the creation of special, solidaristic ties among the citizens and between the citizens and the state. In liberal philosophy, there are many approaches in which the social role of the state is understood in that way (see, for example, Sandel 1982 or Kymlicka 1990). In that sense, Nowak's classification of liberalism as political institutional solidarism appears to be *prima facie* correct.

Still, it is this solidaristic function that liberalism has the most trouble with, and this function seems to be the most fragile basis for the durability of the contemporary liberal society, which becomes especially salient during crisis situations. Nowak formulated the thesis on the solidaristic nature of historiosophy when Western institutional liberalism was in the comfortable situation of triumph over the communist system of Eastern Europe. Thirty years later, that is, in the second decade of the 21st century, we could risk the assertion that a number of crisis situations in liberal democracies have proven that the ideas of social solidarism are the weakest aspect of liberalism (see, for example, Deneen 2018).

It is also very important that Nozick's reconstruction of the model of social evolution from the state of nature to the minimal state demonstrates quite well the fundamental difference between the modeling of the dynamic aspects of social processes in Marxism- and liberalism-derived historiosophies. In the former, the modeled social dynamics usually assumes the form of a particular historical process with subsequent social formations: the primitive society, the slaveholding formation, the feudal formation, and the capitalist formation. In the latter, it assumes the form of a quasi-historical process of a gradual ascension of the society on the abstract ladder of social organization, from the state of nature, through the ultraminimal state, to the minimal state. Such an understanding of social dynamics is, in principle, ahistorical, and it prevents the association of that kind of dynamic process of transitioning from the state of

---

5   On the other hand, it is also possible that the set of assumptions with which Nowak characterizes liberal historiosophy is, in reality, a theoretical hybrid consisting of many concepts and intuitions from various areas of liberal thought. It is quite likely that Nozick's theory only exemplifies points I–II[LN] from Nowak's scheme, while the quoted Fukuyama's concept aligns with points II–III[LN] (although that would require a separate justification).

nature to the minimal state with any actual historical processes. How could we explain that peculiar defect of the liberal modeling of the historical process?

Apparently, it can be explained in three ways. First, it is possible that, as suggested by Nowak, liberal historiosophy only applies to one stage of the historical process, that is, to the development of the capitalist formation and to the line of development of Western societies, in the last, post-war period of that development (see Nowak 1997, pp. 12–13). Another possibility is that Nozick's model is only an initial model, designed with very restrictive conditions and idealized circumstances in mind, and that it should be subjected to the procedure of concretization and completion in order to bring that special historiosophical concept closer to the actual historical process (see Przybysz 2009, pp. 101–103). However, a third answer is possible, namely, that in the case of liberal concepts, we are dealing with a conscious resignation from a description of the historical process, to the benefit of a formulation of normative justifications for the liberal organization of social life and politics. That is achieved with the use of "normative modeling" – a special type of thought constructs, which illustrate the possible and most desirable scenarios of the development of social matters and have the form of 'abstract' or 'idealizing' models capable of depicting, for example, the coveted course of the selection of the principles of justice (Rawls 1971; also see Przybysz 2016) or of the selection of the rules for public decision making (Buchanan, Tullock 1967). In line with the latter section, the difference between Marxian and liberal historiosophies is that the former has explanatory and historicist ambitions, and the latter seeks to explicate the ideals of, for instance, a just society or an ideal quasi-historiosophy process leading to the creation of a state. Thus, liberal historiosophies offer normative and abstract ideals which show what such important processes of social life might look like in an ideal situation.

References

Borbone, G. (2021) *The Relevance of Models. Idealization and Concretization in Leszek Nowak.* GRIN Verlag.

Brzechczyn, K. (2004). *O wielości linii rozwojowych w procesie historycznym. Proba interpretacji ewolucji społeczeństwa meksykańskiego* [On the Multitude of the Lines of Development in the Historical Process: an Attempt at Interpretation of Evolution of Mexican Society]. Poznań: Wydawnictwo Naukowe UAM.

Brzechczyn, K. (2007). On the Application of Non-Marxian Historical Materialism to the Development of Non-European Societies. In: J. Brzeziński, A. Klawiter, T.A.F. Kuipers, K. Łastowski, K. Paprzycka, P. Przybysz et al. (eds.), *The Courage of Doing Philosophy. Essays Presented to Leszek Nowak,* pp. 235–254. Amsterdam-Atlanta: Rodopi.

Brzechczyn, K. (2017). From Interpretation to Refutation of Marxism. On Leszek Nowak's non-Marxian Historical Materialism. *Hybris. Internetowy Magazyn Filozoficzny,* 37, 141–178.

Deneen, P. (2018). *Why Liberalism Failed.* New Haven: Yale University Press.

Fukuyama, F. (1992). *The End of History and the Last Man.* New York.

Kymlicka, W. (1990). *Contemporary Political Philosophy. An Introduction.* Oxford: Oxford University Press.

Nowak, L. (1973). *Anatomia krytyki marksizmu* [The Anatomy of the Critique of Marxism] Warszawa: Ksiażka i Wiedza.

Nowak, L. (1980). *The Structure of Idealization.Towards a Systematic Interpretation of the Marxian Idea of Science.* Dordrecht/Boston/London: Reidel.

Nowak, L. (1983). *Property and Power. Towards a Non-Marxian Historical Materialism.* Dordrecht/Boston/London: Reidel.

Nowak, L. (1985). O konieczności socjalizmu i konieczności jego zaniku [On the Necessity of Socialism and Necessity of its Disappearance]. *Przyjaciel Nauk. Studia z Teorii i Krytyki Społecznej,* 1–2, 105–150.

Nowak, L. (1991a). „Man Vis-a-Vis Others." A Contribution to the Critique of Liberal Social Philosophy. *The Polish Sociological Builletin,* 4, 289–297.

Nowak L. (1991b). *Power and Civil Society. Toward a Dynamic Theory of Real Socialism.* New York: Greenwood Press.

Nowak, L. (1994). O zagadnieniu tak zwanej transformacji ustrojowej [The Problem of the So-Called Social Transformation]. In: K. Zamiara (ed.) *Społeczna transformacja w refleksji humanistycznej,* pp. 117–129. Poznań: Wydawnictwo Humaniora.

Nowak, L. (1997). Marksizm versus liberalizm: pewien paradoks [Marxism vs. Liberalism. A Certain Paradox]. In: L. Nowak, P. Przybysz (eds.) *Marksizm, liberalizm, próby wyjścia,* pp. 7–19. Poznań: Zysk i S-ka,.

Nowak, L. (2011). *Polska droga od socjalizmu. Pisma Polityczne 1980–1989* [*The Polish Road from Socialism: Political letters 1980–1989*], ed. K. Brzechczyn. Poznań: Wydawnictwo Instytutu Pamięci Narodowej.

Nowak, L. (2022a). The Problem of the So-Called Social Transformation On the So-Called Political Transformation. In: K. Brzechczyn (ed.) *New Developments in Theory of Historical Process. Polish Contributions to Non-Marxian Historical Materialism. Poznań Studies in the Philosophy of the Sciences and the Humanities,* vol. 119, pp. 77-95. Leiden/Boston: Brill.

Nowak, L. (2022b). Marxism versus Liberalism: A Certain Paradox. In: K. Brzechczyn (ed.) *New Developments in Theory of Historical Process. Polish Contributions to Non-Marxian Historical Materialism. Poznań Studies in the Philosophy of the Sciences and the Humanities,* vol. 119, pp. 106–118. Leiden/Boston: Brill.

Nozick, R. (1974). *Anarchy, State, and Utopia*. New York: Basic Books.

Popper, K.R. (1957). *The Poverty of Historicism*. London Routledge.

Przybysz, P. (2009). *Modele teoretyczne we współczesnej filozofii politycznej liberalizmu* [The Theoretical Models in Contemporary Political Philosophy]. Poznań: Wydawnictwo Naukowe UAM.

Przybysz, P. (2016). The Choice of the Principles of Justice in the Political Philosophy of John Rawls: An Idealizational Interpretation: In: G. Borbone, K. Brzechczyn (eds.) *Idealization in Science XIV: Models in Science. Poznań Studies in the Philosophy of the Sciences and the Humanities*, vol. 116, pp. 244–269. Leiden/Boston: Brill Rodopi.

Sandel, M. (1998). *Liberalism and the Limits of Justice*. Cambridge: Cambridge University Press.

CHAPTER 4

An Analysis of the Methodology of Leszek Nowak's Non-Marxian Historical Materialism

Krzysztof Kiedrowski

Abstract

This paper is a contribution to Leszek Nowak's non-Marxian historical materialism and it consists of two parts. In the first part, the methodology of this theory is reconstructed. The theory of power and theory of property was constructed by following the method of idealization and gradual concretization. In the second part, the problem of the interdependence between the factors of power, property and spiritual domination is outlined. The main thesis of this section points out that in non-Marxian historical materialism the cultural momentum is, on the one hand, the main factor (similar to political and economic momentum), but on the other hand is a secondary one. Cultural momentum does not determine the basic mechanisms of power and property but only modifies them in the quantitative, not qualitative way. This methodological analysis leads to an enlargement of methodological perspective and supplementing it with the procedures of abstraction and de-abstraction, stabilization and destabilization

Keywords:

Abstraction – concretization – de-abstraction – destabilization – idealization – non-Marxian historical materialism – stabilization – theory of power – theory of property – theory of spiritual production

1 Introduction

In this paper, I try to critically present the methodology Leszek Nowak used for constructing the theory of non-Marxian historical materialism (n-Mhm).[1]

---

1 At this point, I would like to thank Professor Krzysztof Brzechczyn for his generous guidance and precious remarks which helped me write this article.

© KRZYSZTOF KIEDROWSKI, 2022 | DOI:10.1163/9789004507296_005

I am convinced that the methodological layer of n-Mhm merits separate reflection as an example of the effectiveness of using, among other tools, the method of idealization and concretization in the humanities.[2] The specificity of the humanities necessitates the use of a different version of that method, so analyzing it will allow us to better understand the general procedures of idealization and concretization. In the section *A Reconstruction of the Methodology of Non-Marxian Historical Materialism,* I try to reconstruct the methodology of the theory of property (Nowak 1991a; English counterpart: Nowak 1983) and theory of power (Nowak 1991c; English counterpart 1991d). I complement the reconstruction with certain adjustments resulting from the formal properties of the idealization theory and of the method of idealization and concretization.[3]

In the section *The Momentum of Spiritual Production in Non-Marxian Historical Materialism (a Methodological Analysis)*, I discuss and try to argue for the following hypotheses:

1. It is a basic assumption of n-Mhm that three main factors (momentums) interact in every class society, namely, the economic, political, and axiological momentums, and the cultural factor is a derivative factor which modifies the economic and political dependencies quantitatively (mainly as regards the time dimension).

2. For that reason, it is not possible to create a theory of pure culture within the framework of n-Mhm – the axiology must have materialistic 'roots' in the economy and/or politics.

3. Pure theories of property and power are idealizational, but they are also constructed with the use of other methods, namely, abstraction and de-abstraction (what is abstracted from is the occurrence of the remaining main factors and not their influence) as well as stabilization and destabilization (abstracting from the variability of a factor).

One characteristic of Nowak's scientific work is the thesis of methodological monism (see: Nowak 1998b; 2012), that is, the conviction that all mature

---

2 I restrict my analyses to Leszek Nowak's three-volume work from 1991abc entitled *U podstaw teorii socjalizmu* (The Foundations of the Theory of Socialism; English counterparts: Nowak 1983; 1991d), taking into account the appendices to those books. It should be noted that n-Mhm has been developed by a wide circle of Nowak's collaborators (for example, Brzechczyn 1998; 2003; 2004; 2007; 2020; Ciesielski 2013; 2022; Niewiadomski 1989; Siegel 1998; Tomczak 1989 et al.). The restriction is necessary because of the content and aim of this article (the reconstruction and critique of the methodological layer of n-Mhm).

3 Nowak reflected on the methodology of n-Mhm in several articles (see, for example, Nowak 1996a; 1996b; 2003; 2022a; 2022b; Nowak, Nowakowa 2000, pp. 109–184).

AN ANALYSIS OF THE METHODOLOGY OF LESZEK NOWAK'S

scientific disciplines are practiced with the use of the method of idealization and concretization[4] – the life sciences and the humanities alike, although the latter are highly immature when it comes to methodology. Nowak consistently upheld that thesis, and he used it to build concepts in the humanities on the basis of the method of idealization and concretization. Some of them are: the concept of the rational legislator (Nowak 1973), the concept of categorial dialectics (Nowak 1977a), the theory of non-Marxian historical materialism (Nowak 1981; 1983; 1991abc; 1991d), and the concept of negativist unitarian metaphysics (see Nowak 1998a; 2004; 2007).

The essence of the method of idealization and concretization is a deformation of the studied phenomenon, carried out by separating its main and secondary factors, followed by a demonstration, in the subsequent models, of the ways in which those factors influence the studied phenomenon. In the life sciences, which are mathematized, that influence is expressed through quantitative dependencies. In basic philosophical research, it is expressed by expanding the conceptual framework around the studied issue, whereby the structure of a theory can be linear, that is, the subsequent models can be concretizations of the previous ones, or it can be nonlinear, with only the most idealized, central model being concretized.

Nowak also used the method of idealization and concretization for constructing n-Mhm. The whole concept was discussed in the three volumes of *U podstaw teorii socjalizmu* (Nowak 1991abc). It includes the theories of property / economic society (Nowak 1991a; 1983, pp. 18–124) and the theory of power / political society (Nowak 1991c; 1991d). In that work, Nowak wanted to present the specificity of socialism from the materialist perspective – its economic and political dimensions (see Topolski 2003; 2022). The axiological dimension was not thoroughly examined by the author (see, for example, Buczkowski, Nowak, Klawiter 1987; Nowak 1986; 2022c). In this article, I focus solely on the methodological layer of n-Mhm, so I assume that the reader has basic knowledge of this concept (abbreviation, see: Brzechczyn 2017).

---

4 The method of idealization and concretization is discussed the most thoroughly in Nowak 1977b, Nowak 1980, Nowak and Nowakowa 2000. On the Poznań School in Methodology, see: Coniglione 2010, and Nowak's methodological approach see: Borbone 2016; 2021.

2 A Reconstruction of the Methodology of Non-Marxian Historical Materialism

2.1 *The Theory of Property*

Nowak systematized the theory of property in the first volume of *U podstaw teorii socjalizmu* (Nowak 1991a). The theory comprises five models based on five idealizing assumptions (Nowak 1991a, pp. 34–35; see also: Nowak 1983, p. 39–42):[5]

(A) society S only consists of a class of owners the productive forces and of a class of direct producers,

(B) society S is isolated from all other societies,

(C) the level of productive forces in society S is constant,

(D) the number of the areas of production does not grow in society S,

(E) the accumulation fund in society S amounts to o.

Apart from the assumptions enumerated above – the cancellation of which results in a construction of new models of the theory of property – there are also certain special assumptions, which are omitted in the whole theory of property (in accordance with the *ceteris paribus* clause, the factors which have not been introduced into the concept *explicite* are omitted):

– society S is homogeneous;

– society S is not organized into institutional structure,

– every owner has at his or her disposal an appropriate number of employees, and all direct producers find employment, and

– the influence of demographic and geographic factors is not taken into account (see Nowak 1991a, pp. 35–36).

Apart from idealizing assumptions, the following theoretical premises are accepted in particular models of the theory of property:

1) a rationalist conception of human – a rational subject is a subject who selects that action from the available alternative actions which will, according to the subject's knowledge, lead to the result preferred the most by that subject (see Kmita, Nowak 1968; Kmita 1971);[6]

2) an adaptive interpretation of the relations between the owner and the direct producers, which encompasses two laws (Nowak 1991a, p. 37):

---

5   Non-homogeneous as they are, I leave the symbols of Nowak's idealizing assumptions in the theory of property and theory of power unchanged to facilitate possible comparisons of the content of this article with the text of *U podstaw teorii socjalizmu*.

6   Brzechczyn (1998; 2020, pp. 219–235) bases the model of property / economic society on a non-Christian model of man.

AN ANALYSIS OF THE METHODOLOGY OF LESZEK NOWAK'S

I. from a set of historically available systems of the organization of production, that system becomes widespread in society S which brings about the highest newly created value given the level of productive forces which has been achieved in that society;

II. from a set of historically available systems of appropriation, that system becomes widespread in society S which brings about the highest surplus product given the ownership relations in the society and the level of the alienation of work there;

3) a detailed directive for the theory of property concerning the correspondence of "what is logical and what is historical":

> according to that directive, the idealizational theory of the historical process consists of subsequent models which are concretized in the order ("logical order") of the historical succession of social formations described by those models (the "historical order"); thereby, the internal structure of the historiosophical theory as a whole reflects historical development: with new formations, there appear new factors which necessitate the concretization of the model for the earlier formation and, in that way, the creation of a model for the formation which has emerged from the previous one.
>
> NOWAK 1991a, pp. 7–8

4) realistic assumptions (R) that society S consists of individuals (which act in a rational manner) – this is a consequence of the thesis on existential individualism and essential holism (see Nowak 1991a, pp. 29–30; Nowak 2009, pp. 65–66 and pp. 82–83); society S is divided into an class of owners (which has at its disposal the means of production) and a class of direct producers.

In the end, then, the structure of the first two models of the theory of property (the structure of the other models is analogous) takes the following form (Nowak 1991c, pp. 84–85; Nowak 1991d, pp. 52–54):

Model I includes:

1^I) idealizing assumptions **A–E** and special assumptions (the *ceteris paribus* clause),

2^I) realistic assumptions about society S,

3^I) theoretical premises: a rationalist conception of man, an adaptive interpretation of the owner–direct producers relations, an assumption about historiosophical panlogism,

TABLE 4.1   The realistic and idealizing assumptions in the subsequent models of the theory of property

Model	Realistic assumptions	Idealizing assumptions
I	S, K^E	A, B, C, D, E
II	S, K^E, [C, D], non-E	A, B
III-2	S, K^E, C-2, non-E	A, B, non-(C-1), non-(C-3), D
IV	S, K^E, C-2, non-D, non-E	A, B, non-(C-1), non-(C-3)
IP	S, K^E, K^P	non-K^W, B, C, D, E
VP	S, K^E, K^P, c', non-E	non-K^W, B, D

4^I)   linear or branched conclusions (k_1, k_2, ..., kn) which pertain to the modifications of the owner–direct producers relations and are introduced on the basis of premises 1^I, 2^I, and 3.^{I}

Model II contains:

1^{II})   idealizing assumptions **A–D** and special assumptions (the *ceteris paribus* clause),

2^{II})   realistic assumptions about society S which take into account the cancellation of assumption E,

3^{II})   theoretical premises (without changes),

4^{II})   conclusions which pertain to modifying the owner–direct producers relations and are made on the basis of premises 1^{II}, 2^{II}, and 3^{II}.

Table 4.1 presents the contents of the subsequent models of the theory of property, taking into account the realistic and idealizing assumptions. The symbols and assumptions are discussed further in the text, in the parts devoted to particular models.

2.1.1   Model I of the Theory of the Socio-Economic Formation

That model is the core of the theory of property, that is, its most idealized model. It is based on all idealizing assumptions (**A, B, C, D, E**), and it is the starting point for the construction of the remaining models. As regards the realistic assumptions, thesis **S** is proposed: that there is a material foundation for the society and the society is divided into two classes solely on the basis of the disposal of the means of production (K^E – economic classes). That model, then, does not include the division of a society on the basis of two other criteria: the disposal of the means of coercion and of the means of indoctrination.

2.1.2 Model II (Slave Formation)

Model II is a concretization of Model I in which idealizing assumption E is canceled, so the studied society is additionally defined by its economic development (through excess); the other realistic assumptions (S, K^E) remain unchanged. However, as regards methodology, it is somewhat difficult to interpret assumptions C and D in the reconstruction of Model II. When he discusses Model II, Nowak states:

> There is also one more conclusion discordant with current conceptions that follows from the analysis of Model II. It is the slave-labor system, and not capitalism, which turns out to be the paradigmatic ('classical') example of a socio-economic formation. This is so because the slave-labor system *literally satisfies* [emphasis mine] conditions (C) and (D), as it is not disturbed by secondary factors (development of productive forces, emergence of new branches of production) which are disregarded by those simplifying assumptions.
>
> NOWAK 1983, pp. 71–72

The problem here is related to the counterfactual status of idealizing assumptions. The deformation of the studied subject matter (in this case, a society) consists in the indication of the main and secondary factors in order to construct the basic model. To avoid the reification error (see Nowak 1977b, pp. 101–103), assumptions C and D should be treated as quasi-idealizing (see Nowak, Nowakowa 2000, pp. 160–162):

> A quasi-idealizing assumption, then, is an assumption which has – in accordance with the available knowledge – a particular non-empty scope of relations in the considered universe but is not fulfilled for the rest of the universe. It means that the assumption is made – if one takes into account the whole universe – counterfactually.
>
> NOWAK 1996a, p. 39

It follows that for the slave formation, assumptions C and D are not counterfactual but quasi-idealizing assumptions.

2.1.3 Model III (the First Feudalism Phase)

Model III is constructed on the basis of the cancellation of assumption C which postulates that of the level of productive forces is constant. The way in which that condition is rejected, though, is quite complex because on the one hand, productive forces can grow in a periodic or constant manner and on the other hand, it can take place during various phases of the development of the formation. When idealizing assumption C is weakened (full negation does not take place here because the continuous type of technical progress is not taken into account), three realistic conditions are indicated:

(C-1) the level of the productive forces of society S grows in the phase of increasing alienation of work,

(C-2) the level of the productive forces of society S grows in the phase of revolutionary unrest, and

(C-3) the level of the productive forces of society S grows in the phase of the evolution of ownership relations.

When combined, those conditions make it possible to distinguish six variants of Model III (Table 4.2), given the assumption that only the periodic growth of productive forces is taken into account (see Nowak 1983, pp. 78–87; 1991a, pp. 74–84).

From among the possible variants of Model III, Nowak chooses the second variant to be the model description of the first phase of the development of a feudal society, that is, a society in which the level of productive forces increases in the phase of revolutionary unrest and where, consequently, that phase is shortened and multiplied. It is worth noting that that selection is not *a priori*, either – Model III-2 best serves the purpose of 'illustrating' and explaining the history of feudalism until the time when the feudal society is divided as a result of the emergence of a new branch of production (Model IV).

TABLE 4.2   The variants of model III of the theory of property

Variant of model 3	Realistic assumptions	Idealizing assumptions
III-1	S, K^E, C-1, non-E	A, B, non-(C-2), non-(C-3), D
III-2	S, K^E, C-2, non-E	A, B, non-(C-1), non-(C-3), D
III-3	S, K^E, C-3, non-E	A, B, non-(C-1), non-(C-2), D
III-4	S, K^E, C-1, C-2, non-E	A, B, non-(C-3), D
III-5	S, K^E, C-2, C-3, non-E	A, B, non-(C-1), D
III-6	S, K^E, C-1, C-3, non-E	A, B, non-(C-2), D

AN ANALYSIS OF THE METHODOLOGY OF LESZEK NOWAK'S

2.1.4 Model IV (Phase 2 of the Development of Feudalism – Dual Society)

According to Nowak (1991a, p. 84), Model IV constitutes a concretization of Model III-2, and it is constructed on the basis of a cancellation of idealizing assumption D. That makes it possible to propose a model of the emergence – in the second phase of feudalism (circa AD 10), because of the appearance of a new branch of production – of two subsocieties, that is, two pairs of antagonistic classes governed by different rules (Nowak 1991a, pp. 84–87, 92–94). The relation of concretization between models IV and III-2, though, is untenable. If model IV were a concretization of model III-2, then model III-2 could not be applied, in approximation, to phase 1 of feudalism. It follows that we should assume that model IV is a direct concretization of model I. In this approach, the theory of property has a star structure (only Model I is concretized, as the central model) – which is contrary to Nowak's view.

2.1.5 Model IP^7 (Property and Power in Society S).

Nowak claims that this model is a concretization of Model I because it is based on the weakening of assumption **A**, that is, on the presumption that a society is divided into classes based on the criterion of the disposal of not only the means of production but also the means of coercion. That is not a full cancellation of assumption **A**, however, the division into classes based on the disposal of the means of indoctrination is still not taken into account. Therefore, canceling assumption **A** would lead to the formulation of two realistic assumptions:

K^P – society S is divided into two classes on the basis of the disposal of the means of coercion, and

K^W – society S is divided into two classes on the basis of the disposal of the means of indoctrination,

of which only the first one (K^P) is takes into account in the IP model. As regards the subject matter, that model shows the development of a society from the perspective of the mutual influence of two pairs of antagonistic classes, one in the realm of property and one of power.

---

7 Nowak tries to construct Model V for capitalism (Nowak 1983, pp. 101–125; 1991a, pp. 105–146). However, it turns out that with the assumed assumptions – realistic assumptions S, K^E, c' (in society S, productive forces grow in a continuous and uniformly accelerated manner), and non-D and idealizing assumptions A, B, E – "model 5 is, indeed, not constructed properly because it omits the existence of an element indispensable for the capitalist economy, namely, power. The model is invariably based on idealizing assumption A" (Nowak 1991a, p. 143). In order to cancel assumption **A**, Nowak has to form an outline of a theory of power, so he constructs Model IP. That is why in this reconstruction, I do not separately discuss Model V – that model is not a legitimate part of the theory of property.

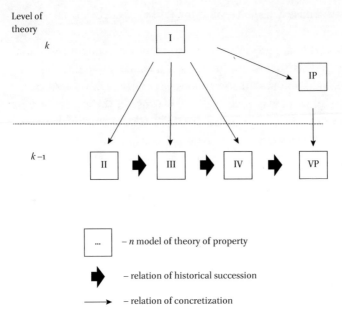

FIGURE 4.1   The structure of the theory of property within the framework of non-Marxian historical materialism

2.1.6   Model vp (Capitalism)

This model constitutes a concretization of Model ip. It is based on partially canceling assumption C, on accepting realistic assumption c' (which postulates that the progress of productive forces in society S is continuous and uniformly accelerated), and canceling assumption E about expanded reproduction. Model vp illustrates the development of capitalism and shows the necessity of transforming late capitalism into political totalitarianism and then socialism.

Taking into account the reconstruction described above and, thereby, the corrections pertaining to the relations between Models i and ii and between Models iii and iv, we can present the structure of the theory of property in Figure 4.1.

The fundamental difference between the structure of the theory of property shown above and the structure proposed by Nowak (see Nowak 1991a, p. 51) boils down to the relation between Models i and ip. In this reconstruction, it is not a relation of a historical concretization (a transition between formations). That is in agreement with the counterfactual status of the most idealized models (the k-th level of the theory). Models from level k-1 are constructed on the basis of the concretization procedure, and they can, with a degree of

AN ANALYSIS OF THE METHODOLOGY OF LESZEK NOWAK'S 67

approximation, provide an interpretive framework for appropriate social for-mations in history. The relation of historical succession only allows one to put the models from that level of the theory in order, but they do not remain in the relation of concretization with respect to one another because they could not be – except for the last one – referred to reality. At this point, I would also like to note that this reconstruction conforms to Nowak's proposal concern-ing the relation of concretization between Models I and IP (and the nature of this reconstruction is not historical). Such an approach to the abovementioned relation, however, creates certain difficulties which I will indicate in the sec-ond part of this article.

2.2   *The Theory of Power*

Volume 3 of *U podstaw teorii socjalizmu* contains a theory of power[8] con-structed within the framework of n-Mhm[9] and complemented with a non-Christian model of man, which provides an anthropological premise for the concept of power. That theory is based on the following idealizing assump-tions (Nowak, 1991c, pp. 81–83; Nowak 1991d, pp. 49–54):

(Z-1) society S (...) is completely isolated from other societies,

(Z-2) society S is only divided in one way: into two political classes, of rul-ers (who have at their disposal the means of coercion) and citizens (the remaining members of society S),

(Z-3) as regards the means of coercion at the disposal of the rulers of society S, we assume that their technical effectiveness is constant,

(Z-4) the rulers of society S not only have at their disposal the means of coer-cion but they also make direct use of them,

(Z-5) society S is not organized in certain political institutions – in particular, the rulers are not organized in a hierarchy of power, and

(Z-6) class consciousness does not exert an influence on the thinking of par-ticular people from the given class.

The list of idealizing assumptions made by Nowak does not include the assumption on which the materialist-institutionalist Model VIII of the theory of power is based (Nowak 1991c, pp. 205–209; 1991d, pp. 157–164). That model is an attempt at conceptualizing the complexity of the class of rulers, taking into account the lack of a single interest ("political fractions"). Thus, it is nec-essary to complement the set presented above with an additional idealizing assumption (formulated but not mentioned by Nowak in the set of idealizing

---

8   Nowak also presented an outline of a theory of power (Model I) in volume 1 of *U podstaw teorii socjalizmu* (see Nowak 1991a, pp. 157–199).

9   That volume is based on a book (Nowak 1988) which was published in English (Nowak 1991d).

assumptions for the theory of power) which will exclude the political hetero-geneity of the class of rulers:

(Z-7) the class of rulers is being led by one, common interest (Nowak 1991c, p. 205; Nowak 1991d, p. 157).

Like in the case of the theory of property, beside the abovementioned ideal-izing assumptions – the successive cancellation of which leads to the con-struction of the theory of power – there are also special simplifications in the whole conception (the *ceteris paribus* clause) (Nowak 1991c, p. 83; Nowak 1991d, pp. 50–51):

- about the constant level of the population of society S,
- about the lack of the influence of environmental conditions,
- about the lack of the influence of demographic conditions,
- about the lack of the influence of economic conditions, etc.

The following theoretical premises also underpin the conceptualization:

1) a non-Christian model of man – it presents a characteristic of human interactions which go beyond rational actions (non-rationality, irratio-nality), and, therefore, it makes it possible to take into account the rela-tions of kindness, hostility, indifference, enslavement, and satanization (Nowak 1991c, 25–54; 1991d, pp. 11–15; 2018); all the simplifying assump-tions which are binding for the non-Christian model of man remain valid for the theory of power;

2) a model of the relations between the authorities and the civil society – it shows those relations from the materialist perspective, that is, it pri-marily characterizes the authorities as a class which actually has at its disposal the means of coercion which make it possible to preserve and broaden the sphere of power regulation, and it shows the subjects' class as maximizing the sphere of the civil autonomy (Nowak 1991c, pp. 51–74; 1991d, pp. 21–48);

3) realistic assumptions – society S consists of individuals (who act in accordance with the characteristic presented within the framework of the non-Christian model of man), which is a consequence of the thesis on social individualism (Nowak 1991a, pp. 29–30); society S is non-homo-geneous because of the disposal of the means of coercion which causes the division into the class of rulers and the civil society.

In analogy to the theory of property, we can present the structure of the first two models of the theory of power in the following way (Nowak 1991c, pp. 84–85; 1991d, pp. 49–52):

Model I includes:

1^I) idealizing assumptions (Z-1)–(Z-7) and special assumptions (the *ceteris paribus* clause),

2^I) realistic assumptions about society S,

3^I) theoretical premises – the non-Christian model of man (an anthropological premise), the model of the relations between the authorities and the civil society (a sociological premise),

4^I) linear or branched conclusions (k_1, k_2, ..., kn) which pertain to modifying the authorities–civil society relations and are introduced on the basis of the abovementioned premises 1^I, 2^I, and 3^I.

Model II contains:

1^{II}) idealizing assumptions (Z-1)–(Z-4), (Z-6)–(Z-7) and special assumptions (the *ceteris paribus* clause),

2^{II}) realistic assumptions S which take into account the cancellation of assumption (Z-5),

3^{II}) theoretical premises (without changes),

4^{II}) conclusions which pertain to modifying the authorities–civil society relations and are based on premises 1^{II}, 2^{II}, and 3^{II}.

The table below (Table 4.3) contains a list of the realistic and idealizing assumptions which constitute the foundation for the subsequent models of the theory of power:

TABLE 4.3 The realistic and idealizing assumptions in the subsequent models of the theory of power

Model	Realistic assumptions	Idealizing assumptions
I	S, K^P	Z-1, Z-2, Z-3, Z-4, Z-5, Z-6, Z-7
II	S, K^P, non-(Z-5)	Z-1, Z-2, Z-3, Z-4, Z-6, Z-7
III	S, K^P, K^W	Z-1, Z-2, Z-3, Z-4, Z-5, Z-7
IV	S, K^P, (z-1a)	non-(z-1b), Z-2, Z-3, Z-4, Z-5, Z-6, Z-7
V	S, K^P, (z-1a), (z-1b)	Z-2, Z-3, Z-4, Z-5, Z-6, Z-7
VI	S, K^P, non-(Z-3)	Z-1, Z-2, Z-4, Z-5, Z-6, Z-7
VII	S, K^P, non-(Z-4)	Z-1, Z-2, Z-3, Z-5, Z-6, Z-7
VIII	S, K^P, non-(Z-7)	Z-1, Z-2, Z-3, Z-4, Z-5, Z-6

2.2.1 Model I

Model I is an elementary (most idealized) model of power of the materialist type. In this model, the nature of society S is assumed to be purely political (K^P), that is, the society divided only on the basis of the actual disposal of the means of coercion. Model I has the full set of idealizing assumptions (Z-1)–(Z-7).

2.2.2 Model II (Materialist-Institutionalist Model).

Model II is based on the cancellation of assumption Z-5, which makes it possible to complement the characteristic of power from Model I by adding the institutional dimension. Thus, the model is a direct concretization of Model I.

2.2.3 Model III (Materialist–Consciousness Model)

In Nowak's approach, Model III is also a direct concretization of Model I because it is constructed with assumption Z-6 canceled, while assumption Z-5 is restored. Thereby, Model III makes it possible to show the influence of social and political consciousness on the elementary concept of power. Since that factor pertains to the disposal of the means of indoctrination, it introduces differentiation at a more elementary level than the factor considered in Model II (I express that by using the K^W symbol which corresponds to the non-(Z-6) symbol; see Nowak 1991c, p. 7).

2.2.4 Models IV and V

The foundation of the construction of Models IV and V, which present the political expansion of society S, is the cancellation of assumption (Z-1) which specifies the isolation of society S. The difference between the indicated models lies in the weakening of assumption (Z-1) in Model IV and on its complete cancellation in Model V. It follows that those models are not in the relationship of concretization, and that the difference between them is technical (instrumental). That difference can be shown by indicating the realistic assumptions introduced as a result of the cancellation of assumption (Z-1):

(z-1a) the aggression of society S against society S' only leads to a conquest of that society;

(z-1b) the aggression of society S against society S' leads to a conquest of that society or to making it dependent on society S.

Therefore, Models IV and V should be considered together, as a concretization of model I.

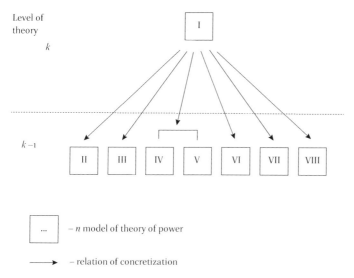

FIGURE 4.2 The structure of the theory of power within the framework of non-Marxian historical materialism

2.2.5   Model VI
Model VI is based on the cancellation of assumption (Z-3), and it shows the influence of technology on power relations. The model is a direct concretization of Model I.

2.2.6   Model VII
Model VII is a concretization of Model I, and it is constructed on the basis of the cancellation of assumption (Z-4), so it shows a realistic separation of the disposal of the means of coercion from their direct application.

2.2.7   Model VIII
In accordance with the correction introduced above, this model entails the cancellation of assumption (Z-7), so it is a concretization of Model I in which the interests of the political power can be diversified.

Taking into account the reconstruction which has been carried out so far, the structure of the theory of power is presented in Figure 4.2.

The presented structure does not, in principle, modify Nowak's proposals, except for the joint consideration of models IV and V. Also, it becomes clear that with regard to methodology, the theory of power has star (non-linear) structure.

3 The Momentum of Spiritual Production in Non-Marxian Historical Materialism (a Methodological Analysis)

The nature of those reflections is almost entirely reconstructive, and they are limited to the methodological dimension of Nowak's social conception presented in volumes 1 and 3 of *U podstaw teorii socjalizmu* (Nowak 1991ac; in English: Nowak 1983, 1991d). At this point, I would like to outline the architectonics of the core of n-Mhm on the basis of an analysis of the momentum of spiritual production[10] and to characterize the procedures which allow the construction of that theory. For this purpose, I will indicate and discuss two issues which have surfaced during Nowak's attempt at conceptualizing a pure cultural model.

Let us note that the following thesis (T) is the foundation of n-Mhm:

In all the most important fields of social activity of man, namely, the economy, politics, and spiritual production, people are divided into huge groups with contrary interests – and in all of them, minorities (owners, rulers, priests) rule thanks to their monopoly on certain material means (the means of, respectively, production, coercion, and indoctrination). The contrariness of the interests of such pairs of antagonistic classes (owners–direct producers, rulers–citizens, priests–the indoctrinated) is, by itself, a source of social resistance in economy, politics, and spiritual production (Nowak 1991c, p. 7; 1991d, pp. 4–5).

Clearly, these social divisions are elementary, in the sense that none of the spheres of domination can be reduced to the other ones. For that reason, n-Mhm is a theory in which property, power, and spiritual authority are considered to be the main factors. That explains the possibility of constructing a pure model of power (Nowak 1991c, 87–103; Nowak 1991d, pp. 55–64) or property (see Nowak 1991a, pp. 25–52; Nowak 1983, pp. 32–62). In Nowak's opinion, the attempts at constructing a pure model of spiritual authority (cultural phenomena, spiritual production) failed:

> [...] The basic hope at the root of this book is that the non-Marxian materialist-historical paradigm described in it can be applied to all three realms of social life: the economy, politics, and culture. I believe that is true with regard to the sphere of property (volume 1) and sphere of power (volume 3), so two-thirds of my hopes have been fulfilled. Having

---

10   Further in this point, I will use the following notions interchangeably: "the momentum of spiritual production," "the cultural factor," "the factor of spiritual authority," and "the value factor."

said that, my many attempts at developing a theory of culture within the framework of non-Marxian historical materialism have been unsuccessful, so I have had little choice but to lose the hope that the said paradigm could be of significant value for attempts at understanding the nature of cultural phenomena. [...]

NOWAK 1991a, p. XI.

This quote is a fragment of *Słowo wprowadzające* (Introduction) to *U podstaw teorii socjalizmu* (Nowak 1991a). Importantly, three years earlier Nowak, Piotr Buczkowski, and Andrzej Klawiter published a text which would later be included as a supplement to volume 1 of *U podstaw teorii socjalizmu* (Nowak 1991a, pp. 271–313) titled *Religia jako struktura klasowa* (Religion as a class structure; Buczkowski, Nowak, Klawiter 1987; Nowak 2022c), which contains an attempt at constructing a pure model of spiritual authority on the basis of the phenomenon of faith. Those reflections went beyond Marx's paradigm (questioning the thesis that social being determines consciousness). In the authors' view, they are in line with the theory of n-Mhm due to their treating spiritual production to be the main factor. On the basis of the quoted fragment, we may infer that this attempt was not, in the end, accepted by Nowak as an integral part of the system of n-Mhm. In other words, there were difficulties on the road to the formulation of a theory of culture within the framework of that social concept, and the author of that conception did not recognize their source.

The second problem is the unequal treatment of social divisions and, thereby, factors within the particular theories of n-Mhm. In the theory of property, the political factor is not viewed as the main factor but as a secondary one (assumption (A)), and the consciousness-related (axiological) factor is not considered at all:

We choose Model I as the starting point for reflections on the influence of power on the regularities of the development of a Marxian society, which means that all the idealizing assumptions of that model except for the first one, (A), remain valid and that idealizing assumption (A) is replaced with a more realistic condition:

(A^1) society S consists of a class of owners (who have means of production at their disposal), a class of rulers (who have the forces of coercion at their disposal), and the people's class.

The remaining assumptions of Model I: (B), (C), (D), (E) are currently maintained. We name this model, based on conditions (A^+)–(E), IP because Model I is corrected here by introducing a political factor, that is, the conflict of political classes.

That model is to determine the role of the political momentum in a Marxian society. However, that characteristic is only an approximation, for two reasons. First, condition (A^+), always idealizing, does not, strictly speaking, define a class society because it always omits the class which has at its disposal the means of indoctrination. In this book, devoted to an analysis of the relations of property and power, we will constantly omit the role of the momentum of spiritual production in our historio-sophical constructions.[11]

NOWAK 1991a, pp. 203–204

In the theory of power, the consciousness factor is taken into account (assumption Z-6), and it is a secondary factor ("the influence of social-political consciousness on the line of development of the system of power is indeed insignificant" – Nowak 1991d, p. 108), and the economic factor appears here within the framework of the interpretation of a special period in the social history of the Soviet Union (the NEP period), so it is not only theoretical (Nowak 1991c, pp. 227–229; 1991d, pp. 195–198), and it is treated as a secondary factor. That situation cannot be explained by reference to the theoretical foundations of the method of idealization and concretization because it appears to indicate that the theory of n-Mhm is based on diverse images of the essential structure.

As regards methodology, the solution to the abovementioned problems boils down to answering both of the following questions:

(1) what ontological perspective and corresponding essentialist hypothesis form the basis of n-Mhm and
(2) what counterfactual procedures are used for the construction of the system.

Let us first take a look at Nowak's answers to those questions. According to thesis (T), quoted at the beginning of this section, understanding social phenomena makes it possible to theorize about three main factors: property, power, and spiritual authority. Those factors are equal and irreducible to one another. By taking into account the dependencies characteristic of the said areas (secondary factors), we can construct particular theories (respectively, of property, power, and spiritual authority). The basic procedures which allow

---

11   See also English version of this methodological comment: Nowak 1983, p. 189.

AN ANALYSIS OF THE METHODOLOGY OF LESZEK NOWAK'S

the construction of those theories and, thereby, the system of n-Mhm, are idealization and concretization.

Since the abovementioned answers do not make it possible to solve the said problems, they must, in my view, be corrected with the use of the following terminological determinations proposed by Renata Zielińska (Zielińska 1989) in relation to the ways in which we can understand abstraction.

> The first way is to abstract from the existence of particular factors, that is, to eliminate them, for a time, from the researcher's area of research. The second way is to abstract from the significance or influence of certain factors on other factors. The third one is to abstract from the variability of those factors, that is, from the possibility of them having different values than the ones temporarily postulated in the given assumption. Each of those kinds of abstraction constitutes the subject matter of a separate procedure: the elimination of factors is related to the procedure of *abstraction*, the omission of their significance – to the procedure of *idealization*, and the omission of their variability – to the procedure of *stabilization*.
>
> ZIELIŃSKA 1979, pp. 89–90[12]

Differentiating abstraction from idealization (the nature of both procedures is counterfactual) appears to be of fundamental importance for theories in the humanities, especially those philosophical theories in which basic concepts ("being," "essence," "subject," "society," "freedom," etc.) are discussed. The thing is that the conceptual apparatus of philosophical theories is based on technical terms which, even if their understanding is borrowed from other scientific disciplines or from everyday life, should be defined and, in that way, introduced to the system based on terms which are already present in it (for obvious reasons, that does not apply to the original terms of the given theory). It is a kind of an ideal of philosophy, practiced in the spirit of analytic philosophy. There is no room for reflecting on the reasonableness, advantages, and disadvantages of that project here. Let us note the fact that a successive construction of a theory on a level of abstraction, that is, in the horizontal dimension, is made possible not by the procedure of idealization but of abstraction.[13]

---

12   Nowak conceptualizes the procedure of abstraction in a different manner (Nowak, Nowakowa 2000, pp. 116–119; Kiedrowski 2016, pp. 223–225).

13   For a more extensive discussion of the method of abstraction and de-abstraction, see: Kiedrowski 2016, p. 238.

One example of this is the theory of property. While constructing the first four models of it, Nowak does not abstract from the influence of the factor of power but its existence. Why is that the case? On the one hand, he can do that because both factors are equal with respect to the power of influence (they are at the same level of abstraction), so the relationship between them cannot be termed idealizational (idealization requires two different levels of abstraction). On the other hand, in order to be included in the system, the concept of power must be defined, at least to a certain extent (Nowak 1991a, pp. 157–182). Abstracting from the existence of a factor (the lack of an appropriate concept in a system) is different from abstracting from its influence (when the concept does exist in the system, but it is not taken into account at the given stage of its construction). Therefore, the relation which connects Models I and IP in the theory of property is one of de-abstraction and not, as claimed by Nowak, concretization (while Models IP and VP are in the relation of concretization).

If those findings are justified for the theory of power as well, the factor that remains to be discussed is value (spiritual authority). In this case, I would like to suggest an essentialist hypothesis that although all three factors – of property, power, and value – are main, the factors of property and power are original, and the factor of value is derivative. One important ramification of this hypothesis is the impossibility of formulating a pure theory of spiritual authority because that factor is always implicated in the sphere of property and/or power, and it determines not so much the mechanics of the development of the relation of property and power as the pace of that development. Thus, the original factors are a kind of a qualitative side of the development of class societies, while value, as a derivative factor, relates to the quantitative side (the time and pace of the development).

It is my belief that this hypothesis is substantiated by many fragments of *U podstaw teorii socjalizmu* (or its English counterpart). Here are a few of them:

> Thus, class consciousness can only be a derivative factor which accelerates or magnifies class conflict, and it cannot be the source of that conflict.
>
> NOWAK 1991a, p. 31

> However, for a historical materialist (in the sense assumed in this book), those are completely insignificant circumstances. Programs, intentions, good will – they are all of secondary importance; at best, they can modify the direction of the process and not determine it. The direction of the political process is determined by the material fact of the unequal position with respect to the means of coercion.
>
> NOWAK 1991a, p. 163

Deviations of the actual systemic line from the normal line, that is, systemic deviations, may be of two kinds: (d) – the functional change is introduced too late (retardation), and

(dd) the functional change is introduced too early (anticipation).

NOWAK 1991d, p. 85

The reason is important in the collective consciousness only if it can be used by collective force.

NOWAK 1991d, p. 105

If the above is true, the influence of social-political consciousness on the line of development of the system of power is indeed insignificant. The modifications included in the picture of interclasss relations are exclusively quantitative corrections, the same holding for the modification of the dynamic model of the system.

NOWAK 1991d, 108

If we accept the differentiation between original and derivative factors, the problem appears what procedure would make it possible to methodically present the relations between them. In line with the quantitative influence exerted by the factor of spiritual authority, I suggest stabilization as the procedure which would make it possible to abstract from that factor (Chwalisz 1979, p. 104; Nowak, Nowakowa 2000, p. 160 and pp. 223–225).[14] Abstracting from variability in the context of broadening or narrowing down the influence of various utopias, ideologies, etc., that is, from the variability of spiritual authority, makes it possible to construct pure theories of property and power. We can find an example of the application of the procedure of destabilization in Model III of the theory of power (Nowak 1991c, pp. 131–166; 1991d, pp. 93–120). The structure Nowak assumes for the momentum of spiritual production is analogous to the two other momentums, so it remains within the scope of the materialist horizon (on alternative conceptualization of spheres of politics, economy and culture, see: Bell 1976; Gellner 1989).

---

14   In my book (Kiedrowski 2013) and article (Kiedrowski 2016), I have viewed the procedure of stabilization as immaterial for the humanities. Considering these reflections, I have to change my position on the said matter. Although the reflections in those works pertained to a metaphysical theory, dealing with time, the conclusion I have made there about the role of stabilization and destabilization in philosophy turns out to be simply wrong, in the light of the analysis carried out in this text.

To sum up, according to Nowak, the basic momentums of a class society which is the subject matter of n-Mhm are: the momentum of property, the momentum of power, and the momentum of value. Contrary to Nowak's determinations, though, the momentums of property and power are original, and the cultural momentum is derivative – it modifies the dynamics of the development of the original momentums. On the one hand, then, Marx's restriction to the economic sphere, indicated by Nowak, remains valid, but on the other hand, the nature of the spiritual momentum in the materialist theory is derivative. Clearly, the thesis that the "social being determines social consciousness" is here interpreted as indicating that the spheres of property and power play the leading role in a class society, and that they are dependent on the factor of value which influences the dynamics of the dependencies in each of those spheres as well as among them. That complexity of the "essence" of a class society can be hypothetically presented with the use of the procedures of abstraction and stabilization. As regards methodology, the elements of the core of n-Mhm and the counterfactual procedures used for its creation are presented in Figure 4.3. That scheme does not contain the method of idealization and concretization because that method is used for developing the theories of particular momentums (in the vertical dimension). It does contain the horizontal dimension of n-Mhm – all the elements of the theory are at the highest level of idealization (abstraction) here.[15]

4   Conclusions

The reflections in this article could be criticized for being purely academic and not contributing anything of value to (especially) the philosophical considerations on social matters. I cannot agree with such criticism, for two important reasons. First, the subject matter of social philosophy are phenomena which create such a dense and complex web of relations that the conceptual system which is to reflect them should, I believe, be developed methodologically, that is, in a way which allows systematic analysis and conceptual synthesis. In this article, I have tried to show that the methods of idealization and concretization as well as of abstraction and de-abstraction, used together, allow a

---

15   In the article (Kiedrowski 2016, 238–241), in relation to the differentiation between the procedures of abstraction and idealization, I introduced a distinction between the terms modules and models. In that approach, modules are the elements of the core of n-Mhm, and the core itself is Model I. I do not use that terminology in this text because I want to avoid interpretive complications.

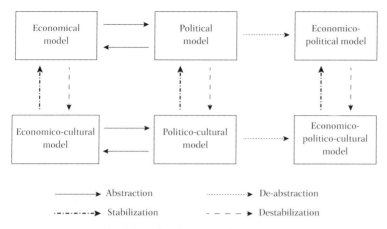

FIGURE 4.3 The methodological architecture of the core of non-Marxian historical materialism

methodologically clear introduction and development of the content of concepts both in isolation and in their relationships with other concepts. On the other hand, the use of qualitative language in philosophy makes the method of idealization and concretization appear to be insufficient for the construction of a holistic philosophical theory. In the humanities, the accurateness and precision afforded to science by mathematics is achieved (off course, to a lesser extent) by methodically developing concepts and, consequently, the conceptual apparatus of the given theory. Thus, the second principal goal of this article was to demonstrate the effectiveness of the use of the methods mentioned above in philosophy, as exemplified by n-Mhm formulated by Nowak. If these reflections are justified, that would be another argument[16] for using the method of abstraction and de-abstraction together with the method of idealization and concretization in philosophy.

References

Bell, D. (1976). *The Cultural Contradictions of Capitalism*. New York: Basic Books.
Borbone, G. (2016). *Questioni di Metodo. Leszek Nowak e la scienza come idealizzazione*. Roma: Acireale.

---

16 I have already tried to demonstrate the necessity of the coexistence of both methods in unitarian metaphysics in my previous works (Kiedrowski 2013; 2016).

Borbone, G. (2021). *The Relevance of Models. Idealization and Concretization in Leszek Nowak*. Műnchen: Grin Verlag.

Brzechczyn, K. (1998). *Odrębność historyczna Europy Środkowej. Studium metodologiczne* [The Historical Distinctiveness of Central Europe: A Methodological Study]. Poznań: Humaniora.

Brzechczyn, K. (2003). Upadek imperium socjalistycznego. Próba modelu [The Fall of the Socialist Empire. An Attempt at a Model]. In: K. Brzechczyn (ed.) *Ścieżki transformacji. Ujęcia teoretyczne i opisy empiryczne*, pp. 135–169. Poznań: Zysk i S-ka.

Brzechczyn, K. (2004). *O wielości linii rozwojowych w procesie historycznym. Próba interpretacji ewolucji społeczeństwa meksykańskiego* [On the Multitude of the Lines of Developments in the Historical Process. An Attempt at Interpretation of the Evolution of the Mexican Society]. Poznań: Wydawnictwo Naukowe UAM.

Brzechczyn, K. (2007). Paths to Democracy of the Post-Soviet Republics: Attempt at Conceptualization. In: E. Czerwińska-Schupp (ed.), *Values and Norms in the Age of Globalization*, 529–571. Berlin: Peter Lang.

Brzechczyn, K. (2017). From Interpretation to Refutation of Marxism. On Leszek Nowak's non-Marxian Historical Materialism. *Hybris. Internetowy Magazyn Filozoficzny*, no. 37, 141–178.

Brzechczyn, K. (2020). *The Historical Distinctiveness of Central Europe: A Study in Philosophy of History*. Berlin: Peter Lang.

Buczkowski, P., L. Nowak, and A. Klawiter (1987). Religia jako struktura klasowa. Przyczynek do nie-Marksowskiego materializmu historycznego [Religion as a Class Structure. A Contribution to non-Marxian Historical Materialism]. *Studia Religiologica* vol. 20, pp. 80–128.

Chwalisz, P. (1979). Stałe w teorii idealizacyjnej [Constant Values in the Idealizational Theory]. In: A. Klawiter, L. Nowak (eds.) *Odkrycie, abstrakcja, prawda, empiria, historia a idealizacja*, 99–104. Warszawa-Poznań: PWN.

Ciesielski, M. (2013). Problem kumulacji podziałów klasowych we współczesnym kapitalizmie. Próba interpretacji teoretycznej [The Problem of the Accumulation of Class Divisions in Modern Capitalism. An Attempt at a Theoretical Interpretation]. In: K. Brzechczyn, M. Ciesielski, E. Karczyńska (eds.). *Jednostka w układzie społecznym. Próba teoretycznej konceptualizacji*, pp. 131–152. Poznań: Wyd. Naukowe WNS UAM.

Ciesielski, M. (2022). The Problem of the Accumulation of Class Divisions in Contemporary Capitalism: An Attempt at a Theoretical Analysis. In: K. Brzechczyn (ed.) *New Developments in Theory of Historical Process. Polish Contributions to Non-Marxian Historical Materialism. Poznań Studies in the Philosophy of the Sciences and the Humanities*, vol. 119, pp. 217–238. Boston/Leiden: Brill.

Coniglione, F. (2010). *Realtà e astrazione. Scuola polacca ed epistemologia post-positivista*. Roma: Bonanno Editore.

AN ANALYSIS OF THE METHODOLOGY OF LESZEK NOWAK'S

Gellner, E. (1989) *Plough, Sword and Book. The Structure of Human History. Chicago:* University of Chicago Press.

Kiedrowski, K. (2013). *Metodologiczne podstawy negatywistycznej metafizyki unitarnej Leszka Nowaka* [The Methodological Foundations of Leszek Nowak's Negativistic Unitarian Metaphysics). Poznań: Wydawnictwo Naukowe Instytutu Filozofii UAM.

Kiedrowski, K. (2016). The Method of Idealization and Concretization on the Ground of Negativistic Unitarian Metaphysics. In: G. Borbone, K. Brzechczyn (eds.) *Idealization XIV: Models in* Science. *Poznań Studies in the Philosophy of the Sciences and the Humanities*, vol. 108, pp. 219–243. Leiden/Boston: Brill Rodopi.

Kmita, J. (1971). *Z metodologicznych problemów interpretacji humanistycznej* [From the Methodological Problems of Humanistic Interpretation]. Warszawa: PWN.

Niewiadomski, M. (1989). Towards a model of economic institutions. In: L. Nowak (ed.) *Dimensions of the Historical Process. Poznań Studies in the Philosophy of the Sciences and the Humanities*, vol. 13, pp. 271–280. Amsterdam: Rodopi.

Nowak, L. (1973). *Interpretacja prawnicza. Studium z metodologii prawoznawstwa* [Legal Interpretation. A Study on the Methodology of Legal Studies]. Warszawa: PWN.

Nowak, L. (1977a). *U podstaw dialektyki marksowskiej. Próba interpretacji kategorialnej* [The Foundations of Marxian Dialectics. An Attempt at a Categorial interpretation]. Warszawa: PWN.

Nowak, L. (1977b). *Wstęp do idealizacyjnej teorii nauki* [The Introduction to the Idealizational Theory of Science]. Warszawa: PWN.

Nowak, L. (1980). *The Structure of Idealization. Towards a Systematic Interpretation of the Marxian Idea of Science*. Dordrecht: Reidel.

Nowak, L. (1981). *Wolność i Władza. Przyczynek do nie-Marksowskiego materializmu historycznego* [Freedom and Power: A Contribution to non-Marxian historical materialism]. Poznań: NZS AR.

Nowak L. (1983). *Property and Power. Towards a non-Marxian Historical Materialism* (Theory and Decision Library, t. 27). Dordrecht/Boston/Lancaster: Reidel.

Nowak, L. (1986). Science, that is, Domination through Truth. In: P. Buczkowski, A. Klawiter (eds.), *The Theory of Ideology and Ideology of Theories. Poznań Studies in the Philosophy of the Sciences and the Humanities*, vol. 9, pp. 106–122. Amsterdam: Rodopi.

Nowak, L. (1988). *Władza. Próba teorii idealizacyjnej* [Power. At Attempt at an Idealizational Theory]. Warszawa: In Plus.

Nowak, L. (1991abc). *U podstaw teorii socjalizmu* [The Foundations of the Theory of Socialism]; vol. 1: *Własność i władza. O konieczności socjalizmu* [Property and Power. On the Necessity of Socialism]; vol. 2: *Droga do socjalizmu. O konieczności socjalizmu w Rosji* [The Road to Socialism. On the Necessity of Socialism in Russia]; vol. 3: *Dynamika władzy. O strukturze i konieczności zaniku socjalizmu* [The Dynamics of Power. On the Structure of Socialism and the Necessity of its Disappearance]. Poznań: Nakom.

Nowak, L. (1991d). *Power and Civil Society. Towards a Dynamic Theory of Real Socialism.* New York/London: Greenwood Press.

Nowak, L. (1996a). Idealizacyjna koncepcja nauki. Przegląd zastosowań i rozwinięć [The Idealizational Concept of Science. An Overview of Applications and Developments]. In: R. Egiert, A. Klawiter, P. Przybysz (ed.), *Oblicza idealizacji*, pp. 11–74. Poznań: Wydawnictwo Naukowe UAM.

Nowak, L. (1996b). Koniec historii czy jej powtórka? [The End of History or its Repetition?] In: W. Heller (ed.), *Świat jako proces*, pp. 31–39. Poznań: Wydawnictwo Naukowe IF UAM.

Nowak, L. (1998a). *Byt i myśl. U podstaw negatywistycznej metafizyki unitarnej* [Being and Thought. The Foundations of Negativistic Unitarian Metaphysics], vol. 1: *Nicość i istnienie* [Nothingness and Existence]. Poznań: Zysk i S-ka.

Nowak, L. (1998b). O skrytej jedności nauk społecznych i przyrodniczych [On the Hidden Unity of the Social and Natural Sciences). *Nauka 1*, 11–42.

Nowak, L. (2003). O prognozie totalitaryzacji kapitalizmu. Próba oceny po dwudziestu latach [On the Prognosis about the Totalitarization of Capitalism. An Attempt at an Evaluation after Twenty Years]. In: K. Brzechczyn (ed.) *Ścieżki transformacji. Ujęcia teoretyczne i opisy empiryczne*, pp. 361–400. Poznań: Zysk i S-ka.

Nowak, L. (2004). *Byt i myśl. U podstaw negatywistycznej metafizyki unitarnej* [Being and Thought. At the Foundations of Negativistic Unitarian Metaphysics], vol. 2: *Wieczność i zmiana* [Eternity and Change]. Poznań: Zysk i S-ka.

Nowak, L. (2007). *Byt i myśl. U podstaw negatywistycznej metafizyki unitarnej* [Being and Thought. The Foundations of Negativistic Unitarian Metaphysics), vol. 3: *Enigma i rzeczywistości* [Enigma and Realities]. Poznań: Zysk i S-ka.

Nowak, L. (2009). *Class and Individual in the Historical Process.* In: K. Brzechczyn (ed.) *Idealization XIII: Modeling in History. Poznań Studies in the Philosophy of the Sciences and the Humanities*, vol. 97, pp. 63–84. Amsterdam/New York: Rodopi.

Nowak, L. (2012). On the Hidden Unity of Social and Natural Sciences. In: K. Brzechczyn, K. Paprzycka (eds.) *Thinking about Provincialism in Thinking. Poznań Studies in the Philosophy of the Sciences and the Humanities*, vol. 100, pp. 15–50. Amsterdam/ New York, NY: Rodopi.

Nowak, L. (2018). *Człowiek, ludzie, międzyludzkie. Eseje z nie-Ewangelicznego modelu człowieka* [Man, People, the Interhuman. Essays from the non-Christian Model of Man]. Warszawa: Semper.

Nowak, L. (2022a). The End of History or its Repetition? In: K. Brzechczyn (ed.) *New Developments in Theory of Historical Process. Polish Contributions to Non-Marxian Historical Materialism. Poznań Studies in the Philosophy of the Sciences and the Humanities*, vol. 119, pp. 96–105. Leiden/Boston: Brill.

Nowak, L. (2022b). On the Prediction of the Totalitarization of Capitalism: An Attempt at an Evaluation after Twenty Years Later. In: K. Brzechczyn (ed.) *New Developments* in *Theory of Historical Process. Polish Contributions to Non-Marxian Historical Materialism. Poznań Studies in the Philosophy of the Sciences and the Humanities*, vol. 119, pp. 150–185. Leiden/Boston: Brill.

Nowak, L. (2022c). Religion as a Class Structure: A contribution to non-Marxian historical materialism. In: K. Brzechczyn (ed.) *New Developments in Theory of Historical Process. Polish Contributions to Non-Marxian Historical Materialism. Poznań Studies in the Philosophy of the Sciences and the Humanities*, vol. 119, pp. 3–51. Leiden/Boston: Brill.

Nowak, L., and J. Kmita (1968). *Studia nad teoretycznymi podstawami humanistyki* [Studies of the Theoretical Foundations of the Humanitites]. Poznań: Wyd. UAM.

Nowak, L., and I. Nowakowa (2000). *Idealization X: The Richness of Idealization. Poznań Studies in the Philosophy of the Sciences and the Humanities*, vol. 69. Amsterdam-Atlanta: Rodopi.

Siegel, A. (1998). Ideological Learning under Conditions of Social Enslavement: the Case of Soviet Union in the 1930s and 1940s. *Studies in Soviet Thought*, 50, 19–58.

Tomczak, G. (1989). The Economic Collapse in Two Models of Socio-economic Formation. In: L. Nowak (ed.), *Dimensions of the Historical Process. Poznań Studies in the Philosophy of the Sciences and the Humanities*, vol. 13, pp. 259–270. Amsterdam: Rodopi.

Topolski, J. (2003). Refleksje o systemie historiozoficznym nie-Marksowskiego materializmu historycznego [Reflections on the Historiosophical System of non-Marxian Historical Materialism). In: K. Brzechczyn (ed.) *Ścieżki transformacji. Ujęcia teoretyczne i opisy empiryczne*, 279–293. Poznań: Zysk i S-ka.

Topolski, J. (2022). Reflections on the Historiosophical System of non-Marxian Historical Materialism. In: K. Brzechczyn (ed.) *Non-Marxian Historical Materialism: Reconstructions and Comparisons. Poznań Studies in the Philosophy of the Sciences and the Humanities*, vol. 120, pp.3–15. Leiden/Boston: Brill.

Zielińska, R. (1979). Przyczynek do zagadnienia abstrakcji [Contribution to the Issue of Abstraction]. In: A. Klawiter, L. Nowak (eds.) *Odkrycie, abstrakcja, prawda, empiria, historia a idealizacja*, 87–97. Warszawa-Poznań: PWN.

Zielińska, R. (1989). Contribution to the Problem of Abstraction. In: J. Brzeziński, F. Coniglione, T. Kuipers, L. Nowak (eds.) *Idealization II: Forms and Applications. Poznań Studies in the Philosophy of the Sciences and the Humanities*, vol. 17, pp. 9–22. Amsterdam: Rodopi.

CHAPTER 5

The Paraphrase Method in Leszek Nowak's Interhuman Model of Man

Aleksandra Gomułczak

Abstract

The aim of this paper is to (1) present the conception of the paraphrase method which can be derived from Leszek Nowak's philosophical works, and to (2) describe how Nowak used this method in order to extract philosophical concepts from literature (in this case from the work of Witold Gombrowicz). I argue that Nowak's examination of Gombrowicz's ideas had a big impact on his own social theory (i.e. the non-Christian Model of Man) since it resulted in creating an improved model, i.e. the Interhuman Model of Man. This model gives more accurate account of the human condition, and the relations between the individual and the society. I also argue that Nowak's conception of the paraphrase method reveals its creative function (as opposed to the reductive function that this method often has in analytic philosophy).

Keywords:

Interpretation – Leszek Nowak – methodology – non-Christian model of man – paraphrase – philosophy of literature – rationality – Witold Gombrowicz

1 Introduction

The paraphrase method plays an essential role in Nowak's methodology. On the basis of his works we can develop an original concept of philosophical paraphrasing. Nowak's procedure is a modification of Ajdukiewicz's method of semantic paraphrase (Ajdukiewicz [1934; 1937] 1978). In Nowak's work, the paraphrase is set between two languages: the language of a philosophical conception T and the language of another philosophical conception T^* – preferred by him. As a paraphrasing language Nowak uses his own conceptions, i.e. the idealization theory of science (Nowak 1979), negativistic unitarian metaphysics (Nowak 1998), the non-Christian model of man (Nowak 1991, pp. 11–15; 1996;

© ALEKSANDRA GOMUŁCZAK, 2022 | DOI:10.1163/9789004507296_006

2000). The main goal of the paraphrase is to incorporate concepts belonging to one theory into another theory. According to Nowak, philosophical conceptions (especially in metaphysics) are incommensurable, i.e. it is not possible to compare one to another (Nowak 1998, p. 77). But one can paraphrase them, if one disposes of a wider theory into which other conceptions can be paraphrased (Nowak 1996, p. 153; 2000, p. 20). This procedure enables one to, for example, compare such two incommensurable conceptions. The paraphrase method has been examined in (Woleński 1989a; 1989b; 1994; Jadacki 1995), and recently in (Będkowski 2019; Będkowski, Brożek, Chybińska *et.al* 2020).

In this paper I consider an example of Nowak's paraphrase from the field of his social philosophy. He applied it in order to make use of the concepts developed by a polish writer, Witold Gombrowicz, in his own theory. Nowak's interest in philosophical aspects of Gombrowicz's work is the subject of his paper (Nowak 1996), and the book (Nowak 2000). The rich content of Gombrowicz's work is also examined by other philosophers connected to Poznań Methodological School (Banaszak 1996; Falkiewicz 1996; Paprzycka 1996; Ciesielski 2012a; 2012b; 2013). However, they don't apply the paraphrase method, and while exploring Nowak's interpretation (e.g. Ciesielski 2013) they do not examine his concept of paraphrasing, which is the focus of this paper.

First, I will describe a conception of the paraphrase method which can be derived from Nowak's works, then I will complete this description by providing some remarks given by authors concerned with the role of paraphrasing in philosophy. I will also provide more general description of the type of the paraphrase method that Nowak applies. I argue that it gives an account of what is essential for this procedure. In the third part I will present an example of Nowak's paraphrasing followed by pointing out the theoretical possibilities of this procedure along with some of its constraints.

2   A Basic Reconstruction of the Conception of the Paraphrase Method in Nowak's Works

Nowak never provided a systematic and detailed description of the paraphrase method. In (Łastowski, Nowak 1979) when introducing the term "critical paraphrase" he gives only a brief characterization of its main features: (1) it is used as a method of translation, (2) which consists of translating the problem P formulated in the conceptual framework T into another, conceptual framework T^*, preferred by him, (3) as a result of paraphrasing, P is changed, since T^* differs essentially from T, although some of the original assumptions of P are preserved, and (4) what is then analysed is P^*. And P^* is not the same problem as P, but *the analogue* of P (see: Nowakowa 1991, p. 82; Quine [1960] 2013, p. 139).

In his book on metaphysics (Nowak 1998), Nowak introduces an "intuitive" definition of philosophical paraphrasing and argues that building a proper definition is a very difficult task:

> The intuitive paraphrase of a notion P from the language of one conception into the language of another, consists of finding in the second language such "a logical place" with which the notion P^* (already constructed or introduced in order to proceed this operation) can be identified; P^* shall keep a series but not all features of P. Thus, the paraphrase would combine the properties of explicating one notion in another language (i.e. the paraphrasing language), and partial definition.
>
> NOWAK 1998, p. 97

This description must be supplemented with the following comments: (1) The subject of the paraphrase here is a notion. (2) The paraphrase method combines the properties of explication and partial definition. Let's assume that we have a notion C belonging to language L. In this language, C is well defined and its meaning is fixed. The paraphrase of C from language L into L^* leads to introduction of C into the framework of L^*. Since the framework of L^* differs from L we obtain a new notion, C^*. C^* is defined using the terms available in L^*. The definition is partial since C^* differs from C in some features (a consequence of the differences between L and L^*).[1] For it is a hitherto unknown notion in L^*, hence by paraphrasing it, we also provide an explication of this notion for L^*.

Nowak also provided some essential comments on the methodological sense of paraphrasing. The paraphrase method serves as a criterion for the "valorization" of philosophical theories (Nowak 1998, p. 79). He argues that if paraphrasing the conception T into T^* fails, it means that the conceptual framework of T^* is too narrow to contain T. And it is not T that is unparaphrasable, it is T^* which needs to be developed in order to be able to provide a proper paraphrase. Moreover, if one is not able to paraphrase T into T^*, one cannot justify e.g. one's criticism of T from the point of view of one's conception T^*, for one simply doesn't have a proper conceptual system to do so.[2]

---

1 A proper definition would require to giving an account of properties belonging to both C and C^*.

2 Nowak argues that if we are not able to paraphrase the theses of a competitive system, we are not allowed to either accept it or reject it. He gives a brief example of this kind of failure: the language of logical positivism was too poor to contain the richness of the Hegelian system,

THE PARAPHRASE METHOD

Nowak claims, that the best conception is the one with the biggest "paraphrasing power," i.e. rich enough to paraphrase the greatest number of elements belonging to other (alternative) conceptions (Nowak 1998, pp. 78–79). This is important if we think about philosophical analysis: the conception T^* with a strong "paraphrasing power" is able to not only give an account of the same phenomena described in the paraphrased conception T, but its conceptual apparatus has the ability to describe phenomena which the latter cannot conceptualize (Nowak 2000, pp. 68, 72).

The idea of paraphrase as a criterion of valorization is a tempting idea and worth developing, nevertheless it is based on some very strong presumptions, which also makes it vulnerable to criticism. One of them is the conviction that we are able to correctly indicate whether two elements E and E^* – each belonging to different conceptions – have something essential in common, and thus whether one can be paraphrased into the other. The main problem here is the lack of a criterion for evaluating the correctness of the paraphrase (see: Jadacki 1995, p. 152).

Moreover, the paraphrase method is described by Nowak in relation to reconstruction (Nowak 2000, pp. 30–31). He claims that there is a very close connection between these procedures. The distinction was described earlier, in detail, by Nowakowa (1991, pp. 82–83). They both argue that the reconstruction is a border case of paraphrasing, i.e. it is "a total" paraphrase, where all the properties of the conception T formulated in language L are paraphrased into T^* formulated in language L^*. We can see that the subject of the paraphrase here is a whole philosophical conception and not just a notion or a problem.

Let's suppose that we have conception T, which we want to paraphrase into our own conception T^*. If we are able to paraphrase every single element belonging to T into the conceptual framework of T^*, we obtain a reconstruction of T in T^*. Nowak argues that it almost never happens, and we often deal with the paraphrase. T^* can be too narrow to paraphrase all the elements of T, but it can also be redundant, and add something to T which was not there before. We can create several paraphrases of one conception T in T^*. In this sense, paraphrases have an approximative function, i.e. a proper reconstruction of T into T^* can be seen as a conjunction of all the paraphrases ($T^*_1 \wedge T^*_2 \wedge T^*_3 \wedge ... \wedge T^*n$).

Let's sum up the overall picture of Nowak's characterization of paraphrasing. There are two levels at which Nowak speaks of the paraphrase. The first

---

thus a positivistic critique of Hegel's metaphysics (and metaphysics in general) is not justified (Nowak 1998, pp. 78–79).

one is (1) methodological, where he describes the procedure of paraphrasing, the elements involved in it, and stresses the problem of the relation between paraphrasing and reconstruction. The second level is (2) metaphilosophical, where he raises the issue of the role of paraphrasing as a method of philosophical inquiry. On the first level Nowak stresses that (1.1) the subject to be paraphrased can be a certain philosophical notion, thesis, problem or a whole conception, (1.2) in consequence of paraphrasing, the subject to be paraphrased loses some of its features, but it can also gain some additional features, (1.3) the paraphrase combines the function of a partial definition and explication of a notion for language L^*, and (1.4) the paraphrase is a step toward a complete reconstruction of one conception into another. On the second level, paraphrase is seen as a (2.1) method of incorporating notions and theses from one conception into the other, and (2.2) the criterion for the valorization of philosophical conceptions.

2.1 The Theoretical Background of the Paraphrase Method

Nowak's conception of the paraphrase method is dispersed in many of his writings. His descriptions of it differ, especially in the case of what the subject to be paraphrased is. Neither did he emphasize strongly enough that paraphrasing is performed on language, which was already emphasized by Ajdukiewicz ([1934; 1937] 1978)[3]. Even when Nowak says that the subject of the paraphrase is a notion or a philosophical conception, it is not the notion or conception itself that is paraphrased, but the names and sentences (theses) that express them. That is why I argue that it is more accurate to describe the paraphrase method as a kind of translation of certain expressions from one language L into another L^*.[4]

However, it is hard to provide one, general definition of the paraphrase method, because there are many types of it depending on various factors (see: Będkowski 2019, pp. 59–63). Moreover, Nowak's conception of paraphrasing differs significantly from the classical examples present in analytic philosophy where the sentences formulated in the natural language are paraphrased

---

3 Unfortunately Ajdukiewicz did not provide a detailed description of the paraphrase method either. See, e.g. the comments on Ajdukiewicz's description by Woleński 1989a, 1989b, 1994 and Będkowski 2019.

4 I am very aware of the problem concerning the notions of translation, language and meaning, nevertheless the paraphrase is performed on language and I prefer to describe it that way. See: e.g. Będkowski's proposition of the typology of paraphrases regarding to how the notions of language, meaning and translation are defined (Będkowski 2019, pp. 40–50).

into certain deductive systems.[5] We already know that Nowak's paraphrases are set between philosophical conceptions, or to be more accurate, between the languages of these conceptions. The description below is thus relativised to the kind of the paraphrases that Nowak talks about:

(*PM*) The paraphrase method involves the translation of expressions (e.g. names, phrases, sentences) which are formulated in language L of a given philosophical theory T (language paraphrased) into language L^* of another philosophical theory T^* (paraphrasing language). The consequence of this translation is a modification of the meaning of the expressions in question. Though, its main intuition is preserved. Theory T^* should satisfy the following conditions:

(1) the conceptual framework of T^* is more precise than T;

(2) the conceptual framework of T^* is able to explain phenomena that T fails to explain.

Philosophers concerned with the paraphrase method discussed its problems, and tried to provide some conditions for its correctness. Będkowski (2019) convincingly showed that the conditions of correctness differ for different types of paraphrases,[6] so it is hard to establish the general conditions for the correct paraphrase. However, I argue that we can provide some approximation of these: (1) the truth conditions between L and L^* should be preserved (Daly 2010, p. 90), and (2) the paraphrase must be validated (Ajdukiewicz [1934] 1978, p. 93).

The first condition is related to the question of whether the same semantic rules hold for T and T^*, thus it is concerned with the formal features of the languages within which these conceptions are formulated. The problem of validation was raised by Ajdukiewicz, and is conceived by Woleński (1989a, pp. 65–66) as the essential element of the paraphrase method. Woleński claims that it is a "meaning-forming" operation. This means that as a result of paraphrasing the sense of the initial expression E is changed to some extent. The problem of validation can be formulated as the following question: how do we justify this

---

5   This is the case in Russell's theory of descriptions (Russell [1905] 2011), Ajdukiewicz's semantic paraphrase ([1937] 1978; see also: Będkowski, Brożek, Chybińska 2020, pp. 66–68), Quine's paraphrases into canonical notation (Quine [1960], 2013, pp. 144–146).

6   In his rich and detailed typology of paraphrases, Będkowski distinguishes, for example the isomorphic and non-isomorphic paraphrases. For the former, e.g. the condition of the similar structure of L and L^* holds. For the latter, it does not (Będkowski 2019, pp. 62–63).

"matching" of expressions belonging to two different conceptions? I already referred to this question when describing Nowak's concept of paraphrasing. For Ajdukiewicz, though he does not express it explicitly, the key is the similarity of the function which given elements perform in the conceptions in question (Ajdukiewicz [1937] 1978). Moreover, he proposes two modes of validation: (1) arbitrary, by definition through postulates (which establishes the new meaning of the expression as an axiom), (2) phenomenological, which consists in looking for the essential intuition standing behind given expressions (Ajdukiewicz [1934] 1978, p. 93).[7] The issue of how to pursue a correct validation of the paraphrase is still open, e.g. it can vary for different paraphrases.

2.2 The Difference between the Paraphrase Method and Other Kindred Methods in Philosophy

There is also a concern about the relation between the paraphrase method and other philosophical methods, like reconstruction, interpretation, explication, definition, reduction, and translation, for certain philosophers use some of these terms as if they were synonymous. This issue was indicated by (Nowakowa 1991; Jadacki 1995; Nowak 2000; Brzechczyn 2013; 2022; Będkowski 2019). A thorough elaboration on this problem requires a separate study that had not been conducted yet. However, this issue was partially raised by Michael Beaney (2009) in the context of the analytic philosophy. He argues that what distinguishes the analytic philosophy from traditional philosophy is not the mere emphasis on the analysis, since this was done by many before, but on the specific kind of it. He calls it "transformative analysis," "interpretive analysis" or "paraphrastic analysis" (Beaney 2009, pp. 197–198, 201). What is specific about it, is that it is based on the translation of the expressions into particular framework. In other words, analytic philosophers transform sentences formulated in natural language into artificial frameworks (deductive systems or theories) in order to analyze them properly. This way of describing what some analytic philosophers do was actually presented earlier by Peter Strawson who, when speaking about the beginnings of analytic philosophy, argues that "a general conception of analysis was that of a kind of translation, or perhaps better, a kind of paraphrase" (Strawson 1957, p. 98).

Beaney shows that for example, Russell's theory of description is based on paraphrasing (Beaney 2009, p. 199). One can also see that Gilbert Ryle too makes use of the concept of paraphrasing, but does it within the natural

---

7 Woleński argues that in his later work, Ajdukiewicz provided validation using complex semantical analysis close to this second way (Woleński 1989a, p. 67).

THE PARAPHRASE METHOD

language (Ryle 1932, pp. 141–143). Certainly, some of the methods mentioned above, i.e. reduction, explication, interpretation, etc. seem to have something in common. And what connects them is that they are based on paraphrasing.[8] But still, it is hard to agree that all of this is the same method. Thus, one has to distinguish between the mere paraphrasing and the paraphrase method in Nowak's or Ajdukiewicz's sense. All these procedures have different aims. And according to Będkowski, Brożek, Chybińska (2020, p. 58) every method is always relativized to the aim. This leads to the following definition of it:

> Method of achieving a given goal is a procedure applied consciously to achieve this goal.
>
> BĘDKOWSKI, BROŻEK, CHYBIŃSKA 2020, p. 59

In Nowak's case, the goal is to incorporate certain philosophical concepts into his own theory, which will allow him to explain certain features of human action. Moreover, this method comprises other specific features. Again, according to Będkowski, Brożek Chybińska, the characterization of a philosophical method M must include: (a) the aim of the application of M, (b) the stages of M, (c) the conceptual tools of M, (d) the methodological status of M, i.e. whether it is reliable (usually effective). However, the last one is not a necessary condition for a procedure to be a method (Będkowski, Brożek, Chybińska 2020, pp. 59–61).

Nowak's goal of applying the paraphrase method was already indicated. The stages of it will be presented in detail in section (3.3.4). The conceptual tools are the concepts provided by Nowak's theory of the non-Christian model of man, which I will describe in section (3.2). The methodological status of Nowak's method is the most problematic one, for we would need more examples of its application.[9]

3 Nowak's Application of the Paraphrase Method

As I pointed out in the introduction, Nowak applied the paraphrase method in many fields he was working in, and ascribed to it a great value. In this section I will focus on the example given in Nowak 1996 and then developed in Nowak

---

8 Będkowski argues that these kinds of methods are based on the "relation of the paraphrase" that is set between two expressions (Będkowski 2019, p. 38).
9 Będkowski, Brożek, Chybińska are concerned about reliability of the philosophical methods in general (2020, p. 59).

2000, where he aims to extract and incorporate into his own theory, an original philosophical conception from the works of one of the most prominent Polish writers – Witold Gombrowicz.

Nowak argues that Gombrowicz's works contain exceptionally mature and deep thought which provides a conceptual framework that is very appropriate for describing the condition of the modern human. But it is expressed in literary language and dispersed across many writings, due to the fact Gombrowicz was a writer, not a philosopher, and thus did not develop, or even aim to develop, a systematic conception.[10] For this reason, according to Nowak, his thought is not appreciated by social philosophers (Nowak 2000, p. 20). Nowak's aim is to "paraphrase this thought into the language of certain social theory in order to make it more explicit than in the original." Through this procedure he also tries to "find the presuppositions and consequences of this conception" which, even if recognized, were not articulated by Gombrowicz (Nowak 2000, p. 16). Thus, at the basic level, Nowak uses a paraphrase to extract a philosophical conception from literature and frame it into a more systematic theory.[11]

The structure of Nowak's analysis consists of five main parts: (1) a basic interpretation of Gombrowicz's ideas, i.e. introducing the conception T, (2) the presentation of Nowak's theory T^* into which T will be paraphrased, (3) the extension of T^* in order to paraphrase T, (4) the paraphrase of T into T^*, resulting in obtaining T^{**}, and (5) the application of the obtained framework to analyze certain problems in order to show the usefulness of the model. Finally, Nowak also highlights some limitations of T^{**} and presents some ideas for further improvement.

3.1 Nowak's Interpretation of the Main Concepts Introduced by Gombrowicz

What Nowak finds crucial in Gombrowicz's thought is its potential to be used to (1) give an account of the condition of the modern human, (2) criticize a dominant (in contemporary Western culture) conception of "a rational man" or rationality in general (characteristic for liberalism). Although Gombrowicz does not refer to liberalism and the concept of rationality directly, his description of, what he calls, *interhuman*, stands in clear opposition to it (Nowak 2000, pp. 39–41). The modern, liberal concept of rationality claims that humans make decisions based on their calculation of what state or situation is the

---

10   See, for example Falkiewicz's analyses of philosophical aspects of Gombrowicz's works (Falkiewicz 1996).

11   The concept of a human or an individual presented in Gombrowicz's work was also explored by Ciesielski 2012a; 2013.

THE PARAPHRASE METHOD   93

most preferred by them. Each individual establishes his or her own hierarchy of preferences.[12] The model of a rational man states that the essential feature of an individual is his or her autonomy, which reveals itself on both axiological and epistemological level (Nowak 2000, p. 40).

Gombrowicz's view is the opposite, he claims that

> the human is subjected to the interhuman (…) he is infused with people, often he doesn't know what is going on with him. This creature, elusive, interhuman, unknown, sets his possibilities.
>
> GOMBROWICZ 1969, p. 47

Nowak argues that in this understanding, the human being is not an autonomous individual. Man does not establish his own preferences. The individual copies the values of the community to which he belongs. It is the community, and not he himself, that defines his own conscience. Thus, initially preferences can be ascribed only to communities, not to individuals. There are no "private" preferences, only "public" ones (imposed by the interhuman). Gombrowicz's human is not a rational individual – it is not a person in the liberal understanding. The interhuman is embodied in Gombrowicz's conception of *the form*. The form is founded by individuals who first create and then belong to the community. It defines them, it sets rules of how one shall behave, determines what is good and bad, and it even shapes one's mindset (Nowak 2000, pp. 44–45; Gombrowicz 1961). According to Nowak's interpretation, the form generates certain pretensions: (1) monopoly: one can respect the preferences generated by nothing but one form, (2) total internalization: one cannot respect any "private preferences," all the preferences of the individual are created by the form, and (3) completeness: the form regulates every situation happening within the form, it doesn't contain any axiological gaps (Nowak 1996, pp. 169–170).

But this is only one side of Gombrowicz's conception. In addition to the great importance of the interhuman, the individual is also defined by what can be called *intrahuman*.[13] This manifests in the human being's constant striving for rebellion against interhuman. It is his own, independent drive to break or deconstrue the form. This dialectic game and tension between interhuman and intrahuman is the core of Gombrowicz's conception. Nowak calls

---

12   About the concept of a liberal individual see also Przybysz 1997.

13   I introduce this term since I think that it fits well as a name for this concept. In psychology there is a term "intrapersonal" defined as "relating to or within a person's mind" https://dictionary.cambridge.org/dictionary/english/intrapersonal). The prefix "intra" can be used to describe one's relation to oneself.

it "Gombrowicz's paradox" (Nowak 2000, p. 50). He points out that there are two kinds of conceptions of the human: idiogenic and allogenic (Nowak 1996, p. 153). According to the former, the essence of the human is to be found within himself. These conceptions presume that the individual is the essential entity from which certain facts about human nature in general can be derived, (e.g. liberalism). The latter, in contrast, aims to derive it from the external conditions (e.g. behaviourism). Nowak argues that the conception reconstructed from Gombrowicz's works is neither idiogenic, nor allogenic. There are two levels of the human psyche, the first is basic and unconscious, filled with content incorporated from the form, while the other, higher level, is itself an awareness of the conditioning to which one is subjected to (Nowak 1996, p. 164). Both of these levels are essential for the human being's motivational structure. In his *Diary 1953–1956* Gombrowicz writes: "not only do I give meaning to myself. The others also give me meaning. The clash of these two interpretations gives rise to the third meaning, which designates myself" (Gombrowicz 1986, p. 231). The interhuman and intrahuman represent, according to Nowak, the static and dynamic components of Gombrowicz's conception (Nowak 2000, p. 101). Hence, the static component refers to the impact which other humans have on the individual (the form), while the dynamic component refers to the individual's ability to obtain strong awareness of this influence, and his own actions caused by this awareness (the destruction of the form).

This key – though paradoxical – element of Gombrowicz's vision, when systematized into the theory, grasps an essential feature of human nature. This feature can be observed only if this contradiction between the interhuman and intrahuman is transcended into the new theory. And this is the main result of Nowak's enquiry.

3.2   *The Basis for the Paraphrase: The Non-Christian Model of Man*

In his work on Gombrowicz Nowak uses his own social theory as a basis for the paraphrase,[14] i.e. non-Christian model of man (Nowak 1991; 1996), which can be abbreviated to NCMM. Later, Nowak uses the term Interhuman Model of Man (Nowak 2000), so let's refer to this as IMM. I propose to use NCMM as a name for the paraphrasing conception, and IMM to describe the result

---

14   Nowak constantly calls his method a reconstruction, even if he introduces the distinction between the paraphrase and reconstruction in the same book (Nowak 2000). Moreover, he admits that the interhuman model of man "uses Gombrowicz's conception only partially." The aim is to expose the key fragment of it (Nowak 2000, p. 61). Thus, it is not a reconstruction in Nowak's own terms.

THE PARAPHRASE METHOD   95

of paraphrasing Gombrowicz's notions using *NCMM*.[15] Nowak argues that the conception extracted from Gombrowicz's works (1) lies at the basis of the *NCMM* and (2) enables this model to be approximated to the real state of affairs (Nowak 2000, p. 61). In this section, I'll describe the non-Christian model of man and its origins, and then (in section 3.3) the paraphrase resulting in the Interhuman Model of a Man.

The non-Christian Model of Man was introduced in opposition to the Christian Model of Man (*CMM*). According to Nowak, *CMM* does not provide a correct account of how human beings actually behave (Nowak 1991, pp. 11–13). In a nutshell, we can distinguish two levels of this model: descriptive and normative. Nowak claims that every norm is based on the certain recognition of the actual state of affairs (Nowak 1991, p. 6). Following this reasoning, we have to agree that Christian normative ethics is based upon a quite concrete knowledge. In Nowak's interpretation, *CMM* consists of two main notions: *benevolence* and *hostility*, which describe some dispositions ascribed to humans.[16] *CMM* assumes that: if we have two individuals, X and Y, then the relation between them can be seen as the following: (1) the kinder X is toward Y, the kinder Y is toward X. (2) the greater the hostility X manifests toward Y, the greater the hostility Y manifests toward X. This assumption is the basis for the crucial norm of Christian ethics i.e.

> (*N*) You shall love your neighbour as yourself.
> Matthew 22:40

The norm (*N*) is developed with complete consistency, since "neighbor" means here *every one*; even if one is our enemy, we are obligated to love him. This norm presumes that humans act in certain way, and demands them to act differently in certain cases. It assumes that if Y is kind towards X even if X is hostile towards Y, then X will realize that he is wrong and will change his behaviour (Nowak 1991, p. 7). Christian ethics, and thus (*N*) have, moreover, a strong claim to universality.

According to Nowak's description, *CMM* does not correctly identify how humans actually act, thus (*N*) is based on false presuppositions about human

---

15   Nowak calls it the non-Christian Model of Man with a Gombrowiczian Correction (Nowak 1996) or the Interhuman Model of Man with a Gombrowiczian Correction (Nowak 2000) respectively.

16   Nowak admits that his interpretation is adaptative, not historical. *CMM* is an idealization and it is based on certain strong presuppositions.

nature,[17] and therefore cannot be established as universal (Nowak 1991, pp. 11–13). The criticism of CMM results in his own conception. It is rich enough (1) to absorb CMM in its framework, (2) to criticize CMM on the one hand and make use of some of its notions on the other, and (3) to contain a set of notions which can describe human behaviour in the way that corresponds more accurately with the actual state of affairs.

Above all CMM works only in the cases of what Nowak calls *normal situations*, it does not work in *extreme situations*, i.e. (1) extreme evil, and (2) extreme benevolence. Nowak describes $NCMM$ in the following terms. The relation of preference is linear: P_{-1}, P_0, P_{+1}. P_0 is a neutral situation, P_{+1} are the situations preferred by an individual – good ones. P_{-1} are situations which aren't preferred by the individual – evils ones. Let suppose we have the individual X (actor) and individual Y (recipient) of the interaction.

Nowak proposes the following definitions:

(B) X is kind towards Y when X consciously realizes good situations of Y.

(H) X is hostile towards Y when X deliberately realizes what Y views as bad for him.

The relations between X and Y:

A. Normal situations (described by CMM)
    (a)   the more X is kind toward Y, the more Y is kind toward X.
    (b)   the more X is hostile toward Y, the more Y is hostile toward X.

B. Situations of extreme evil:the reaction of Y to the extreme evil inflicted by X is extreme benevolence (*the enslavement* of Y by X).

C. Situations of extreme benevolence:the reaction of Y to the extreme kindness inflicted by X is *the satanization* of Y.

CMM doesn't perceive (B) and (C) in CMM's conceptual framework. And the norm (N) based on it demands Y to be kind in (B) and X to be kind in (C).

Christian ethics does not universally work in this model since its framework only holds for normal situations. In extreme cases, the demand of love actually leads individuals to immoral behaviour. In the situation of the extreme evil, extreme enslavement, one starts to manifest love toward one's oppressor. In this kind of situation, the slave (Y) is deprived of his humanity, for the oppressor (X) intentionally treats him as if he is not a human. The norm (N) demands that Y stay in this condition (see: 1 Cor, 7: 20–21). Thus, it demands that he give up his humanity. In this way, according to Nowak, this norm leads one to act immorally – against one's own humanity. There is only one thing which Y can

---

17   At the same time Nowak agrees to the uniqueness and novelty of Christian ethics and claims that up until today "our moral sensibility was unable to digest this norm" which strongly struck our "sense of obviousness" (Nowak 2000, p. 73).

THE PARAPHRASE METHOD 97

do to regain it, and this thing is *rebellion* against X. In this case harming the oppressor (our neighbour) is morally justified – even morally demanded (!).

In the second case, the extreme benevolence of X toward Y results in the growth of hostility of Y toward X. This situation is called satanization of Y. Nowak claims that by following (N), X is obliged to manifest kindness towards Y unconditionally, despite how Y acts. This kind of behaviour is also immoral, since X lets Y be immoral. In order to be corrected Y needs to be *punished*. To punish Y (to do what he thinks is bad for him) is morally justified and demanded. For it is for his own sake (and for the sake of the community to which Y belongs, actually).

These are the basic features of this model. It is important to notice that this is an idealization which intentionally overlooks some properties (Nowak 2000, p. 64). But it is enough to become a conception within which Gombrowicz's thought can be paraphrased.

3.3   *The Paraphrase of Gombrowicz's Conception into* NCMM

First, it is necessary to indicate that Nowak makes some important remarks about both NCMM and the paraphrase. (1) NCMM contains some idealizing assumptions, e.g. the actor X is defined as the omnipotent partner of Y, (2) not all the elements of Gombrowicz's thought are paraphrased in the model, and (3) in order to paraphrase Gombrowicz's ideas, NCMM must be extended (Nowak 1996, p. 184). This extension is directed in a quite concrete way, but it is not the only way of possible extension.

Another comment must be made here, namely that, Nowak's procedure is certainly not a "classical" paraphrase.[18] Its peculiarity is the following: the main role of this procedure is not actually to systematize T into better framed conception T^* but to improve T^* itself. Since T consists of concepts unknown in T^* before, and introducing them in T^* enables the conceptualization of phenomena which T^* did not allow to be perceived within its own conceptual apparatus. Thus, as a result of paraphrasing, T^* is changed to the extent that it becomes a different conception, T^{**}.

To summarize, in pursuing this operation the following steps are taken: (1) the extension of NCNN, (2) the paraphrase of the following

---

18   In more classical paraphrases, which can be found in Russell's ([1906] 2011), Ajdukiewicz's ([1937] 1978) or Quine's ([1960] 2013) works, the paraphrasing conception T^* is already fixed, and paraphrasing T into T^* does not change the conceptual structure of T^*. An exception can be found in Ajdukiewicz's articles ([1949] 1978), where T^* (Leśniewski's Ontology) is extended by additive theses and primitive terms in order to paraphrase some theses of idealism. But the goal here is completely different than in Nowak's case.

notions: (a) the conception of the form (a static component of Gombrowicz's idea), (b) the process of creating and destroying the form (a dynamic component in Gombrowicz's idea). The paraphrase results in a new model being obtained, i.e. Interhuman Model of Man.

3.3.1 The Extension of the NCMM

Extension of the *NCMM* is based on introducing the idea that the basic social relation is the relation between the individual and the community (or the society), and not between the individuals. The community imitates the omnipotent partner. What is changed in the model is, then, that the independent variable switches from individual Y to community S (Nowak 1996, pp. 185–186). Nowak claims that the relations between the individual and society differ in some manners from the relations between the two individuals X and Y. The main instant is the relation of indifference. In *NCMM* this relation is symmetrical: when individual X is indifferent toward another individual Y, Y is also indifferent toward X. But when this very relation happens between individual and community, it is not symmetrical: when individual X is indifferent toward society S, S is also indifferent toward X. But when it is S that is indifferent toward X, X responds with kindness toward S. The reason for this is that an individual is always strongly bound to his environment, he has a strong need to belong to the community. Through this extension, the notion of the community as the main partner of individual X is introduced into NCMM. This extension enables Nowak to paraphrase Gombrowicz's ideas in his model.

3.3.2 The Paraphrase of the Conception of the Form

In *IMM* the conception of the form is paraphrased into the conception of the *social form*. The social form is extracted from the environment:

> the social form is a set S of persons; the line of action of every person belonging to S is to some extent dependent on the community created by all the other persons belonging to S. This area is called the *field of dependence* of the person on the form S. The rest of this line of action is called the *field of autonomy* of this person within the form S.
>
> NOWAK 1996, p. 187

Within the form there are three types of possible positions: the individual can be (1) totally dependent on the form, (2) partially dependent on the form, and (3) totally independent from the form[19]. (1) and (3) are idealizations and are

---

19   For a comparison see Ciesielski's interpretation of the types of Gombrowicz's humans in view of their relation to the form (Ciesielski 2013, pp. 32–37).

described as the *ideal representative* of the form and the *ideal outsider* respectively. The ideal representative of the form is a person whose line of action is in every part dependent on the form, it precisely satisfies *IMM*, and plays a role of a regulative idea, to which all real members of the community submit their action. The social form is divided into layers in accordance with the level of internalization of this ideal. The group of members which imitates the ideal representative to the highest extent create *an elite*. The opposite sphere is constituted by the members of the community who imitate the ideal outsider and thereby create a *margin*. Between these two border oppositions a wide range of medium layers are situated (Nowak 1996, p. 188). And most of the members of the community belong to the latter.

The paraphrase of the conception of the form into the social form enables *IMM* to describe in detail how the form is structured, and what possible positions an individual can be ascribed to. The question here is, whether and how the individual can choose the position within the social form. The answer to this question is provided in Nowak's paraphrase of the dynamic component of Gombrowicz's vision of human.

3.3.3 The Paraphrase of the Process of the Creation and Destruction of the Form

The construction of the ideal representative of the form is created by someone much more real, i. e. *a leader* (Nowak 2000, p. 115). Someone who is able to impose his own way of action on other people. This concept of a leader is a paraphrase of Gombrowicz's idea of "possession": the goal of the human being is to possess other humans (Gombrowicz 1986, p. 116). A leader is someone who is able to dominate others. But he does not acquire this ability instantly. Let's suppose that an individual X enters into a community, and that X has the nature of a leader. At first, he draws about him a smaller group of individuals, creating his own form. When a number of this group surpasses the so-called *threshold of social gravity*, the attractiveness of the form grows very quickly, until it acquires a proper number. A leader, as the closest to the ideal representative of a social form, takes the highest position within the form, he possesses strong *social power*. But, at the same time, in order to maintain this position X must be completely and constantly subordinate to it; he becomes a slave of the form which he himself created (Nowak 2000, p. 105). If, however, he reaches the strongest awareness of this subordination, and reveals his own "private" preference, he blasts the form and starts to create another one.

The conceptual framework of this paraphrase helps Nowak to bring out the *Gombrowiczan Rules of Action*:

I. The rule of the choice of the basic community: an individual enters the community within which he believes he can acquire the greatest social power.

II. The rule of social success: if an individual acquires a social power demanded by himself, he becomes a loyal participant of the form, if not, he abandons it and looks for another.

III. The rule of social attraction: if an individual calculates his limit of social power as higher than that possible to acquire in any existing community, he aims to establish his own form by becoming a leader.

IV. The rule of self-transgression: when social form acquires a proper number of members, a leader stops to maximize the growth of his social power and destroys the form in order to create another one (Nowak 2000, p. 118).

Rules I-II represent the common way of action taken by people. Rules III-IV describe people who are unique. And the individual who respects Rule IV is called the "Gombrowiczian human," since Gombrowicz positively values such people (Nowak 2000, pp. 120–121). The Gombrowiczian human is the one who constantly creates and destroys forms, who migrates from one form to another in a never-ending cycle.

3.3.4 Summary

Nowak uses $NCMM$ in order to extract the crucial part of Gombrowicz's thought, i.e. the conception of the interhuman and intrahuman, which are described in terms of the form. But in order to do so, $NCMM$ had to be extended, the variable "individual Y" is replaced by the variable "community S" as the main partner of the individual X. This extension can also be seen in terms of paraphrasing, based on the similar (but not identical) functions which these variables perform in these conceptions. The modification of $NCMM$ resulted in opening the possibility of introducing the conception of the form using the conceptual apparatus available in the transformed model, i.e. IMM. The whole argument consists of the following steps:

A. preparatory steps:
    (1) intuitive interpretation, resulting in the conception T;
    (2) presentation of the paraphrasing conception T^*;
(2) extension of the paraphrasing conception T^*;

B. the main step:
    (3) paraphrase of the chosen notions from T into T^*;

C. the consequences of the paraphrase:
    (4) application of the result of paraphrasing (new theory T^{**}) into philosophical analysis;

THE PARAPHRASE METHOD   101

D.   self-reflecting step:
    (5)   indication to the constraints of the theory, and the ideas of how it
        can be developed.[20]
We can see that only steps A-B belong to the procedure itself; the last two present the possibilities of a new theory: the application and some limitations of
the obtained model. They will be briefly described in the following section.

3.4   *Theoretical Value of the Interhuman Model of Man*

Nowak argues that the significant value of *IMM* is that this model has the
advantage over other models of man (Nowak 2000, p. 89). He indicated the
limitations of these models, and showed that *IMM* is not only more general,
but is also able to unify them in one theory. Nowak distinguishes three main
models: (1) Christian Model of Man (*CMM*), (2) Model of a Rational Individual
(*MRI*), (3) Marxist Model of Man (*MMM*) (Nowak 2000, p. 72).

    The limitations of the Christian Model of Man (*CMM*) were already pointed
out in section (3.2), along with the advantage of *IMM* over it. Hence, let's move
on to the next two models. First, *MRI* is characteristic for liberal philosophy
and is based on the presumption about the rationality of an individual: human
beings use their reason in order to realize their aims, which are based on their
preferences. This concept is called *the principle of rationality* (Nowak 1991,
pp. 5–6; 2000, p. 79):

> (*R*) a rational subject selects from among the alternative actions avail-
> able, the one action that, according to his or her knowledge, will lead to a
> result that he or she prefers the most.

Nowak argues that when we are dealing with normal situations there is no
reason to object (*R*). But with the change of circumstances toward extreme
situations, the limitations of *MRI* are exposed. Let me remind you that the
two extreme situations are extreme hostility (the enslavement of *Y*), and
extreme benevolence (the satanization of *Y*). In the first case, if *Y* is enslaved,
Y doesn't realize *Y*'s own preferences, but the preferences of *X* who enslaves
Y. And it could be the case that *Y* realizes what is contrary to *Y*'s preferences.
Then, this individual acts in line with, what Nowak calls, *the principle of
counter-rationality*:

---

20   For other reconstructions of the steps of the paraphrase procedure see: e.g. Będkowski,
    Brożek, Chybińska 2020, p. 67; Woleński 1989a, p. 66.

(*cR*) *Y* (the enslaved) selects from among the alternative actions available, the one action that leads to the maximization of the preferences of *X* (the oppressor).

By contrast, in the situation of the extreme benevolence, where *Y* is satanized, *Y* realizes not *Y*'s own preferences, but what is a counter-preference of *X*. *Y* acts in line with, what Nowak calls, *the principle of irrationality*:

(*iR*) *Y* (the satanized) selects from among the alternative actions available, the one action that leads to the maximization of the counter-preferences of *X* (the benefactor).

Therefore, in the circumstances of extreme hostility and extreme benevolence one does not act rationally, since in these situations one does not maximize one's own preferences. Hence, *MRI* is based on the presupposition (*R*) that is not always correct (Nowak 2000, pp. 80–81).

Now, let's move on to the third model. Nowak excerpts the concept of man from the late Marx, where the human being is seen as a "totality of the relations of production." He realizes these relations for as long as they fit the current level of technological advancement (the means of production), and allow for the progress of production. However, when they start to disturb the development of the economy, man becomes apt to rebellion. The rebellion is based on a simple reliance: the stronger the exploitation, the stronger tendency to rebellion by the exploited. According to Marx's historiosophy, at some point in history, the proletarian becomes the embodiment of the idea of humanity. His rebellion makes the way for creating the new system that is based on the community property, which then enables the progress of the forces of production. Marxist man is *homo economicus*, "the free producer." Nowak argues that there are some valuable discoveries in this model. Marx recognized that the basic element of the nature of the individual is the attitude of other people toward him. Human nature is not rooted within the individual, but between him and his social environment. However, the problem with Marx is that his concept of the social environment was pretty narrow, limited to the economic classes and groups that are class-derived. Moreover, his concept of the relations between humans is also blinkered, for it includes only the relations of production, exchange, and rebellion in the face of exploitation (Nowak 2000, p. 81).

In the next step, Nowak provides a generalization of *MMM* that includes its valuable concepts but avoids its limitations. This was done on the ground of Nowak's conception of the non-Marxian historical materialism.[21] Let's call it the Extended Marxian Model of Man (*EMMM*). According to this theory, humans are not only free producers but also free citizens whose freedom encompasses the choice of the world-view. According to the non-Marxian historical materialism,

> the division [of the society] into large social groups of conflicting interest occurs in all important spheres of human social activity – economics, politics, spiritual production. In all three areas, the supremacy of the minority (owners, rulers, and priests) is based on their monopoly of certain material means (respectively, means of production, coercion, and indoctrination). The conflict of interest between pairs of antagonistic classes (owners – direct producers; rulers – citizens; priests – the indoctrinated) constitutes an autonomous source of social resistance in the economy, politics, and spiritual production.
>
> NOWAK 1991, p. 4

The rebellion happens at all of these three levels. Within the framework of the non-Marxian historical materialism, humans accept economic, political, and spiritual coercion on the low level, rebel against them on the medium level, but surrender when the exploitation becomes overwhelming (Nowak 2000, pp. 83–84).

The overall picture of *EMMM* has two significant features: (1) it comprises a wider understanding of social relations that are essential for this model, i.e. there are not only relations of production, but also the relations that tie the individual with the rulers, and spiritual relations that tie him with the given world-view and its priests; (2) the rebellion against exploitation at all these three areas does not satisfy the linear reliance indicated by Marx. According to the non-Marxian historical materialism, this reliance is bell-shaped. There is a spectrum of tolerance (low level of coercion). But, the reinforcement of coercion causes resistance that results in rebellion. However, a consistent reinforcement of coercion eliminates all the tendencies toward rebellion. As a result, we gain the anti-Marxian reliance, i.e. the stronger coercion, the weaker resistance (Nowak 2000, p. 85). Nowak emphasizes that this conception assumes *MRI*, because "the rulers and citizens, as well as priests and the indoctrinated, act according to their own preferences, and their own knowledge" (Nowak 1991, p. 5). Therefore, because *EMMM* does not avoid the limitations of *MRI* it has

---

21 On the concept of the non-Marxian historical materialism see Nowak 1983; 1991.

to be corrected. And this correction is done through the developing *NCMM*, which itself is the correction of *CMM* using the basic framework developed by *EMMM*. And, as we already know, the final extension of *NCMM* is *IMM*, which is based on paraphrasing Gombrowicz's concepts.

All four models described by Nowak: Christian, rational, Marxian, and Extended Marxian have significant limitations: (1) the *CMM* is based on the norm (N) that doesn't work for extreme situations, (2) the same problem applies to the *MRI*, and the rule (R), moreover the *MRI* doesn't recognize the weight of the relations between individuals, (3) which was achieved by Marx in the *MMM*, but his concept of the essential relations was narrowed down to the relations of production. (4) Nowak's theory of the non-Marxian historical materialism (*EMMM*) provides a wider concept of the relations between the individuals that includes not only economical but also political and spiritual relations. However, it also presumes (R), the concept of individual rationality. Nowak argues that Christianity, liberalism, and Marxism have one thing in common, i.e. they hold the faith in the independent individual. And as we've already seen, Gombrowicz showed that this kind of thinking about the human being is erroneous (Nowak 2000, p. 90). That is why Nowak decided to incorporate his concepts into *NCMM*, which resulted in *IMM*.

To sum up, Nowak argues that his model unifies all the other models, for all of them say something important about humans, and *IMM* allows to recognize these features. But it is also able to explain the phenomena that contradict certain findings of these models that don't account for the reality of human actions (Nowak 2000, p. 89). Moreover, Nowak shows how to apply *IMM* as a critical tool that provides insightful analysis of, for example, Christian ethics (Nowak 2000, pp. 136–144), or the concept of individual beliefs (Nowak 2000, pp. 152–160).[22] However, *IMM* does not pretend to state any claims about "human nature." It ignores many dimensions of it, hence it is merely focused on the relations between humans.[23] Nowak also states that his proposition is only one of the possible ways of extending *IMM* by paraphrasing Gombrowicz's ideas (Nowak 2000, p. 61).

---

[22] Nowak briefly describes how *IMM* helps to explain the phenomenon of revolution (Nowak 2000, pp. 87–88).

[23] Nowak also indicates some limitations of Gombrowicz's thought, e.g. his attitude toward science (Nowak 2000, pp. 123–124, 212–225).

4   Conclusions

The use of a variety of paraphrase methods in analytic philosophy is pervasive (see: Beaney 2009, Woleński 1989b, Będkowski 2019). The way in which Nowak applies paraphrasing is further indication of the uniqueness of his thought. Not only in terms of his modification of the method itself, but also the aim which it serves. Generally, paraphrasing is a tool used to criticize certain conceptions (Ajdukiewicz [1937] 1978; Quine [1960] 2013) or to show some formal features of the propositions (Russell [1906] 2011; Ryle 1932). The significant feature of Nowak's paraphrasing is that it's role is creative. It not only transforms some ideas occurring in literature into the more systematized language of philosophical theory, but above all, it transforms this very theory itself and improves it in order to describe some phenomena which would not have been possible to grasp through the use of its former conceptual apparatus.

References

Ajdukiewicz, K. ([1934] 1978). On the Applicability of Pure Logic to Philosophical Problems. In: *The Scientific World-Perspective and other Essays 1931–1963*. J. Giedymin (ed.). pp. 90–94. Dordrecht: D. Reidel Publishing Company.

Ajdukiewicz, K. ([1937] 1978). The Semantical Version of the Problem of Transcendental Idealism. In: *The Scientific World-Perspective and other Essays 1931–1963,* edited by J. Giedymin, pp. 140–154. Dordrecht: D. Reidel Publishing Company.

Ajdukiewicz, K. ([1949] 1978). On the Notion of Existence. In: *The Scientific World-Perspective and other Essays 1931–1963,* edited by J. Giedymin, pp. 209–221. Dordrecht: D. Reidel Publishing Company.

Banaszak, T. (1996), Kilka uwag o pojęciu wolności u Gombrowicza [Some Remarks on Gombrowicz's Concept of Freedom]. In: A. Falkiewicz, L. Nowak (eds.) *Przestrzenie świadomości. Studia z filozofii literatury,* pp. 193–204. Poznań: Zysk i S-ka.

Beaney, M. (2009). Conceptions of Analysis in Early Analytic and Phenomenological Traditions: Some Comparisons and Relationships. In: M. Beaney (ed.) *The Analytic Turn. Analysis in Early Analytic Philosophy and Phenomenology,* pp. 196–216. New York/London: Routledge.

Będkowski, M. (2019). *Parafrazu – metoda – analiza* [Paraphrase – Method – Analysis]. Warszawa: Semper.

Będkowski, M., Brożek, A., Chybińska, A. Ivanyk, S., Traczykowski, D. (2020). *Formal and Informal Methods in Philosophy. Poznań Studies in the Philosophy of the Sciences and the Humanities.* vol. 113. Leiden/Boston: Brill Rodopi.

Brzechczyn, K. (2013). Zwycięska rewolucja i przegrana modernizacja. Próba parafrazy teorii rewolucji społecznych Thedy Skocpol w aparaturze pojęciowej niemarksowskiego materializmu historycznego [A Victorious Revolution and a Lost Modernization. An Attempt to Paraphrase Theda Skocpol's Theory of Social Revolution in the Conceptual Apparatus of non-Marxian Historical Materialism]. In: K. Brzechczyn, M. Ciesielski, E. Karczyńska (eds.) *Jednostka w układzie społecznym. Próba teoretycznej konceptualizacji,* pp. 223–252. Poznań: Wyd. WNS.

Brzechczyn, K. (2022). A Victorious Revolution and a Lost Modernization. An Attempt to Paraphrase Theda Skocpol's Theory of Social Revolution *in the Conceptual Apparatus of non-Marxian Historical Materialism.* In: K. Brzechczyn (ed.) *Non-Marxian Historical Materialism: Reconstructions and Comparisons.* Poznań Studies in the Philosophy of the Sciences and the Humanities, vo. 120, pp. 161–194. Leiden-Boston: Brill – Rodopi.

Ciesielski, M. (2012a). Human on the Periphery of the Community. Witold Gombrowicz on Provincialism. In: K. Brzechczyn, K. Paprzycka (eds.) *Thinking about Provincialism in Thinking. Poznań Studies in the Philosophy of the Sciences and the Humanities,* vol. 100. pp. 103–119. Amsterdam/New York: Rodopi.

Ciesielski, M. (2012b). *Zagadnienie ograniczeń racjonalnego modelu działań ludzkich: próba ujęcia działania nawykowo-racjonalnego* [The Issue of the Limitations of the Rational Model of Human Activities: an Attempt to Grasp the Habitual-Rational Action]. Poznań: Wydawnictwo Poznańskie.

Ciesielski, M. (2013). Człowiek Gombrowicza a model jednostki racjonalnej [Gombrowicz's Human and the Model of a Rational Individual]. In: K. Brzechczyn, M. Ciesielski, E. Karczyńska (eds.) *Jednostka w układzie społecznym. Próba teoretycznej konceptualizacji,* pp. 23–43. Poznań: Zysk i S-ka.

Daly, Ch. (2010). *An Introduction to Philosophical Methods.* Peterborough/Buffalo: Broadview Press.

Falkiewicz, A. (1996). Gombrowicz: filozof i filozofujące dzieło [Gombrowicz: a Philosopher and Philosophizing Work]. In: A. Falkiewicz, L. Nowak (eds.) *Przestrzenie świadomości. Studia z filozofii literatury,* pp. 125–138. Poznań: Zysk i S-ka.

Gombrowicz, W. (1961). *Ferdydurke,* Kraków: Wyd. Literackie.

Gombrowicz, W., de Roux D. (1969). *Rozmowy z Gombrowiczem* [Conversations with Gombrowicz]. Paryż: Instytut Literacki.

Gombrowicz, W. (1986). *Dziennik 1953–1956* [Diary 1953–1856]. Kraków: Wyd. Literackie.

Jadacki, J. (1995). Definition, Explication, and Paraphrase in the Ajdukiewiczian Tradition. In: V. Sinsi, J. Woleński (eds.) *The Heritage of Kazimierz Ajdukiewicz. Poznań Studies in the Philosophy of The Sciences and the Humanities,* vol. 40. pp. 139–152. Amsterdam/Atlanta: Rodopi.

Łastowski, K., Nowak L. (1979). Zabieg krytycznej parafrazy [The Procedure of the Critical Paraphrase]. In: K. Łastowski, L. Nowak (eds.) *Konfrontacje i parafrazy. Poznańskie Studia z Filozofii Nauki,* pp. 5–13. Warszawa/Poznań: PWN.

Nowak, L. (1979). Problem adekwatności teorii w idealizacyjnej koncepcji nauki (The Problem of Adequacy of the Theory in Idealization Conception of Science). In: K. Łastowski, L. Nowak (eds.). *Konfrontacje i parafrazy,* pp. 29–38. Warszawa/Poznań: PWN.

Nowak, L. (1983), *Property and Power. Towards a Non-Marxian Historical Materialism.* Dordrecht: D. Reidel Publishing Company.

Nowak, L. (1991). *Power and Civil Society. Toward a Dynamic Theory of Real Socialism.* New York: Greenwood Press.

Nowak, L. (1996). Gombrowicza model świadomości (między)ludzkiej [Gombrowicz's Model of (inter)Human Consciousness]. In: A. Falkiewicz, L. Nowak (eds.) *Przestrzenie świadomości. Studia z filozofii literatury,* pp. 139–192. Poznań: Zysk i S-ka.

Nowak, L. (1998). *Byt i myśl. U podstaw negatywistycznej metafizyki unitarnej* [Being and Thought. Introduction to the Negativistic Unitarian Metaphysics]. Poznań: Zysk i S-ka.

Nowak Leszek (2000). *Gombrowicz. Człowiek wobec ludzi* [Gombrowicz. Man toward People]. Warszawa: Prószyński S-ka.

Nowakowa, I. (1991). *Zmienność i stałość w nauce* [Stability and Change in Science]. Poznań: Nakom.

Paprzycka, K. (1996), Gombrowicz a analityczne teorie działania (Gombrowicz and Analytic Theories of Action). In: A. Falkiewicz, N. Nowak, (eds.) *Przestrzenie świadomości. Studia z filozofii literatury,* pp. 205–218. Poznań: Zysk i S-ka.

Przybysz, P. (1997). Liberalna koncepcja jednostki a marksizm [Liberal Conception of the Individual and Marxism]. In: L. Nowak, P. Przybysz (eds.) *Marksizm, liberalizm, próby wyjścia,* pp.135–157. Poznań: Zysk i S-ka.

Russell, B. ([1906] 2011). On Denoting. In: A. P. Martinich, D. Sosa (eds.), *Analytic Philosophy. An Anthology,* pp. 35–43. Malden: Wiley-Blackwell.

Ryle, G. (1932). Systematically Misleading Expressions. *Proceedings of the Aristotelian Society* vol. 32, pp. 139–170.

Strawson, P. F. (1957). Construction and Analysis. In: A.J. Ayer, W.C. Kneale, G.A. Paul, (eds.) *The Revolution in Philosophy,* pp. 97–110. London: Macmillan & Co. Ltd.

Quine. W. van O. ([1960] 2013). *Word and Object.* Cambridge/Massachusets: MIT Press.

Woleński, J. (1989a). *Logic and Philosophy in the Lvov-Warsaw School,* Dordrecht/Boston/London: Kluwer Academic Publishers.

Woleński, J. (1989b). Kierunki i metody filozofii analitycznej [Directions and Methods of Analytic Philosophy]. In: J. Perzanowski (ed.), *Jak filozofować. Studia z metodologii filozofii,* pp. 30–77. Warszawa: PWN.

Woleński, J. (1994). *Metamatematyka a epistemologia* [Metamathematics and Epistemology]. Warszawa: PWN.

PART 2

Non-Marxian Historical Materialism: Paraphrases and Comparisons

∴

CHAPTER 6

The Class Structure of Hydraulic Societies: An Attempt at a Paraphrase of Karl August Witttfogel's Theory in the Conceptual Framework of Non-Marxian Historical Materialism

Tomasz Zarębski

Abstract

The aim of this paper is to reconstruct Carl August Wittfogel's concept of agrarian despotism. In the first part of the paper, I present two issues: (i) the hydraulic hypothesis and (ii) class divisions in hydraulic societies. In the second part, Wittfogel's ideas will be explicated in the conceptual apparatus on non-Marxian historical materialism. This paraphrase clarifies the problem of the analogy between the class structures of hydraulic and socialist societies. It leads to the conclusion that the societies analyzed by Wittfogel do not fit in with the theory of socialist societies in n-Mhm. Therefore, Wittfogel's claim about the 'hydraulic' genesis of real socialism is undermined.

Keywords:

Agrarian despotism – class structure – geographical materialism – hydraulic society – non-Marxian historical materialism – real socialism – theocracy

1   Foreword

This aim of this article is to reconstruct of Carl August Wittfogel's theory of agrarian despotism in the light of the conceptual apparatus of non-Marxian historical materialism (Nowak 1983; 1991ab). First, I will discuss two main elements of his theory: the hydraulic hypothesis and the findings concerning the nature of class divisions in hydraulic societies. The issue of developmental differences between the West and the East was a traditional topic of interest of many philosophers and philosophically oriented historians. Therefore, Wittfogel's propositions were not created in a theoretical vacuum and his ideas

© TOMASZ ZARĘBSKI, 2022 | DOI:10.1163/9789004507296_007

were vividly discussed by many scholars.[1] In the second part of this paper, I present an expanded typology of societies in non-Marxian historical materialism (n-Mhm). In the last part of this article, I attempt to present Wittfogel's ideas a little more precisely, with the use of the extended conceptual apparatus of non-Marxian historical materialism.

2   Selected Elements of the Concept of Hydraulic Societies

Wittfogel's analysis of the specificity of the agrarian-bureaucratic despotism of oriental societies is a comprehensive study of many theoretical and empirical issues. It is one of the most significant studies of the idea of the separate development of Eastern societies. By virtue of that fact, it is an important argument against the position of unilinearists who try to explain the nature of agro-managerial despotism with the use of standard categories of Marxian historical materialism.

Wittfogel criticizes Marx for not having created, for ideological reasons, a complete theory of the Asiatic manner of production. Supposedly, the experiences of oriental despotism brought to mind the politically inconvenient supposition that the nationalization of the means of production postulated in programs of communist parties would strengthen the economic and political oppression of workers rather than contribute to the abolition of all social inequalities. Wittfogel was of the opinion that the hidden fears of the author of *Capital* were justified. As he looked at the societies of the states within the sphere of the influence of the USSR, he concluded that social relations there were similar to those in Asiatic despotisms. In a sense, the concept of hydraulic societies pertains to the historical origins of 20th-century totalitarianisms.

In order to avoid any misunderstandings, I would like to emphasize that I only discuss certain elements of Wittfogel's analysis here. One important issue omitted in this article is the division into the core, the margin, and the submargin of hydraulic societies, which, according to Wittfogel, was particularly useful for analyzing the structural stagnation of those systems.

2.1   *Geographic Materialism and the Historical Origins of Hydraulic Societies*

Wittfogel's conception is rooted in his conviction that environmental factors helped shape the agro-managerial system of despotism in Eastern countries. In his opinion, there are many geographic areas on our planet where water was

---

1   See for example: Borowska (1996); Bratkiewicz (1989); Chmielewski (1987); Davies (2009); Dunn (2011); Graca, Zingarelli (2015); Morgan (2017); Price (1994); Sawer (1977); Ulmen 1977).

THE CLASS STRUCTURE OF HYDRAULIC SOCIETIES 113

a factor of special significance. Wittfogel claims that while Western Europe could – thanks to regular precipitation – rely on virtually unlimited water resources, a large part of the Eastern world had to find ways to protect itself from either the excess or great scarcity of water. What are the organizational consequences of such a challenge for small and big communities facing the forces of nature? Wittfogel answers:

> Irrigation farming always requires more physical effort than rainfall farming performed under comparable radical social and political adjustments only in a special geohistorical setting. Strictly local tasks of digging, damming, and water distribution can be performed by a single husbandman, a single family, or a small group of neighbors, and in this case no far-reaching organizational steps are necessary. Hydroagriculture, fanning based on small-scale irrigation, increases the food supply, but it does not involve the patterns of organization and social control that characterize hydraulic agriculture and Oriental despotism.
>
> These patterns come into being when an experimenting community of farmers or proto farmers finds large sources of moisture in a dry but potentially fertile area. If irrigation farming depends on the effective handling of a major supply of water, the distinctive quality of water-its tendency to gather in bulk-becomes institutionally decisive. A large quantity of water can be channeled and kept within bounds only by the use of mass labor; and this mass labor must be coordinated, disciplined, and led.
>
> WITTFOGEL 1957, pp. 17–18.

In short, societies which made use of pre-industrial technologies did not have much choice. Apparently, alternative solutions would not have been as effective in managing irrigation works on such a large scale as the agro-managerial system was. How did it function in practice?

Wittfogel notes that hydraulic agriculture requires many time-consuming preparatory (irrigating) and preventive (flood-controlling) actions which can only be carried out by a large group of people. It becomes necessary to divide the work and choose managers:

> All teamwork requires team leaders; and the work of large integrated teams requires on-the-spot leaders and disciplinarians as well as over-all organizers and planners. The great enterprises of hydraulic agriculture involve both types of direction. The foreman usually performs no menial work at all; and except for a few engineering specialists the sergeants and officers of the labor force are essentially organizers.
>
> WITTFOGEL 1957, p. 46

The management includes individuals with the greatest organizational talents, which increases the effectiveness of collective work in hydraulic agriculture. Effectiveness is also boosted by another phenomenon: "To be sure, the physical element-including threats of punishment and actual coercion is never absent" (Wittfogel 1957, p. 46).

The whole community can only survive if the organizational order is constantly reproduced. What consequences does this have for a hydraulic society as a whole?

2.2 *Class Divisions in Hydraulic Societies*

According to Wittfogel, the class structure of societies which are organized around hydraulic agriculture was shaped, in the process of their historical development, in a very specific manner. By way of simplification, we could say that the specificity of oriental despotism consisted in the fact that the network of relations which were binding on the macrosocial scale was reflected in every agricultural-irrigatory enterprise on the microsocial scale.

2.2.1 The Primacy of Politics

One of Wittfogel's main theses is:

> In hydraulic society the first major division into an order of superior and privileged persons and an order of inferior and underprivileged persons occurs simultaneously with the rise of an inordinately strong state apparatus. The masters and beneficiaries of this state, the rulers, constitute a class different from, and superior to, the mass of the commoners-those who, although personally free, do not share the privileges of power. The men of the apparatus state are a ruling class in the most unequivocal sense of the term; and the rest of the population constitutes the second major class, the ruled
>
> WITTFOGEL 1957, p. 303.

Thus, the basic class division recognized by the author of *Oriental Despotism* is that into political power and the people. However, the main interest maximized by the class of rulers is the surplus product (profit). Two crucial factors shape the long-term realization of their economic interest: the management optimum and the consumption optimum:

> The rulers' managerial optimum is maintained whenever the government collects a maximum revenue with a minimum hydraulic effort. [...] The rulers' consumptive optimum is maintained whenever the masters

> of the hydraulic state arrogate to themselves a maximum of goods, which they may consume with a maximum of conspicuousness ("splendor").
>
> WITTFOGEL 1957, p. 129

According to Wittfogel, the rulers of a hydraulic state have almost total control over their subjects' lives. The dominance of political power is so great that other social classes can only exist in its shadow – the degree to which they can develop in the conditions of agro-bureaucratic despotism depends solely on the degree of the realization of the abovementioned interest of the ruling class.

2.2.2 The Private Class of Owners is Subordinate to the Political Class of Rulers

Although, in principle, politics had a priority in Eastern despotism, that fact has almost never led to a complete disappearance of the private class of owners. Moreover, the hydraulic form of government is flexible enough to allow for structural differentiation. Within hydraulic civilizations, which often encompass huge territories, the availability of alternative solutions is understandable and, from the rulers' point of view, rational. The degree of openness to private ownership could not be universal, and it appears in hydraulic societies in three main variants:

(i)   simple – when both the immovable (farmland) and movable (capital, trade goods) private property is of secondary importance,

(ii) semicomplex – when private property is very significant in industry and trade, but does not encompass agriculture,

(iii) complex – when private property develops intensely in all three sectors of the hydraulic economy.

According to the author of *Oriental Despotism*, the private class of owners could not grow in significance in the first variant of the "patterns of ownership complications." In that variant, small industry, in the form of craft, is completely dependent on the greatest client and cooperator, namely, hydraulically organized agriculture. The same can be said about the second fundamental sector of the hydraulic economy – construction works on a great scale. Both sectors of oriental economic systems remain at the disposal of the state apparatus; the monopoly appears to be absolute and completely secure.

The situation is a little different in the case of semicomplex hydraulic societies – private property is more important there than in simple systems. Particular sectors of economy, especially trade, are managed by the class of private owners to a greater degree – trade is often the second power of a semicomplex hydraulic system. However, in those systems, the "such developments did not result in anything that can be called the rule of hydraulic merchants"

(Wittfogel 1957, p. 269). The third variant is the most complicated model of the coexistence of private ownership and the system of agro-managerial power. That is because immovable property, especially land, can have different forms in it:

> In order to establish the extent of private land we have to clarify the extent of government-controlled land. This last comprises three main types: (1) government-managed land, (2) government-regulated land, and (3) government-assigned land.
>
> WITTFOGEL 1957, p. 271

The first case concerns management of land "farmed under the direction of government functionaries and for the immediate and exclusive benefit of the government" (Wittfogel 1957, p. 271). The second one occurs when land is managed by a private person, but it is the government and not the manager that takes the profits. The third one is when land is handed over for farming to state officials, representatives of the dominant religion, or outstanding individuals who, for various reasons, were able to ingratiate themselves with the despotic rulers.

There was often much movable property in complex hydraulic societies: "Under certain conditions, the representatives of Oriental despotism found it economically advisable to have the bulk of all trade handled by private businessmen" (Wittfogel 1957, p. 297). Still, the riches obtained by some traders never changed the global position of that group within an agro-managerial system.

To sum up, we could say that each of the abovementioned forms of private ownership present in hydraulic societies can only be properly characterized by through reference to the set of ownership prerogatives of the state apparatus. That apparatus determines and controls the admissible level of the development of private disposal of ownership. Only the rulers of a hydraulic society are at complete liberty to make economic decisions. The economic autonomy of private entities is very restricted. The subordination of private ownership to political power is one of the fundamental and most durable features of oriental despotisms.

2.2.3   The Subordination of the Class of Priests to Political Rulers

According to Wittfogel, "The majority of all hydraulic civilizations are characterized by large and influential priesthoods" (Wittfogel 1957, p. 88). That does not mean that priests enjoy true autonomy. When he analyzed the interrelationships between political power and religion in hydraulic societies, Wittfogel

THE CLASS STRUCTURE OF HYDRAULIC SOCIETIES   117

emphasized the general subordination of the priesthood to political rulers. To
be more precise: religion is pulled into a complex system of relations, with the
state apparatus being of the utmost importance:

> The hydraulic state, which permitted neither relevant independent mil-
> itary nor proprietary leadership, did not favor the rise of independent
> religious power either. Nowhere in hydraulic society did the dominant
> religion place itself outside the authority of the state as a nationally (or
> internationally) integrated autonomous church.
>
> WITTFOGEL 1957 , p. 87

Religion and political power were combined in various ways. Priests were rarely
members of the power elite, and if they were, their double-class status was
quickly terminated as they resigned from their religious functions – Wittfogel
calls that solution "quasihierocratic" (Wittfogel 1957, p. 88).

As a rule, though, state authorities used religious symbols for their ideological and propagandist goals. All authorities need an ideology. A despotic power
can do very much in that regard – the highest ruler was often declared a god
or fulfilled the role of the highest priest. Wittfogel described this solution as
"theocratic."

He claimed that proper hierocracy, understood as "priestly rule," never
existed in agrarian despotisms. Members of the state apparatus were never
required to prepare for fulfilling religious duties in order to take positions in
the hierarchy of political power. The influence of priests on political power was
apparently too small to enable them to restrict it in any way.

3   The Typology of Hydraulic Societies on the Basis of Wittfogel's Conception

The review above shows the whole set of hydraulic societies – the initial general category is divided into a series of subcategories of a narrower scope of
application. Within the framework of his concept, Wittfogel proposes two
typologies. In one of them, the classification criterion is the scope of the presence of private ownership in a given hydraulic society. With the use of that
criterion, we obtain the following scheme in Figure 6.1 (page 118).

The second classification criterion is focused on the relations between political power and religious power in a given hydraulic society. With that criterion,
we obtain the following scheme in Figure 6. 2 (page 118).

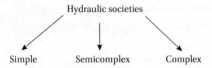

FIGURE 6.1   The classification of hydraulic societies in terms of the presence of private ownership

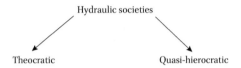

FIGURE 6.2   The classification of hydraulic societies in terms of the relations between politics and religion

It should be noted that the two classifications are independent from each other in Wittfogel's theory, but when we combine them, we obtain the following variants of hydraulic societies:

(1)   the simple theocratic society,
(2)   the simple quasi-hierocratic society,
(3)   the semicomplex theocratic society,
(4)   the semicomplex quasi-hierocratic society,
(5)   the complex theocratic society,
(6)   the complex quasi-hierocratic society.

In each of those systems, the class of political rulers is dominant – it strongly dominates owners in the first two types of hydraulic societies, and it strongly dominates priests in the simple theocratic society; in the simple quasi-hierocratic society, the dominance over the class of priests is weakened. In the two subsequent cases, the relationships between state authorities and the class of priests are analogous, but the social position of the class of owners is different. The owners are less dependent on the authorities than in the simple variants. In the last two types of societies, the relationships between state authorities and religious authorities remain the same, but private owners enjoy the greatest possible autonomy – which is visible in all sectors of hydraulic economy.

As we can see, this typology introduces *explicite* the possible relations between the class of rulers and the subdued classes. However, the relations between the private owners' class and the class of priests is only taken into account *implicite*, so we can only intuit which class is the 'second' power in the given variant of hydraulic society. In order to avoid, among other things, that interpretive difficulty, I propose expressing Wittfogel's findings in the terms of n-Mhm because its conceptual framework is broad enough to allow us to determine those issues unequivocally.

4 The Class Structure of Hydraulic Societies. An Attempt at a Paraphrase in Terms of Non-Marxian Historical Materialism

4.1 *The Typology of Societies in Non-Marxian Historical Materialism*[1]

Within the framework of n-Mhm, it is assumed that we can distinguish three basic social momentums – politics, the economy, and culture – in every society with a sufficiently large population. There are class divisions in each of those momentums. The criterion of that classification is access to the material means of coercion, production, and indoctrination. The classes can be clearly separate, or there can be an accumulation of class divisions in the process of historical development. In the first case, we speak about class (three-momentum) societies, and in the second case – about supra-class societies (two-momentum or one-momentum societies).

Krzysztof Brzechczyn expanded that original typology of societies in n-Mhm in such a way that the theory became "capable of grasping the multiplicity of lines of developments in the historical process)" (Brzechczyn 2007, p. 244). The expanded typology is based on the following criteria:

(i)   the indication of the dominant type of class interest in the given society,

(ii)   the determination of the level of the accumulation of class divisions in that society,

(iii)   the indication of the relationships between the dominated classes of social potentates (Brzechczyn 2007, p. 244).

As regards three- and two-momentum societies, the first criterion indicates the dominant type of class interest in the given society, which can be political (the maximization of the sphere of power regulation), economic (the maximization of the surplus product), or spiritual (the indoctrination of followers). In the case of one-momentum societies, the first criterion indicates the type of interest prioritized by the triple class of social potentates and determines the type of the line of development of the given social system.

---

1   I only present those elements of n-Mhm which are directly related to the subject matter of this research. For a systematic presentation of the foundations of that theory, see Nowak (1983, 1991a, 1991b); summaries of this theory are in Brzechczyn 2017; 2020, p. 171–219.

The second criterion determines the level of the accumulation of class divisions in a given society, that is, whether the dominant class is a single, double, or triple one – it determines which *variant* characterizes the given type of society.

Finally, the third criterion determines: for three-momentum societies – the relations between the realization of the interests of the classes which are subjugated to the main class, for one-momentum societies – the relations within the derivative interest of the triple class, for two-momentum societies – the relations between the realization of the derivative interest of the double class and the interest of the subjugated class. Taking that criterion into account makes it possible to indicate the version in which a variant of a given type of a society can exist. In that way, as many as "eighteen types of societies, which initiate separate lines of development" (Brzechczyn 2007, p. 246) are distinguished in n-Mhm (see also: Brzechczyn 2004, p. 76 and the scheme included in that work).

4.2 An Attempt at Broadening the Typology of Economic One- and Two-Momentum Societies

4.2.1 Economic One-Momentum (E-Socialist) Societies

The strong variant of socialist societies consists of two classes: the class of triple lords and the people's class. Weak variants of this type of societies can additionally have a class of owners and a class of priests, and/or a class of rulers. In that way, apart from three strong variants of the one-momentum society, that is, systems in which the class of triple rulers maximizes, respectively: power regulation, profit, or spiritual authority, there are nine weak variants. The following weak variants of E-socialism are especially important for this text:

(1)   the political variant (the presence of a class of rulers),
(2)   the spiritual variant (the presence of a class of priests),
(3)   the politico-spiritual variant (the presence of a class of rulers and a class of priests).

It seems that this division can be expanded. Let us note that from the conceptual point of view, apart from the indicated variant, there is also an alternative with the single class of owners accompanying the triple class of owners, priests, and rulers. In such a society, there exists private ownership of the means of production. Therefore, we can distinguish:

(4)   the economic variant of the E-socialist society (the presence of a class of owners).

Having isolated that variant, we can further expand the initial typology by distinguishing the following varieties:

THE CLASS STRUCTURE OF HYDRAULIC SOCIETIES   121

(5)   the economic-political variant (the presence of classes of owners and rulers),

(6)   the economic-spiritual variant (the presence of classes of owners and priests), and

(7)   the economic-political-spiritual variant (the presence of classes of owners, rulers, and priests).

4.2.2   Two-Momentum E-Totalitarian Societies

The strong-variety of two-momentum societies are systems with three classes: the double class of social potentates, the single class of social potentates, and the people's class. In the weak variety, those systems consist of four classes: the double potentate class, two single potentate classes, and the people's class. Hence, in addition to the twelve strong variants already encompassed by n-Mhm, we can distinguish twelve new weak variants.

Let us consider the E-totalitarian system in greater detail. The strong variant of such a society consists of three classes: of owners-rulers, priests, and people. The weak variant of it also allows for the existence of the single class of rulers. The class structure of the weak variant of the E-totalitarian system is as follows:

(1)   owners-rulers, owners, priests, people. However, let us note that this is the political variety of E-totalitarianism. Apart from the double class of owners-rulers and the class of priests, there is the single class of rulers.

There exists another weak variant of the E-totalitarian society. It may have the following form:

(2)   owners-rulers, owners, priests, people – in this case, apart from the double class of owners-rulers and the class of priests, there is a single class of the owners of the means of production. Therefore, we call it the economically weak variant of E-totalitarianism.

That is not all, however. The E-totalitarian class system can have the form of a structure consisting of five elements:

(3)   owners-rulers, owners, rulers, priests, and people – with, once again, private ownership of the means of production, and the separate class of political rulers. By way of analogy with the determinations above, that system can be called the political-economic variant of E-totalitarianism.

4.3   *An Attempt at Expanding the Concept of the Ownership of the Means of Production within the Framework of Non-Marxian Historical Materialism*

Within the framework of n-Mhm, it is assumed that the owner of the means of production (that is, of the material-economic forces of a given society) is the person who makes the actual (real) decisions concerning the manner in which they will be used.

It is worth noting that that approach to the issue of ownership is based on individual actions, that is, it situates ownership within the realm of microsocial phenomena. In the case of a theory which, like n-Mhm, mainly operates on the level of macrosocial phenomena, global determinations which concern the system as a whole are equally important. That problem is clearly visible in the case of the weak variants of the E-socialist society and the E-totalitarian society introduced above when the disposal of the means of production is distributed among separate classes of social potentates. We should ask what the possible patterns of coexistence between triple (E-socialism) and double (E-totalitarianism) class of owners' class with the single class of owners are.

Let us note that the owners who belong to the single class of owners are not the 'first' social power in the abovementioned types of societies. They are subordinated to the classes which accumulate the disposal of several kinds of the material means of a society. Therefore, the scope of the presence of private ownership will depend on the degree to which the interests of the double or triple class are realized. It seems that there are two solutions to that problem. First, private ownership may only be allowed in selected sectors of the economy of a given society. In such cases, we can refer to private ownership of the means of production. Second, private ownership can be allowed in all sectors of the economy of a given society. In such cases, we refer to unlimited private ownership of the means of production. We should add that the lack of limits is structural in nature and does not mean a lack of control on the part of the triple or single class which dominates that society.

4.4 *The Types of Hydraulic Societies in N-Mhm*

Below, I will try to paraphrase Wittfogel's hypotheses concerning the class structure of hydraulic societies within the conceptual framework of n-Mhm. As has been noted earlier, we can distinguish six types of hydraulic societies on the basis of Wittfogel's reflections. In my opinion, each of them has a counterpart in a certain type of society in the expanded n-Mhm typology.

4.4.1 The Simple Theocratic Hydraulic Society

This type of society can be interpreted in n-Mhm categories as a strong variant of the E-socialist society. It consists of two classes: the triple class of owners-rulers-priests and the people's class. The most important interest is to maximize the surplus value (profit), and the maximization of power regulation, along with the maximization of spiritual authority, is subordinated to the realization of the economic interest. Let us remember that private ownership is marginalized in simple hydraulic societies, and that it has hardly any influence on social life as a whole. State property is the only socially significant property. In theocratic hydraulic societies, the class of priests is a functional 'addition' to the power apparatus. Therefore, from the perspective of n-Mhm, we can speak about the triple accumulation of class divisions in their strong, economic variety.

4.4.2   The Simple Quasihierocratic Hydraulic Society

Within the framework of n-Mhm, the weak spiritual variant of E-socialism could be viewed as an analog of that social structure. In the case of that society, the authorities maintain the disposal of the means of production, but the class of priests is allowed a certain degree of autonomy. That society consists of: the triple class of owners-rulers-priests, the class of priests, and the people's class.

4.4.3   The Semicomplex Theocratic Hydraulic Society

Within the conceptual framework of n-Mhm, this system could be called the weak economic variant of E-socialism with limited private ownership of the means of production. In such societies, religion remains a part of the system of political power. However, there appears a group of people who could be called the single class of the owners of the means of production. Thus, we have three classes: a triple class of owners-rulers-priests, a single class of the owners of the means of production, and the people's class. However, private ownership only exists in trade and small (artisanal) industry – it does not extend to the most important sector of the hydraulic economy, namely, agriculture. Thus, we can say that the scope of private ownership is limited to selected areas of production.

4.4.4   The Semicomplex Quasihierocratic Hydraulic Society

In n-Mhm, the counterpart of that society is the weak economic variety of E-totalitarianism with limited private ownership of the means of production. It is characterized by the presence of a double class of owners-rulers, a single class of owners, a single class of priests, and a people's class. However, private ownership of the means of production is still restricted, and it only pertains to smaller sectors of the hydraulic economy, that is, trade and craft.

4.4.5   The Complex Theocratic Hydraulic Society

In n-Mhm, that society is the weak economic variant of E-socialism with unlimited private ownership of the means of production. In such societies, there are the following classes: a triple class of owners-rulers-priests, a single class of the owners, and the people's class. Private ownership exists in all sectors of the hydraulic economy – agriculture, trade, and craft – so we can assume that it is unlimited. There is no separate class of priests.

4.4.6 The Complex Quasihierocratic Hydraulic Society

In terms of n-Mhm, we can call that society the weak economic variant of E-totalitarianism with unlimited private ownership of the means of production. The class structure of such a society is as follows: a class of owners-rulers, a class of owners, a class of priests, and the people's class. Private ownership exists in all sectors of the hydraulic economy, which means it is unlimited.

5 Conclusions

On the basis of the above paraphrase, we can draw the following conclusions. To identify hydraulic societies – within the meaning given to that term by Wittfogel – with systems historically classified as real socialist societies would be unwarranted. From the point of view of n-Mhm, socialism is a system with a class structure consisting of only two classes: a triple class of rulers-owners-priests, and the people's class. The main interest realized by the triple class of social potentates is to expand the sphere of power regulation. It follows that real socialism is a strong variant of political socialism (P-socialism).

No type of the hydraulic society can be classified as a strong variant of P-socialism. Some of them could, admittedly, be classified as socialist societies; however, the dominant interest of the triple class in those systems is not to expand the sphere of power regulation but to maximize (or optimize) the surplus value (profit). That is why the correct category in this case is E-socialism. The remaining types of hydraulic societies distinguished on the basis of Wittfogel's reflections are not socialist societies at all and should rather be considered to be elements of the set of E-totalitarian systems.

At the end, I would like to express my belief that a successful reconstruction of selected elements of the concept of Wittfogel's conception is an indirect confirmation that the aspiration of n-Mhm to be transformed into a scientific research program which would allow for an empirically adequate analysis of the historical development of societies outside of Europe is justified.

THE CLASS STRUCTURE OF HYDRAULIC SOCIETIES

References

Borowska, E. (1996). *Indie, Chiny, Rosja w badaniach Marksa. Przyczynek do ontologii wspólnoty* [India, China, and Russia in Marx's Research. A Contribution to Community Ontology]. Warsaw: Wydawnictwa Uniwersytetu Warszawskiego.

Bratkiewicz, J. (1989). *Teoria przedkapitalistycznej formacji społecznej w kulturach orientalnych* [A Theory of a Pre-Capitalist Social Formation in Oriental Cultures]. Wrocław: Ossolineum.

Brzechczyn, K. (2004). *O wielości linii rozwojowych w procesie historycznym. Próba interpretacji ewolucji społeczeństwa meksykańskiego* [On the Multitude of the Lines of Development in the Historical Process. An Attempt at Interpretation of Evolution of Mexican Society]. Poznań: Wydawnictwo Naukowe UAM.

Brzechczyn, K. (2007). On the Application of Non-Marxian Historical Materialism to Development of Non-European Societies. In: J. Brzeziński, A. Klawiter, T.A.F. Kuipers, K. Łastowski, K. Paprzycka, P. Przybysz (ed.), *The Courage of Doing Philosophy. Essays Presented to Leszek Nowak*, pp. 235–254. Amsterdam – New York, NY: Rodopi.

Brzechczyn, K. (2017). From Interpretation to Refutation of Marxism. On Leszek Nowak's non-Marxian Historical Materialism. *Hybris. Internetowy Magazyn Filozoficzny*, 37, 141–178.

Brzechczyn, K. (2020). *The Historical Distinctiveness of Central Europe: A Study in the Philosophy of History*. Berlin: Peter Lang.

Chmielewski, P. (1987). Teoria państwa Karla A. Wittfogla [Carl A. Wittfogel's Theory of the State]. *Colloquia Communia* 6 (35).

Davies, M. (2009). Wittfogel's Dilemma: Heterarchy and Ethnographic Approaches to Irrigation Management in Eastern Africa and Mesopotamia. *World Archaeology*, 41(1), 16–35.

Dunn, St P. (2011). *The Fall and Rise of the Asiatic Mode of Production*. New York Routledge Taylor &. Francis Group.

Graca, da L., A. Zingarelli (2015) (eds.) *Studies on Pre-Capitalist Modes of Production*. Leiden/Boston: Brill.

Morgan, R. (2017). The Anthropocene as Hydro-social Cycle: Histories of Water and Technology for the Age of Humans. *Icon,* 23, 36–54.

Nowak, L. (1983). *Property and Power. Towards a non-Marxian Historical Materialism*. Dordrecht: Reidel.

Nowak, L. (1991a). *U podstaw teorii socjalizmu* (The Foundations of the Theory of Socialism); vol. 1: *Własność i władza. O konieczności socjalizmu* (Property and Power. On the Necessity of Socialism); vol. 2: *Droga do socjalizmu. O konieczności socjalizmu w Rosji* (The Path to Socialism. On the Necessity of Socialism in Russia); vol. 3: *Dynamika władzy. O strukturze i konieczności zaniku socjalizmu* (The Dynamics of Power. On the Structure and Necessity of the Disappearance of Socialism). Poznań: Nakom.

Nowak L. (1991b). *Power and Civil Society. Toward a Dynamic Theory of Real Socialism.* New York: Greenwood Press.

Price, D. (1994). Wittfogel's Neglected Hydraulic/Hydroagricultural Distinction. *Journal of Anthropological Research,* 50(2), 187–204.

Sawer, M. (1977) (ed.). *Marxism and the Question of the Asiatic Mode of Production.* Haque: Martinus Nijhoff.

Ulmen, G. L. (1978). *Society and History.* The Hague: Mouton Publishers.

Wittfogel, K. A. (1957). *Oriental Despotism: Comparative Study of Total Power.* New Haven/London: Yale University Press.

CHAPTER 7

The Image of a Social Structure in *Manusmṛti*: An Attempt at a Theoretical Analysis

Marta Bręgiel-Pant

Abstract

The article presents an interpretation of the social structure specific to Indian society as shown in the Indian sacral text called *Manusmṛti*. In the process of interpretation, the author employs terms coined within the framework of non-Marxian historical materialism. The content and characteristics of the treatise are presented in the Foreword. The next part contains reconstruction guidelines. It specifies types of interpretation, the social structure introduced by non-Marxian historical materialism, and deformational procedures (taking into consideration especially the forms of ideological and utopian thinking about society, with a detailed list of them and a description of their characteristics). In the main part of the article, the social class divisions presented in *Manusmṛti* are reconstructed. That chapter contains an in-depth description of the meta-doctrinal layer of the treatise, along with the social stratification and the interrelations between particular social strata. Finally, the author presents her conclusions and hypothesis, as well as suggestions for further research proposals.

Keywords:

Classes – Indian society – *Manusmṛti* – non-Marxian historical materialism – social structure

1 Foreword

It is quite a common belief that the historical evolution of Indian society – as it is different from the history of the societies of the Western civilization – can only be explained in categories developed within the framework of Indian civilization, and that applying concepts and theories created in one civilization to another is ahistorical and doomed to failure – it can even be criticized as Eurocentric or as cultural imperialism.

© MARTA BRĘGIEL-PANT, 2022 | DOI:10.1163/9789004507296_008

Therefore, in this article, I seek to show that such attempts can be made successfully. For that purpose, I have chosen *Manusmṛti* – an Indian normative text. On its basis, I will interpret the class structure of Indian society, from the perspective of non-Marxian historical materialism. *Manusmṛti*, also called *Mānavadharmaśāstra* ("The Law Book Originating from Manu"), translated into English by Ganganath Jha,[1] is the earliest from a large set of texts called *dharmaśāstra* (teachings concerning the sacred law), which evolved from *dharmasutras*, that is, concise aphorisms containing rules for a virtuous life. In time, prose *dharmasutras* grew into long, verse *dharmaśāstras*. Both *sūtras* and *śāstras* are classified as *smṛti* (remembered) literature, juxtaposed with *śruti* (heard) literature which is believed to have been manifested and is held to be sacred (Basham 1954, pp. 112–113).

It is estimated that *Manusmṛti* was written between the 2nd century BCE and the 2nd century CE, at which time there appeared references to *Manusmṛti* in other works. There are no clues as to the possible place where the work was written. Traditionally, the authorship of *Manusmṛti* is ascribed to Manu[2] (*Manu Svayambhuva* – "self-manifested"[2]), the great-grandfather of humanity (Thapar 2002, p. 28). The character of Manu also appears in *Mahābhārata*, as the first king-god sent by Brahma to lead humanity out of the state of chaos, lawlessness, and permanent danger.

The book encompasses twelve chapters, called discourses in the English translation. The chapters consist of 2694 couplets called *ślōkas*.[3] Discourses one and twelve contain philosophical reflections on morality and cosmogony.[4] From discourse two to discourse six, particular stages of an excellent life are characterized. Also, women's virtue is discussed there. Discourse seven teaches about rulers' rights and obligations. Discourse eight is a lecture on civil and criminal law; it also contains directives concerning court proceedings. Discourse nine is about family law, and chapter ten completes that lesson by discussing the structure of social classes and the ramifications of mixing social classes, as well as teachings about the work of representatives of particular classes during unrest or in trouble. Discourse eleven contains a detailed

---

1 *Manusmṛti with the 'Manubhāṣya' of Medhātithi*, transl. Gangānātha Jhā, University of Culcutta, Delhi 1926.

2 In his article (1962), Eugeniusz Słuszkiewicz writes about the relationship between the name Manu and the English word *man*, the German word *Mann*, and the Polish word *mąż*.

3 In Sanskrit, *ślōka* means a 32-syllable stanza.

4 It is in that part that a description of the stratification of Indian society is described for the first time. Those chapters complete the composition of the work and they are the ones considered to have been written later, whenever the non-uniform and compilatory nature of *Manusmṛti* is discussed.

discussion of the social position of the class of priests, and a prescription for how to atone for particular sins.

In this article, I present reconstructive assumptions, paying especially attention to forms of ideological and utopian thinking about society. The core of my reflections is in the third part of this article where I reconstruct the class divisions in the image of society sketched in *Manusmrti*. At the end, on the basis of these reflections, I draw conclusions and put forward hypotheses and research proposals.

In my article, Sanskrit terms are transcribed in accordance with the ISO 15919 standard. Still, some of the quoted authors use different transcriptions, which is the reason for the disparities in this text.

2 Theoretical Assumptions

2.1 *On Varieties of Interpretation*

There are at least three interpretive paradigms which can be used in a heuristic analysis of any text: formal-axiological, functionalist-sociological, and antagonicist-sociological (Nowak 1988, p. 232; 1991a, pp. 273–276; Nowak 2022, pp. 7–10). In the formal-axiological approach, a field of culture is ascribed a value (e.g. of truth, beauty), and a discussion ensues about what characteristics that field should have in order to realize those values. In the functionalist-sociological approach, particular choices of values are justified, usually by a reference to the social functions of a cultural work, such as improving social integration or identity building. In the antagonicist-sociological approach, the question is the material interest of which social class is realized when particular cultural content is popularized.

Each of these interpretive types has two varieties: historical and adaptive (Nowak 1975). It is common knowledge that every literary work consists of several – main and secondary – motifs and their interrelations. The task of the historical interpretation is to recreate the hierarchy of those motifs in such a way as would reflect the views of the interpreted author. In the adaptive interpretation, the starting point is usually the interpreter's question or problem. In order to find the answer to the interpretive question, the interpreter can reformulate the motifs in the oeuvre of the interpreted author in a way which may not reflect the author's intentions. In the analysis of *Manusmrti*, I use the adaptive interpretation. My questions or problems are as follows:

– What image of social structure (solidaristic or antagonistic) is presented in *Manusmrti*?
– What social classes are distinguished?

- What relationships are there among the distinguished social classes?
- A manifestation of what type of thinking about social reality (ideological or utopian) is in the analyzed text?

We can understand the distinguished interpretive categories in various ways. In this article, I use the concept of social divisions and the characteristics of an ideology and a utopia assumed in non-Marxian historical materialism (n-Mhm; Nowak 1983; 1991c; 1991d). For the purpose of my analysis of ideological and utopian thinking, I have also used the typology of deformational procedures developed in the idealizational theory of science (Nowak 1980; 1998; 2012; Nowak Nowakowa 2000).

2.2 Class Divisions

In n-Mhm, it is assumed that class divisions arise spontaneously in three areas of human activity (politics, the economy, and culture). Their basis is the relation to material social means. The relation to the means of coercion determines the division of the society into the class of rulers and the class of citizens. Those social groups have contrary interests – it is in the interest of the rulers to increase the range of their control over social life, while it is in the citizens' interest to increase the range of their autonomy. In economy, the division into the class of owners and the class of direct producers is determined by the relation of those two social groups to the means of production. It is in the owners' interest to maximize the surplus product, while the direct producers want to increase the variable capital.

There are material means in the sphere of culture, too. They are tools for imposing certain ideas. On the basis of access to the cultural material means, we can distinguish two classes: of priests and of followers. The class of priests attempts to dominate the set of ideas professed by the followers so as to make them decide in all matters related to their enterprises in accordance with the world view forced on them by the priests. Any beliefs considered to be contrary to or deviating from the propagated ones are stigmatized. To broaden the scope of spiritual power means to strive for a state in which any autonomous relations of faith and intellectual activity will be subordinated to the propagated worldview, or even mediated by the presence of a priest. In that way, autonomous spiritual relations are eliminated.

It should be emphasized that the social antagonisms which occur in all three momentums of social life are mutually autonomous although they can influence one another and strengthen or weaken class struggle.

The assumption of three autonomous class divisions makes it possible to construct a typology of societies in which the basic criterion is the type of the class interest (political, economic, spiritual) which is assigned the highest priority in a given society, at a given time. Based on that criterion, we can distinguish, respectively, political, economic, and hierocratic societies. Class divisions can also be accumulated when one social class takes control over more than one type of material social means (for example, the means of coercion and the means of production). On that basis, a classification into triple-, two-, and one-momentum societies is introduced. Two- and one-momentum societies are called supraclass societies (for a full typology of societies, see Brzechczyn 2004; 2007, for further developments, see: Ciesielski 2013; 2022, Zarębski 2013; 2022), three-momentum societies are class societies .

2.3 Deformational Procedures

Idealization is one of many deformational procedures which consist in conscious, counterfactual presentation of the studied phenomenon. However, science is not the only field of application of deformation. We can find that procedure in many fields of culture because cultural practice by nature deforms the explored phenomena.

There are weak and strong deformational procedures (Nowak 1998; 2012, pp. 30–35). Positive and negative potentialization are examples of weak (quantitative) deformational procedures. Potentialization consists in presenting an object to have one of its properties in a degree that is different from an actual one. In the case of positive potentialization, a value attributed to property A is greater than the actual one. In the case of negative potentialization, a value attributed to property A on the given object is smaller than the actual one. A special case of positive potentialization is mythization: some or all properties of an object are presented as having maximal values i– that procedure is characteristic of religion. When we minimize the value of a given property of an object, we carry out ideation.

Reduction and transcendentalization are examples of strong deformational procedures, Reduction consists in depriving the object by subtracting some of its properties. The opposite of reduction is transcendentalization, in which an object is ascribed a property it does not actually possess.

All these procedures deform reality and create distorted images of existing objects. Still, although they have been presented here in a slightly formalized way, those procedures are natural foundations of all human intellectual activity. They are used in various areas of human spirituality that are only apparently different. For instance, scientific cognition – or, more precisely, the idealizational method is combination of reduction and negative potentialization (usually ideation). First, a scientist assumes that some properties do not influence an object under study. Second, s/he assumes that some of remaining properties do not have a great impact on the object and attributes them the minimal (usually zero) value different than the actual value.

Fictionalization is combination of reduction and positive potentialization (including mythization). It is a characteristic feature of human emotional life and its immensely rich manifestations as art. Friendship, love, affection – they are all based on the creation of an image of an actually existing object by eliminating some of its features (for example, a friend or a beloved person never says boring things, even if everybody around that person perceives such a characteristic) and by magnifying those features which are the direct reason for our warm feelings for the person (even a very average woman will be the most beautiful woman in her lover's eyes). The same procedures are used – much more consciously – in art: only selected features of a person or object are captured in a work of art with the use of the means of artistic expression because of either formal restrictions or the artist's intention, while some features are exaggerated for a more distinct effect.

Positive potentialization (in extreme cases, mythization) in combination with transcendentalization creates absolutization which is commonly used in the realm of faith (both religious and ideological). All kinds of deities are equipped with many features which are not found in any real beings. Moreover, deities usually possess those features with exaggerated (or absolute) degree. In a similar fashion, to humans, a hero, an idol seems to have superhuman characteristics which situate him on the border of human and gods' worlds.

2.4   *The Ideological and Utopian Determinants of Social Thought*

Social classes are social groups constituted by the realization of their respective social interests. The main division line is between the oppressors and the oppressed, with appropriate positions assigned to the classes of, on the one hand, rulers, owners, and priests and, on the other hand, subjects, direct producers, and followers. Each class creates a particular form of collective consciousness – a class consciousness:

> Class consciousness consists of these convictions (cognitive or valuating) which motivate the members of this class to actions that comprise collective activities necessary to realize the interest of that class in given objective conditions.
>
> NOWAK 1986, p. 28

It is worth noting the difference between class consciousness and the consciousness of a class. The latter term means a set of beliefs held by the members of a given class, and it roughly – but never completely – overlaps with

THE IMAGE OF A SOCIAL STRUCTURE IN *MANUSMRTI*

class consciousness which is a kind of an ideal type. The consciousness of a class and class consciousness are matched by eliminating those individuals whose beliefs are contrary to the class interest and by the class members gradually relinquishing the 'wrong' beliefs for the sake of beliefs which are conducive to the maximization of the class interest.

My presentation of the properties of ideological and utopian thinking is based on descriptions by authors who work within the framework of non-Marxian historical materialism (Nowak 1984; 1986; 1991b, pp. 293–306; Brzechczyn 2002). The basic determinants of the ideological form of collective consciousness are: auto-ideology, a solidaristic vision of social order, a reformist model of social change, and the self-image of an ideal representative of the dominant class. Utopian thinking is characterized by: auto-utopia, an antagonistic vision of social order, a radical model of social change, and the self-image of an ideal representative of the dominated class. The characterization of an ideology should be complemented by such features as: the universalization of the interest of one's own class, the particularization of the social interest of the dominated class, and the creation of the image of representatives of the dominated class through the strategy of exclusion or stereotyping. The characterization of a utopia can be complemented with: the universalization of the interest of one's own class, the particularization of the interest of the privileged class, and the creation of the image of representatives of the dominant class through the strategy of exclusion or stereotyping. Table 7.1 (on the next page) contains a breakdown of the above-mentioned elements.

I will now provide brief descriptions of the distinguished properties of ideological and utopian thinking.

2.4.1 Autoideology

Every social ideology has a meta-doctrinal dimension – this part of a social ideology makes statements about the status of the given form of social thinking (which is called, for instance, a scientific view, the only true view, a view given from God). Autoideology motivates ideologists to fulfill their social roles and increases persuasiveness as well as, consequently, the degree of a given ideology's popularity among the members of a social class.

2.4.2 A Solidaristic Vision of the Social Order

With the view to realizing the interest of the privileged class, the mechanisms which are crucial for the functioning of the system are hidden from the subjugated classes. The presented image of the social structure masks the main dependencies among classes. In contrast to the actual aim of its actions (increasing political power, economic profit, or control over the followers'

TABLE 7.1   Basic determinants of ideological and utopian thinking

Ideology	Utopia
Auto-ideology	Auto-utopia
A solidaristic vision of the social order	An antagonistic vision of the social order
A reformist model of social changes	A radical model of social changes
Universalization of one's own class interest; particularization of the social interest of the dominated class	Universalization of one's own class interest; particularization of the social interest of the privileged class
The self-image of an ideal representative of the dominant class	The self-image of an ideal representative of the dominated class
The image of representatives of the dominated classes (the exclusion/stereotyping strategy)	The image of representatives of the dominant classes (the exclusion/stereotyping strategy)

consciousness), the ideology of dominant classes affirms their solidaristic attitude toward the masses.

2.4.3   A Reformist Model of Social Changes

Since the basic interest of the the dominant classes is to broaden the sphere of their social influence, their ideology minimizes the significance of the resistance of the oppressed and promotes reformism, that is, actions which allow for changes which do not violate the social order. The ideology also hides the fact that only resistance can bring about an improvement in the situation of the oppressed.

2.4.4   Universalization of One's Own Class Interest and Particularization of the Social Interest of the Dominated Class

This phenomenon consists in the presentation of one's own class interest as a realization of the general human interest: of serving mankind, civilization, society, of fulfilling a mission received from higher forces. The realization of this task results in assigning privilege to one social class at the expense of another, which is justified by the laws of nature, the sacred order of things, harmony, etc. The social interest of the dominated class is particularized by treating the attempts at the realization of that interest as manifestations of egoism, immaturity, etc.

2.4.5 The Self-Image of an Ideal Representative of the Dominant Class

Every ideology shapes an image of an ideal representative of the given class, with the use of deformational procedures (positive potentialization, transcendentalization, etc.).

2.4.6 The Image of Representatives of the Dominated Classes

The image of representatives of the dominated classes is created by means of deformational procedures. Two strategies are used: exclusion (for example, Aristotle excludes slaves from the social structure by denying them the status of people) and stereotyping (ascribing negative nature, social immaturity to them).

Just like the privileged and the oppressed classes constitute the opposite poles of a society, an ideology (the rulers' vision of social order) and a utopia (the subjects' vision of it) constitute the opposite poles of thinking about social reality. Let us, then, outline the utopian vision of the social world.

2.4.7 Autoutopia

The status of a utopian doctrine is defined by introducing elements of meta-consciousness (for example, the doctrine is called the only true one, the liberating one). The meta-doctrinal layer increases the influence of the doctrine on the oppressed.

2.4.8 An Antagonistic Vision of Social Order

While an ideology tries to hide the mechanisms of social domination, a utopia unmasks the structures of social rule and the fact of oppression. A utopia explains the specificity of social life in terms of a struggle of contrary interests, and it contradicts the harmonious ideological vision.

2.4.9 A Radical Model of Social Changes

A utopia underlines the significance of class resistance and presents it as an effective tool for improving the fate of the oppressed.

2.4.10 The Universalization of One's Own Class Interest and the Particularization of the Interest of the Privileged Class

Contrary to an ideology, a utopia presents the realization of the social interest of the dominated class as beneficial to the whole society, while the realization of the interest of the ruling class is discredited as a manifestation of its members' egoism.

2.4.11   The Self-Image of an Ideal Representative of the Dominated Class
Every utopia creates an image of an ideal representative of the oppressed class. That image is constructed with the use of deformational procedures.

2.4.12   The Image of Representatives of the Dominant Class
By analogy with ideologies, in a utopia, the image of a representative of the dominant class is created by way of stereotyping or exclusion. It is emphasized that representatives of that class strive to (illegally) oppress other people, are morally corrupt, duplicitous, etc.

Both a utopia and an ideology deform social reality, and present such an image of it as best serves the realization of the interests of particular classes. The image of a social system presented in an ideology or a utopia reflects a desired state which is ideal from the points of view of the social classes creating that vision (Kościelniak 2003). Such projects have an axiological dimension and a propaganda function – they promote the realization of particular interests. That happens with the use of deformational procedures: the rejection of certain aspects of real society, their omission of them, or even their negation of them, while other aspects are magnified and assigned key importance:

> A standard component of those forms of social thinking which are called utopias –which actually often applies to ideologies, too – are projects of ideal social systems. However, they are evaluative projects constructed on the foundation of a theoretical image of social life, which are usually formed by negating those components of the image which are negatively evaluated or by extrapolating and magnifying those components which are evaluated positively. Both a utopia and an ideology are, then, based on theoretical models of an existing society.
>
> NOWAK 1991b, p. 299

3   The Image of the Indian Society in *Manusmṛti*

Let us now, guided by the interpretive assumptions sketched above, analyze the image of society presented in *Manusmṛti*.

3.1   *The Meta-Doctrinal Layer of Manusmṛti*
Let us take a look at the first discourse of *Manusmṛti*. The starting point are these words:

THE IMAGE OF A SOCIAL STRUCTURE IN *MANUSMṚTI* 137

The Great Sages, having approached Manu,
paid their respect to him in due form,
and finding him seated with mind calm and collected,
addressed him these words, May Thou, O blessed One,
explain to us, in due form and in proper order,
the duties of all castes
and intermediate castes!
Thou alone, O Lord,
art conversant with what ought to be done,
which forms the true import of this entire Veda,
– which is eternal, inconceivable
and not directly cognisable.

> (*Manusmṛti* I, 1–3).

"The duties of all castes", that is, *dharma*, which is ascribed to representatives of particular social classes, is to be told, explained, in its fullest form. Only Manu knows it and can transmit it because it does not come from any earthly lawmaker but is rooted in the "eternal" order which, as we learn, is "inconceivable" and "not directly cognisable." Thus, the treatise is expected to be different from other texts in that it is rooted in the absolute order. With this introduction, a potential follower is deterred from potentially rejecting the doctrinal content – the addressee should accept that it is the godly lawmaker Manu ("possessed of illimitable vigour" I, 4: here and in other quoted passages concerning the mythical author of *Manusmṛti*, we find examples of absolutization) that teaches the rules of conduct. They are not justifiable by any rule graspable by reason as they came into existence together with all categories:

Thereafter, the supreme being Hiraṇyagarbha, self-born, unmanifest and
bringing into view this (universe),
appeared,– dispelling darkness
and having his (creative) power operating
upon the Elemental Substances
and other things.
He,– who is apprehended beyond the senses,
who is subtle, unmanifest and eternal,
absorbed in all created things
and inconceivable,
– appeared by himself.

> (I, 6–7)

The lawmaker transmits to humanity what has been revealed to him by the godly, absolute, unknowable Creator himself. Manu, however, has learned those secrets because he is a descendant of the Creator:

> Having divided his body into two halves,
> with the one half, the Lord became Male,
> and with the other half, Female;
> from her he produced Virāj.–
> O best of Brāhmaṇas,
> know me, the creator, of this whole (would),
> to be that whom the said Being Virāj himself,
> after having performed austerities, produced
> (I, 32–33).

Such a source of the law does not require an empirical confirmation – actually, it excludes it. The Absolute, in the act of creation, reveals the category of Virtue, *dharma* which is the basic category of the social structure in *Manusmṛti:*

> For the due discrimination of actions,
> he differentiated Virtue and Vice;
> and he connected these creatures
> with such pairs of opposites
> as Pleasure-Pain and the like.
> (I, 26)

That work speaks about Virtue, and the knowledge passed on to people should be a faithful description of the original *dharma*. Crucially, knowledge itself is absolutized. Its immense authority is emphasized in *Manusmṛti* many times:

> This (treatise) is ever conducive to welfare;
> it is most excellent;
> it expands the understanding
> brings fame and constitutes the highest good.
> Herein has been expounded Dharma in its entirety:
> the good and bad features of actions of all the four castes;
> as also eternal Morality.
> Morality [Right Behaviour] is highest Dharma;
> that which is prescribed in the śruti and laid down in the Smṛti.

THE IMAGE OF A SOCIAL STRUCTURE IN *MANUSMRTI* 139

> hence the twice-born person, desiring the welfare of his soul,
> should be always intent upon Right Behaviour.
>> (1, 106–108).

The separation of the meta-doctrinal layer in itself does not allow us to draw a conclusion as to whether the text is a product of ideological or utopian thinking (both types include that element). We can only determine that by analyzing the manner in which particular social classes are described.

3.2   The Genesis of Social Divisions

In *Manusmrti*, social divisions are presented as a result of a creative process. The Creator determines the nature of human beings, which will remain with them throughout their whole stay on Earth.

> Each being,
> when created again and again,
> naturally conformed to that same act
> to which the lord had, at first, directed him.
>> (1, 28)

Human characteristics are presented as innate, assigned during the process of creation:

> Hurtfulness or harmlessness,
> tenderness or hard-heartedness,
> virtue or vice, truthfulness or truth-lessness,
> – each of these accrued
> to that being in which he implanted it
> at creation.
>> (1, 29)

In the very first discourse, which is the ideological foundation for later reflections, we find the genesis of social divisions:

> With a view to the development of the (three) regions,
> He brought into existence the Brāhmaṇa,
> the Kṣatriya, the Vaiśya and the Śūdra,
> from out of His mouth, arms, thighs and feet (respectively).
>> (1, 31)

That image refers to the myth of Puruṣa (*Hymny Rigwedy* 1971, p. 106)[5] and is to emphasizes the ritual chastity of every *varṇa*. In the original situation, human beings are formed from particular sets of characteristics, and they assume those characteristics as their own. However, individuals are not ascribed to particular status groups on the basis of their characteristics which manifest as they function in the society. Belonging to a particular status group is determined by birth. At this point, there is a significant shift of emphasis, from "you are a Brahmin because you are wise, chaste, and truthful" to "you are wise, chaste, and truthful because you are a Brahmin." That is absolutization of the image of a Brahmin. In short, it is not the case that a good person is Brahmin, but that a Brahmin is good. What are Brahmins' features, then? They are: truthfulness, chastity, understanding of Virtue. Why are those features ascribed to Brahmins and not to another status group? Because they were born from the mouth of Brahma, so they are ritually clean. How do we know they were born that way? It is confirmed in the *Vedas*. The following stanza teaches about the inappropriateness of looking for knowledge outside of the authority of the *Vedas*:

> An epileptic, one having a string of scrofulous swellings,
> One who suffers from leucoderma, the backbiter, the lunatic,
> The blind man, and the derider of the Veda –
> All these should be avoided.
>> (III, 161)

3.3   *Social Stratification*

The division into four *varṇas* is absolute. From the following description, we learn how belonging to a class is associated with the types of activities which are considered to be admissible:

> For the Brāhmaṇas
> he ordained teaching, studying,
> sacrificing and officiating at sacrifices,
> as also the giving
> and accepting of gifts.
> For the Kṣatriya he ordained
> protecting of the people,
> giving of gifts, sacrificing and studying,

---

5   For an elaborate interpretation of the hymn, see: Kudelska 2003, 14–35; Brown 1931.

THE IMAGE OF A SOCIAL STRUCTURE IN *MANUSMṚTI* 141

as also abstaining from being addicted to the objects of sense.
For the Vaiśya,
tending of cattle,
giving of gifts, sacrificing and studying;
as also trade, money-lending and cultivating of land.
For the Śūdra
the Lord ordained only one function
 the ungrudging
service of the said castes.

(1, 88–91)

Following that breakdown, let us find counterparts for particular *varṇas* within the conceptual framework of non-Marxian historical materialism. Brahmins are the only status group which can teach and which has at its disposal the means of spiritual production (as we read in the chapter on learning). Therefore, they are a counterpart of the class of priests. Kshatriyas could be identified with rulers, the class which has at its disposal the means of coercion. Trade, usury, and farming could be viewed as activities proper to those who have at their disposal the means of production. Thus, Vaishyas would be the class of owners. The Shudras, who are deprived of any means and whose only role is to obey and serve the three higher social layers, must be a counterpart of the people's class.

However, the genesis of the social stratification is not earthly, that is, based on unequal access to the material social means – it is divine, that is, it results from the Creator's will. That perspective could be seen as a manifestation of the ideologization of social divisions.

The text contains the following description of a hierarchical social order:

Man is described as purer above his navel;
hence the Self-existent One
has declared the mouth
to be his purest part.
In matters regarding 'Dharma',
the Brāhmaṇa is the Lord of this whole world;
– because he sprang
out of the best part of (Prajāpati's) body,
because he is the eldest of all,
and because he upholds the Veda.

(1, 92–93)

Knowledge of rituals is emphasized here as a factor which guarantees the highest position in the social hierarchy because it gives great power in a society where all activities, in order to be beneficial for the actor, must be, as postulated in *Manusmṛti*, mediated by magical activities:

> For the twice-born persons
> corporeal consecration,
> beginning with 'Conception,'
> should be performed
> with auspicious Vedic rites;
> it purifies in this world
> and also after death.
> Of twice-born men
> the taint of seed and womb is removed
> by the 'Libations in connection with Pregnancy'
> and by 'Jātakarman' (Rites attendant upon birth),
> 'Chauḍa' (Tonsure)
> and 'Mauñjībandhana' (Tying of the grass-girdle).
> (II, 26–27).

3.4   *The Class of Priests*

The top social layer, as has already been said, consist of Brahmins. The image of a Brahmin, constructed with the use of procedures of positive potentialization and transcendentalization, is devoid of negative characteristics. Thus, a Brahmin is presented as the best of people:

> Him the Self-existent one, created, in the beginning,
> after performing austerities,
> out of his own mouth,
> for the conveying of offerings (to the gods) and of oblations (to the Pitṛs),
> and for the preservation of this entire creation.
> What being is superior to him
> through whose mouth
> the gods always eat the offerings
> and the Pitṛs the oblations?
> Among beings, animated ones are regarded as foremost;
> among animated ones, those that subsist by reason:
> among rational beings men are foremost; and among men, Brāhmaṇast.
> (I, 94–96)

THE IMAGE OF A SOCIAL STRUCTURE IN *MANUSMRTI* 143

In the last verses which justify the priestly rule, members of that social class are absolutized. Brahmins' ritual purity is emphasized, as well as their predestined role as keepers of the original harmony of the world. That harmony which guarantees perfect social order can be seen as a manifestation of ideological thinking in *Manusmṛti*. Brahmins are assigned certain special attributes which predestine them for playing a superior social role.[6] The ideological mystification here consists in hiding the material sources of social power and accentuating the unique characteristics of representatives of that class. Priests have a distinguished position because of Virtue. But who has learned what Virtue is? Brahmins themselves. Here is the rather enigmatic legitimization of the great claims of the class of priests:

> The very genesis of the Brāhmaṇa
> is the eternal incarnation of Virtue;
> for he is born for the sake of Virtue;
> and this (birth) leads to the state of Brahman.
> The Brāhmaṇa, on coming into existence,
> becomes supreme on earth;
> he is the supreme lord of all beings,
> serving the purpose of guarding the treasure of Virtue.
> Whatever is contained in this world
> is all the property of the Brāhmaṇa;
> the Brāhmaṇa verily deserves all
> by virtue of his superiority and noble birth.
>> (1, 98–100)

Manusmṛti also introduces an additional assumption: a Brahmin does not only know the rules of Virtue – for that very reason, he cannot act against them:

---

6 Likewise: "When a small boy only has eyes for his father, he ascribes to his parent numerous characteristics about which that father could not even dream, and he greatly exaggerates his father's actual characteristics. The same paradigm is observed in religion: the postulated beings are ontologically richer than real ones, and their characteristics must be of the 'highest' order: the Highest Power, the Greatest Good, Omniscience, etc. An atheistic credo is often based on similar assumptions. György Lukács's proletariat, which has a border consciousness and the ability to break the laws of history and to create new laws, is but an absolutization of the actual working class (Nowak 1996, p. 298).

> The Brāhmaṇa studying these institutes,
> and (thence) discharging all prescribed duties,
> is never defiled by sins of commission (or omission),
> proceeding from mind, speech or body.
> He purifies his company,
> and also his kindreds–
> seven higher (ancestors) and seven lower (descendants).
> He alone deserves this entire earth.
>> (I, 104–105)

A Brahmin is protected from doing evil simply by virtue of studying the rules of behavior. The important implication is that a Brahmin must be respected whatever his conduct might be – just out of regard for the truth he has found in the course of his studies.

Brahmins' dominance over other *varṇas* is mentioned many times in *Manusmṛti*. Their prestige is to be so great that they deserve greater respect than the elderly. That is likewise justified by Virtue being the Brahmins' domain:

> The Brāhmaṇa, who brings about his Vedic birth,
> and teaches him his duty,
> – even though he be a mere child,
> – becomes in law the father of the old man (whom he teaches).
>> (II, 150)

Manusmṛti even teaches that Brahmins sanctify the people around them. The very presence of Brahmins is sanctifying:

> Now listen to the full description
> of those chief of twice-born men,
> the sanctifiers of company,
> by which best of the twice-born a company
> defiled by men unworthy of company
> becomes purified.
>> (III, 183)

Brahmins deserve a recompense for that propitious influence. The tradition of amply rewarding them is elaborated upon in *Manusmṛti* – it is applauded as being in perfect agreement with the natural order of things. The sacredness and excellence of Brahmins are sufficient reasons for endowing them with riches:

Whatever may be agreeable to the Brāhmaṇas,
that he shall give ungrudgingly.
He shall relate stories
told in the Veda
as this is liked by the Pitṛs.

(III, 231)

Being happy himself,
he shall bring delight to the Brāhmaṇas;
he shall feed them, gently and slowly,
with dishes, and urge them repeatedly
by means of seasonings.

(III, 233)

Some regulations surprise us with the amount of detail, but it is those description that give some insight into the Brahmins' vision of the desirable state of things. The fantasy which allows for a combination of recommendations about how to feed a Brahmin and how to observe rituals is amusing:

He shall then inform them
of the food that may be left after they have eaten;
being permitted by the Brāhmaṇas he shall do as they tell him.
At the rite in honour of the Pitṛs, one should say
"svaditam" (well-dined); at the Goṣṭha,
"suśṛtam" (well-cooked);
at the Ābhyudayika rite, "sampannam" (accomplished);
and at the rite in honour of the gods, "rucitam" (agreeable).

(III, 253–254)

Many stanzas in *Manusmṛti* concern sanctions against disobedience to the rules of Virtue, in particular, offenses against Brahmins. Those sanctions are not, however, presented as originating "from this world." Those stanzas, also fulfill ideological functions – the described crimes are punishable with a horrible spell, and the punishment is meted out by supernatural powers:

The man of evil conduct
becomes deprecated among men;
he is constantly
suffering pain, is sick –
and short-lived.

(IV, 157)

The twice-born person
who threatens a Brāhmaṇa,
with the intention of striking him,
wanders about in the tāmisra hell
for a hundred years.
Having, in anger,
struck him intentionally,
even with a straw,
he is born, during twenty-one births,
in sinful wombs.

(IV, 165–166)

Brahmins should be obeyed regardless of how they behave:

Similarly even though they betake themselves
to all sorts of undesirable acts,
yet Brāhmaṇas should be honoured in every way;
for they are the greatest divinity.

(IX, 319)

The identification of Brahmins with gods is a manifestation of absolutization, and it completes the ideal image of that social class and its rule, which fulfills ideological functions in *Manusmṛti* – at no point in the description can information about the earthly sources of that dominance be found. Nor is Brahmins' dominance ever associated with oppression. On the contrary, it is presented as natural and organic, as a form of beneficial leadership. The realization of the interest of the class of priests is thus identified with the good of the whole society. Their class interest is universalized and included in a solidaristic vision of the social order. Such a vision is a characteristic of ideological thinking.

3.5   *The Class of Rulers*

The second class we read about in *Manusmṛti* is rulers, specifically, the king, who is the personification of all political power. In the very first verses about him, the king is presented as a supernatural power of divine origins. He is horrific, but he provides security to the society, which can be interpreted as another manifestation of ideological thinking: the king is not a ruler who pacifies his subjects with the use of the means of coercion in order to broaden the scope of his power – he is almost a god, a caring guardian who destroys evil and crime. He makes it possible to transcend the wild and scary natural state:

THE IMAGE OF A SOCIAL STRUCTURE IN *MANUSMṚTI* 147

At a time when the people were without a King,
and were utterly perturbed
through fear,
the Lord created the King
for the protection of all this;
taking out the essential constituents
of Indra, Vāyu,
Yama, Sūrya,
Varuṇa, Chandra and Kubera.
(VII, 3–4)

Even though an infant,
the King shall not
be despised as if he were
merely human; because he is
a great divinity in human form.
(VII, 8)

Those are a rulers' tasks: showing generosity, collecting taxes, controlling citizens by means of a network of spies, keeping enemies away, punishing criminals, taking care of citizens' welfare, zealously protecting morality, and supporting poor subjects (IX, 304–311). An ideal representative of the ruling class, then, would possess the features necessary to fulfill those obligations. The role of political authorities is to serve. We read about the king's mission and incessant sacrifice in this excerpt:

When however, having subdued love and hatred,
he deals with cases justly,
his subjects turn towards him,
as the rivers towards the ocean.
(VIII, 175)

At the very beginning, we read that the law prescribes that the function of a ruler should be fulfilled by a member of the Kshatriya *varṇa*:

The protection of all this
shall be done according to law,
by the Kṣatriya who has received
the Vedic training in due form.
(VII, 2)

On the basis of these quotes, we can infer that the king occupies a superior position with respect to the whole social hierarchy; however, we soon learn more about his duties, which are very interesting from the point of view of the most intriguing social relationship of the system designed in *Manusmṛti*, namely, the relationship between political and spiritual power.

Among other things, the king is the judge in cases between citizens, and he punishes the guilty party. The concept of punishment is strongly emphasized in *Manusmṛti* and shown as inextricably linked with the concept of Virtue:

> That punishment is the 'King',
> the 'Man'; that is the 'Leader'
> and the 'Ruler' and that has been declared to be the 'surety'
> for the Law
> of the Four Stages.
> (VII, 17)

The king administers just punishments, which is another element of the solidaristic vision of society presented in *Manusmṛti*. The king sacrifices himself selflessly, fulfilling his mission of the defendant of the people:

> If the King did not untiringly
> mete out punishment to those
> that deserve punishment,
> the stronger would have roasted the weaker,
> like fish, on the spit.
> (VII, 20)

Such an image of the king – whose role is to maintain social order and mind his subjects' welfare – proves the ideological status of these fragments of *Manusmṛti*. In those excerpts, the ruler's role of being of service is emphasized, while the antagonistic dimension of power is never mentioned. Moreover, the image of an ideal representative of the rulers' class is built with the use of deformational procedures, mainly positive potentialization.

3.6 The Relationships between the Class of Priests and the Class of Rulers

The king is said to mete out punishments according to the rules of Virtue. It follows that there must be guardians of those rules. Let us examine how the relationship between priests and rulers is depicted in *Manusmṛti*:

THE IMAGE OF A SOCIAL STRUCTURE IN *MANUSMRTI* 149

After rising in the morning,
the King shall wait upon the Brāhmaṇas,
who are accomplished students of the Threefold Science and learned;
and shall follow their advice.

(VII, 37)

Political power is wielded with the assistance of a sizable number of officials, managers, and spies (VII, 81; VII, 233). The most important ones are ministers, who are recruited from Brahmins. Their scope of their power appears to be huge, their presence – indispensable, and their opinion – decisive, so they appear to have a very privileged position.

He shall appoint
seven or eight ministers,
with respectable status, versed in law,
of heroic temperament,
experienced in business,
born of noble families,
and thoroughly tested.

(VII, 54)

With the learned Brāhmaṇa, however,
who is the most distinguished of them all,
the king shall discuss
the highest secrets pertaining to the six-fold state-craft
He shall always, in full confidence,
entrust all business to him;
and having, in consultation with him, formed his resolution,
he shall do what has to be done.

(VII, 58–59)

In *Manusmṛti*, we can find a complete set of ruling methods. I have already mentioned spies and officials. It is also worth noting that the ruler has the right to impose taxes, although that power is, of course, interpreted in terms of solidarity:

He should cause the yearly revenue
to be collected by trusted men.
In his business he shall stick to the scriptures;
and towards the people

he shall behave like a father.
(VII, 80)

The ruler also has the right to use force in order to defend against an enemy.

He shall have his force
always operative;
his manliness always displayed,
his secrets constantly concealed,
ever following up
the weak points of his enemy.
(VII, 102)

For the prosperity of kingdoms
the wise ones always recommend
Conciliation and Force
from among the four expedients,
conciliation and the rest.
(VII, 109)

The detailed laws, however, do not give a clear picture of the scope of priests' dominance over the rest of the society, including political rulers and owners. Instead, we can find passages in which Brahmins' interest is universalized by being identified with the good of the whole society. For instance, taxes do not apply to Brahmins. On the contrary, the king should pay their living costs, and if the Brahmins were reduced to poverty, this would bring about supernatural punishments for the state:

Even though dying,
the King shall not levy a tax
on the Śrotriya;
and no Śrotriya
living in his kingdom
shall suffer from hunger.
The kingdom of that King
in whose realm the Śrotriya suffers from hunger,
shall, ere long,
pine with hunger.
Having ascertained
his learning and character,

THE IMAGE OF A SOCIAL STRUCTURE IN *MANUSMṚTI*   151

he shall provide for him a fair living;
and he shall protect him against all things,
even as the father protects his lawful son.
> (VII, 133–135)

The detailed content of the regulations confirms the privileged position of the class of priests. Their rights are much greater than the rights of other status groups, including the king:

A learned Brāhmaṇa,
having found treasure buried by his forefathers,
shall take it wholly;
as he is the master of everything.
When the king himself
finds a hoard buried of old under the ground,
he shall give one-half of it to the Brāhmaṇas
and have the other half put in his treasury.
> (VIII, 37–38)

In a similar fashion, when Brahmins commit crimes, the penalties are much milder. The most salient example of this principle are the punishments for verbal abuse. When we compare the ones for the Kshatriya *varṇa*, including the king, and the class of priests, we learn that the former occupies a lower position than the latter:

On abusing a Brāhmaṇa
the Kṣatriya
should be fined one hundred; [...].
For abusing a Kṣatriya,
 the Brāhmaṇa should be fined fifty
[...].
> (VIII, 267–268)

There is also a general rule of imposing the lowest possible punishment on a Brahmin, and a punishment of average severity – on a Kshatriya.

Brahmins have an advantage in courts, which operate in accordance with the principles of Virtue; what is more, their testimony is irrefutable:

On a conflict among witnesses,
the king shall accept the majority;

in the case of equality (of number)
those possessed of superior qualifications;
and in the case of conflict between equally qualified witnesses,
the best among the twice-born.

(VIII, 73)

The relationship between political power and spiritual power is accurately summed up in the following fragment:

Even when fallen in the deepest distress,
the king shall not provoke the Brāhmaṇas;
for if provoked,
they would ruin him,
along with his army and conveyances.
Who could escape ruin
after having provoked those
by whom fire was rendered all-devouring,
by whom the ocean was made undrinkable
and by whom the moon was made
to wax and wane?
Who could prosper
after injuring those who,
on being provoked, would create other worlds
and other guardians of the regions,
and who would make the Gods
cease to be Gods?

(IX, 313–315)

The king, despite all his privileges, still has to accept the Brahmins' opinion as final. The postulated higher authority of Brahmins with respect to the king is justified by their suprahuman competences. The image of priests is highly absolutized – they are raised above the gods and ascribed a power which exceeds political power by far – it extends to other worlds. Brahmins are expressly called the creators of the world, so there is no need to further justify their dominance in society. There is also no need to explain why a person who can order the elements around has greater power than an army general. One can hardly argue with such a justification – indeed, it is virtually indisputable. The relationship between Brahmins and Kshatriyas is ideologically mystified by the presenting Brahmins' earthly dominance – which results from their monopoly of the means of indoctrination – as the supernatural dominance

THE IMAGE OF A SOCIAL STRUCTURE IN *MANUSMRTI* 153

of guarantors of ritual preservation of the world, a function which is fulfilled for the good of the society, including the rulers. The deformational procedures of mythization and transcendentalization are used to substantiate the priests' dominance over the rulers' class.

3.6   *The Lower Classes: The Class of Owners and the People's Class*

For this presentation of the social structure to be complete, the class of owners and the people's class have to be described. Both are described in a rather cursory manner in *Manusmrti*.

As regards Vaishyas, we only learn that they should perform the duties of a host, cattle grower, trader, or money-lender. The attribute of Vaishyas is wealth, so they can be called the class of owners. The regulations on Virtue encourage asset accumulation because Vaishyas provide financial resources to the society.

> He shall put forth his best effort
> towards increasing his property
> in a righteous manner;
> and he shall zealously give food
> to all beings.
>> (IX, 333)

Shudras are only advised to humbly fulfill their only function of serving the twice-born. Obviously, to serve Brahmins is the greatest distinction:

> If he is pure,
> attendant upon his superiors,
> of gentle speech, free from pride,
> and always dependent upon the Brāhmaṇa,
> – he attains a higher caste.
>> (IX, 335)

In relative terms, much space is devoted to descriptions of Shudras' negative nature. Representatives of the dominated class are portrayed through stereotyping, and it is those abhorrent characteristics of members of the people's class that are to determine its low social status. The interdependence which has been described above is at play here as well: people are assigned to a social class based on their birth, without awaiting the manifestation of their personal characteristics. All *varṇas* are advised to hold the people's class in contempt. For Brahmins, any contact with a Shudra entails ritual contamination. Shudras are compared to the dirtiest objects:

> In a village where a corpse still lies,
> in the presence of low people [...]
> – it is unfit for study [...].
>> (IV, 108)

Shudras' unfortunate condition is reflected in the cruel punishments recommended for them:

> If a once-born person
> insults a twice-born one
> with gross abuse,
> he should suffer the cutting off of his tongue;
> as he is of low origin.
> If he mentions the name
> and caste of these men with scorn,
> a burning iron nail
> ten inches long
> shall be thrust into his mouth.
> If through arrogance,
> he teaches brāhmaṇas their duty,
> the king shall pour heated oil
> into his mouth and ears.
>> (VIII, 270–272)

Importantly, Shudras do not belong to the community of the twice-born, do not study, cannot even listen when other people study (horrible physical tortures are a punishment for such a transgression), and are not subjected to the ritual of initiation. Actually, their being a part of the society is in itself questionable. In every possible realm of social life, they are the oppressed: they do not own property or have political power. Their exclusion from the society of the twice-born eliminates inter-class antagonism from the Aryan community. The remaining *varṇas* form a harmonious sequence of groups of increasing status in a solidaristic vision of society.

The text of *Manusmṛti* actually advocates for slavery of the people's class, as if Shudras' very nature predestined them for that role. That kind of an explanation given by one class for the oppression of another can be interpreted as ideological:

> But a Śūdra, whether bought or unbought,
> he shall make to do servile work;

THE IMAGE OF A SOCIAL STRUCTURE IN *MANUSMṚTI*   155

> since it is for doing servile work for the Brāhmaṇa
> that he has been created by the self-born one.
> Even though set free by the master,
> the Śūdra is not released
> from service; since that is
> innate in him,
> and who can release him from it?
>> (VIII, 413–414)

According to this precept, a Shudra does not have the right to own property, and whatever Shudras have "on them" can be taken away at any moment by the master (VIII, 417).

4   Conclusions

The image of society presented in *Manusmṛti* fulfilled an ideological function for the class of priests and, to a lesser extent, the class of rulers, as evidenced by the solidaristic vision of social order and by the obfuscation of the conflict between the higher classes (priests/rulers/owners) and the people's class, as well as of the contradiction between the interests of the former and the latter. Deformational procedures are used to paint the priests' extraordinary predispositions which are then used to justify the Brahmins' dominance. The people's class is excluded from the social continuum by means of the concept of being 'twice-born.' At the same time, religion legitimizes actions which preserve the existing social order.

Nonetheless, there is a direct mention of the threat of an open outbreak of a class conflict in *Manusmṛti*:

> Even though he be able,
> the Śūdra shall not amass wealth;
> for having acquired wealth,
> the Śūdra harasses the Brāhmaṇas.
>> (X, 129)

One can hardly resist the temptation to ask the question what type of a social structure is ideologically mythicized by *Manusmṛti*. There are grounds for supposing that the Indian society in the classical period was theocratic – the class of priests took over some of the prerogatives of political power and the landowners. In order to evaluate how advanced that process was and to see if we can talk about the formation of a triple class of priests-rulers-owners, we would have to do separate research on the literature on the subject.

As early as about 200 BC, when merchant guilds grew in importance, despite ideological objections, Brahmins had to strike a compromise with the incoming people. One example of this could be the assigning of the status of 'fallen Kshatriyas' to groups of influential foreigners who Brahmins could not afford to ignore. At the same time, with the development of trade and the necessity of employing more and more artisans, representatives of the lower classes had an opportunity to improve their situation through a change of profession or through migration. Vaishyas (active traders) became more significant, and attempts were made to softening the rigors of social stratification so as to meet the needs of the developing society. There was greater pressure to create more precise regulations of the relationships among the *varnas*. It was then that Law Books (*Dharmaśāstras*) were written. They postulated the Brahmins' privileged position (also with respect to Vaishyas).[7] Brahmins remained the arbiters of morality and continued to determine what was or was not compliant with *dharma*. The central Hindu concept of that time, that of *karman*, helped broaden the scope of the Brahmins' social impact. About 300 years BC, trade was developing very dynamically and guilds were becoming even stronger. Brahmins, however, maintained that traveling on a ship, called "crossing the black water," was a horrible sin punishable by expulsion from the *varna*. Obsessive care for ritual purity prevented people from leaving their country as they feared contact with the impure – the foreigners – who did not observe Hindu rigors (*mleccha*). That hindered the development of the merchantry; consequently, their profit-based power was less threatening to Brahmins. Romila Thapar notes the strengthening of Brahmins' position during the reign of the Gupta dynasty:

> In the Gupta period, the Aryan model was adopted in Northern India, and Brahmins gained much more power. Numerous texts were rewritten to reinforce Brahmins' point of view, which implies their relatively influential and mighty status. Their superiority was also augmented by numerous land grants. They retained their position in society not only

---

7 "During this period there was much activity in the writing of Law Books (*Dharmashastras*) [...] The rising importance of the *vaishyas* and the creation of new sub-castes, owing to the more liberal atmosphere of urban life, must doubtless have caused concern to the upholders of traditional social law and usage, and the time had come when social relations had to be precisely defined. Not surprisingly the most important of Law Books reiterate at every step that a brahman is inherently superior in every way to other members of society and is to be shown the utmost respect, even by the wealthy vaishyas" (Thapar 2002, 123).

THE IMAGE OF A SOCIAL STRUCTURE IN *MANUSMṚTI*

> by proclaiming themselves the main heirs of the Aryan tradition but also by monopolizing power through their own system of education and by using that monopoly as an additional source of power.
>
> THAPAR, 2002, p. 166

The king's importance diminished at that time, despite royal titles suggesting great power. The king rewarded people who rendered services for him with land, as we learn from inscriptions and observers' reports. Only soldiers were rewarded in cash. A specific type of grant was *agrahara* – a tax-free grant reserved for Brahmins which, according to Romila Thapar, was another factor contributing to Brahmins' privileged position.

> Although they were not so frequent as in later times, land grants made in the Gupta period weakened the king's authority. The endowed owners, often state officials, stayed far from the reach of the central power. Although the king could, in theory, withdraw a grant, it rarely happened because Brahmins or officers offended by the withdrawal could easily express their dissatisfaction as political opposition.
>
> THAPAR 2002, pp. 145–146

Jan Kieniewicz also emphasizes that the grants expanded the scope of the immunity of their beneficiaries, lay and ecclesiastical, as well as their independence from the ruler, which effectively prevented the creation of a strong centralized power – instead, the king had to seek support with more grants (Kieniewicz 1985, pp. 109–113).

Presumably, then, the Vaishyas' growing economic potential threatened the Brahmins' position. *Manusmṛti* may have been one defense strategy against that, at least in the ideological realm. On the one hand, the text sanctioned the existing theocratic system, on the other hand – it was meant to 'protect' Brahmins against the increasing power of the class of owners'. The aim of these remarks is to indicate the heuristic potential of non-Marxian historical materialism rather than to make unequivocal interpretations – the latter would require further, much deeper historical studies.

References

Basham, A.L. (1954). *The Wonder That Was India.* London: Sidgwick & Jackson.

Brown, W. N. (1931). The Sources and Nature of purusa in the Purusasukta (Rigveda 10.91). *Journal of the American Oriental Society* 51 (2): 108–118.

Brzechczyn, K. (2002). Świadomość a klasy społeczne. Próba rozszerzenia stratyfikacji społecznej w nie-Marksowskim materializmie historycznym [Consciousness and Social Classes. An Attempt at Broadening Social Stratification in Non-Marxian Historical Materialism]. In: P. Orlik (ed.) *Światłocienie świadomości*, pp. 213–235. Poznań: Wydawnictwo Naukowe IF UAM.

Brzechczyn, K. (2004). *O wielości linii rozwojowych w procesie historycznym. Próba interpretacji ewolucji społeczeństwa meksykańskiego* [On the Multitude of the Lines of Developments in the Historical Process. An Attempt at Interpretation of the Evolution of the Mexican Society]. Poznań: Wydawnictwo Naukowe UAM.

Brzechczyn, K. (2007). On the Application of Non-Marxian Historical Materialism to Development of Non-European Societies. In: J. Brzeziński, A. Klawiter, T.A.F. Kuipers, K. Łastowski, K. Paprzycka, P. Przybysz (ed.), *The Courage of Doing Philosophy. Essays Presented to Leszek Nowak*, pp. 235–254. Amsterdam – New York, NY: Rodopi.

Ciesielski, M. (2013). Problem kumulacji podziałów klasowych we współczesnym kapitalizmie. Próba analizy teoretycznej [The Problem of the Accumulation of Class Divisions in Contemporary Capitalism]. In: K. Brzechczyn, M. Ciesielski, and E. Karczyńska *Jednostka w układzie społecznym. Próba teoretycznej konceptualizacji,* pp. 131–152. Poznań: Wydawnictwo Naukowe WNS UAM.

Ciesielski. M. (2022) The Problem of the Accumulation of Class Divisions in Contemporary Capitalism: An Attempt at a Theoretical Analysis. In: K. Brzechczyn (ed.) *New Developments in Theory of Historical Process. Polish Contributions to Non-Marxian Historical Materialism. Poznań Studies in the Philosophy of the Sciences and the Humanities*, vol. 119, pp. 217–238. Boston/Leiden: Brill.

Hymny Rigwedy (1971). Translated by S.F. Michalski. Warszawa: Ossolineum.

Kieniewicz, J. (1985). *Historia Indii* [History of India]. Warszawa: PIW.

Kościelniak, C. (2003). Utopia, antyutopia, kontrutopia. Przyczynek do analizy metodologicznej [Utopia, Anti-Utopia, Counter-Utopia. A Contribution to the Methodological Analysis]. In: K. Brzechczyn, *Ścieżki transformacji. Ujęcia teoretyczne i opisy empiryczne*, pp. 401–413. Poznań: Zysk i S-ka.

Kudelska, M. 2003. *Karman i Dharma. Wizja świata w filozoficznej myśli Indii* [Karman and Dharma. The Vision of the World in the Philosophical Thought of India]. Kraków: Wydawnictwo Uniwersytetu Jagiellońskiego.

Manusmṛti with the 'Manubhāṣya' of Medhātithi (1926). Transl. Gangānātha Jhā, University of Culcutta.

Nowak, L. (1975). Próba interpretacji adaptacyjnej [On Adaptive Interpretation]. In: J. Kmita (ed.) *Wartość, dzieło, sens*, pp. 211–227. Warsaw: Książka i Wiedza.

Nowak L. (1983). *Property and Power. Towards a non-Marxian Historical Materialism* (Theory and Decision Library, t. 27). Dordrecht/Boston/Lancaster: Reidel.

Nowak, L. (1984). Ideologia a utopia [Ideology and Utopia]. In: J. Brzeziński and L. Nowak (eds.) *Świadomość społeczna a świadomość jednostkowa,* pp. 37–68. Warsaw – Poznań: PWN.

Nowak, L. (1986). Ideology versus Utopia. A Contribution to the analysis of the Role of Social Consciousness in Movement of Socio-Economic Formation. In: P. Buczkowski, A. Klawiter (eds.) *Theories of Ideology and Ideology of Theories. Poznań Studies in the Philosophy of the Sciences and The Humanities,* vol. 9, pp. 24–52. Amsterdam: Rodopi.

Nowak, L. (1988). Spiritual Domination as a Class Oppression: A Contribution to the Theory of Culture in non-Marxian Historical Materialism. *Philosophy of Social Sciences,* 18, 231–238.

Nowak, L. (1991abc). *U podstaw teorii socjalizmu* [The Foundations of the Theory of Socialism]; vol. 1: *Własność i władza. O konieczności socjalizmu* [Property and Power. On the Necessity of Socialism]; vol. 2: *Droga do socjalizmu. O konieczności socjalizmu w Rosji* [The Road to Socialism. On the Necessity of Socialism in Russia]; vol. 3: *Dynamika władzy. O strukturze i konieczności zaniku socjalizmu* [The Dynamics of Power. On the Structure and Necessity of the Disappearance of Socialism]. Poznań: Nakom.

Nowak L. (1991d). *Power and Civil Society. Toward a Dynamic Theory of Real Socialism.* New York: Greenwood Press.

Nowak, L. (1996). Kilka uwag na temat miejsca logicznego empiryzmu w dwudziestowiecznej filozofii [A Few Remarks on the Position of Logical Empiricism in the 20th-century Philosophy]. In: R. Egiert, A. Klawiter, P. Przybysz (eds.) *Oblicza idealizacji,* pp. 293–310. Poznań: Wydawnictwo Naukowe UAM.

Nowak, L. (1998). O skrytej jedności nauk społecznych i przyrodniczych [On the Hidden Unity of Social Science and Natural Science]. *Nauka* 1, pp. 11–42.

Nowak, L., I. Nowakowa (2000). Idealization X: The Richness of Idealization. *Poznań Studies in the Philosophy of the Sciences and the Humanities,* vol. 69. Amsterdam/Atlanta: Rodopi.

Nowak, L. (2012). On the Hidden Unity of Social and Natural Sciences. In: K. Brzechczyn, K. Paprzycka (eds.). *Thinking about Provincialism in Thinking.* Poznań Studies in the Philosophy of the Sciences and the Humanities, vol. 69, pp. 13–50. Amsterdam/Atlanta: Rodopi.

Nowak, L. (2022). Religion as a Class Structure: A Contribution to non-Marxian Historical Materialism. In: K. Brzechczyn (ed.) *New Developments in Theory of Historical Process. Polish Contributions to Non-Marxian Historical Materialism. Poznań Studies in the Philosophy of the Sciences and the Humanities,* vol. 119, pp. 3–51. Leiden/Boston: Brill.

Słuszkiewicz, E. (1962). Społeczna funkcja *Manavadharmaśastry* [Social Function of *Manavadharmaśastra*]. *Euhemer. Przegląd Religioznawczy,* 3 (28), 3–40.

Thapar, R. (2002). *A History of India*. New Delhi: Penguin Books.

Zarębski, T. (2013). Struktura klasowa społeczeństw hydraulicznych. Próba parafrazy teorii Karla Augusta Wittfogla w aparaturze pojęciowej nie-Marksowskiego materializmu historycznego [The Class Structure of Hydraulic Societies. An Attempt at a Paraphrase of Karl August Wittfogel's Theory in the Conceptual Apparatus of Non-Marxian Historical Materialism]. In: K. Brzechczyn, M. Ciesielski, and E. Karczyńska *Jednostka w układzie społecznym. Próba teoretycznej konceptualizacji,* pp. 207–221. Poznań: Wydawnictwo Naukowe WNS UAM.

Zarębski, T. (2022). The Class Structure of Hydraulic Societies. An Attempt at a Paraphrase of Karl August Witttfogel's Theory in the Conceptual Framework of non-Marxian Historical Materialism. In: K. Brzechczyn (ed). *Non-Marxian Historical Materialism: Reconstructions and Comparisons. Poznań Studies in the Philosophy of the Sciences and the Humanities,* vol. 120, pp. 111–126. Boston/Leiden: Brill.

CHAPTER 8

A Victorious Revolution and a Lost Modernization: An Attempt to Paraphrase Theda Skocpol's Theory of Social Revolution in the Conceptual Apparatus of Non-Marxian Historical Materialism

Krzysztof Brzechczyn

Abstract

The aim of this paper is to paraphrase Theda Skocpol's theory of social revolutions with the use of the conceptual apparatus of non-Marxian historical materialism. In the successive sections of this paper, the concepts of modernization, the nature of state power, an agrarian bureaucracy, and the mechanism of a victorious revolution are paraphrased. This paraphrase makes it possible to distinguish two kinds of agrarian bureaucracies, each resulting in social revolutions with different outcomes. A victorious revolution led to successful modernization in the case of an economic agrarian bureaucracy, but not in the case of a political agrarian bureaucracy.

Keywords:

Comparative historical sociology – Leszek Nowak – modernization – non-Marxian historical materialism – social revolution – Theda Skocpol

1 Foreword

This article constitutes an attempt to paraphrase Theda Skocpol's theory, presented in *States and Social Revolutions* (1979), in the conceptual apparatus of non-Marxian historical materialism (n-Mhm), a historiosophical theory formed by Leszek Nowak. The first work within the framework of Nowak's theory, *U podstaw teorii procesu historycznego* (*The Foundations of the Theory of the Historical Process*), was also published in 1979, but it was only available as a samizdat edition at the time.

© KRZYSZTOF BRZECHCZYN, 2022 | DOI:10.1163/9789004507296_009

Both theories, to varying degrees, concern the modernization of societies. In order to characterize the two theoretical frameworks, I propose the following classification of theories of modernization, based on two questions-criteria. The first criterion is the manner – revolutionary or evolutionary– in which a society can be modernized. The second criterion is the type of factors which stimulate the modernization of a society – they can be internal or external with respect to the society which undergoes modernization. When we combine the two criteria, we obtain four types of theories of modernization:

- evolutionary-endogenous, according to which modernization is an internal social process which leads to gradual transformations of the social structure and the economic structure;
- evolutionary-exogenous, according to which the external conditions of a political (for example, international rivalry) or economic kind (for example, international trade and exchange) lead to a gradual transformation of the social and economic structures of traditional societies;
- revolutionary-endogenous, according to which the internal contradictions of traditionalist societies lead to a revolution which allows them to modernize themselves;
- revolutionary-exogenous, according to which external conditions cause a revolutionary crisis and, in the end, a modernization of the given society.

Walt Rostow's theory, which presupposes a five-stage process of modernization stimulated by internal factors (at the first stage, the main factors are: the development of science, agriculture, and industry), is an example of the evolutionistic-endogenous type (Rostow 1964). One example of the evolutionistic-exogenous type is the theory of a global economic system created by Immanuel Wallerstein (e.g. Wallerstein 1974; 1976). The incorporation of the economies of particular societies into the global capitalist system took place gradually (through the development of trade), under the influence of core countries: England (later Great Britain) and the Dutch Republic in the 16th and 17th centuries. Marxism is a representative of the revolutionistic-endogenous type – it presupposes that the internal contradictions of feudal societies will lead to a revolution which, if victorious, guarantees the modernization of the given society. Theda Skocpol's theory can be classified as revolutionistic-exogenous. In her view, the worsening situation of traditionalist countries in the international arena, the symptoms of which are defeats wars and the loss of spheres of influence to the benefit of capitalist countries, forces the elites which govern those traditionalist societies to implement reforms which result in their revolutionary transformation (modernization).[1] It seems that non-Marxian historical materialism is an evolutionistic-endogenous approach – the transformation of feudal ownership relations into capitalist ones takes place through social evolution (Nowak 1983; 1991a), under the influence of unsuccessful protests of the oppressed classes.

Let us take a closer look at the paraphrase procedure. A paraphrase procedure consists in translating problem Q, formed in theoretical language T, into the language of the paraphrasing-theory, T^*, which is considered to be better than T in some respects (more precise/abstract). If all the assumptions of question Q are recreated in the language of the paraphrasing theory and are solved by its means, we can refer to it as a reconstruction of that problem. Sometimes, the theory into which problem Q is translated is too meager. In such a case, only some of the assumptions of problem Q are reconstructed, and the translation becomes a partial reconstruction, that is, a paraphrase. A paraphrase, then, consists in forming, in the language of theory T^*, an analog of Q^*, which has certain assumptions in common with Q (Nowakowa 1991, 81–83).[2]

Therefore, the paraphrased problem gains a different theoretical rank within the framework of the new theoretical system. The result of a paraphrase can be positive or negative, depending on whether the theses of the paraphrased theory turn out to be, respectively, true or false in the language of the paraphrasing theory (Łastowski, Nowak 1979, pp. 3–4; Nowak 1998, pp. 77–79).[3]

This article consists of two main parts. In the first part, I intuitively reconstruct Skocpol's theory of revolution – I present her theoretical assumptions and conceptualization of: modernization processes, the nature of state power, societies of agrarian bureaucracy, and the mechanism of a victorious revolution. In the second part, I paraphrase her theory within the conceptual framework of non-Marxian historical materialism, in four steps. I paraphrase: the

---

1 For a more systematic comparison of Marx's and Skocpol's visions of politics and concepts of revolution, see Brzechczyn 2009, and for a description of the influence of a revolution on democratization in comparative historical sociology, see Brzechczyn 2010b.

2 Incidentally, in the heuristic inspired by the idealizational theory of science, a number of interpretive procedures are distinguished, for example, historical interpretation, adaptive interpretation, idealizing reconstruction, intuitive reconstruction, or paraphrase, the interrelationships of which are not entirely clear, or at least they have not been the subject of systematic research. On methodology of Nowak and Poznań School, see: Borbone 2016; 2021l Coniglione 2010.

3 Various theories have been paraphrased within the framework of the idealizational theory of science, by such scholars as Nowakowa (1992) and Egiert (2000). Nowak (2000) paraphrased Gombrowicz's social concepts within the framework of the non-evangelical model of the human being.

process of modernization, the status of political power, the structure of an agrarian bureaucratic society, and the mechanism of a revolution itself.

2 The Theory of Social Revolutions. An Attempt at a Presentation

2.1 *Theoretical Assumptions*

Skocpol's theory of social revolutions is based on the following methodological directives:

> In the first place, an adequate understanding of social revolutions requires that the analyst take a nonvoluntarist, structuralist perspective on their causes and processes. [...]. In the second place, social revolutions cannot be explained without systematic reference to *inter*national structures and world-historical developments [...]. In the third place, in order to explain the causes and outcomes social revolutions, it is essential to conceive of states as administrative and coercive organizations – organizations that are potentially autonomous from (though, of course conditioned by) socio-economic interests and structures.
>
> SKOCPOL 1979, p. 14

In her conception, the author combines certain ideas of Marx – his class analysis of the economic structure of society – with theories of political conflict. She writes:

> The Marxist conception of class relations as rooted in the control of productive property and the appropriation of the economic surpluses from direct producers by nonproducers is, in my view, an indispensable theoretical tool for identifying one sort of basic contradiction in society.
>
> SKOCPOL 1979, p. 13

As regards theoreticians of political conflict, Skocpol believes that they make it possible to answer the following question:

> [...] when and how do dominant classes have the capacity for collective political actions? For answering such question, the political-conflict argument that collective action is based upon group organization and access to resources, often including coercive resources, is especially fruitful.
>
> SKOCPOL 1979, p. 13–14.

She asserts that revolutions are very rare historical events, because they are:

> [...] rapid, basic transformations of a society's state and class structures; and they are accompanied and in part carried through by class-based revolts from below. Social revolutions are set apart from other sort of conflicts and transformative processes above all by the combination of two coincidences: the coincidence of societal structural change with class upheaval; and the coincidence of political with social transformation
>
> SKOCPOL 1979, p. 4.

Additionally, the author distinguishes rebellions, that is, social movements limited to the economic sphere, and political revolutions which entail the transformation of only the political aspect of social life. In short, Skocpol defines a revolution as a transformation of both the economic and the political sphere of life.

2.2 *Modernization*

In Skocpol's theory, modernization is understood as a transnational process of economic development, characterized by industrialization, widespreading of wage labor and of processes of exchange by means of market mechanisms. Those changes, in turn, lead to changes in other spheres of social life, especially in political and legal institutions, and they contribute to the creation of a modern, bureaucratic (within the meaning given to that word by Max Weber) state. In the first phase, in the 18th century, England modernized itself. In the 19th century, modernization reached other European countries and some non-European societies (Japan). It led to the creation of the international economic market which included capitalist countries as well as those which, for various reasons, remained outside of the range of such modernizing processes.

Modernization was taking place in a particular international context: that of an international system of competing countries. Europe was specific in that no imperial state controlled the whole area of Europe and its overseas territories. According to Skocpol, the international rivalry of countries stimulated the colonial expansion of Spain in Latin America. Later, the competition between England and France led to the construction of the first colonial empire by the former country. England owed its advantageous position in the international rivalry to its earlier start on the path of capitalist development. Finally, in the 19th century, the competition among the European countries led to the conquest of the whole world. Once more, European countries owed their advantageous position over the rest of the world to their having been the first to undergo modernization. The mechanism of international competition overlapped with the modernization processes although it was independent from them:

> [...] nation states are, more fundamentally, organizations geared to maintain control of home territories and populations and to undertake actual or potential military competition with other states in the international system. The international state system, as a transnational structure of military competition, was not originally created by capitalism. Throughout modern world history, it represents an analytically autonomous level of transnational reality – *interdependent* in its structure and dynamic with world capitalism, but not reducible to it. The militarily relevant strengths and international advantages (or disadvantages) of states are not entirely explicable in terms of their domestic economies or international economic positions. Such factors as state administrative efficiency, political capacities for mass mobilization, and international geographical position are also relevant.
>
> SKOCPOL 1979, p. 22

2.3   *The Nature of State Power*

According to Skocpol, the process of modernization takes place in an international system – which is autonomous with respect to that process – of countries which compete with one another. Therefore, it is worth taking a look at the state as the basic unit of that international system. Its autonomy is based on the fact that "the state, in short, is fundamentally Janus-faced, with an intrinsically dual anchorage in the class-divided socioeconomic structures and an international system of states" (Skocpol 1979, p. 32). Skocpol views the state as potentially autonomous from the dominant class in a society.

State organizations inevitably compete to some extent with the dominant class(es) in appropriating resources from the economy and society. And the objectives to which the resources, once appropriated, are devoted may very well be at variance with the existing dominant class interest. Resources may be used to strengthen the bulk and autonomy of the state itself – something necessarily threatening to the dominant class unless the greater state power is indispensably needed and actually used to support the dominant-class interest. But the use of state power to support the dominant-class interest is not inevitable. Indeed, the attempts of state rulers merely to perform the state's "own" functions may create conflicts of interests with the dominant class. The state normally performs two basic sets of tasks. It maintains order and it competes with other actual or potential, states (Skocpol 1979, p. 30).

Skocpol agrees with the Marxian approach which assumes that state organizations "usually do function to preserve existing economic and class structures, for that is normally the smoothest way to enforce order" (Skocpol 1979, p. 30). However, in crisis conditions, a state, motivated by its own interest, can also have a policy regarding the oppressed classes.

Although both the state and the dominant class(es) share a broad interest in keeping the subordinate classes in place in society and at work in the existing economy, the state's own fundamental interest in maintaining sheer physical order and political peace may lead it – especially in periods of crisis – to enforce concessions to subordinate-class demands. These concessions may be at the expense of the interests of the dominant class, but not contrary to the state's own interests in controlling the population and collecting taxes and military recruits (Skocpol 1979, p. 30).

2.4   *Agrarian Bureaucratic Societies*

One element of the international system are traditionalist states in which revolutions take place. Skocpol analyses revolutions in three countries: France, Russia, and China. In my presentation of Skocpol's conceptualization and in my paraphrase of that theory in the conceptual apparatus of non-Marxian historical materialism, I will omit the Chinese case and limit the discussion to the societies which belong to the European line of development. The author notes:

> [...] comparative historical analysis works best when applied to a set of a few cases that share certain basic features. Cases need to be carefully selected and the criteria for grouping them together made explicit.
>
> SKOCPOL 1979, p. 40.

The three states mentioned above were chosen by Skocpol for three reasons: first, none of them was subject to the colonial rule of more developed (that is, capitalist) states in its history; second, in each of these three states, the outbreak of revolution was preceded by a longer or shorter period of international crisis and internal political conflict – In France, in 1787–1789, in China, in 1911, and in Russia, in 1917; third, the selected societies represent the same type of a social system, that is, agrarian bureaucracy. The author describes the system of agrarian bureaucracy as follows:

> An agrarian bureaucracy is an agricultural society in which social control rests on a division of labor and a coordination of effort between a semi-bureaucratic state and a landed upper class. The landed upper class typically retains, as an adjunct to its landed property, considerable (though

varying in different cases) undifferentiated local and regional authority over the peasant majority of the population. The partially bureaucratic central state extracts taxes and labor from peasants either in directly through landlord intermediaries or else directly, but with (at least minimal) reliance upon cooperation from individuals of the landed upper class. In turn, the landed upper class relies upon the backing of a coercive state to extract rents and/or dues from the peasantry. At the political center, autocrat, bureaucracy, and army monopolize decisions, yet (in varying degrees and modes) accommodate the regional and local power of the landed upper class and (again, to varying degrees) recruit individual members of this class into leading positions in the state.

SKOCPOL 1976, pp. 178–179

Following that initial characterization, we can reconstruct the social relations among the social entities: the authorities, the landed class, the merchant-bourgeois classes, and the peasantry. In that type of society, there were social tensions between the higher classes (bourgeoisie, landed gentry, the state) and the peasantry (see Figure 8.1). There was social peace between the merchants-bourgeoisie, on the one hand, and the state together with the landed class, on the other hand. In that model of a society, the key relationships were those between the state power and the landed class. In conditions of social stabilization, there was social peace between those social entities; in conditions of a political crisis, it changed into a conflict.

In an agrarian bureaucracy society, the state was a proto-bureaucratic structure. That meant that administrative and military power functioned within the institutional framework of an absolute monarchy. In that kind of a state, offices were partially specialized and officers were subjected to hierarchical control which, however, did not extend to all their functions. The functions

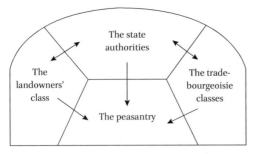

FIGURE 8.1 The social structure of an agrarian bureaucracy. Abbreviations used: ↔ common social interests; → conflict of social interests

A VICTORIOUS REVOLUTION AND A LOST MODERNIZATION

of holding of an office and managing one's assets became partially independent from each other. Still, the state did not become fully bureaucratic because power was not centralized to the degree characteristic of a nation state. The author notes:

> It is worth emphasizing in particular that the imperial states of old-regime France, Russia [...] were not in a position to control directly, let alone basically reorganize, local agrarian socio-economic relationships. Rather, they were limited to variations or extensions of the functions they had, so to speak, been built up to perform: waging war abroad; supervising society at home to maintain some semblance of general order; and appropriating socioeconomic resources through military recruitment and through taxes on land, population or trade (but not on anything so difficult to assess and individual income).
>
> SKOCPOL 1979, p. 48

Market economy, trade, and industry developed in that type of a society, and capitalist relations of production appeared, which, however, did not dominate the economy. Consequently, the merchant and bourgeois classes were interrelated on many levels with the landed class and the proto-bureaucratic state with which they lived – in Skocpol's words – in a symbiosis.

I will now present the relationships between the landed gentry and the state. In that social system, the state and the landed class were partners – in the exploitation of peasantry – but also competitors. Skocpol describes it as follows:

> The dominant classes could not defend against peasant rebellions on a local basis; they had all come to depend, albeit in varying degrees, upon the centralized monarchical states to back their class positions and prerogatives.
>
> SKOCPOL 1979, p. 49

Nevertheless, the author notes that:

> [...] the imperial states and the landed classes [...] were also competitors in controlling the manpower of the peasantry and in appropriating surpluses from the agrarian-commercial economies. Monarchs were interested in appropriating increased resources from society and channeling them efficiently into military aggrandizement or state-sponsored and centrally controlled economic development. Thus, the economic interests

of the landed upper classes were in part obstacles to be overcome; for the landed classes were primarily interested either in preventing increased state appropriation or in using state offices to siphon off revenues in ways that would reinforce the domestic socio-economic status quo.

SKOCPOL 1979, p. 49

One characteristic of agrarian bureaucracy societies was that representatives of the owners held lower offices in the power apparatus. The author explains this as follows:

... in preindustrial states, monarchs found it difficult to channel sufficient resources through the 'center' to pay simultaneously for wars, culture and court life on the one hand, and a fully bureaucratic officialdom on the other. Consequently, they often had to make do with 'officials' recruited from wealthy backgrounds, frequently, in practice, landlords. In addition, central state jurisdiction rarely touched local peasants or communities directly; governmental functions were often dele- gated to landlords in their 'private' capacities, or else to non-bureaucratic authoritative organizations run by local landlords.

SKOCPOL 1976, p. 184

What is more, the dominant classes had become accustomed to having opportunities for private fortune-building through state service. And, indeed, such appropriation of surpluses indirectly through state office-holding had become very important in old regime France, Russia, and China alike.

SKOCPOL 1979, p. 49

On the other hand, that state of things had the following consequences.

But to the extent the dominant-class members gained a capacity for self-conscious collective organization within the higher levels of the existing imperial state structures they might be in a position to obstruct monarchical undertakings that recounter to their economic interests. Such obstruction could culminate in deliberative challenges to autocratic political authority – and at the same time, it could have quite unintended effect of destroying the administrative and military integrity of the imperial state itself.

SKOCPOL 1979, p. 49

That caused constant conflicts between the state elite, which strove for greater centralization of power, and the owners' classes, which wanted to maintain the *status quo* with its guarantee of privileges:

> The fundamental politically relevant tensions in all three Old Regimes were *not* between commercial-industrial upper classes and/or very dependent upon the imperial states. Instead, they were centered in the relationships of producing classes to the dominant classes and states, and in relationships of the landed dominant classes to the autocratic-imperial states. As in all agrarian states, the potential for peasant (and urban – popular) revolts was endemic.
>
> SKOCPOL 1979, p. 48

> Peasants are primarily agricultural cultivators who must, because of political and cultural marginality and relative socio-economic immobility, bear the burden of varying combinations of taxes, rents, corvée, usurious interest rates, and discriminatory prices. Peasants always have grounds to rebellion against landlords, state agents, and merchants who exploit them. What is at issue is not so much the objective potential for revolts on grounds of justifiable grievances. It is rather the degree to which grievances that are always at least implicitly present can be collectively perceived and acted upon.
>
> SKOCPOL 1979, p. 115

The social situation of the peasantry was a potential ground for an outbreak of peasants' dissatisfaction. Peasants' ability to rebel depended on three factors:

> (1) the degrees and kinds of solidarity of peasant communities; (2) the degree of peasant autonomy from the direct, day-to-day supervision and control by landlords and their agents; and (3) the relaxation of state coercive sanctions against peasant revolts.
>
> SKOCPOL 1979, p. 115

As we can see, a revolution can break out if there is a certain level of organization of peasant communities. The first two conditions depend on the structure of agricultural ownership – when it obstructs the organization of peasant communities, it prevents the outbreak of a revolt. That may be the case on great estates where the owners supervise the peasants directly, or when the class of owners controls the administrative and executive power at the local level. The third condition, which is crucial for an outbreak of revolution, is determined by the relationship between the state and the landed gentry. When the international situation of the state is stable, the authorities and the landed gentry are partners in the exploitation of the peasantry. A crisis only begins when:

> [...] old regime states became unable to meet the challenges of evolving international situation. Monarchical authorities were subjected to new threats or to intensified competition from more economically developed powers abroad. And they were constrained or checked in their responses by the institutionalized relationship of the autocratic state organization to the landed upper classes and the agrarian economies. Caught in cross-pressures between domestic class structures and international exigencies, the autocracies and their centralized administrations and armies broke apart, opening the way for socio-revolutionary transformations spearheaded by revolts from below.
>
> SKOCPOL 1979, p. 47

2.5 The Mechanism of a Victorious Revolution

I will now present the mechanism of a social revolution. Skocpol discusses an international system consisting of capitalist societies and agrarian bureaucracies. In international rivalry, agrarian bureaucracy systems encounter challenges they cannot rise up to. In order to compete successfully with states which have embarked on the road of modernization, agrarian bureaucracy societies must construct an effective tax system, move more resources toward military development, and build an economy capable of fulfilling national objectives (Skocpol 1976, p. 180). However, because of the landowners' resistance, central power has limited ability to carry out internal, peaceful reforms. In particular, it cannot rationalize the tax system. Because of the political structure of agrarian bureaucracies, the authorities also have restricted access to financial and human resources, which are controlled by the landed classes. Moreover, the government has a limited ability to mobilize the society because such an action would be against the interests of the landed class, which acts as both the state and an employer as regards the peasantry.

Meeting the challenges of international competition requires an effective economy capable of financing the costs of maintenance of an army, administration, and diplomatic service, so the state solves the crisis by modernizing the economic and political structure. The reforms weaken the relationships between the state structure and the class of owners. When the state no longer protects the interests of the aristocracy, the possibility of an outbreak of peasant rebellions arises, because:

> Agricultural regimes featuring large estate worked by serfs or laborers tend to be inimical to peasant rebellion – witness the East Elbian Junker regime – but the reason is not that serfs and landless laborers are economically poor, rather that they are subject to close and constant supervision and discipline by landlords or their agents.
>
> SKOCPOL 1976, p. 193

Finally, the fourth factor was the influence of the radical political elites which formed on the margins of societies:

> Although peasant insurrections played a decisive role in each of the great historical social revolutions, nevertheless an exclusive focus on peasants – or on the peasant situation in agrarian bureaucracies – cannot provide a complete explanation for the occurrences of social revolution.
>
> SKOCPOL 1976, p. 201

Such a complete explanation can only be obtained by taking into account the influence of marginal political elites. Generally speaking, members of those social groups came from the intelligentsia. They had knowledge and skills which qualified them for service in the state apparatus, but they did not have traditional sources of prestige (such as noble birth) which would give them the right to independently wield power. That is why it was natural for the elites of the opposition to demand equality, the abolition of status-group privileges, and the introduction of political democracy. French marginal political elites originated chiefly from the third status group. The main leaders of national assemblies of the French Revolution belonged to a professional group called notables – they were lawyers and lower-rank officials. They were marginal in that they held lower offices in the administrative structure of the pre-revolutionary order or came from provincial towns. The marginality of members of political elites of the opposition in Russia was determined by their social origins or belonging to radical political groups. Bolsheviks were often the graduates of universities which prepared them for a career in the state. However, during their studies, they joined radical political movements, and they became professional revolutionaries instead of state officials.

The participation of marginal political elites in the revolution helped translate the practical postulates of mass peasant revolts into the language of political postulates which transformed the structure of the state and society; it also built the internal communication between the naturally dispersed and decentralized peasant communities. Moreover, those political elites which opposed the old order – Jacobins and communists – had at their disposal a universal ideology which encouraged the cooperation of people from various social environments and facilitated the political mobilization of the masses. That ideology was also a world view which justified using unlimited (that is, immoral) means to realize limited aims (that is, moral aims, in the light of a given ideology). As noted by Skocpol, although revolutionary ideology was a necessary component of social revolutions, their course and results cannot be explained by referring to the content of the ideology – instead, one should look at its functions.

To sum up Skocpol's theory, we could say that for a victorious social revolution to take place, the four analyzed factors must be at play: external modernizing pressure, a political crisis caused by the weakening of the relations between the authorities and the owners, peasant revolts, and the influence of marginal political elites (see Figure 8.2). External modernizing pressure worsens the international position of agrarian bureaucratic states. State elites try to meet the challenges of the international situation by carrying out reforms which weaken the relationship between the political power and the class of owners. That, in turn, causes an internal political crisis which is aggravated by peasant rebellions made possible precisely by the reduction of the range of the authorities' political control over the peasantry. When the political elites of the opposition form an alliance with grassroots peasant revolts, the actions of the peasantry can be coordinated on a national scale, and a separate vision of the social order can be expressed. Consequently, the state authorities are overthrown, and a new state order is built.

In Skocpol's model, the distinguished factors appear to be operating in a somewhat automatic, mechanistic fashion. I suppose this results from the

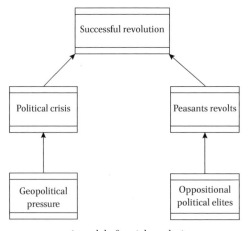

FIGURE 8.2 A model of social revolution

author's focus on the macrostructural dimensions of revolutions and the consequent omission of the subjective aspect of the historical process. Were that aspect taken into account, it would be possible to enquire about the circumstances in which political elites decide to carry out internal reforms. Modernizing pressure can lead to internal reforms, but state elites can oppose this in different ways: by importing military technology from more developed states, by isolating the society from other states so as to avoid the pressure, or by making better use of the existing resources. State elites will choose a particular action based on their value system, ideology, and knowledge – all factors which are omitted, on principle, in the presented analysis.[4]

For Skocpol, a revolution only ends when the revolutionary elites have created an alternative political order. In her view, the significant features of that order are discernible in all three analyzed cases. Peasant revolutionary movements changed the agrarian structure of the states in which they took place.

Centralized and completely bureaucratized nation states replaced autocratic and proto-bureaucratic monarchies. In particular societies, the pre-revolutionary class of great owners lost its privileged position to the benefit of lower classes and of the hitherto marginal political elites which seized power in post-revolutionary states. Most importantly, the great class of owners lost any possibility of politically controlling the peasants.

The new elites defeated counterrevolutions and fended off external interference. Consequently, the new state organizations were more centralized and rationalized than the pre-revolutionary systems. Hence, as noted by Skocpol, "they were more potent within society and more powerful and autonomous over and against competitors within the international system of states" (Skocpol 1979, pp. 161–162). Let us consider those processes as exemplified by two states: France and Russia.

The French monarchy was transformed into a centralized and fully bureaucratized state. The greatest changes were introduced in the army: a completely professional officer corps was created, and the army was nationalized. The total number of soldiers in Napoleon's army from 1804 to 1813 has been estimated to have been about 2.4 million (Skocpol 1979, p. 198). Another indicator of the

---

4 Michael Burawoy (1989, p. 772), Elizabeth Nichols (1986), and Michael Taylor (1988) voice similar reservations about Skocpol's model. According to Taylor, who analyzes peasant revolts, an important disadvantage of Skocpol's conception is that it lacks microfoundations, that is, assumptions about the rationality of the peasantry and peasant communities. Such assumptions would make it possible to recreate the system of peasants' preferences, vision of the world, and knowledge about social conditions of action. Only then, according to Taylor, can a revolution be fully explained.

centralization of a state could be the growth of bureaucracy – in France, it grew from 50 to 250 thousand people during the revolution, including an increase from 420 officials of central offices in 1788 to 5 thousand in 1796 (Skocpol 1979, p. 199). Also, the range of the power of the bureaucracy over civil society was broadened. The state began to control higher and middle level education, subjugated the Catholic church by paying priests regular wages, improved the tax apparatus, and established a central bank which issued the national currency (Skocpol 1979, p. 202).

Similar changes were made in Russia, where professional, hierarchized bureaucracy was formed, which nationalized the economy and took control over all areas of social life. Unlike in France, the state administration in Russia was subject to the communist party and secret police.[5] Skocpol explains the differences between the results of revolutions in France and Russia as follows.

> The results of the French revolution, to begin with, contrasted to those in the Soviet Russia [...] in ways suggested by the usual labeling of the French outcomes as "bourgeois." The Russian [...] revolution gave rise to party-led state organizations that asserted control over the entire national economies [...] and (in one way or another) mobilized the populace to propel further national economic development. In France, however, no such results occurred. Instead, the French Revolution culminated in a professional-bureaucratic state that coexisted symbiotically with, and indeed guaranteed the full emergence of, national markets and capitalist private property.
>
> SKOCPOL 1979, p. 162

The author attributes the differences to the disparate courses of the peasant revolts, of the paces of the revolutionary crises, and of the international positions of the two countries. In France, peasant revolts did not disturb the ownership structure because the peasants were satisfied with the abolition of

---

5   The differences between, on the one hand, France, and, on the other hand, Russia and China, as exemplified by the control of the internal movement of populations, are also noted by Torpey (1988). He claims that various forms of migration control in France and in Russia existed before the revolutions. At the beginning of the two revolutions, those forms of control were abolished, but they were later reintroduced because of, among other things, threats to the revolutionary authorities. However, that is where the differences between post-revolutionary France and Russia end. In France, after the Napoleonic Wars had ended in the middle of the 19th century, population control was almost completely abolished, while in Stalinist Russia it was tightened up to a considerable degree in comparison with the tzarist period. That was the state of things until Mikhail Gorbachev's reforms.

feudal privileges. In Russia, however, there was a redistribution of land. Skocpol explains this by referring to the differences between the internal structures of the peasant classes in France and in Russia. The French peasant class was more layered than the Russian one. In France, there was a group of rich peasants who appreciated private ownership and did not demand that property be taken away from feudal lords, for fear that there might be a backlash against them. For that reason, after the feudal privileges had been abolished – which was in the interest of all peasants – the French peasantry was not capable of further cooperation. In Russia, there was a long tradition of (*Obshchina*). Village communities were more integrated because of various forms of communal farming, so their demands for division of feudal land could be effective, and the Bolsheviks readily granted their wishes in the first phase of the revolution.

Moreover, the revolutionary crises in France and Russia developed at different paces. In France, the process was slower, so Jacobins could make use of pre-revolutionary experience and resources for the construction of their army and administration. In Russia, it was more violent, so Bolsheviks had to build an army and an administration for the party virtually from scratch. Also, the international situation of the two countries was not the same. After the revolution, "France's strong position on the Continent favored the channeling of revolutionary mobilization into militarily expansionist nationalism rather than further politically directed transformation at home" (Skocpol 1979, p. 234). Russia was exposed to attacks from abroad, which necessitated violent industrialization and a transformation of the society, effected primarily with the use of the omnipresent structures of the party-state.

3   Modernization through a Victorious Revolution. An Attempt at a Paraphrase with the Use of the Conceptual Framework of Non-Marxian Historical Materialism

3.1   *A Paraphrase of Modernization*

I will now paraphrase Theda Skocpol's conception in the conceptual apparatus of non-Marxian historical materialism. A paraphrase of problem Q formulated in language T in the language of theory T^* consists in the search, in paraphrasing theory T^*, for analogs of theory T. If the language of theory T^* is too poor, it can be expanded. The ability to paraphrase, then, is a kind of a test for theory T^*, because that is how the range of the application of T^* can be expanded. Therefore, we should look for analogs of the distinguished elements from Skocpol's theory in non-Marxian historical materialism.

In this theory, modernization is a result of the development of the capitalist formation.[6] In contrast to the previous slavery and feudal formations, capitalist society may be characterized by:

(1) a separation and balance between the class of rulers, the class of owners and the class of priests;

(2) wage-labor replaced earlier coercive forms of employment and this guarantees a level of working class autonomy and productivity that is higher than in the previous formation;

(3) a high level of civil autonomy owing to widespread political democracy, which is an institutional form of the control of the authorities by the class of citizens;

(4) the conflict of interest between the class of owners and the class of the direct producers is solved by increasing the variable capital and the redistributive policy of the state (class of rulers),

(5) the balance between classes of disposers (owners, rulers and the priests) guarantees the spiritual freedom of the believers and the autonomy of different spheres of culture (science, art);

(6) constant technological progress, which resulted from the joint tendencies (1), (2), (4) and (5).[7]

In contrast to Skocpol's approach to modernization as a revolutionary and exogenous process, in n-Mhm modernization processes are presented as endogenous and basically evolutionary.[8] Taking into account the international dimension, that is, not only capitalist states but also states with pre-capitalist economies, makes it possible to broaden that vision of social transformations in non-Marxian historical materialism. For that purpose, however, the nature of state power must be paraphrased within the conceptual framework of that theory.

3.2 *The Status of State Power. An Attempt at a Paraphrase*

Such definitions of the authorities as: "state organizations" or "organizations which have administrative power and the means of coercion at their disposal"

---

6 The model of a capitalist society is presented in Nowak 1981, pp. 116–156 and 244–263 (English version: Nowak 1983, pp. 101–125 and 211–235), and its concretization including the influence of political institutions and ideologies is in Nowak 1989.

7 In n-Mhm, the term modernization is used to mean, in accordance with the common understanding of that word, technological progress, and it is not a synonym of social progress. The criterion of social progress depends on the type of society. In societies of the economic type, it is growing liberation of labor, while in political societies – increasing citizens' autonomy.

8 I used the adverb "basically' because Nowak formulated a mechanism of 'social progress by lost revolutions.' According to this view, revolutions prompt the reform process introduced by the political elites. However, these revolutions should not be victorious. In the event of their victory, the new post-revolutionary dictatorship is restored and the whole reform process is blocked, see Nowak 1989.

suggest that Skocpol characterizes state authorities at the institutional level (Skocpol 1979, p. 31). The state has a double nature, in that it upholds social order internally and competes with other states externally. However, Skocpol's institutionalist perspective prevents her from consistently conceptualizing the phenomenon of the authorities' external aggressiveness. Let us take a closer look at her explanation:

> As events of the eighteenth century unfolded, it became more and more apparent that the French monarchy could not fulfill its raison d'être. The victories in war necessary for the vindication of French honor on the international scene, not to mention the protection of seaborne commerce were beyond its grasp.
>
> SKOCPOL 1979, p .60

Skocpol explains the growing ineffectiveness of pre-revolutionary France in international affairs through a reference to idealistic ("the honor of France") and economic ("protection of *seaborne commerce*") factors. However, the materialist theory of power in non-Marxian historical materialism makes it possible to conceptualize power without these inconsistencies. In n-Mhm, the authorities are a social class constituted by having at their disposal the material means of coercion. That social inequality generates an autonomous social conflict because the class of rulers wants to maximize the sphere of power regulation at the cost of the autonomy of citizens' class as well as at the cost of citizens from other societies. That is how we can explain the mechanism of external aggressiveness and the activity of the state (that is, the institutionalized ruling class) on the global arena. In n-Mhm, the specificity of the societies discussed by Skocpol can be explicated as follows: the nature of state power is solidaristic inside a society and antagonistic outside of it. The reason for this is not the metaphysical assertion that "the state, in short, is fundamentally Janus-faced, with an intrinsically dual anchorage in the class-divided socioeconomic structures and an international system of states" (Skocpol 1979, p. 32) but the fact that in agrarian bureaucratic societies, the increase of power regulation is blocked by the owners' class, and the rulers' class can only maximize the external spheres of power regulation. In order to gain a better understanding of that phenomenon, we should paraphrase the description of agrarian bureaucracy societies with the use of the conceptual apparatus of non-Marxian historical materialism.

3.3   *Agrarian Bureaucratic Societies. An Attempt at a Paraphrase*
An agrarian bureaucratic society is a social system with a class of rulers and a class of owners which is divided into two sub-classes: owners of the means of

production in the urban sector and owners of the means of production (land) in the agrarian sector of the economy. This type of a society is characterized by fusion between the authorities and the class of landowners – representatives of the landed class have positions in state administration which gives them political control over the peasantry.

In n-Mhm, there are two basic types of societies (Nowak 1991a, p. 177–181; for a full classification of societies, see: Brzechczyn 2004, p. 73–86; 2007, for further developments see: Ciesielski 2013; 2022). The first are class societies with separate classes of rulers, owners, and priests. The second are supraclass societies in which there is accumulation of social divisions so that one and the same social class can control, for example, the means of coercion and the means of production (a totalitarian society), the means of production and the means of propaganda (a fascist society), or the means of coercion, production, and propaganda (a socialist society).

However, it would not be correct to apply the term 'supraclass system' to the phenomenon of symbiosis as defined by Skocpol. Therefore, in order to paraphrase such inter-class relationships, we must broaden the conceptual framework of non-Marxian historical materialism. For that purpose, we have to apply the conceptual apparatus created in the theory of power to other areas of social life. In this theory, the original vision of the structure of political life was dichotomic, with a division only into rulers and citizens. In the expanded theory of power in non-Marxian historical materialism, that dichotomic image of the political sphere was replaced with a trichotomic one (Nowak 1991c, pp. 57–60). In that approach, there are two political classes: the class of rulers, that is, the class which has at its disposal the means of coercion, and the class of citizens, that is, the rest of the society, people without such influence, and there is a social category of a servant within this class – servants are those citizens who trade their own freedom for the ability to enslave others. Let me present this division in a more systematic manner. Let us assume that there are three people: A, B, and C. Person A has a sphere of influence which encompasses a fragment of the field of activity of person B. It follows that person B is enslaved by A. It is also possible that there could be a situation in which B has a sphere of influence which encompasses person C. Person C, then, is enslaved by B. If person B has obtained his or her sphere of influence from A in return for becoming subjected to enslavement by A, then A, B, and C form a chain of enslavement. The foundation of that chain is the exchange of one's freedom for the possibility of enslaving other people. The division into the class of rulers and the class of citizens does not overlap with the division into the ruling and the ruled. In the discussed approach, the criterion for being a ruler is purely materialistic: a ruler is the person who has at his or her disposal the means of coercion, while a citizen is a person devoid of those resources. The criterion of being a servant is relational: a servant is a person who participates in the structure of enslavement.

That trichotomic image of the political dimension of life can be generalized, and the social role of a servants can be distinguished in the two remaining spheres of social life: economy and culture. Generally speaking, we can say that a servant is a person who obtains the possibility of (political, spiritual, economic) domination over other people at the cost of facilitating (through subjugation) the realization of class interest by the person (a ruler, priest, owner) who has at his or her disposal a particular type of material social means. Let us consider the relationship between the economic and political spheres.

In the economic sphere, that person is a servant who agrees to being exploited by the owner in return for the possibility of (co)exploiting others. Therefore, economic servants will be all people without property rights who will manage the owner's economic property on his behalf.[9] Within the framework of the permissions received from the owner, servants can influence the direct producers' working conditions in an economic unit, for example, shape their profits (lower or raise bonuses), define production standards, or determine the working time. An institutional counterpart of the servant position will be, for instance, a director (or members of the management board) of an economic unit, foremen, or shift managers.[10]

When we take into account the categories of political and economic servants, we can distinguish two basic types of class symbiosis. In the first case, the ruler becomes an economic ruler. At the cost of being subjugated economically to the owner, he obtains the possibility of influencing decisions about the use of the means of production, and uses them to increase his political influence. In the latter scenario, the owner becomes a political servant– at the cost of becoming politically subjugated, he obtains political influence which he can use to further his own economic interest.

The classification of cases of class symbiosis will be enriched when we take into account various types of a class society and various forms of realization of class interest. We can distinguish two forms of realization of class interest: optimization and maximization[11]. The class of rulers maximizes its interest

---

9   At this point, I generalize the concept of an economic servant known from history, for example, a bailiff.

10   For a more detailed discussion of the institutional level of economy in non-Marxian historical materialism, see Niewiadomski 1989.

11   According to Nowak (1996, pp. 276–280 see also Ciesielski 2012, pp.71–97), the principle of rationality states that the individual maximizes her/his preferences, that is, she/he undertakes that activity from a set of activities which – in the light of her/his knowledge – leads

by increasing power regulation and, in that way, decreasing the range of civil autonomy, which leads to growing resistance of the class of citizens. Power regulation is optimized by maintaining such a level of political rule (or such growth of power regulation) as does not lead to civil resistance and guarantees the class of citizens certain level of autonomy.

The class of owners maximizes its interest by increasing owners' income and, in that way, decreasing the income of direct producers, which leads to growing resistance from the class of direct producers. The interest of the class of owners is optimized by maintaining such a level of income (or such growth of income) as does not lead to resistance from direct producers.

There are two types of class society with separate political and economic classes: a political one and an economic one (Brzechczyn 2004, pp. 73–86). In a class society of the political type, the class of rulers is the dominant class while in a class society of the economic type, the owners' class is dominant. The domination of class A over class B means that should there be a conflict of interest between the two classes, then, given a sufficiently long period of time, the interest of class A will be realized.

In a class society of the political type, an owner who is a political servant (i) optimizes only his own economic interest, at the cost of being politically subjugated, while an owner who is an economic servant (ii) can maximize his political rule at the cost of being economically subjugated.

In a class society of the economic type, an owner who is a political servant (iii) can maximize his economic interest at the cost of being politically subjugated, while an owner who is an economic servant (iv) can optimize his political rule.

In the conceptual apparatus of n-Mhm, we can distinguish two types of agrarian bureaucratic societies – political and economic – and four cases of

---

to the result she/he prefers the most. The standard model of rational action is based on numerous idealizing assumptions. For example, it is assumed that an individual is able to perform any activity that leads to the result that she/he prefers in the highest way. However, sometimes an individual is not able to perform activities that would lead to the most preferred state of affairs. Therefore, for each individual some activities are feasible, some are unfeasible, and others are feasible on condition that she/he learns what a certain set of actions consists of. In some cases, the process of learning may be too long, tedious or just impossible for an individual. In this situation the principle of rationality is replaced by the principle of preference optimization. This means that an individual chooses such an activity that leads to the state of affairs more preferred by her/him than any other state of affairs achieved at a given activity's level of difficulty, and the state of affairs of which is at the same time lower in the preferential order than states of affairs achieved by activities which are too difficult for the individual to perform.

class symbiosis with various social ramifications. The class symbiosis case described by Skocpol belongs to type (iii): an owner becomes a political servant and gains the additional possibility of maximizing his own profits, while blocking the realization of the political interest of state authorities. That is possible in an agrarian bureaucratic society of the economic type, such as France.

From the broadened perspective of n-Mhm, we can see what Skocpol does not notice: that the same case of class symbiosis – distinguished by her – can lead to diverse social outcomes in two types of agrarian bureaucratic societies.

In an agrarian bureaucratic system of the economic type, owners (or, to be more precise, a segment of that group), at the cost of becoming subjugated to political rulers – for example, by becoming officers in the state apparatus – can exploit the direct producers in their employment more effectively. They are a special kind of servants because they also have at their disposal the means of production. The owners-political servants' loyalty to the state authorities extends to the degree to which it is a condition for realizing their social interest – maximizing the surplus product. That means following the state authorities' recommendations if it is beneficial to the realization of the class of owners' interest and resisting them if the opposite is the case. The level of political control is determined by the owners' interest, which severely limits the rulers' ability to strengthen their position in the agrarian society. The owners-servants block the mechanism of internal maximization of power regulation, so the need to recompense it by maximizing external power regulation arises. Skocpol believes that this is what happened in France.

In an agrarian bureaucratic society of the political type, where the state authorities are the dominant party, the situation is different. In such a case, the owners' loyalty to the state authorities only guarantees the optimization and not maximization of the interest of that class. In that kind of a social system, the stronger partner, that is, the state authorities, decides about the forms and degree to which the class of owners will exploit the direct producers. In such a society, the rulers have greater possibilities of strengthening their political rule than in the economic variant of an agrarian bureaucratic society – although not as great as they would be if average citizens, devoid of any material social means, were the servants.

Thus, we can see that the "class symbiosis," defined by Skocpol, between the landed class and the class of rulers means that an owner is simultaneously a political servant in the power hierarchy. That is a special case in the whole spectrum of the varieties of class symbiosis which can be distinguished in the appropriately broadened conceptual apparatus of non-Marxian historical materialism (Brzechczyn 2004, pp. 95–100 and pp. 300–303). Within that framework, an agrarian bureaucratic society has its counterpart in a class society of the economic or political type, in which the owners have the additional social role of political rulers. In agrarian bureaucratic societies of the economic type, the owners can trade their political independence for the possibility of increasing their political control over the direct producers employed in their enterprises and, in this way, maximize their profits more efficiently. In agrarian bureaucratic societies of the political type, when the owners submit themselves to the state power, they can only optimize the realization of their class interest because in the end it is the rulers that decide how the owners' interest is to be realized.

Skocpol did not notice the possibility that that type of inter-class relationships can occur in two types of class societies – political and economic ones – because of her Marxian inspirations and institutionalist perspective on power. Skocpol claims that economic classes in agrarian bureaucracy societies are *ex definitione* dominant classes, and the autonomy of the state from economic structures can only be potential. Such a postulate makes it difficult to conceptualize Russian society. Skocpol declares:

> this Russian *dominant class* [emphasis mine – K. B.] appropriated surpluses, both directly from the peasantry and indirectly through renumeration services to for the state. But in sharp contrast to the French and Chinese dominant classes, the Russian landed nobility was economically weak and politically dependent vis-à-vis Imperial authorities.
>
> SKOCPOL 1979, p. 85

At this point, we might wonder what kind of a dominant class would be "economically weak and dependent" on the state? The further (empirical) description of the Russian social structure subverts what Skocpol has (theoretically) declared. It turns out that:
- the status of the Russian nobility, as well as its property, passed on from generation to generation, was dependent on service to the tzar,
- the land of the hereditary nobility was confiscated by the state and given to the so-called service nobles – as a reward for its services to the state,
- in order to weaken the social influence of this social class, the lands given to the service nobility by tsars were not located in the same area,
- the service nobility was obligated to serve the state for many years; that obligation was abolished in the 18th century (Skocpol 1979, 85–90).

As admitted by Skocpol, as a result of the disturbed balance between rulers and owners: "ironically, though, as the serf-owning nobility continued to depend upon the Imperial state, the autocracy became less dependent upon the landed nobility" (Skocpol 1979, p. 87). What can only be "ironically" perceived in the language of one theoretical concept, can be quite "seriously" paraphrased in the language of another social theory.

That possibility – of greater freedom of conceptual maneuvers – is offered by the theoretical perspectives of n-Mhm which makes it possible to explicate another type of agrarian bureaucratic society, in addition to the economic one: the political type. The two types of class societies are represented by the pre-revolutionary societies of France and Russia. To paraphrase Skocpol's conception in the conceptual apparatus of n-Mhm, in both societies – French and Russian – there existed a class symbiosis which led to the owners becoming the political servants. The difference between the two was that Russian society was a class society of the political type,[12] while French society was of the economic type. That difference had an impact on the course of the revolutions in the two states.

Let us now consider how n-Mhm can help explain the lower effectiveness of agrarian bureaucratic economies in comparison to capitalist economies. It seems that in capitalist economies, where political power is separated from ownership and the authorities give up regulation of the economy for the sake of ownership, the social conflict between the owners and the direct producers is solved by way of a compromise which is beneficial to both parties. In a purely economic state, an economic conflict can only be solved if the owners make concessions to the benefit of the direct producers. Such concessions can be in the form of a revision of ownership relations, that is, they involve increasing the direct producers' economic autonomy and, in that way, work efficiency or variable capital (which grows in proportion to technological progress).

In agrarian bureaucratic systems, symbiotic relationships between the state power and the owners have an influence on both politics and the economy. On the one hand, the pure class of rulers does not have direct political control over the citizens, that is, the direct producers (of the agrarian sector of the economy – the peasantry), but only indirect control, through the class of owners

---

12   It ought to be added that a stronger thesis is put forth within the framework of n-Mhm, namely, that in certain periods of its history, Russian society was a totalitarian society of the political type, with the accumulation of power and ownership – Nowak's analyses (1999ib) prove that political power was combined with the disposal of the means of production in the 16th century, leading to the creation of a double class of rulers-owners. The rivalry between landowners (Russian: помещик), who combined property owning with political rule, and boyars, who were a class of single owners, was a crucial component of the whole modern social history of Russia. Because of that totalitarian anomaly, state feudalism transformed into state capitalism, and later into socialism – in which political rulers took control over the means of production and propaganda – without the free-market stage.

who fulfill the social role of peasants' servants. In this social system, the degree of the owners-servants' loyalty to the state power depends on their maximization of the surplus product. Those orders of the state power which are in line with the interest of the class of owners-rulers are realized, while those which are incompatible with it are not. For that reason, the maximization of political control by the state power – in Skocpol's terms, social mobilization – is limited.

On the other hand, the fact that the owners can make use of state coercion has an impact on the functioning of the economy (Nowak 1991b, pp. 63–65). The owners-political rulers backed by the political structure can solve a conflict with the direct producers not by way of social compromise but with the use of force. If they can permanently enslave the direct producers, it is even better, because this prevents a possible new outbreak of opposition. In that way, the political rulers become engaged in the economic conflict as every protest against exploitation turns into a protest against the social order. Because of the possibility of the declassation of the direct producers, the owners derive profits mainly by decreasing variable capital and not, for example, stimulating technological progress. Consequently, the economy becomes less efficient, which leads to technological stagnation.

Since the economy produces not only the means of production and consumption but also the means of coercion, its condition has an impact on the ability of the state power to increase external power regulation. If the army is technologically backward, the rulers find it more and more difficult to expand the external spheres of power regulation and to maintain control over already subjugated countries.

3.4 A Paraphrase of the Mechanism of Social Revolution

In Skocpol's approach, the modernizing pressure which catalyzes a social revolution does not exert that influence in all non-capitalist states but only in imperial states. Therefore, it would not be justified to apply the analysis to revolutions in colonial states, such as Vietnam, Mexico, or Algeria (Skocpol 1979, pp. 287–290). Since Skocpol does not characterize that category of states or other entities of the international system in greater detail, I will attempt to do this, within the framework of the theory I have adopted.[13] The following types of states can be distinguished:

(i) an imperial state which has internal spheres of power regulation in the form of provinces created as a result of having conquered other societies and removed the native class of rulers from there, as well as of

---

13   I base my distinctions on Models IV and V of a political society: Nowak 1991d, pp. 129–148, see also Norkus 2018, pp. 69–196.

having conquered satellite states and subjugated them, while preserving their original authorities;

(ii) a sovereign state which does not have an external sphere of power regulation and does not constitute other societies' sphere of influence;

(iii) a satellite state which preserves its original class of rulers but depends on another society; it can be influenced by more than one state and can have its own spheres of influence (or provinces);

(iv) a provincial state – that is, a society which has been conquered by an empire – in which the original class of rulers has been replaced by the imperial one.

The paraphrase of an empire state made in the conceptual framework of n-Mhm and the categories of states distinguished with the use of that theory are partially in agreement with and partially contrary to Skocpol's thesis. In the light of n-Mhm, modernizing pressure does have an impact on all states but to varying degrees. It has the greatest influence – Skocpol is right about this – on imperial states because the imperial class of rulers has the greatest external spheres of power and is the most susceptible to economic backwardness, which prevents it from competing with other states. Modernizing pressure has a smaller influence on the remaining categories of states: sovereign, satellite, and provincial ones. A backward economy makes it difficult for a sovereign state to retain its autonomy in decision making, for a satellite state – to decrease the degree of its dependence on other entities on the international arena, and for a conquered state – to win independence.

The difficulties in achieving extraordinary growth in their spheres of power regulation make the state authorities decide to modernize the economy, that is, eliminate the relations between state power and ownership. The withdrawal of the state authorities from regulation of the economy brings about a social crisis in the relationship between the rulers and the owners and opens the way for peasant revolts. Thanks to the participation of political elites from the intelligentsia, spontaneous peasant revolts created their own institutional structures and utopian consciousness and transformed into full revolutions.[14] According to Skocpol's paraphrased theory, only such revolutions can be victorious.

---

14 In Tomczak's (1989) view, social movements have three components: material, institutional, and awareness-related. Simple revolutions only disturb the material relations of class subordination. If revolutionary actions are channeled into institutions which are independent from the ruling class, then a social movement will have an institutional component. If a revolutionary movement gains its own social self-awareness, it will have an ideological component. Complete revolutions, unlike simple ones, contain the three levels of social life: material, institutional, and level of social consciousness.

In the paraphrase within the framework of n-Mhm, though, it turns out that, contrary to Skocpol's thesis, not every victorious revolution leads to successful modernization. A victorious revolution results in successful modernization in class societies of the economic type. At this moment, I would like to recall that in the light of n-Mhm, the result of successful modernization is the separation of power and ownership (1), a high level of autonomy of the working class (2), and constant technological progress. In societies in which the state authorities are a dominant class, a victorious revolution does not lead to a severance of the relationship between state power and ownership but to the accumulation of the means of coercion and production in the hands of one social class. One example of this phenomenon can be the different outcomes of the revolutions in France and in Russia. Skocpol explains these differences by referring to the factors which she considers to be secondary: different stratification of the Russian versus the French peasantry, different courses of political crises in the two countries, and the international positions of France and Russia. However, the paraphrase within the framework of n-Mhm leads to a different answer, namely, that the different outcomes of the revolutions can be ascribed to the types of those class societies. In the light of that paraphrase, France was an agrarian bureaucratic society of the economic type, and Russia – of the political type. That is why in France the state authorities originating from the revolution did not disturb the ownership structures of the state as it maximized the external spheres of power regulation during the Napoleonic era. Because of that, class symbiosis – so characteristic of the pre-revolutionary era – disappeared there, and a high level of citizens' autonomy was maintained. In Russia, the revolution did not disturb the domination of the state authorities over the owners, so the political loop created by the Bolshevik revolution was a triple social loop: the authorities also seized the means of production and indoctrination. In the longer term, the subordination of the economy to the political authorities explains the failure of the modernization of that state during the Stalinist era and the later economic stagnation during the Brezhnev period. There is an additional argument for the presented thesis: Gorbachov's *perestroika* in the second half of the 1980s, would not have been necessary, had Russia successfully modernized. Gorbachev's reforms can be interpreted as another manifestation of the top-down modernization processes taking place as a result of the lost arms race in the 1980s, which ended in the disintegration of the empire (Brzechczyn 2003; 2006; 2007a; 2010a) and the fall of the system of triple rule.

4 Summary

With the use of the appropriately broadened conceptual apparatus of non-Marxian historical materialism, the following paraphrases were made:
- of modernization processes,
- of agrarian bureaucratic societies,
- of imperial states and the remaining entities in the international system, and
- of outcomes of victorious revolutions.

The modernization process resulted (see paragraph 2.1) from the growth of the social autonomy of the lower classes: the direct producers, citizens, and the faithful, which is strengthened by a separation and balance between the higher classes: rulers, owners and priests (secular and religious).

Pre-capitalist societies are social systems in which symbiotic relationships between the state authorities and the owners are dominant. However, in the light of the paraphrase made above, we can distinguish not one but two types of agrarian bureaucratic societies: the economic type, in which the class of owners dominates the society, and the political type, in which the class of rulers is dominant.

The inter-state system consists of capitalist (class) societies and traditionalist states (with symbiotic relationships among classes) of the economic and political type. Contrary to Skocpol's statements, the pressure of modernization, exerted by the capitalist societies, is felt – to varying degrees – in all states. Pre-capitalist imperial states which need a modern economy as they compete with other states for influence are the most susceptible to that pressure. With an inefficient economy, it is not easy for the state authorities to increase (or maintain) their external sphere of power regulation, so they have to introduce reforms which weaken the bond between politics and the economy. When the state authorities cease to control economic life, the class of direct producers in the agrarian sector of economy resists and, in alliance with the marginal political elites, overthrows the existing social order.

However, a victorious revolution does not always initiate a successful modernization, which is another limitation of Skocpol's theory, which is evident in that paraphrase. The outcome of such a revolution depends on the type of the agrarian bureaucratic society. In France, an agrarian bureaucracy of the economic type, post-revolutionary changes caused class symbiosis to disappear, and the state embarked on the path toward capitalism. In Russia, an agrarian bureaucracy of the political type, the post-revolutionary transformation weakened the symbiotic relationships between the state authorities and ownership, but it led to an accumulation of control over the means of coercion, production, and indoctrination. Consequently, the politically forced industrialization in the 1930s was not accompanied by the growth of civil autonomy. Contrary, the Soviet society was more enslaved than pre-revolutionay Russian one.

The paraphrase, then, provides some good results, which confirm certain of Skocpol's claims paraphrased in the conceptual apparatus of n-Mhm, and produces some negative outcomes, which are contrary to several theses of the paraphrased concept. Obviously, the results of the paraphrase can only be accepted if the conceptual framework used for paraphrasing is accepted. For that reason, they will not be binding for a person who does not see n-Mhm as useful for the purpose of this paraphrase.

In the paraphrase, Skocpol's theses, made in historical-empirical language, are reformulated in the conceptual apparatus of n-Mhm. That allows a reconsideration of the methodological issue of the range of Skocpol's theory – the question whether it is limited, as originally intended by the author, to the three cases she distinguishes: China, Russia, and France, or whether it can be used for explaining revolutions in other societies – and, if the answer is yes, on what conditions. Skocpol's position on that matter is not clear because she initially restricted the range of the application of her conception to three states: France, Russia, and China, and later she attempted to use a modified version of her theory to explain revolutions in Iran[15] and in third world countries (Skocpol 1982b). Skocpol's theory was also modified by Walter Goldfrank, who tried to explain the outbreak of the Mexican revolution.[16] Having paraphrased Skocpol's theory in the language of n-Mhm, we can say that her theory finds its fullest application in those class societies with class symbiosis which have the position of an empire. It can only be applied partially, with varying degrees of approximation, to other societies of that type, which have the status of an independent, satellite or conquered state on the international arena.

---

15   Skocpol (1982a) broadened the range of the explanatory factors by adding cultural and ideological ones (compare with, for example, Nichols 1986, p. 183), and she replaced external modernizing pressure with conducive international conditions. In her approach, Iran does not fit in with the definition of an agrarian bureaucratic society, either – she sees it as a rentier state which earns most of its income by selling oil. See Eqbal Ahmad's (1982), Walter L. Goldfrank's (1982), and Nikki R. Keddie's (1982) comments and the presentation of the discussions about Jarosław Chodak's Iran (2012, pp. 153–154). For a discussion of the methodological status of Skocpol's theory and its relationships with other concepts created within the framework of comparative historical sociology, see Brzechczyn 2007b.

16   Goldfrank (1979, p. 148) replaced the factor of external modernizing pressure from Skocpol's model with the factor of tolerant or permissive world context. That is not merely a stylistic procedure, because in my reconstruction, Skocpol's external modernizing pressure is a factor which indirectly influences a social revolution, while Goldfrank's tolerant or permissive world context is a factor with direct impact on the course of a revolution.

References

Ahmad, E. (1982). Comments on Skocpol. *Theory and Society* 11, 293–300.

Borbone, G. (2016). Questioni di Metodo. Leszek Nowak e la scienza come idealizzazione. Roma: Acireale.

Borbone, G. (2021). *The Relevance of Models. Idealization and Concretization in Leszek Nowak.* Műnchen: Grin Verlag.

Brzechczyn, K. (2003). Upadek imperium socjalistycznego. Próba modelu [The Fall of the Socialist Empire. An Attempt at a Model]. In: K. Brzechczyn (ed.) *Ścieżki transformacji. Ujęcia teoretyczne i opisy empiryczne,* pp. 135–169. Poznań: Zysk i S-ka.

Brzechczyn, K. (2004). *O wielości linii rozwojowych w procesie historycznym. Próba interpretacji ewolucji społeczeństwa meksykańskiego* [On the Multitude of the Lines of Developments in the Historical Process. An Attempt at Interpretation of the Evolution of the Mexican Society]. Poznań: Wydawnictwo Naukowe UAM.

Brzechczyn, K. (2006). Próba konceptualizacji rozwoju politycznego w republikach postradzieckich [The Dynamics of Democratization. An Attempt at a Conceptualization of Political Development in Post-Soviet Republics]. In: K. Brzechczyn, J. Silski (eds.), *Demokracja. Między teorią a empirią, ideałem a praktyką,* pp. 86–121. Poznań: Wyższa Szkoła Nauk Humanistycznych i Dziennikarstwa.

Brzechczyn, K. (2007a). Paths to Democracy of the Post-Soviet Republics: Attempt at Conceptualization. In: E. Czerwińska-Schupp (ed.) *Values and Norms in the Age of Globalization,* pp. 529–571. Berlin: Peter Lang.

Brzechczyn, K. (2007b). Rozwój teorii rewolucji w socjologii historyczno-porównawczej. Próba analizy metodologicznej [The Development of the Theory of Revolution in Historical-Comparative Sociology. An Attempt at a Methodological Analysis]. In: K. Brzechczyn, M. Nowak (eds.) *O rewolucji. Obrazy radykalnej zmiany społecznej.* pp. 37–64. Poznań: Wydawnictwo Naukowe IF UAM.

Brzechczyn, K. (2009). Polityka jako proces rewolucyjnej zmiany społecznej. Od Marksa do współczesnych teorii rewolucji w socjologii historyczno-porównawczej [Politcs as a Process of a Revolutionary Social Change. From Marx to Contemporary Theories of Revolution in Sociology]. In: W. Wesołowski (ed.) *Koncepcje polityki,* pp. 273–317. Warsaw: Scholar.

Brzechczyn, K. (2010a). O ścieżkach upadku imperium sowieckiego. Próba uzupełnienia nie-Marksowskiego materializmu historycznego [On the Paths of the Fall of the Soviet Empire. An Attempt at Complementing of non-Marxian Historical Materialism]. In: A. Nowak (ed.) *Ofiary imperium. Imperia jako ofiary. 44 spojrzenia,* pp. 571–582. Warsaw: IPN – IH PAN.

Brzechczyn, K. (2010b). Przegrana wojna czy przegrana rewolucja? Próba parafrazy kontrowersji wokół mechanizmów demokratyzacji społeczeństw zachodnich w socjologii historyczno-porównawczej [A Lost War or a Lost Revolution?

An Attempt at a Paraphrase of the Controversy Concerning the Mechanisms of the Democratization of Western Societies in Historical-Comparative Sociology]. *Politeja. Pismo Wydziału Studiów Międzynarodowych i Politycznych Uniwersytetu Jagiellońskiego* 14 (2), 389–406.

Burawoy, M. (1989). Two Methods in Search of Science. Skocpol versus Trotsky. *Theory and Society* 18, 759–805.

Chodak, J. (2012). *Teorie rewolucji w naukach społecznych* [Theories of Revolution in Social Science]. Lublin: UMCS.

Ciesielski, M. (2012). *Zagadnienie ograniczeń racjonalnego modelu działań ludzkich. Próba ujęcia działania nawykowo-racjonalnego.* Poznań: Wydawnictwo Poznańskie.

Ciesielski, M. (2013). Problem kumulacji podziałów klasowych we współczesnym kapitalizmie. Próba analizy teoretycznej [The Problem of the Accumulation of Social Divisions in Contemporary Capitalism: An Attempt at Theoretical Analysis]. In: K. Brzechczyn, M. Ciesielski, E. Karczyńska (eds.). *Jednostka w układzie społecznym. Próba teoretycznej konceptualizacji,* pp. 223–252. Poznań: WN WNS UAM.

Ciesielski, M. (2022). The Problem of the Accumulation of Class Divisions in Contemporary Capitalism: An Attempt at a Theoretical Analysis. In: K. Brzechczyn (ed.) *New Developments in Theory of Historical Process. Polish Contributions to Non-Marxian Historical Materialism. Poznań Studies in the Philosophy of the Sciences and the Humanities,* vol. 119, pp. 217–238. Boston/Leiden: Brill.

Coniglione, F. (2010). *Realtà e astrazione. Scuola polacca ed epistemologia post-positivista.* Roma: Bonanno Editore.

Egiert, R. (2000). *Parafrazy idealizacyjne. Analiza metodologiczna szkoły w Groningen* [Idealizational Paraphrases. A Methodological Analysis of the School in Groningen]. Poznań: Wydawnictwo Fundacji Humaniora.

Goldfrank, W. L. (1979). Theories of Revolution and Revolution without Theory. The Case of Mexico. *Theory and Society* 7, 135–165.

Goldfrank, W. L. (1982). Commentary on Skocpol. *Theory and Society* 11, 301–304.

Keddie, N. K. (1982). Comments on Skocpol. *Theory and Society* 11, 285–292.

Łastowski, K., L. Nowak (1979). Zabieg krytycznej parafrazy. Przedmowa [The Procedure of Critical Paraphrase. Foreword]. In: K. Łastowski, L. Nowak (eds.) *Konfrontacje i parafrazy,* pp. 1–4. Poznań: PWN.

Nichols, E. (1986). Skocpol on Revolution: Comparative Analysis versus Historical Conjuncture. *Comparative Social Research* 9, 163–186.

Niewiadomski, M. (1989). Toward a Model of Economic Institutions. In: L. Nowak (ed.) *Dimensions of the Historical Process. Poznań Studies in the Philosophy of the Sciences and the Humanities* vol. 13, pp. 271–281. Amsterdam: Rodopi.

Norkus, Z. (2018). *An Unproclaimed Empire: The Grand Duchy of Lithuania From the Viewpoint of Comparative Historical Sociology of Empires.* London: Routlegde.

Nowak, L. (1979). *U podstaw teorii procesu historycznego* [On the Foundations of the Theory of the Historical Process]. Poznań: samizdat.

Nowak, L. (1981). *Wolność i władza. Przyczynek do nie-Marksowskiego materializmu historycznego* [Freedom and Power. A Contribution to Non-Marxist Historical Materialism]. Poznań: NZS AR.

Nowak, L. (1983). *Property and Power: Towards a non-Marxian Historical Materialism.* Dordrecht: Reidel.

Nowak, L. (1989). An Idealizational Model of Capitalist Society. In: L. Nowak (ed.). *Dimensions of the Historical Process. Poznań Studies in the Philosophy of the Sciences and the Humanities,* vol. 13, pp. 217–259. Amsterdam: Rodopi.

Nowak, L. (1991abc). *U podstaw teorii socjalizmu* [The Foundations of the Theory of Socialism]; vol. 1: *Własność i władza. O konieczności socjalizmu* [Property and Power. On the Necessity of Socialism]; vol. 2: *Droga do socjalizmu. O konieczności socjalizmu w Rosji* [The Road to Socialism. On the Necessity of Socialism in Russia]; vol. 3: *Dynamika władzy. O strukturze i konieczności zaniku socjalizmu* [The Dynamics of Power. On the Structure and Necessity of the Disappearance of Socialism]. Poznań: Nakom.

Nowak, L. (1991d). *Power and Civil Society. Toward a Dynamic Theory of Real Socialism.* New York: Greenwood Press.

Nowak, L. (1996). On the Limits of the Rationalistic Paradigm. In: A. Zeidler-Janiszewska (ed.) *Epistemology and History. Poznań Studies in the Philosophy of the Sciences and the Humanities,* vol. 47, pp. 267–282. Amsterdam-Atlanta: Rodopi.

Nowak, L. (1998). *Byt i myśl. U podstaw negatywistycznej metafizyki unitarnej* [Being and Thought. The Foundations of Negativist Unitarian Metaphysics]; vol. 1: *Nicość i istnienie* [Nothingness and Existence]. *Poznań: Zysk i S-ka.*

Nowak, L. (2000). *Gombrowicz. Człowiek wobec ludzi* [Gombrowicz. A Man and People]. Warsaw: Prószyński i S-ka.

Nowakowa, I. (1991). *Zmienność i stałość w nauce. Przyczynek do metodologii między-teoretycznych związków diachronicznych* [Variability and Stability in Science. A Contribution to the Methodology of Intertheoretical Diachronic Relationships]. Poznań: Nakom.

Nowakowa, I. (1992). Uwagi o problemie indukcji. Próba parafrazy idealizacyjnej [Notes on the Problem of Induction. An Attempt at an Idealizational Paraphrase]. In: E. Pakszys, J. Such, and J. Wiśniewski (eds.) *Nauka w świetle współczesnej filozofii,* pp. 168–178. Warsaw: PWN.

Rostow, W.W. (1964). *The Stages of Economic Growth. A Non-Communist Manifesto.* Cambridge: Cambridge University Press.

Skocpol, Th. (1976). France, Russia China: A Structural Analysis of Social Revolutions. *Comparative Studies in Society and History,* 2, 175–210.

Skocpol, Th. (1979). *States and Social Revolution*. Cambridge: Cambridge University Press.

Skocpol, Th. (1982a). Rentier State and Shi'a Islam in the Iranian Revolution. *Theory and Society* 11, 265–283.

Skocpol, Th. (1982b). What Makes Peasant Revolutionary? In: S. E. Guggenheim, R. P. Weller (eds.) *Power and Protest in the Countryside*, pp. 157–179. Durham, DC: Duke University Press.

Taylor, M. (1988). Rationality and Revolutionary Collective Action. In: M. Taylor (ed.). *Rationality and Revolution. Studies in Marxism and Social Theory*, pp. 63–98. Cambridge: Cambridge University Press.

Tomczak, G. (1989). Struktura ruchów masowych. Przyczynek do problematyki rewolucji [The Structure of Mass Movements. A Contribution to the Problems of Revolution]. In: J. Brzeziński, K. Łastowski (eds.). *Filozoficzne i metodologiczne podstawy teorii naukowych*, pp. 253–263. Poznań: PWN.

Torpey, J. (1998). Revolutions and Freedom of Movement: An Analysis of Passport Controls in the French, Russians, and Chinese Revolutions. *Theory and Society* 4, 837–867.

Wallerstein, I. (1974). Immanuel The Modern World-System. New York: Academic Press.

Wallerstein, I. (1976). From Feudalism to Capitalism: Transition or Transitions? Social Forces, 55 (2), 273–283.

CHAPTER 9

The Elitarian versus Class Theory of Democracy: An Attempt to Paraphrase the Mechanism of the Absorption of the Elites from Eva Etzioni-Halevy's Theory in the Conceptual Apparatus of Non-Marxian Historical Materialism

Karolina Rutkowska

Abstract

In this paper, the author presents the Eva Etzioni-Halevy's democratic elite theory and compare it with Leszek Nowak's theory of power in non-Marxian historical materialism. In Nowak's theory of power main mechanism of social development is political evolution through lost revolutions, in Halevy's theory – through the mechanism of elite absorption. According to Eva Etzioni-Halevy, absorption of elites through cooptation of oppositional movement's leaders into existing power structures leads primarily to the stabilization of democracy and consequently to desired political changes. In theory of power in non-Marxian historical materialism it is assumed that civil revolutions are always followed by repressive actions against the citizens. In order to incorporate Halevy's mechanism of absorption of elites in the theoretical framework of non-Marxian historical materialism, the author enriches the conceptual apparatus of Nowak's theory of power.

Keywords:

Absorption of elites – elite theory – Eva Etzioni-Halevy – Leszek Nowak – non-Marxian historical materialism – progressive absorption – regressive absorption

1 Foreword

The founders of the theory of elites, such as Vilfredo Pareto or Gaetano Mosca, are rightly considered to be critics of democracy. Therefore, the theory of elites itself and the authors who make references to it are believed to be more or less

© KAROLINA RUTKOWSKA, 2022 | DOI:10.1163/9789004507296_010

camouflaged critics of the democratic system. As the example of Eva Etzioni-Halevy shows, that does not have to be the case. In her theory, the very existence of political and social elites constitutes a foundation of the functioning of a democratic system. According to Marek Żyromski, Etzioni-Halevy's theory "constitutes one of the more interesting (and elaborate) theoretical proposals which indicate the possibility of reconciling the existence of elites (especially a political elite) with the functioning of a system of representative democracy in the contemporary world" (Żyromski 2007, p. 45). That is why it is worth presenting here the main concepts of Etzioni-Halevy's theory, in comparison with the theory of political society in non-Marxian historical materialism, and paraphrasing the key elitist mechanism of the development of the concept of democracy, that is, the mechanism of absorption of elites, in appropriately expanded conceptual apparatus of non-Marxian historical materialism.

2 The Elite Theory of Democracy. An Attempt at a Presentation

2.1 *The Main Assumptions of the Theory of Democratic Elites*
Etzioni-Halevy's theory of democratic elites is based on a few elementary concepts: power, resources, elites, sub-elites, their relative autonomy, and democracy, and on key statements based on those concepts. Etzioni-Halevy defines power as "the ability to constraint or shape other people's action, volitions, values, beliefs, and life chances through control over (or having at one's disposal) resources on which these others are dependent, of which they have a need, or which may otherwise affect their life" (Etzioni-Halevy 1989, p. 25). She defines those resources as "deficit goods which have an influence on peoples lives, which are needed by many people, and for which there is greater demand than supply" (Etzioni-Halevy 1989, 25). The author distinguishes the following types of resources (Etzioni-Halevy 1993, pp. 98–99):
– pertaining to physical coercion,
– administrative and organizational,
– symbolic,
– material end economic,
– psychological and personality-related.
Having at one's disposal resources of a particular type constitutes elites which are "groups of people who hold power and influence, that is, as people who have disproportionate control on resources (on which others are dependent, or by which they are affected) in a given sociopolitical system" (Etzioni-Halevy 1989, p. 25). On the basis of that definition, Etzioni-Halevy divides society into three parts: elites, sub-elites, and the people.

Elites occupy the highest level of the social structure. They include: members of the government, members of parliamentary committees, leaders of the main opposition parties, bureaucratic elites, members of the army, the police, the judiciary, business elites, leaders of trade unions, the media, and intellectual elites. They are not only the most privileged but also the most active group of people. They fight for victims and strive for greater justice and equality.

Sub-elites, consisting of lower-rank elite members, have at their disposal some resources and, by virtue of that, they enjoy some autonomy and power. As they occupy the second position (right after the elites) in the social and political hierarchy, they often represent elites before the people, as a mediator.

The last element of social structure, the people, is perceived not as a passive category ruled by elites but as a group with a great potential. By supporting their representatives and actively participating in demonstrations or strikes, this group can influence the social and political situation and, consequently, the development of the system.

Since economic and material resources are not seen as superior to other types of resources in the elitist theory of democracy, many elites can be distinguished that control various kinds of resources in contemporary societies, and none of those elites is singled out as in any way special. Still, having observed the democratic practice in Western states, Etzioni-Halevy does give priority to those political elites that are chosen by way of democratic elections. Together with the state bureaucracy, the military, and the judiciary, they are generally acknowledged as the ruling elite. Social elites also include the leaders of big political parties, the parliamentary opposition, the economic elite, trade union elites, and the media elite – they are called non-ruling elites. Ruling elites differ from non-ruling ones with respect to the scope of power, which is greater, but can be reduced to the benefit of the latter group by incorporating its members in the structure of the state authorities.

Another term which needs to be defined is democracy. Etzioni-Halevy defines democracy as a "sociopolitical system in which two people or more persons, groups, or organizations (such as parties) participate in the contest for government power in a state (or for elite position)" (Etzioni-Halevy 1989, p. 27). The rivals compete in regular free elections attended by all citizens with the right to vote. Parties refer to the past, their political programs, and their external image. The competition takes place in a political system which ensures basic freedoms, such as freedom from persecution, freedom of information, freedom of speech, freedom of association, freedom of organization, and freedom to participate in political life, and which respects the specific division of power in the state. The principle of equal value of all votes in an election is important for reflecting the will of the majority of the electorate. The existence of other elites, relatively independent from the ruling elite, is guaranteed by freedom of organization and by the separation of power. According to Etzioni-Halevy, the presence of elites that provide a partial counterbalance to the state elite and that limit its power is the essence of democracy. Free elections are the basic mechanism of selecting elites and an important component of their relative autonomy which limits the power of the state elite.

Elites are a constant element of a democracy, and, according to the theory of democratic elites, their presence in the system is inevitable because resources are disproportionately distributed in all societies. Some people collect more resources than others, so there is a great probability that the individuals who have resources at their disposal will institutionalize their advantageous position, taking control over the actions and views of people who are dependent on their resources. Those individuals acquire the elite status through institutionalization or by incorporating resources in an organizational structure. Another function of free elections and freedom of organization (which are the essence of democracy) is to select elites or to deprive them of power (when voters do not support them). What is more, political mechanisms (for example, referendums) aimed at intensifying mass participation in democracy require an elite to initiate and organize them, and to implement the outcomes. Even direct participation in the form of a demonstration or protest movements (including movements the goal of which is to overthrow the existing elites) creates new elites, that is, groups of people who have at their disposal appropriate resources, such as: time, motivation, leadership skills, or charisma. In contemporary societies, state elites have the most resources at their disposal. They control both the means of physical coercion and the economic sphere (through monetary, fiscal, and legislative policies). They also have 'pure power' resources based on the means of coercion or, more often, control over the regulation and coordination structures, such as: legislation, administration, and adjudication. Admittedly, economic elites have at their disposal most of the material resources which are not controlled by the state; however, state elites own the means of coercion, power coordination structures, and the possibilities of shaping fiscal and monetary policies, which gives them advantage over the first group. Still, that does not mean that state elites have total control over economic elites and all remaining, non-ruling elites.

Although non-ruling elites are partially dependent on state elites, the foundations for resource control are very different for those two groups. The main non-ruling elites derive power from different sources than ruling ones, and the difference is even greater in the case of the remaining non-ruling elites, which gives them a great deal of independence. That relative autonomy allows those elites that have not been chosen by way of a free election to partially restrict the power of the elected elites, and it makes it possible for non-ruling elites to counterbalance state elites.

2.2   *The Relative Autonomy of Elites and Sub-Elites*

In order to determine the relative autonomy of elites precisely, it is necessary to differentiate between this term and 'elite pluralism' (the two terms are often used synonymously, see Etzioni-Halevy 1989; 1993). Elite pluralism is determined by the number of social elites, while relative elite autonomy is based on the autonomy of the resources which constitute the basis of their power and position (Etzioni-Halevy 1993, p. 98). In other words, the autonomy of elites depends on whether they can dispose of resources of a given type in a free, undisturbed manner.

The first type of resources are the means of physical coercion. An elite or a sub-elite will be considered to be autonomous if its members are not subject to repression by other elites. In the case of material resources, an elite or a sub-elite is perceived to be autonomous if it does not depend on resources belonging to other elites and if it has resources which are not controlled by other elites. As regards administrative and organizational resources, we can speak of autonomous elites and sub-elites when they are not under the administrative and organizational supervision of other elites, when their resources cannot be determined by external powers, when their members are not controlled and obligated to follow instructions from other elites, and when their members constitute a separate unit within a larger organization. With respect to symbolic resources, elites and sub-elites are perceived to be autonomous when they are not dependent on external symbolic resources, when their symbols are not controlled, and when foreign symbols are not forced on them. Furthermore, the autonomy of elites and sub-elites can be based on various combinations of resources. When we analyze any socio-political system, we can unequivocally conclude that the absolute autonomy of the elites and sub-elites cannot exist because the division of resources between the elites and sub-elites is never proportional. Some resources of an elite are always controlled by external forces, so their autonomy can only be viewed as relative, in accordance with the theory of democratic elites.

Relative elite autonomy means partial independence from other elites, especially those which, thanks to their resources, could take control of the resources of another elite. The elite with the greatest 'imperialist' desires is the state elite which has both the means of coercion and the administrative, organizational, and material resources. The relative autonomy of elites and sub-elites with respect to the state elite is a key element of democracy – a prerequisite for preserving democratic principles. It is also a necessary condition for the development of the system, as exemplified by contemporary Western societies. Although democratic principles do not directly refer to elite autonomy, the two phenomena are closely related. According to Etzioni-Halevy: "without freedom of elections and of organization there can be no institutionalized independent opposition" (Etzioni-Halevy 1993, p. 103). Moreover, freedom of speech and association allows the existence of relatively autonomous media elites. As regards the doctrine of the separation of powers, it is a guarantee of the independence of legislative, executive, and judicial elites. The above-mentioned freedom of association also facilitates collecting resources, for example, economic ones (leading to the appearance of relatively independent economic elites), and it enables trade union and social movement activity. The dependence between democratic principles and elite and sub-elite autonomy is not one-sided. Elites and sub-elites strive to preserve democratic principles which are a foundation of their relative independence. The relative autonomy of the elites does not only protect democratic principles but also allows their implementation. Independent elites (for example, media elites) play an important role in elections by providing society with information which is not controlled by the state. That, in turn, allows public discourse on the basis of which people make independent choices and vote either for the existing ruling elite or the opposition. Bureaucratic elites fight election-related corruption, and police elites protect the opposition against persecution during elections. Autonomous academic-intellectual elites take part in public social and political discourse. By popularizing scientific texts, views, and ideas about contemporary reality, they initiate reflections on threats to democracy and on its development. In addition, through their incessant verification of the actions of the ruling elite, the relatively autonomous opposition, media, and courts, allow people to form opinions and make conscious decisions about the socio-political sphere.

2.3   *Relative Elite Autonomy and Stabilization of Democracy*

According to Etzioni-Halevy, the most important factor responsible for democracy development and stabilization of democracy is relative elite and sub-elite autonomy. Principles of democracy guarantee the existence of elite and sub-elite autonomy. They are the basis of the social influence of elites, so it is in the interest of the elites to preserve them. Let us assume –Etzioni-Halevy proposes – that democracy has been overthrown, and a despotic ruler takes control of the country and decides to use the means of coercion against the autonomous elites. In the first phase of the introduction of the dictatorship, the elites and sub-elites would protect their autonomy and, at the same time, fight to restore the violated principles of democracy. Thus, a democracy without elites and sub-elites which would protect both their autonomy and democratic principles would be much more vulnerable in the face of attacks of non-democratic forces and the threat of destabilization.

Elite autonomy is also a condition for introducing a democratic form of government because it can develop in a non-democratic regime even before democratic principles (free elections, universal suffrage, civil rights) are introduced in the political system. As they strive for greater power, relatively autonomous elites and sub-elites pave the way for the development of democracy, and they later contribute to its stabilization.

2.4 A Historical Outline of the Development of Democracy in Western and Eastern Europe

Eva Etzioni-Halevy tests her thesis on the relationship between relative elite autonomy and the development and stabilization of democracy. In states with a stable democratic form of government, previously developed, relatively autonomous elites and sub-elites should exist. In states where the development of democracy was disturbed, the relative autonomy of elites should be restricted. These assertions are confirmed by examining the history of the democratization of the United Kingdom, Germany, USSR, and Poland in the 19th and 20th centuries.

Etzioni-Halevy's comparison of the United Kingdom and Germany proves that relative elite autonomy is a necessary condition for stabilizing democracy. In the United Kingdom – a state where democracy is stable – the four analyzed elites and sub-elites: of business, the trade unions, the media, and the universities, were largely successful in their fight for independence from the state authorities, which contributed to the stabilization of democracy there. In Germany, where democracy fell, none of those elites or sub-elites obtained relative autonomy. They were subdued and controlled by the German government and deprived of resources independent from the ruling elite, and they became largely subjugated to it and obedient. The differences between the autonomy levels of the British and German elites resulted mainly from the different positions of the state authorities in those societies. In the United Kingdom, the authorities were dominant until the end of the 16th century. Then, the power of the state was gradually restricted in accordance with the assumptions of liberal philosophy which assigned greater priority to civil liberties and personal freedoms than to the ruling elite which was losing its position. In Germany, the role of the state authorities was perceived in a different way. The state, legitimized by Hegel's philosophy, dominated social life. It is worth noting that while state power was being gradually restricted in the United Kingdom, democracy was becoming more stable there with the growth of personal freedoms and civil liberties, along with the autonomy of the elites and sub-elites which protected those freedoms. In Germany, the dominance of the state authorities prevented the stabilization of democracy: it forced authoritarian rule on the German society and deprived the elites and sub-elites of relative autonomy, so they could not protect democratic freedoms. The relative autonomy of elites and sub-elites is not only an important element of democracy but also a factor which protects other components of this form of government and contributes to its development and stabilization.

Etzioni-Halevy came to similar conclusions after she had made a historical comparison of Poland and the USSR. Her analysis of the autonomy of religious, union, and university-intellectual elites in both states proved once more that elite independence is a crucial factor in the development of democracy. In the USSR, where the ruling party had a monopoly on power, and elites and sub-elites were weak, the road to democracy was much longer than in Poland where the ruling elite was relatively weak, and the autonomy of elites and sub-elites was correspondingly greater.

2.5 The Mechanism of the Development of Democracy in Western European States

Stable Western democracies have "dynamic and progressive potential" (Etzioni-Halevy 1993, p. 199). Its sources can be traced to the "democratic meta-principle of the autonomy of elites" Etzioni-Halevy 1993, p. 199). According to the author, the "a major linchpin which connects this principle to change consists of social protest movements and their elites and sub-elites" (Etzioni-Halevy 1993, p. 199). Elite autonomy not only makes it difficult to subdue social protests but also makes the government use alternative political strategies for dealing with them. The aim of those strategies is to stabilize the system by absorbing the protest and gradually changing the system.

The author distinguishes between, on the one hand, social movements – which appear during the development of Western democracies – and, on the other hand, interest or pressure groups. Like pressure groups, social movements strive for a redistribution of resources, but they do that not only for their own good but also for the good of the general public. Unlike interest groups, social movements cross the legal boundaries of the social system. Moreover, social movements become engaged in less institutionalized or non-institutionalized forms of action, such as demonstrations, rebellions, or strikes. Just like pressure groups, social movements differ with respect to their size and the degree of their influence. Most of the time, that influence is not big enough to overthrow the system, but sometimes the position of the leaders of the main social movements is very strong. For instance, leaders of the most active trade unions are closely connected with both their society and the state elite, and they become a kind of a mediation channel which may, at a certain point, pose a threat to the existing ruling elite. What is more, thanks to their active interaction with the people, they incite grassroots political participation and, consequently, participatory democracy.

Despite the threat posed by social movements to the state elite, they cannot be eliminated form politics because they are protected by the principle of relative elite autonomy, which says that the ruling elite cannot use the means of coercion against other social elites. That is why the means of coercion cannot be used against social movements in Western democracies. Nevertheless, in the face of the emergence of counter-elites, state elites can use other strategies of control. One such strategy is protest absorption. It differs from the repression strategy in two respects. First, in the absorption strategy, the means of direct coercion are not used, even though "coercion is always there in the background, and available as a last resort, the actual strategy of control is a step removed from coercion" (Etzioni-Halevy 1993, p. 204). Second, it is not the goal of the absorption strategy to completely change a social movement – rather, the aim is to mitigate the radicalism of the counter-elites. The strategy of protest absorption is not contrary to democratic principles – it is quite different from the subordination of counter-elites to the state authorities. It is like an exchange transaction in that social movements give up those of their postulates which destabilize the system, while the governing elite, in return, realizes some of their other demands. That dependence is an important channel of social and political changes in Western democracies. In order to illustrate that statement, we should analyze the main absorption strategies used by the government.

It has already been mentioned that the ruling elite controls many assets: the means of physical coercion as well as symbolic, administrative-organizational, and material resources. They may be used in the form of a penalty imposed on a social movement and its elites – when their activity eludes the control of the state authorities – or in the form of a reward for moderate activity. In other words, the ruling elite may use the strategy of absorption (a positive strategy) or the strategy of repression (a negative strategy) against the elites of social movements. The exact tactics used within the framework of those strategies depends on the type of resources possessed by the state elite. Having at its disposal symbolic resources, the state elite can use the strategy of repression and slander or intimidate members of social movements. Choosing the strategy of absorption, it can also publicly express support for and interest in goals of social movements as well as attempt to contribute to their realization.

With the use of administrative and organizational resources, the state authorities can pass restrictive laws, for example, regulations which prohibit or control the course of street marches or demonstrations, and in that way implement the repressive strategy. Absorption tactics in this sphere would mean, for instance, abolishing legal restrictions or even co-opting leaders of social movements to the organizational structures of the state, on condition that the opposition mitigates its demands. As regards material resources, the government can deprive some social movements or their leaders of financial means or – if it chooses the absorption strategy – assign additional funds to the realization of the postulates of those movements. It is worth noting that the state elite does not resort to one type of resources but uses all its resources as it implements the protest absorption or repression strategy.

Protest absorption leads to elite co-option and mitigates the threat posed by social movements as well as weakening their potentially radical goals. When the absorption strategy has been used with success, the leaders of social movements accept the partial realization of their postulates and give up the system-destabilizing ones. Thus, the development of democracy on the basis of the mechanism of elite absorption can be described as follows:

> The state authorities distribute resources in the non-egalitarian way → there grows a social protest movement led by own elite → the authorities absorb that protest by co-opting this social elite, which leads to a more egalitarian distribution of resources → the renewed elites distribute resources in non-egalitarian way → there grows another social protest movement led by own elite.

That mechanism, although devoid of violent rebellions or revolutions, contributes to the democratization of the social system. Since the counter-elites and sub-elites of social movements in Western democracies began to represent the interests of unprivileged groups, the system has been developing in the direction of the egalitarian distribution of power and material resources. Additionally, "since leaders and activists of social movements can maintain their positions only if they deliver at least some achievements to their supporters, there is always a likelihood that they will push for a more egalitarian distribution of resources" (Etzioni-Halevy 1993, p. 211) which, according to the author, is a criterion of social progress. Social movements were the most efficient at redistributing material resources at the turn of the 19th century. Their behavior has not changed much since that time. As a result of that process, the leaders of social movements have partially abandoned their postulates of a redistributing of material resources and begun to emphasize post-material values and improvement of the quality of life. Obviously, that does not mean that all social movements in Western democracies have dropped the issue of a redistributing of resources. Nowadays, the leaders and activists of social movements are striving for greater autonomy of individuals and for participatory politics. In other words, they want to implement more egalitarian principles of power distribution, that is, greater democratization leading to the development of Western democratic societies.

One important factor of that development is relative elite and sub-elite autonomy. However, the main reason for system changes is not the activity of those movements but the actions of the ruling elite, based on the strategy of protest absorption. It is those actions, especially co-option, that make it possible to 'mitigate' the demands made by social movements. The process of 'coming to terms' with social movements entails certain concessions on the part of both the government and current or future leaders and activists of social movements. In response to relative elite autonomy, the ruling elites use stabilization strategies which lead to changes of the form of government. The concessions of the ruling elite to the benefit of social movements, made in return for the 'mitigation' of their postulates, are a mechanism of power in Western democracies which both protects the system and triggers its development.

> [...] recurring cycles of the generation of relatively autonomous movements, the absorption of their protest by co-option of their elites, according some limited concessions to them, their consequent acceptance of the status quo, and finally the generation of yet other relatively autonomous counter-elites to take their place, may be seen as a major 'learning mechanism', or a major channel through which progress in Western democracies takes place.
>
> ETZIONI-HALEVY 1993, p. 213

The process of co-opting the elites of social movements will probably continue because it makes democracy a more democratic, just, and egalitarian system.

3 The Theory of Political Society in Non-Marxian Historical Materialism and the Theory of Democratic Elites. An Attempt at a Comparison

Let us compare Eva Etzioni-Halevy's theory of democratic elites with Leszek Nowak's theory of political society in non-Marxian historical materialism (1983; 1989; 1991abc; 1991d). Any analogies between those concepts would point to their similar theoretical assumptions. A comparative analysis of such complex theories will be carried out, according to the following criteria:

- the foundation of social divisions,
- the main social categories and the method of distinguishing them,
- the presence or absence of accumulated social divisions,
- the optimal mechanism of social development, and
- the conditions of democratic stability.

In non-Marxian historical materialism, social divisions are founded on the relationship with material social means, which comprise:

- the means of production,
- the means of coercion, and
- the means of spiritual production.

They belong to the material level of the three spheres of social life: the economy, politics, and culture. The approach to particular material social means is the basis for the division of society into the following social classes: the dominant ones (rulers, owners, priests) and the dominated ones (citizens, direct producers, the faithful). The dominant classes have at their disposal material means of a given type, while the dominated classes have no influence on the use of those means.

In the case of the theory of democratic elites, the basis of the division of society into classes are various kinds of resources defined as "any goods having an impact on people's lives". In this theory – in contrast to non-Marxian historical materialism – resources are not considered only at the material level of social life because – let us remember – Etzioni-Halevy distinguishes resources pertaining to physical coercion, organizational-administrative, symbolic, material-economic, and psychological.

In non-Marxian historical materialism, the basis of social division is the relationship to social material means, while in the theory of democratic elites it is the relationship to resources. In Nowak approach, the relationship to social material means in each of the three domains of social life determines the division of society into social classes. In the economic sphere they are: the class of owners (which has at its disposal the means of production) and direct producers (deprived of such means); in the political sphere they are: the class of rulers (which has at its disposal the means of coercion) and the class of citizens (deprived of such means); and in the cultural sphere they are: the class of priests (which has at its disposal the means of indoctrination) and the class of the faithful (deprived of such means).

In the elitist theory, the basic social category are social elites distinguished at the institutionalist level. One's social class is determined by the position one occupies in particular social and political structures. That privileged position is based on the unbridled disposal of resources. In Eva Etzioni-Halevy's classification, which encompasses five types of resources, elites include, among other people, members of the government, heads of the main opposition parties, military forces, the police, courts, trade unions leaders, the media, bureaucratic elites, intellectuals, and business leaders.

Another comparative criterion is the possibility of the occurrence of accumulated social divisions. Nowak's theory admits the possibility of one social class having more than one type of material social means at its disposal (Nowak 1983, pp. 169–186; 1991a, pp. 178–179). Hence, in non-Marxian historical materialism, we can distinguish single classes which only have one type of material means at their disposal, double classes which control two types of material social means, and triple classes which have at their disposal all types of material social means. Double and triple classes constitute a new type of societies: supraclass societies (for a full typology of societies, see Brzechczyn 2004b, pp. 73–86; 2007).

In the case of the theory of democratic elites, Etzioni-Halevy distinguishes one additional category apart from the five basic types of resources, namely, that of mixed resources. Since various resources are interrelated, various combinations of them can be used by the elites. That is why one elite can have at its disposal several types of resources. Nevertheless, according to the author, such a social situation does not lead to the creation of a social system the main principle of which would be different from the one in which the elites only have one type of resources at their disposal.

In non-Marxian historical materialism, the optimal mechanism of social development is the mechanism of evolutionary progress through lost revolutions (Nowak 1991c, pp. 95–97; 1993). All such revolutions end in a defeat, but rulers make concessions to the civil society in order to avoid another defeat. After a time, those concessions are withdrawn, which contributes to the outbreak of another revolution, on a greater scale than the previous one. That revolution also ends in a defeat and forces the authorities to make greater concessions than the previous time. Gradually, the concessions become bigger while power regulation is decreases. In that way, through the ebb and flow of social struggle, the society evolves slowly, until the moment when social peace is achieved.

In the theory of democratic elites, the optimal mechanism of social development is the mechanism of elite absorption. This consists in the co-option of the emerging elites of social movements into the ruling elite in order to weaken the radicalism of those movements. The elites of the social movements absorbed into the authorities give up some of their postulates in return for partial realization of other goals. The ruling elite also agrees to make certain concessions to the social movements. Thus, the co-option strategy used by the ruling elite stabilizes the system and, consequently, leads to a change of the form of government. The mechanism of system evolution in the theory of democratic elites differs from the cycle of social changes in non-Marxian historical materialism mainly in that it is devoid of violent rebellions or mass revolutions. That is why it can stabilize and correct a political system at the same time.

The last comparative criterion concerns the conditions of the stability of democracy. In non-Marxian historical materialism, the stability is based on the balance of the influence of the classes of priests, rulers, and owners (Brzechczyn 2003, pp. 42–48; 2004a). In Etzioni-Halevy's theory of democratic elites, it depends on the autonomy of the elites of the democratic system. For the comparison of both theories, see: Table 9.1.

TABLE 9.1   A comparison of Nowak's and Etzioni-Halevy's theories

The comparative criterion	Leszek Nowak	Eva Etzioni- Halevy
The basis for the social division	material social means of: – production, – coercion, – indoctrination	resources: – physical coercion – organizational-administrative – symbolic material-economic – psychological and personality-related
The main social actors	classes	elites
The level at which the main social categories are distinguished	materialist	institutionalist
Accumulated social divisions	single classes double classes triple classes	mixed elites having at their disposal combined resources
The optimal mechanism of social development	evolutionary progress through lost civil revolution	elite absorption mechanism
The conditions for the stability of democracy	balance among single social classes: rulers, owners, and priests	relative elite autonomy

4 An Attempt at a Paraphrase of the Elite Absorption Mechanism in the Conceptual Apparatus of the Theory of Power of Non-Marxian Historical Materialism

As has been mentioned, Etzioni-Halevy believes the absorption mechanism to be the basic mechanism of the development of democracy. It consists in the co-option of elites of social movements into the state authorities in order to weaken the radicalism of those movements. The elites of social movements absorbed into the authorities give up some of their postulates in return for certain concessions on the part of the ruling elite. Thus, the co-option strategy used by the ruling elite stabilizes the system, and then the desired changes of the form of government can be made. Let us remind that in the theory of democratic elites, the mechanism of the development of society works as follows:

> The state authorities distribute resources in the non-egalitarian way → there grows a social protest movement led by own elite → the authorities absorb that protest by co-opting this social elite, which leads to a more egalitarian distribution of resources → the renewed elites distribute resources in non-egalitarian way → there grows another social protest movement led by own elite.

In the conceptual framework of non-Marxian historical materialism, the counterpart of the resources at the disposal of the authorities in the democratic elite theory is the rulers' ability to control the class of citizens (the scope of power regulation), while the counterpart of the resources of the class of citizens is the scope of political autonomy. In standard social conditions, increasing the scope of power regulation leads to a decrease of citizens' autonomy, while increasing citizens' autonomy leads to a decrease of power regulation.

4.1 The Mechanism of the Absorption of Elites and the Mechanism of Evolutionary Progress through Lost Revolutions

In non-Marxian historical materialism, the optimal mechanism in the development of a political society is the mechanism of lost revolutions. In the last two phases of the development of a political society: the phase of cyclical declassations and the phase of cyclical revolutions, after the defeat of the citizens' revolution, the rulers use repressions against the class of citizens. Moreover, the authorities decrease their sphere of power regulation (concessions) in order to protect themselves against another citizens' revolution. Consequently, there is an increase of the autonomy of civil society and a separation of the spheres of social life which are once more subjected to the control by the authorities.

The mechanisms of competition for power increase citizens' alienation, which leads to another revolution. Each subsequent citizens' revolution has a greater scope, so the number of concessions grows, power regulation decreases, and the sphere of social autonomy expands. That cycle of the development of a political society "lasts until there is a revolution on such a large scale, involving so many citizens that mass repressive action becomes unfeasible and the authorities must immediately make concessions" (Nowak 1991c, p. 93). Those concessions must be big enough to lead to class peace. As they grow in size, the cycle of class development (concessions – a revolution – concessions) changes. It continues until "the sphere of power regulation decreases to the threshold of public order" (Nowak 1991c, p. 93), until the role of the state authorities is reduced to the administration of social life. This model can be illustrated in the following way:

> A revolution → repression and concessions → etatization → a revolution with a broader social base → repression and concession → etatization → a revolution which necessitates concessions which reach the threshold of class peace.

The mechanism of evolutionary progress through lost revolutions differs from Etzioni-Halevy's mechanism of elite absorption. First, in non-Marxian historical materialism, it is assumed that citizens' revolutions will grow in size, while Etzioni-Halevy clearly underlines the limited scope of social mobilization in most, if not all social events called a revolution. Second, the mechanism of lost revolutions presupposes the use of repressions against citizens directly after each revolution, while Etzioni-Halevy assumes that a social conflict is always followed by the use of the strategy of elite co-option. Third, Nowak uses the term 'the class of citizens" and ignores, at least in Model I of the theory of power, the internal differentiation of that social category. Etzioni-Halevy distinguishes between social elites (or sub-elites) and ordinary members of social movements. For that reason, the mechanism of evolutionary progress through lost revolutions cannot be the basis for a paraphrase of Etzioni-Halevy's mechanism of elite absorption.

4.2 The Mechanism of the Absorption of Elites in Non-Marxian Historical Materialism

In non-Marxian historical materialism, the abovementioned final stage of the evolution of a political society has been concretized by Krzysztof Brzechczyn, who has defined the concept of the absorption of elites within the framework of that theory. In non-Marxian historical materialism, Model I of the theory of power is concretized by the introduction of three types of a revolution and taking into account the internal differentiation of the class of citizens.

THE ELITARIAN VERSUS CLASS THEORY OF DEMOCRACY 211

Nowak only defines one type of revolution, namely, a mass revolution. Brzechczyn distinguishes three types of revolution: mass, local, and balanced. He defines a mass revolution as a kind of a social conflict in which "the participation of a greater part of the civil class leads to the elimination of the old class of rulers and its substitution with the revolutionary elite" (Brzechczyn 1993, p. 278; 1997, p. 401). A local revolution is defined as a revolution which involves "only a small part of the civil class" (Brzechczyn 1993, p. 278; and for that reason, "it ends in a defeat" (Brzechczyn 1993, p. 278). In the case of a balanced revolution, "the forces of both sides are more or less balanced, and the social conflict cannot end in the defeat of one of them" (Brzechczyn 1993, p. 278).

Moreover, the author discusses the internal differentiation of the class of citizens and divides it into the elite and ordinary citizens (Brzechczyn 2004c; 2010). Brzechczyn considers the elite of the civic movement only at the material level because that elite has at its disposal the material means of social communication and decides about their use. Thus, it "not only coordinates but also controls the actions of the class of citizens" (Brzechczyn 1997, p. 402). Since the elite can both block and support certain initiatives of the class of citizens, there is a risk that some members of the elite will want to increase their influence and, in that way, gain power. In the face of a revolution, rulers decide to make certain concessions to the benefit of the revolutionary elite which is then co-opted by the class of rulers, while, at the same time, repressions are used against ordinary members of the class of citizens. The renewed rulers' class can once more broaden the scope of its power regulation. Consequently, another protest movement grows. Once more, it has its own revolutionary elite. As the next balanced revolution cannot end in the victory of either of the sides, the rulers use the elite absorption strategy again. Thus, according to Brzechczyn, the mechanism of the development of a political society takes the following form:

> A balanced revolution → elite absorption and repressions → etatization → another balanced revolution → elite absorption and repressions.

Brzechczyn's approach to that process differs, however, from Etzioni-Halevy's mechanism of the absorption of elites. First, Brzechczyn assumes that the co-option of elites into the structures of power is followed directly by the use of repression by the rulers against the remaining participants of the citizens' protest movement. Etzioni-Halevy's mechanism of the absorption of elites precludes the use of repression. Second, according to Brzechczyn, when elites are co-opted, power regulation grows, while in Etzioni-Halevy's theory, the result is more egalitarian resource distribution. For that reason, the mechanism of the absorption of elites as conceptualized by Brzechczyn cannot be the basis for a paraphrase of the mechanism of the absorption of elites from Etzioni-Halevy's theory.

4.3 On the Mechanism of Progressive Absorption

Apart from Brzechczyn's concept of the absorption of elites, which is called regressive absorption, the conceptual framework of non-Marxian historical materialism also makes it possible to present a new type of absorption which I call progressive absorption. In the case of progressive absorption, the class of rulers' co-opts the revolutionary elite, but it does not, at the same time, use repressions against the class of citizens. Instead, the rulers decide to make concessions to the benefit of the whole class of citizens which leads to greater social autonomy. However, that growth of autonomy is smaller than in the case of the standard mechanism of social evolution (through lost revolutions). The mechanism of progressive absorption can be expressed with the following scheme:

Balanced revolution → elite absorption and concessions → etatization → balanced revolution

The concept of progressive absorption can be the basis for a paraphrase of the mechanism of protest absorption in Etzioni-Halevy's theory of democratic elites. The counterpart of the social protest movement is the phenomenon of a balanced revolution, that is, a revolution with a limited social base. The absorption consists in the co-option of the elites of the protest. In Etzioni-Halevy's approach, the result is more egalitarian resource distribution; in the case of progressive absorption – it is greater citizens' autonomy.

The paraphrase confirms the truthfulness of Etzioni-Halevy's intuition that when social mobilization is limited, social elites play the main role in social development. They cease to play that role when there is a true mass revolution. However, that aspect of social development is ignored by the author. Therefore, we could say that non-Marxian historical materialism is a more general theory which takes into account the influence of a mass protest movement and a limited one which leads to a balance of powers between the rulers and the citizens' society and, consequently, contributes to social development. The paraphrased mechanism of absorption is a variant of the political development assumed in non-Marxian historical materialism.

Another problem concerns the social and political conditions that are conducive to progressive or regressive absorption. At that level of idealization, it is not possible to give a clear answer to that question. The answer will depend on a number of factors, such as the structure, ideology, or type of leadership of the social movement, which are omitted at this stage of the reflections.

5   Conclusions

The analogies between the theory of political society in non-Marxian historical materialism and Etzioni-Halevy's theory of elites point to certain theoretical assumptions those two concepts have in common, such as:
- the autonomy of the political sphere and
- the antagonistic nature of the political sphere.

The autonomy of the political sphere consists mainly in the relative independence of political elites from economic and cultural elites. The ruling elite has the power to decide about both its own fate and that of the citizens. Citizens may influence the social and political situation but do not participate directly in the decision-making process of the elites.

The antagonistic understanding of politics allows contrary interests which generate a social conflict between the elites and non-elites, but that conflict can be solved by way of social compromise. Because of those analogies, the theory of power in non-Marxian historical materialism can be considered as another version of the elite theory of politics. The theory of power in non-Marxian historical materialism and Etzioni-Halevy's elite theory differ with respect to the manner in which social divisions are determined: in non-Marxian historical materialism, class divisions are discerned at the material level, so political classes are distinguished (in this approach, elites are a part of those political classes: the classes of rulers and the citizens), while in the elite theory, class divisions are discerned at the institutional level, so only elites are distinguished, and social classes are omitted.

References

Brzechczyn, K. (1993). Civil Loop and the Absorption of Elites. In: L. Nowak and M. Paprzycki (eds). *Social System, Rationality and Revolution. Poznań Studies in the Philosophy of the Sciences and the Humanities*, vol. 33, pp. 277–282. Amsterdam-Atlanta: Rodopi.

Brzechczyn, K. (1997). Zapaść obywatelska i absorpcja elit. Próba poszerzenia teorii ewolucji społeczeństwa politycznego [Citizens' Inertia and the Absorption of Elites. An Attempt at Expanding the Theory of the Evolution of a Political Society]. In: L. Nowak and P. Przybysz (eds). *Marksizm, liberalizm, próby wyjścia*, pp. 399–404. Poznań: Zysk i S-ka.

Brzechczyn, K. (2003). Upadek realnego socjalizmu w Europie Wschodniej a załamanie się hiszpańskiego imperium kolonialnego w Ameryce Łacińskiej. Próba analizy porównawczej [The Fall of Real Socialism in Easter Europe and the End of the

Spanish Colonial Empire in Latin America. An Attempt at a Comparative Analysis].
In: K. Brzechczyn (ed.) *Ścieżki transformacji. Ujęcia teoretyczne i opisy empiryczne,*
pp. 37–81. Poznań Zysk i S-ka.

Brzechczyn, K. (2004a). The Collapse of Real Socialism in Eastern Europe versus
the Overthrow of the Spanish Colonial Empire in Latin America: An Attempt
at Comparative Analysis. *Journal of Interdisciplinary Studies in History and
Archaeology,* 1 (2), 105–133.

Brzechczyn, K. (2004b). *O wielości linii rozwojowych w procesie historycznym. Próba
interpretacji ewolucji społeczeństwa meksykańskiego* [On the Multitude of the Lines
of Developments in the Historical Process. An Attempt at Interpretation of the
Evolution of the Mexican Society]. Poznań: Wydawnictwo Naukowe UAM.

Brzechczyn, K. (2004c). Porozumienie przy Okrągłym Stole w świetle koncepcji kom-
promisu klasowego. Próba modelu [The Round Table Agreement in the Light of the
Concept of Class Compromise. An Attempt at a Model]. In: S. Drabczyński and M.
Żyromski (eds.). *Rola wyborów w procesie kształtowania się społeczeństwa obywatel-
skiego w Polsce,* pp. 24–47. Poznań: WSNHiD.

Brzechczyn, K. (2007). On the Application of non-Marxian Historical Materialism
to Development of non-European Societies. In: J. Brzeziński, A. Klawiter, T.A.F.
Kuipers, K. Łastowski, K. Paprzycka, P. Przybysz (eds.), *The Courage of Doing
Philosophy: Essays Dedicated to Leszek Nowak,* pp. 235–254. Amsterdam/New York,
NY: Rodopi.

Brzechczyn, K. (2010). The Round Table Agreement in Poland as a Case of
Class Compromise: An Attempt at a Model. *Debatte: Journal of Contemporary
Central and Eastern Europe,* 18(2), 185–204.

Etzioni-Halevy, E. (1989). *Fragile democracy – The Use and Abuse of Power in Western
Societies.* New York: Transaction Publishers.

Etzioni-Halevy, E. (1993). *The Elite Connection – Problems and Potential of Western
Democracy.* Cambridge: Polity Press.

Nowak L. (1983). *Property and Power. Towards a non-Marxian Historical Materialism.*
Dordrecht/Boston/Lancaster: Reidel.

Nowak, L. (1989). An Idealizational Model of Capitalist Society. In: L. Nowak (ed.),
*Dimensions of the Historical Process. Poznań Studies in the Philosophy of the Sciences
and the Humanities,* vol. 13, pp. 217–258. Amsterdam: Rodopi.

Nowak, L. (1991abc). *U podstaw teorii socjalizmu* [Foundations of Theory of Socialism],
vol. 1: *Własność i władza. O konieczności socjalizmu* [Property and Power. On the
Necessity of Socialism]; vol. 2: *Droga do socjalizmu. O konieczności socjalizmu w Rosji*
[The Road to Socialism. On the Necessity of Socialism in Russia], vol. 3: *Dynamika
władzy: o strukturze i konieczności zaniku socjalizmu* [The Dynamics of Power. On
the Structure and the Necessity of the Disappearance of Socialism]. Poznań: Nakom.

Nowak L. (1991d). *Power and Civil Society. Toward a Dynamic Theory of Real Socialism.* New York: Greenwood Press.

Nowak, L. (1993). Revolution is an Opaque Progress but a Progress Nonetheless. In: L. Nowak and M. Paprzycki (eds). *Social System, Rationality and Revolution. Poznań Studies in the Philosophy of the Sciences and the Humanities,* vol. 33, pp. 237–250. Amsterdam-Atlanta: Rodopi.

Żyromski, M. (2007). *Teoria elit a systemy polityczne* [*The Elite Theory and Political Systems*]. Poznań: Wydawnictwo Naukowe UAM.

CHAPTER 10

Leszek Nowak's non-Marxian Historical Materialism and Pareto's Elite Theory: Similarities and Differences

Giacomo Borbone

Abstract

This paper takes into account the main similarities and differences existing between the following two social theories: Leszek Nowak's non-Marxian Historical Materialism and the Élite-theory, as the latter was elaborated and developed by Vilfredo Pareto and other outstanding Italian representatives of this social theory, that is to say Gaetano Mosca and Roberto Michels (who was a German-born Italian). I think that there are some similarities between Nowak's social theory and élite-theory, especially concerning the adopted methodology, cyclical revolutions and social progress, but nonetheless there are also some differences that can be found, especially in the role of the masses.

Keywords:

Elite theory – Vilfredo Pareto – Leszek Nowak – revolution

1 Introduction

Leszek Nowak's non-Marxian historical materialism is one of the most innovative contemporary contributions to the development of social theory and it provided a very interesting explanation of the socialist society that arose after the Russian Revolution. The conceptual apparatus of Nowak's social theory is obviously indebted to his previously elaborated epistemological reflections on the idealizational nature of scientific theories. It is well known that Nowak largely used the method of idealization, concretization and gradual approximations in order to enucleate the main theoretical fallacies of Marxian social theory. According to Nowak, mature science makes use of idealizational statements (see Galileo, Newton, and so on) instead of generalization from empirical facts (Aristotelian abstraction), and he found this methodology also to be

© GIACOMO BORBONE, 2022 | DOI:10.1163/9789004507296_011

at work in Marx' economic works (see, for instance, the theory of value, which is a typical idealizational law). In line with this scientific approach, Nowak employs several idealizational models for his analysis and critique of Marxian Historical Materialism. Through this methodological move, Nowak criticized and then generalized Karl Marx's social theory from a classist point of view that, at the end of the day, was more extreme than the Marxian one. In fact, Nowak extended Marxian Historical Materialism out of the mere economic sphere, by taking into account both the political and ideological spheres. According to Marx these three dependences – *the economy*, *politics* and *culture* – allow us to outline the three main aspects of social totality, but the economic one, as Marx holds, is the *fundamental one*, from which politics and culture arise only as super-structural manifestations. Nowak, after the study of mechanisms and dynamics of *real socialism*, understood very well that the main factor was indeed the political one and not, as the classical Marxian scheme up-holds, the economic one. In this way Nowak showed that the three material levels characterize each Marxian level, respectively: the material level (means of production, means of indoctrination and means of indoctrination in culture), the institutional level (economic organizations, political organizations and cultural organizations), and the level of social consciousness (economic ideologies, political ideologies and, finally, cultural ideologies).

In this paper I will also compare the main aspects of Leszek Nowak's non-Marxian historical materialism with Italian élite-theory as it was elaborated and developed by Vilfredo Pareto and other outstanding Italian rappresentatives of this social theory, that is to say Gaetano Mosca and Roberto Michels (who was a German-born Italian). I think that there are some similarities between Nowak's social theory and élite-theory, especially concerning the methodology adopted, the cyclic revolutions and social progress, but nonetheless there are also some differences that can be found, especially in the role of the masses.

2   From Trier to Poznań

Even though, as I previously said, the methodological aspects of Nowak's reflections on science are strictly linked to his social theory, unfortunately a discourse on this topic would be extremely wide, so I am forced to suggest to readers the following volumes and essays on the method of idealization and concretization (Nowak 1980; Coniglione 2010; Borbone 2016; Borbone, Brzechczyn 2016). Having said that, let's turn our gaze to the way Leszek Nowak generalized the so-called Materialist Conception of History. In fact, it is extremely important to understand the reasons why Nowak considered Marxian social theory as a case of economic determinism or economicism. As it is well known, the best exposition of Karl Marx' Historical Materialism can be found in his *Preface of A Contribution to the Critique of Political Economy* (1859), where he set up three fundamental dependencies: 1) *structure*, 2) *political* and *legal super-structure*, 3) *definite forms of social consciousness*. Marx writes that:

> The first work which I undertook to dispel the doubts assailing me was a re-examination of the Hegelian philosophy of law. [...] The general conclusion at which I arrived and which, once reached, became the guiding principle of my studies can be summarized as follows. In the social production of their existence, men inevitably enter into definite relations, which are indipendent of their will, namely relations of production appropriate to a given stage in the development of their material forces of production. The totality of these relations of production constitutes the economic structure of society, the real foundation, on which arises a legal and political superstructure and to which correspond definite forms of social consciousness. The mode of production of material life conditions the general process of social, political and intellectual life. It is not the consciousness of men that determines their existence, but their social existence that determines their consciousness. At a certain stage of development, the material productive forces of society come into conflict with the existing relations of production or – this merely expresses the same thing in legal terms – with the property relations within the framework of which they have operated hitherto. From forms of development of the productive forces these relations turn into their fetters. Then begins an era of social revolution. The changes in the economic foundation lead sooner or later to the transformation of the whole immense superstructure.
>
> MARX 1859, p. 263

It is clear that, according to Marx, society is the result of the mutual action of mankind but, as Engels clarifies in a letter to Annenkov, his "material relations form the basis of all his relations. These material relations are but the necessary forms in which his material and individual activity is realised" (Engels 1846, p. 96). Obviously, historical materialism is an *ideal* scheme, a method that Marx used to apply to his political, economical and social studies. Once again, let's see what Engels wrote about it in a letter to Werner Sombart: "Marx's whole way of thinking [*Auffassungsweise*] is not so much a doctrine as a method. It

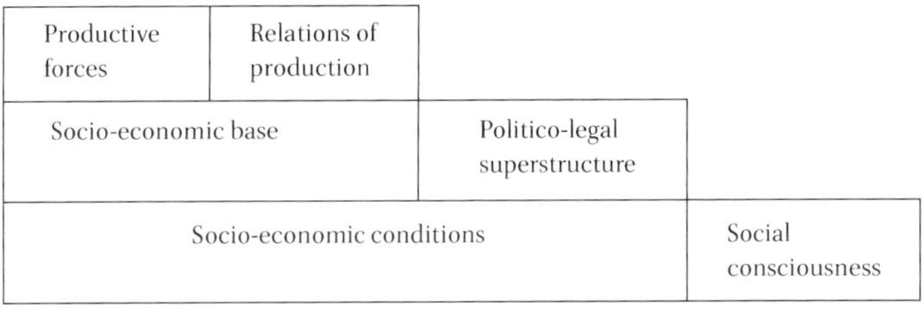

Productive forces	Relations of production		
Socio-economic base		Politico-legal superstructure	
Socio-economic conditions			Social consciousness

FIGURE 10.1 The structure of economical momentum

provides, not so much ready-made dogmas, as aids to further investigation and the method for such investigation" (Engels 1895, p. 461).

In fact, the main theses of Marxian historical materialism hold that at the base of everything there is nature, which, through its obstacles, pushes men to develop the so-called *productive forces* (for example, man's hand, intruments, machines, energy, scientific knowledge incorporated in science, technology, information technology, and so on). At this stage, to this given development of productive forces, corresponds given relations of production (that is to say, modes of production, and at this phase a social revolution can occur, which arises from the conflict between relations of production and productive forces). And then arises the *structure* (relations of productions: for example the relationship between capitalist and worker, feudal master and slave, and so on, where a class struggle can occur). On the basis of Marxian assumptions, we can state that the so-called *structure* gives its mark to the *political and legal superstructure* (State, Constitutions, laws, political parties) to which correspond definite forms of *social consciousness* (morals, habits, arts, religion, literature, and so on). Marx and Engels never conceived this scheme in a deterministic way, just because even the forms of cosciousness act on the superstructure, which, in turn, sanctions the relations of production that, in turn, produce a development of those productive forces that allow an intense exploitation of nature (see Figure 10.1).[1]

This is the point at which Nowak's critique of Marxian historical materialism begins, even though the Polish philosopher never denied the Marxist roots of his thought: "First, historical materialism as proposed here assumes the Marxian methodology and the Marxian dialectics. [...] Second, the theoretical conception outlined here employs the Marxian conceptual apparatus" (Nowak

---

1 This scheme is taken from Nowak (1979), p. 61.

1983, p. 61). Nonetheless, Nowak noticed some theoretical mistakes in Marxian social theory and he aimed to overcome these fallacies through a materialistic critique. First of all, for Nowak historical materialism cannot satisfy the three fundamental requirements for a Marxist theory of historical process. These requirements are the following:

– the idealizational nature of the theory;
– dialectical accuracy;
– social progressiveness.

We already mentioned the idealizational nature of the models used by Nowak for his reflections on Marxist social theory, so there is no need to examine the question in depth. It is enough to say that Marxian theories and modern science share the same methodological structure, that is to say a sequence of models that are subsequently concretized. The requirement of dialectical accuracy, instead, refers to the essential structure of magnitudes; it means that in this case we have to start from the set of factors that influence a given magnitude F (these factors are obviously necessary for the explanation of F). Furthermore, we have to put in order this set, which Nowak calls the "space of essential magnitudes" for F. Once the set has been built, which is composed of $k+1$ elements: $H, \ldots, p_k, \ldots, p_1$, where H is the main factor for F and the others are gradually less essential, we can then proceed to the formation of its essential structure. Anyway, at the base of Nowak's conception of dialectics there is a complex and profound reflection. In fact, dialectics has nothing to do with the mere concepts of movement and change as they can be found in common sense (that is to say, the becoming of things), but rather with

> the changeability of hierarchies of factors influencing phenomena occurring in things themselves. The thesis of dialectics so conceived would not, then, be that things change but rather that their essential structure changes and, hence, that regularities governing things vary over the time.
>
> NOWAK 1983, p. 12

This is the so-called categorial interpretation of dialectics. So, the dialectical accuracy of a theory consists of its capacity to identify, in an appropriate manner, the entire list of the main factor for a given investigated phenomenon. The third requirement, that is to say the one of social progressiveness, comes from the Marxian theory of ideology. In fact, the class of owners gives birth to an image of associated life that must hide the most decisive aspects of it. The real interest of private property is to impose, on the subordinate masses, an essentially false image of social reality.

What Nowak does, in this respect, is apply these three requirements to Marxian historical materialism, and what he finds out is that Marxian materialism satisfies only the first one, that is to say the idealizational nature of the theory. The second one is not satisfied because, on the one hand, if according to Marx it is true that the productive forces determine the relations of production, it is also true, on the other hand, that this situation does not occur in a socialist society. In the latter the relations of production are not adapted to the level of the productive forces but rather to the will of the power hierarchy. While in a capitalist society the state was simply a superstructural manifestation, in a socialist society it is rather the opposite. Even the third requirement is not satisfied by Marxian Materialism, just because in a socialist society it was paradoxically a reactionary theory. Nowak arrives at this conclusion after the analysis of the three main theoretical curves or trends of Marxism during the period of Russian socialism: the orthodox one, the nomological one and the praxistic one. For Nowak, the orthodox interpretation has a rather low systematic value, inasmuch it does not try to overcome the ambiguities of historical materialism. The praxistic and nomological ones are instead considered by Nowak with more attention. The praxistic interpretation, briefly, holds the impossibility of any reduction of history to isomorphic natural laws. It does not consider history as an entity subjected to strict laws of a naturalistic kind; history, that way, has a meaning just because we impose to it through our actions. The nomological interpretation, which we can trace back to the Marxism of the Second International, does exactly the opposite, namely it is based on the idea that there are laws of development of history that refer to the contradiction between the economic base and the superstructure.[2]

Nonetheless, Nowak postulates the inadequacy of both the nomological interpretation and the praxistic one (as it can be found, for instance, in Lukács) for the following reasons:

> The former entirely ignores the role of the (antagonistic) class struggle, interpreting it as the means of realization of the regularities working

---

2 Nowak finds an example of nomological intepretation in the reflections of the economist O. Lange, according to which "the structure of a socio-economic formation is determined by two laws: the law of a necessary agreement between production relations and the nature of productive forces, and the law of a necessary agreement between the superstructure and the base; these laws determine the conditions of the 'inner harmony, the internal balance of social formations' " (Nowak 1983, p. 29). There is also a third law, which determines the way a formation develops itself, that is to say the law of the progressive development of productive forces.

outside human actions. The latter, in turn, abandons what seems to be the greatest contribution of historical materialism to social sciences, namely, the idea of socio-economic formations whose structure and motion undergo objective laws.

NOWAK 1983, p. 32

The fundamental point, in this respect, is the one concerning the way we can conjoin the idea of class struggle with the idea of socio-economic formations. This is the starting point of Nowak's solution of this problem, namely so-called non-Marxian historical materialism, characterized, in line with his methodological approach, by several models that are subsequently concretized.[3]

3 *Über Marx.* Non-Marxian Historical Materialism

The importance of non-Marxian historical materialism (on this topic, see: Brzechczyn 2007; 2008) is linked to Nowakian effort to put into light, with a fresh perspectival view, the main fallacies of its historical predecessor, and in addition it provided quite a satisfying explanation of real socialism, thereby solving the ambiguities concerning the distance existing between Marxian predictions and the disastrous outcomes of Stalinism. If there is a remarkable distance between what Marx predicted and the Stalinist gulags, it means that there was a basic error in Marxian social theory but, on the other hand, if it is true that Marx was the Galileo of social sciences, it means that we should use Marx's methodology against Marx himself. This is, briefly, Nowak's idea of a Marxist critique of Marx. Nowak begins his critique of Marx by taking into account the three main factors that Marx used to form the conceptual base of his social theory: economy, politics and culture.

Nowak, Buczkowski and Klawiter (1982, pp. 110–121) share the same Marxian hypothesis, according to which these three fields characterize the associated life in its entirety, but they also highlight their isomorphic structure by showing that each of them, in turn, is composed of three levels: the material level, the institutional level and the level of consciousness. At each successive level, one can conceptualize these fields in a solidaristic or antagonistic manner, where the first approach underlines the function of the social order and of general agreement that lies at its base, while according to the second one,

---

3 For the sake of truth, we have to reiterate that in a series of models (from the more abstract one to the more concrete one) the last model should not be conceived as describing the entire reality; in fact, it approximates to reality but it does not complete it in its totality.

coercion constitutes the fundament of social order, and history is characterized by class conflicts between the oppressed majority and the minority that oppresses it. For Nowak, Marxian Materialism is an economicist materialism, just because the author of *Das Kapital* circumscribes the antagonistic level to the mere economic base, that it to say, to the economic field. This means that Marx conceives the political aspects or political sphere in solidaristic terms, so the State is conceived as a social power that aims to mantain the main kind of conflict, that is to say the economic class struggle. The consequence is that the Marxian approach is unilaterally limited to the sphere of the economy. The main intent of Nowak, once he highlighted the main Marxian fallacies, consists in overcoming the solidaristic limitations that can be found in Marx and in the extension of the classist and antagonistic paradigm to the political and cultural fields. That is why Nowak holds that the extension of Marxian historical materialism to real socialism is inadequate, just because the main factor for a socialist society is political power and not property (Nowak 2009, p. 68). Therefore, in each field of the three levels outlined by Marx, one can identify the following three:

- material level;
- institutional level;
- the level of *consciousness*.

In this way, Nowak tries to generalize and radicalize Marxian historical materialism, by extending the materialist critique also to political aspects. As Nowak says in his *Introduction* to *Property and Power*, "it is only a Marxist criticism of the Marxian theory which makes it possible to reveal the mistakes in question" (Nowak 1983, p. xxvii). In effect, it is not possibile to explain real socialism through Marxian historical materialism alone, but it is also true that it cannot be rejected, but rather generalized and radicalized. So, the political power consists of the fact that a certain minority is materialistically characterized by the disposal of the material means with the purpose of controlling human behaviour. In this respect, on the one hand we have the *rulers* (or "political class") and on the other the *ruled* (or "citizens").

Hence, it is simple to notice the formal analogy between the main aspects of the economical field analyzed by Marx and the ones of the non-Marxian historical materialism that Nowak extends to political power. Needless to say, this tripartition occurs also in the third level of social life, that is to say the ideological one.

In conclusion, there are three moments of society and for each of them it is possible to describe their *inner structure*, but while according to Marx they are an undifferentiated aggregate, Nowak confers full autonomy on them. Nowak provides several models and momentums of society, that is to say the economic, political and ideological momentums, but a deep analysis of these would require too many pages, so we are forced to stop our discussion at this point. In this case, it is enough to list the main theses of non-Marxian historical materialism:

– class divisions do not only exist in the economy; they emerge also in other human spheres, such as politics and culture;
– in political relationships, the means of coercion determine the division of a society into the class of rulers – which controls the means of coercion – and the class of citizens, deprived of this chance;
– in the economy, the material level is characterized by the means of production, which determines a division into the class of owners and the class of direct producers;
– in culture, the material level is characterized by the spiritual means of production, which determines a division into the class of priests and the class of believers.

Hence, for Nowak there are three autonomous class divisions not only in the economic sphere – as Marx holds – but also in politics and culture; as a consequence, the remaining two class divisions are indispensable, just like the economic division. Marxian Historical Materialism is inadequate for explaining the development of social movements like Fascism, Socialism and Capitalism, unless one applies it to class societies, just like slave society or feudal society (see: Nowak 1979, p. 68). After all, Nowak's main purpose is to explain, through the idealizational procedure employed by Marx, the phenomenon of real socialism, which cannot be explained in an adequate manner through historical materialism alone.

Nowak proposes a model which is based on the assumption that socialism consists in the possession of the triple monopoly on all the material means for the control of mass-actions. This means that this kind of control is under the influence of political power, just because in socialist societies the main factor is not property but rather political power. Here is the main Marxian theoretical mistake, that is to say the assumption that political and ideological aspects are subordinated to the economy; this assumption is quite correct in a society where private property exists. The class which possesses all the three powers together – politics, ideology and the economy – also possesses the means of coercion, production and indoctrination; this class corresponds to the one that Nowak calls "the triple-ruling class." Hence, Marx was wrong when he thought that the structure of class societies was characterized by owners and direct producers only. Slave, feudal and capitalist societies experienced three classes of oppressors: owners, rulers and priests.

Unfortunately, I cannot take into account the several models that Nowak exposed in his main books on non-Marxian Historical Materialism, such as *Property and Power* or *Power and Civil Society*, for reasons of length. In this case I will take into account Nowak's reflections on revolution, which are strictly linked to the problem of social progress.

4 Revolution and the Masses

We have seen that Russian Socialism was mainly characterized by the triple-ruling class, which holds all the three powers together, but at some point a revolution can occur. According to Nowak, a revolution is characterized by three phases: the state of class peace, the revolutionary state and, finally, the state of declassation. A revolution can be won or not, but in the first case there is the so-called post-revolutionary terror; its function consists of breaking up autonomous social relations through the elimination of the most active citizens. That way, the only factor that can stop the repression of power, that is to say the civil resistance, has been eliminated. When a revolution is won by the citizens, its result does not fulfill any articular change, especially if we analyze the revolutionary process from a materialistic point of view. In fact, in this case, the revolutionaries simply become an élite power just because they own new means of coercion, so the revolutionary masses become instruments of repression and control. From that perspective, the new revolutionary élite become the seed of a new political ruling class, so the civil revolution is, from a materialist point of view, only a struggle between the actual political ruling class and the emerging one. According to Nowak, this is quite evident if we take into account what happens when the masses win a revolution. The revolutionary élite gets the monopoly of the instruments of coercion and become, in that way, the new political ruling class, which is subjected to the same regularities that occurred in the previous regime. Among the revolutionaries some individuals appear, and they love power for power itself and aim to amass in their hands an always-growing number of important decisions. That way, the sphere of control grows incessantly, and the civil loop is thereby brought to an end. In this case, there are two possibilities: the masses lose the new revolution = declassation; victory = a new civil loop. The declassation process gives to the political class the chance to subsequently extend the sphere of control, in order to dominate everything: this is the phase of totalitariansim. As Brzechczyn points out,

The declassation of citizens at that stage of social development allows rulers to further maximize the sphere of state regulation, without any resistance on the part of citizens. When all spheres of social life are controlled by the rulers, the system reaches the state of total enslavement. In that phase of development there are no longer any autonomous spheres of social life which could be subdued.

BRZECHCZYN 2017, pp. 159–160

But, in this respect, the following question arises: how, in such a scheme, is social progress possible? In this case, Nowak analyzes two positions: the revolutionary one and the evolutionary one. The former thinks that the only way to change a social system is the fast and global action of very large masses, but a victorious revolution can only postpone the process that would lead the new élite to reach power (Nowak 1983, p. 280). The latter, just like Karl Popper's *piecemeal engineering*, (Popper [1945] 2013, p. 147) is based on the assumption that the social costs of a revolution are too high, so it is recommended to make use of little, gradual and partial changes in a pre-determined direction, in order to achieve social progress. According to the assumptions of non-Marxian historical materialism, both the revolutionary position and the evolutionary one are unacceptable. If we start from the revolutionary strategy, it is clear that a victorious revolution brings us to a civil loop, while with the evolutionary one we have to ask ourselves: what kind of *piecemeal engineering* is possible for the atomized masses? From that point of view there are no gradual methods able to free society from totalitarianism. According to Nowak's non-Marxian historical materialism, the only way to improve, effectively, the condition of citizens lies in the lost or defeated revolutions, because that way the ruling class is forced to introduce some evolutionary changes (or concessions) into the system, in order to avoid another revolution. If the concessions are too limited, the revolution cannot be avoided and the political class will be forced to make new concessions, but only if the new revolution will also be lost. So, progress can be realized only through evolutionary corrections, but they are only possible through defeated revolutions.

The consequences of a socialist revolution could not have been foreseen by Karl Marx, even in its essentials outlines, just because according to the thinker of Trier the structure of societies was characterized by two classes only, that is to say the owners and direct producers. But slave societies, like feudal society, experienced three classes of oppressors: owners, rulers and priests, who took position against those who were economically oppressed, politically ruled and ideologically or spiritually hegemonized. After the Russian revolution, the new ruling class, once the class of owners and the class of priests were eliminated, accumulated triple power and then it became the triple-ruling class. Nowak uses the following scheme in order to explain the natural succession of state political systems:

democracy → autocracy → dictatorship → dispotism → dictatorship → autocracy → democracy

Nowak, against Marxian economicism, demonstrates that the conflicts that occur in the other two main social spheres (politics and culture) follow an inner logic which is irreducible to the mere economic factor.

5 Non-Marxian Historical Materialism and Élite-Theory

As we have seen, Russian Socialism was mainly characterized by the class of triple-lords, which holds all the three powers together, but at some point a revolution can occur. According to Nowak, a revolution is characterized by three phases: the state of class peace, the revolutionary state and the state of declassation. At this point, it would be interesting to compare the Nowakian analysis of socialism with the élite-theory as it was developed by Vilfredo Pareto, Gaetano Mosca and Roberto Michels.[4] I think that between non-Marxian historical materialism and the élite-theory (especially with the Paretian one, see: Busino 2010) there is a convergence concerning the dynamics of social progress. In fact, according to Nowak, social progress is guaranteed by the so-called lost revolutions, which allow the ruling élite to provide some concessions in order to curb potential revolutionary outbursts. The élite-theory, in summary, affirms that there is always an organized minority which rules over a disorganized majority[5]; so, in this case, the phenomenon of authority is the preferential object of study. Authority, according to the conceptual scheme of élite-theory, is conceived as the capacity to get the approval of masses in order to rule over them. The popular mass is unfit to express its authority and it is also technically unfit to take on its own any decision-making responsibilities. The minority rules over the majority just because the first is able to get organized, while the second is not.[6] This way of conceiving authority is quite analogous to the Gramscian concept of hegemony, which is a pre-condition for attaining power, and it is obviously linked to an *intellectual* and *moral reform*.

---

4 An interesting attempt at an explanation of the relationship between Nowak and the èlite-theory (especially the one of Eva Etzioni-Halevy) can be found in Rutkowska (2013; 2022).

5 Other interesting analysis on the concept of élite can be found in Barach (1967), Keller (1963) and Parry (1969).

6 See Bettin Lattes (2011), p. 16.

But the originality of Gramsci's *Prison Notebooks* lies in conceiving the getting of *consensus* just *before* attaining power, through the gradual conquest of the so-called *earthworks* (see: Gramsci 2001 pp. 2010–2011 and Borbone 2012). In this instance, a comparison between élite-theory and non-Marxian historical materialism is quite interesting; in fact, both these social theories try to explain and outline the essential features of the passage from one ruling élite to another by taking into account, firstly, the role that ideologies play during this passage and, secondly, the phenomenon of social change that occurs during the dynamics for the conquest of power. At the core of the perspective of Nowak's social theory there is the passage from one revolutionary élite to another, but the innovative aspect of the Nowakian approach consists in considering the victorious revolutionary élite as the author of a sophisticated work of ideological mystification aimed at concealing its real interests. Obviously, this reasoning is strongly linked with the idea that the three main spheres of social life (the economy, politics and culture) share the same internal structure; in fact, Nowak says, it is "somewhat trivial that three domains can be distinguished in social life: the economy, politics, and spiritual production. It is probably less trivial that all these domains possess a similar internal structure" (Nowak 1994, p. 77). Nowak conceives the passage from a revolutionary élite to another is in agreement with the concept of political class of the classical élite-theory (especially with Gaetano Mosca's concept of *political formula*). For Nowak, revolutionaries simply form a power élite just because they possess new means of coercion. So, the new revolutionary élite is the embryo of a new political ruling class and the civil revolution is nothing but a collision between the political ruling class and the one that is gradually emerging. Vilfredo Pareto said something similar in his work *I sistemi socialisti* (*Socialist systems*), where he wrote that "actually the new ruling classes that, in some country, get the power, have the same privileges of the previous ruling classes" (Pareto [1902] 1987, p. 231). After all, Pareto conceives the socialist political class as composed of a ruling élite and an essential part of the socialist élite can be found

> in the interest of a part of its members. No social class is homogeneous, there are always rivalries at its core; a political party forms itself that way and later on it can find its foothold in the subordinate classes. This phenomenon is very general. Almost all the revolutions had as leaders some dissident members of an *élite*.
>
> PARETO [1902] 1987, p. 181

According to Pareto, socialism was destined to give birth to a ruling élite and not to a proletarian dictatorship; in fact he wrote that even though "the socialist religion, one day, will rule over some country, we will maybe still see the same distance between the equality principles that it declares and the hierachy that it will establish" (Pareto [1902] 1987, p. 306). Even Gaetano Mosca, as I prevously said, up-holds something similar through his concept of *political formula*, which is used by the *political class* in its strong ideological pregnancy in order to legitimate its own power; after all, according to Mosca, is not the political formula that determines the way a political class forms itself, rather the opposite (Mosca ([1884] 1982, p. 227). On the same level of analysis we can also find Roberto Michels who – especially in his work entitled *Zur Soziologie des Parteiwesens in der modernen Demokratie. Untersuchungen über die oligarchischen Tendenzen des Gruppenlebens* (Michels 1911; comparison between Michels and Nowak conceptions, see: Menke 2022) and dedicated to his friend Max Weber – exposes his well known *iron law of oligarchy*, according to which all the political parties reach an oligarchical form that, in one way or another, brings us back to the "Mosca-Pareto School". But let us now look in more detail at Pareto's ideas on the élite in order to make a comparison between his theories and non-Marxian historical materialism.

The importance of the Italian sociologist Vilfredo Pareto is mainly linked to his *opus magnum*, that it to say the *Trattato di sociologia generale*, where can be found not only his conception of sociology as a science, but also his fundamental ideas concerning the concept of the élite. Here I will not take into account Paretian sociology in its entirety, but rather the issue of the élite and a comparison between it and Nowakian reflections on cyclical revolutions. We already showed the convergence existing between Pareto and Nowak with regard to the passage from one élite to another, but the similarities between them can also be found in their methodological views. In brief, according to Nowak the method of idealization and concretization can be used not only in the natural sciences but also in the social sciences and Pareto, who devoted many pages in his main works to the issue of method, used a methodology which is substantially congruent with an idealizational approach to science (on idealization in Pareto see: Guala 1998, pp. 23–44). Obviously, some ambiguities remain, just because on many occasions Pareto postulated the superiority of the inductive method and a conception of truth in line with the well-known *adaequatio rei et intellectus*, but in this case we will apply to Pareto's scientific practice the same methodological reconstruction that Nowak applied to Marxian economic works. In effect, Pareto wrote that "the only truth criterion of a the ory consists of its correspondence with facts" (Pareto [1902] 1987, p. 499), but this conception of truth cannot be reconciled with an idealizational approach to science. Nonetheless, once again it is Pareto who wrote that in the case of human sciences, if we want to catch the essential aspects of phenomena, it is fundamental to make a distinction between *real movements* and *virtual movements* or, to put this distinction in modern epistemological terms, between reality and model:

> [...] one can distinguish even for human sciences real movements from virtual ones. Let's suppose there is a heavy material point, which is forced to move itself on a surface. The line that it will cover is entirely determined. Its real movement will occur on this line. But, for a moment, we can abstract from gravity and in this case the point can cover whatever line on this surface: that way one will have *virtual movements*. Their study can be useful to set the conditions of the equilibrium of the point on a surface, but also to find some properties of the curve covered by the point [...] Let's suppose there is a man living in a society. The environment where he lives, his nature and other circumstances determine his actions. This is a real movement. Let's abstract, for a moment, from some of the circumstances that determine the actions of this man: we will have other possible actions that correspond precisely to virtual movements. The study of these actions is very useful if we want to find the conditions of the equilibrium and also to find certain features of the real actions.
>
> PARETO [1902] 1987, pp. 186–187

This methodological reflection of Pareto is very far away from a correspondence idea of truth, just because he is upholding *de facto* a modeling approach taken from the natural sciences and extended to social phenomena. An interesting aspect of Pareto's scientific practice is the distance between what he used to say and what he used to do. He used to consider himself a positivist scientist, but in his scientific practice he basically used the method of idealization and concretization. For instance, in the chapter of his *Trattato* entitled "Parole e cose" ("Words and things") he wrote that

> geometrical entities such as a straight line, a circle or chemical substances *absolutely* pure, can never be found in the tangible reality [...] even though there are no chemical substances that are *absolutely* pure, nonetheless the laws of chemistry hold with great approximation for the substances that our means of analysis show us to be pure.
>
> PARETO [1916] 1988, vol. I, pp. 121–122

This quotation shows us that Pareto is making a very important epistemological distinction, that is to say the one concerning the difference between reality and model, a difference between the ontological level and the epistemic one.

Pareto applies this distinction also to economics, especially when he exposes the passage from pure economy to applied economy: "from rational mechanics we arrive at applied mechanics by adding some considerations to concrete phenomena, and analogously we arrive at applied economy from pure economy. For instance, rational mechanics gives us an ideal lever, while applied mechanics teaches us to construct concrete levers; pure economy lets us know the function of a coin, while applied economy let us know the existing monetary systems" (Pareto [1916] 1988, vol. I, p. 1924). As we can see, Pareto used to conceptualize social phenomena through a modeling approach taken from the natural sciences: "We do not know, and we will never know, a concrete phenomenon with all its particular features; we can only know ideal phenomena that approximate more and more to the concrete phenomenon" (Pareto ([1897] 1942, p. 24) even the well-known Paretian difference between logical and non-logical actions (see: Boudon 2013) is based on an idealizational approach to science. If we compare Pareto's methodological ideas with the Nowakian idealizational approach we can notice an almost perfect convergence.

Let us now compare Pareto's theory of the élites-circulation with the Nowakian analysis of cyclical revolutions. The starting point for an analysis of Paretian theory of the élite finds its roots in the already mentioned distinction between logical and non-logical actions. Pareto uses this distinction in order to explain the use, by the individuals, of values and ideologies (called *derivations*), which in turn produce determined mental states and instincts (called *residuals*). The explanation of this distinction is very simple: by logical actions Pareto means "actions that link, in a logical way, the actions to the purpose" (Pareto [1916] 1988, vol. I, p. 147), while the non-logical ones do not have this logical nexus. If the logical actions are the result of reasoning, the non-logical ones find their root rather in determined psychic states, just like feelings. In this case, the most original aspect of Pareto's reflection consists of upholding the primacy of the non-logical actions, so in the light of this perspective the idea of man conceived as a rational animal loses its validity (in effect, Pareto considered man as an *ideological animal*). According to Paretian terminology, ideologies correspond to derivations and their function consists in providing a logical mask to feelings and to non-logical actions. Pareto reduces these residuals to six classes and the most important of them are the following: the instinct of combination (which promotes innovation, change) and the persistance of the aggregates (conservative and stable). These residuals, according to Pareto, are not equally spread or equally powerful along the various strata of the same society (Pareto [1916] 1988, vol. I, p. 1629), so inside the social fabric there will be individuals who are depositaries of these residuals, that is to say the components of an élite, which own "the most elevated indexes in their sector of activity"; in turn, Pareto divides them in two classes: "those who, directly or indirectly, play a remarkable part in the government will constitute the *elected government class*", while "the remaining ones will be the non-government elected class" (Pareto [1916] 1988, vol. I, pp. 1944–1945).[7] As we can see, Paretian approach is psychological and individualistic, because the main goal of the Italian sociologist is to highlight the individual nature of ideology (which, in his view, is absolutely constant), while the Marxian one emphasizes its social nature. According to Norberto Bobbio, their different way of explaining the nature of ideology is at the base of their different approaches to the critique of ideology; in fact, for Bobbio, Marx "carries out a *political* critique of ideologies, Pareto aims mainly to a *scientific* critique" (Bobbio 2001, pp 103–104). What Pareto refuses to accept in Karl Marx's historical materialism is the deterministic interdepence between economic phenomena and social factors:

> *Historical Materialism* was a remarkable scientific progress, because it sheds light on the contingent aspect of some phenomena [...]. Furthemore, it is undoubtedly partially true because there is an interdependence between the economic phenomenon and social phenomena: the mistake consists in having turned this inderdependence into a cause-effect relation."
>
> PARETO [1916] 1988, vol. I, p. 830

For Pareto, the materialistic conception of history on the one hand "approximizes us to reality and it possesses all the features of a scientific theory" (Pareto [1902] 1987, p. 739), but on the other he criticizes its deterministic value, as well as the concept of class struggle. In fact, according to Pareto, the subject that has power is always a ruling élite and not a class of great dimension such as the proletariat; for that reason, behind a mass movement such as Socialism, there is always the phenomenon of the élite-circulation (which in Pareto's view is a characteristic trait of the political phenomenon). We can sum-up the Paretian critique of democracy by highlightning the demagogical aspect of democracy. In this case, an aristocracy or élite passes off its own particular claims as if they were of general interest, in order to replace the old élite: "A new aristocracy wants to replace the old one, it fights in the name of the greatest number of the population. An aristocracy that is gradually arising, has often the mask of democracy" (Pareto [1906] 1994, p. 414). While Immanuel Kant wrote "so act that

---

7 For the sake of truth we must highlight the almost perfect convergence between Pareto's concept of residuals and that of Gustav Le Bon, who coined for the first time the term "residual" with the same semantic value of the Paretian one. See Le Bon (1895).

you treat humanity, whether in your own person or in the person of any other, always as the same time as an end, never merely as a means" (Kant [1797] 1996, p. 429), Pareto instead overturns the famous Kantian categorical imperative, because the masses, for élites, "are a means and not an end" (Pareto [1902] 1987, p. 159). In this case, the main subject of history is not a class (as in the Marxian view), but the élite; nonetheless, élites or aristocracies, analogously to natural phenomena, are subjected to generation and corruption, so in this sense "aristocracies do not last. [...] History is a cemetery of aristocracies" (Pareto [1916] 1988, vol. III, p. 1954). In order to explain how the aristocracies retain power, Pareto resorts to Machiavelli's images of the fox and the lion, which represents, respectively, the consensus and the strength. All those élites which are good at keeping in balance these two qualities or virtues, will also mantain their status of elected class but, according to the Paretian theory of the élite-circulation, at some point an élite will not be able anymore to manage in a cautious way both consensus and strength, which are used in a perfect balance by the new emerging élite. However, for Pareto social equilibrium rarely occurs, because there is an imbalance between the residuals that previously favoured the rise of the old élite. In this way, the élite-circulation occurs and Pareto reduces it to three main stages: by evolution, by degrees and by revolution.

Let us now compare now Pareto's élite-circulation theory with Nowak's theory of cyclical revolutions, which are respectively characterised by some affinities and divergences. In fact, as we have already seen, for Nowak a victorious revolution represents the greater danger for society, while for Pareto the élite that replaces the old one gives birth to a new positive and healthy phase for the social fabric. Nowak and Pareto look at ideology in the same way, that is to say as a means for getting the consensus of the masses and for replacing the old élite; even though for Nowak this function finds its higher expression during the civil loop. The Polish philosopher, nonetheless, outlines some differences between his theory and the Paretian one, such as the one concerning the main historical subject. In this case, Nowak agrees with Marx, according to whom the main historical subject is a class, while according to Pareto it is the élite. Between civil classes and the élites there are some remarkable differences; in fact, Nowak says that if an élite is composed of those individuals who excel in their activity it means that "the number of elites is practically unlimited in society, whereas there are only three single dominating classes (rulers, owners, priests) plus their combination" (Nowak 1991, p. 207). The second difference concerns the role, crucial or not, played by the residuals in the phenomenon of the élite-circulation, which Nowak considers to be quite irrelevant in the case of the civil loop:

The rotation of the elites consists in the fact that the possessors of new residuals acquire the highest positions and the previous possessors are eliminated. In contrast, a civil loop consists in a change of those who dispose over the means of coercion, and whether or not the new masters are possessors of new residuals is hardly decisive. [...] It turns out that there occurs a consciousness analogue of civil loop (the ideological loop). But a civil loop is possibile under the name of consciousness ("residuals") of the new and the old class of rulers ("elites").

NOWAK 1991, p. 207

6 Conclusion

Between Nowak's social theory and the Paretian élite-theory we discovered some interesting affinities, concerning first of all the same methodological approach, namely an idealizational conception of science extended also to the sphere of social phenomena. Both criticized the overly deterministic value of the Marxian conception of history and the economic sphere conceived as the base of social changes. But, as we have seen, the way they explained social progress shows the great distance between these two social theories.

To sum up, Nowak, coherently with his generalization of historical materialism, believed that what is fundamental is not the élite that possesses the new residuals, but rather the passage of the means of coercion from an élite to another in the case of the civil loop. In fact, Nowak writes that "Pareto mantained that we cannot determine in a general manner the conditions under which an exchange of elites occurs. As for a civil loop, it is possible to do so, albeit in highly idealized models" (Nowak 1991, p. 207). To be honest, Nowak's reasoning is not totally correct, because according to Pareto this is possible, and precisely when we are able to determine the composition of the élite, as well as residuals and derivations. Another difference concerns the élite-circulation:

"[...] it is perhaps worth of stressing a difference of an "ideological" nature. For Pareto the exchange of elites is healthy and necessary for social development. In non-Marxian historical materialism, a class loop is the main threat to society. For the most class-ridden societies, socialist societies, actually come into existence through class loops.

NOWAK 1991, p. 207

So, while Pareto considers the élite-circulation as something healthy for society, Nowak, in direct contrast, considers it as fatal, just because the victorious revolutions gave birth to totalitarian pheomena such as Russian socialism.

References

Barach, P. (1967). *The Theory of Democratic Elistism*. Bosto-Toronto: Little Brown and C.

Bettin Lattes, G. (2011). Autorità. In G. Bettin Lattes-L. Raffini (eds.), *Manuale di sociologia*, vol. I. Lavis (Tn): Cedam.

Bobbio, N. (2001). L'ideologia in Pareto e in Marx. In: *Saggi sulla scienza politica in Italia*. Rome-Bari: Laterza.

Borbone, G. (2012). *From Cosmopolitism to National-Popular Culture. Gramscian Attempt at Overcoming Provincialism*. In: Brzechczyn, K. and Paprzycka, K. (eds.), *Thinking about Provincialism in Thinking* (*Poznań Studies in the Philosophy of the Sciences and the Humanities,* vol. 100). pp. 87–102. Leiden-Boston: Rodopi-Brill,.

Borbone, G. (2016). *Questioni di metodo. Leszek Nowak e la scienza come idealizzazione*. Acireale-Rome: Bonanno.

Borbone, G. and K. Brzechczyn (2016) (eds.). *Idealization XIV: Models in Science. Poznań Studies in the Philosophy of the Sciences and the Humanities,* vol. 108. Leiden-Boston: Rodopi-Brill.

Boudon, R. (2013). Les actions «logique» et «non-logique» selon Pareto. *Revue européenne des sciences sociales*, 51 (2), 19–46.

Brzechczyn, K. (1993). Civil Loop and the Absorption of Elites. In: L. Nowak-M. Paprzycki (eds.), *Social System, Rationality and Revolution. Poznań Studies in the Philosophy of the Sciences and the Humanities*, vol. 33, pp. 399–403. Amsterdam-Atlanta: Rodopi.

Brzechczyn, K. (2007). *On the Application of Non-Marxian Historical Materialism to Development of Non-European Societies*. In: K. Łastowski, A. Klawiter et al. (eds.), *The Courage of Doing Philosophy. Essays Presented to Leszek Nowak,* pp. 235–254. Amsterdam-Atlanta: Rodopi.

Brzechczyn, K. (2008). Polish Discussion on the Nature of Communism and Mechanisms of its Collapse. *East European Politics and Societies*, 22 (4), 828–855.

Brzechczyn, K. (2017). From Interpretation to Refutation of Marxism. On Leszek Nowak's non-Marxian Historical Materialism. *Hybris*, 37, 159–160.

Buczkowski, P., A. Klawiter, and L. Nowak (1982). Historical Materialism as a Theory of the Social Whole. In: L. Nowak (ed.), *Social Classes, Action and Historical Materialism. Poznań Studies in the Philosophy of the Sciences and the Humanities,* vol. 6, pp. 110–121. Amsterdam: Rodopi.

Busino, G. (2010). Pareto oggi. *Revue européenne des sciences sociales*, 48 (1), 113–127.

Coniglione, F. (2010). *Realtà e astrazione. Scuola polacca ed epistemologia post-positivista*. Acireale-Rome: Bonanno.

Engels, F. ([1846] 1982). Letter to P. V. Annenkov, 11 December 1846. In: K. Marx-F. Engels, *Collected Works*, vol. 38. London: Lawrence & Wishart.

Engels, F. ([1895] 2004). Letter to W. Sombart, 11 March 1895. In: K. Marx-F. Engels, *Collected Works*, vol. 50. London: Lawrence & Wishart.

Gramsci, A. (2001). *Quaderni del carcere*, edited by V. Gerratana, 4 voll. Turin: Einaudi.

Guala, F. (1998). Pareto on Idealization and the Method of Analysis-Syntesis. *Social Science Information*, 37, 23–44.

Kant, I. ([1797] 1996). Groundwork of the Metaphysics of Morals. In: *Practical Philosophy*, translated by Mary Gregor. Cambridge: Cambridge Univ. Press.

Keller, S. (1963). *Beyond the Ruling Class. Strategic Élites in Modern Society*. New York: Random House.

Le Bon, G. (1895). *Psychologie des Foules*. Paris: Réédition.

Marx, K. ([1859] 1987). Preface of A Contribution to the Critique of Political Economy (1859). In: K. Marx-F. Engels, *Collected Works*, vol. 29. London: Lawrence & Wishart.

Michels, R. (1911). *Zur Soziologie des Parteiwesens in der modernen Demokratie. Untersuchungen über die oligarchischen Tendenzen des Gruppenlebens*. Leipzig: Dr. Werner Klinkhardt.

Mosca, G. ([1884] 1982). Sulla teorica dei governi e sul governo parlamentare. In: *Scritti politici*, vol. I, edited by G. Sola. Turin: UTET.

Menke, R. (2022). Iron Law of Oligarchy versus Rule of Political Competition. An Attempt at Comparison between Robert Michels' and Leszek Nowak's Approaches to Power. In K. Brzechczyn (ed.) *Non-Marxian Historical Materialism: Reconstructions and Comparisons. Poznań Studies in the Philosophy of the Sciences and the Humanities,* vol. 120, pp. 238–257. Leiden/Boston: Brill.

Nowak, L. (1979). Historical Momentums and Historical Epochs. An Attempt at a Non-Marxian Historical Materialism. *Analyse und Kritik*, vol. 1, pp. 60–76.

Nowak, L. (1980). *The Structure of Idealization*. Dordrecht: Reidel.

Nowak, L. (1983). *Property and Power. Towards a Non-Marxian Historical Materialism*. Dordrecht-Boston-Lancaster: Reidel.

Nowak, L. (1991). *Power and Civil Society: Towards a Dynamic Theory of Real Socialism*. New York: Greenwood Press.

Nowak, L. (1994). Political Theory and Socialism. On the Main paradigms of Political Power and their Methodological and Historical Legitimation. In: M. Krygier (ed.), *Marxism and Communism: Posthumous Reflections on Politics, Society, and Law. Poznań Studies in the Philosophy of the Sciences and the Humanities,* vol. 36, pp. 77–97. Amsterdam-New York: Rodopi.

Nowak, L. (2009). Class and Individual in the Historical process. In: K. Brzechczyn (ed.), *Idealization XIII: Modeling in History. Poznań Studies in the Philosophy of the Sciences and the Humanities,* vol. 97, pp. 63–84. Amsterdam-New York: Rodopi.

Pareto, V. ([1897] 1942). *Corso di economia politica,* 2 vol. Turin: Einaudi.

Pareto, V. ([1902] 1987). *I sistemi socialisti,* edited by G. Busino. Turin: UTET, Torino.

Pareto, V. ([1906] 1994). *Manuale di economia politica,* edited by S. Lombardini. Pordenone: Edizioni Studio Tesi.

Pareto, V. ([1916] 1988). *Trattato di sociologia generale,* 4 voll., edited by G. Busino. Turin: UTET.

Parry, G. (1969). *Political Élites.* London: Allen & Unwin.

Popper, K. ([1945] 2013). *The Open Society and its Enemies.* Princeton: Princeton University Press.

Rutkowska, K. (2013). Elitarystyczna versus klasowa teoria demokracji. Próba parafrazy mechanizmu absorpcji elit w teorii Evy Etzioni-Halevy w aparaturze pojęciowej nie-Marksowskiego materializu historycznego [The Elitarian versus Class Theory of Democracy. An Attempt to Paraphrase the Mechanism of the Absorption of the Elites from Eva Etzioni-Halevy's Theory in the Conceptual Apparatus of *non-Marxian Historical Materialism*]. In: K. Brzechczyn, M. Ciesielski, E. Karczyńska (eds.), *Jednostka w układzie społecznym. Próba teoretycznej konceptualizacji,* pp. 253–272. Poznań: WN WNS UAM.

Rutkowska, K. (2022). The Elitarian versus Class Theory of Democracy. An Attempt to Paraphrase the Mechanism of the Absorption of the Elites from Eva Etzioni-Halevy's Theory in the Conceptual Apparatus of *Non-Marxian Historical Materialism.* In: K. Brzechczyn (ed.) *Non-Marxian Historical Materialism: Reconstructions and Comparisons. Poznań Studies in the Philosophy of the Sciences and the Humanities,* vol. 120, pp. 195–215. Leiden/Boston: Brill.

CHAPTER 11

The Iron Law of Oligarchy versus the Rule of Political Competition: An Attempt at a Comparison between Robert Michels' and Leszek Nowak's Approaches to Power

Regina Menke

Abstract

In *Political Parties. A Sociological Study of the Oligarchical Tendencies of Modern Democracy*, the German-born Italian sociologist Robert Michels (1962) provides an extensive yet non-systematic analysis of non-democratic tendencies in modern democracy. Describing the emergence and behavior of elites within political parties, the work was seen as an important contribution to the elite theory of democracy. Though derived from a different historical context, the theory has certain similarities to the theory of power that Leszek Nowak presents in *Power and Civil Society. Toward a Dynamic Theory of Real Socialism* (1991). This paper interprets Nowak's book as a work belonging to the elite theory paradigm, in the sense that it attempts to explain the constant tendency to domination of the class of rulers over a class of citizens. Making use of Nowak's typology of levels of power analysis (materialist, institutionalist and consciousness), the paper aims to systematize the resources in the hands of party elites that Michels describes as serving to secure power. The paper also states that Michels adds the perspective of an anthropological level of power to Nowak's theory.

Keywords:

democracy – civil society – elite theory – historical materialism – idealization – iron law of oligarchy – Leszek Nowak – political leadership – Robert Michels – theory of power

1   Introduction

1.1   *Milner versus Nowak: a Sketch of Intellectual Biographies*

This paper aims to discuss two approaches towards democratic theory that can be interpreted as the elite theory of democracy. Democratic theory is an established subfield of political theory that aims to examine, on the one hand, the definition and meaning of the concept of democracy, and its moral foundations, challenges, and overall desirability on the other hand. Democratic theories typically operate on multiple layers of orientation; mixing normative, empirical and descriptive approaches (see: Laurence 2017). In his article on democracy in the *Stanford Encyclopedia of Philosophy,* Tom Christiano mentions the problem of democratic citizenship that asks "whether ordinary citizens are up to the task of governing a large society," as a specific problem of the theory of democracy (Christiano 2006). Christiano introduces the elite theory of democracy as one of several theoretical fields that offer solutions to this problem. Elitist theorists of democracy argue "that high levels of citizen participation tend to produce bad legislation designed by demagogues to appeal to poorly informed and overly emotional citizens" (Chistiano 2006). The role of elites in this specific theory of democracy, which evolves from the assumption that ordinary citizens are rather incapable of taking responsibility for the maintenance of a democratic system becomes clearer in the definition of the sociologists Murray Milner. He describes the elite theory of democracy as arguing "that power is concentrated in a relatively small number of elites" (Milner 2015, p. 8) and seeing the emergence of elites as "a virtual inevitability in any large organization or complex society" (Milner 2015, p. 8).

The works that will be compared in this paper with regards to their view of oligarchizational processes are *Political Parties. A Sociological Study of the Oligarchical Tendencies of Modern Democracy* by Robert Michels (1962) and *Power and Civil Society* by Leszek Nowak (1991). *Political Parties* is regarded as an important work of elite theory from the first half of the 20th century (even though its relation to "classical" elite theory can be qualified, as I will try to explain in section *An Interpretation of* Political Parties *in Relation to Elite Theory*). The work can be read as expressing concerns about non-democratic tendencies in modern democracy. Michels' elaborations constantly return to one main argument: the realization of democracy requires a strong form of organization, but a strong form of organization requires a self-perpetuating leadership cadre. Such a leadership cadre is incompatible with true democracy. Thus, the realization of true democracy is impossible (see: Ansell 2001 and others).

The theoretical starting point for the German-Italian sociologist Robert Michels is a specific historical experience: He writes from the perspective of a member of the German Social Democratic Party in the first decade of the 20th century. The analysis he provides is motivated by a certain disillusionment with the reality of socialism he experienced there. Harald Bluhm and Skadi Krause, in their preface to a publication that was released on the occasion of the anniversary of the release of *Political Parties,* point out the uncertainty concerning the first publication of the book (Bluhm, Krause 2012). In the first edition, the year 1911 is noted, while according to Michels and others the book was published for the first time in 1910 (see: Bluhm / Krause 2012, pp. 1–8). According to Dirk Käsler's short biography (Käsler 1994) of Robert Michels, Michels joined the German Social Democratic Party (SPD) in 1903, and in 1907 he stopped his political activities in the party. Later he accepted Italian citizenship and started to sympathize with Italian patriotism and nationalism. In 1922, he joined Benito Mussolini's *Partito Nazionale Fascista.* However, most commentators avoid mentioning this twist in Michels' biography when interpreting *Political Parties.* Even though Michels presents the oligarchization of parties as a natural process, his book can be read as advocating the shaping of democracy within the determined frames. There are no phrases in *Political Parties* that would make it plausible to read and interpret the work as encouraging a turn away from democracy as such (see also Lipset 1962, p. 38).

In *Power and Civil Society* Leszek Nowak (1991) provides several models that aim to analyze dynamic elements of power. The work can be interpreted as a contribution to the elite theory of democracy since with its *Rule of Political Competition*, it attempts to explain the constant domination of a ruling class over a ruled class. According to Nowak's own statement in the preface, the work is an elaboration of lectures he gave in 1982 to fellow activists of the Solidarity movement in Kwidzyn Prison. In an interview (Nowak [1985] 2011, p. 592), Nowak points out that even though his reconstruction of Marxism had a strictly scientific character, he conducted it with a social intention: After the experience of March 1968 (which he presents as an emotional and personal experience, see also: Nowak 1988, pp. 36–37), Nowak started to deal with Marxism, convinced of the need for a nonconformist theory that would reveal the hidden mechanisms of Marxism. He aimed to create a theory that criticizes the political praxis of the system and its ideology but stays loyal to the Marxian message.

It can be stated that the theoretical starting point for both Michels and Nowak was the experience of disillusionment with the reality of socialism, in Michels' case with the structures in the Social Democratic Party in early 20th century Germany, in Nowak's case with socialism during the period of real socialism in Poland (1944–1989). *Political Parties* and *Power and Civil Society* can be related to each other as they both analyze the occurrence of spontaneous political divisions and the tendency of political leaders to maximize power for the sake of maximizing power. As I will point out in section *Remarks on Michels' and Nowak's Methodological Approaches*, in *Political Parties* Michels operates simultaneously on various methodological layers. Nowak on the other hand has a very clear methodological approach: He starts by creating a first, highly idealized model that only considers the most important factors of interest to him and then undertakes a process of concretization, creating subsequent models by omitting some of the idealizing assumptions. My attempt at a comparison of *Political Parties* and *Power and Civil Society* shall thus be preceded by an attempt at reconstructing certain aspects of Michels' theory, making use of Nowak's distinction between different levels of power as a tool for methodological systematization and reconstruction.

1.2   *An Interpretation of Political Parties in Relation to Elite Theory*

Even though *Political Parties* is commonly claimed as a work belonging to elite theory, this relation can be qualified, especially with regards to the elite theory developed by Max Weber and Joseph Schumpeter. In order to contextualize the following comparison, I want to present two possibilities of interpreting the relation between *Political Parties* and elite theory of democracy.

Firstly, one can see *Political Parties* as stating the impossibility of true democracy. A reading that interprets the *Iron Law of Oligarchy* as a summary of Michels' analysis (opposed to, for example, Harald Bluhm and Skadi Krause, who claim that such a reading ignores the complexity of the work, Bluhm, Krause 2012, pp. 9–19) would support this interpretation. Seymour Martin Lipset in his introduction to the English translation of *Political Parties*, puts Michels together with Pareto, Mosca and Sorel, in the context of the Machiavellian school of politics (Lipset 1961, p. 34). Whereas the elite theory of democracy as elaborated by Weber and Schumpeter stresses that "the distinctive and most valuable element of democracy is the formation of a political elite in the competitive struggle for the votes of a mainly passive electorate" (Lipset 1961, p. 33), Michels (according to Lipset) would be radicalizing the elite theory of democracy in the sense that it claims the impossibility of democracy "by *seeing any separation* between leaders and followers as *ipso facto* a negation of democracy" (Lipset 1961, p. 34).

Secondly, one can read *Political Parties* as a suggestion that there is a "need for a more realistic understanding of the democratic potential in a complex society" (Lipset 1961, p. 35), and as an encouragement to create more room to manoeuvre within the determined political processes and structures of a society. For example, in his *Final Considerations*, Michels writes:

> The writer does not wish to deny that every revolutionary working-class movement, and every movement sincerely inspired by the democratic spirit, may have a certain value as contributing to the enfeeblement of oligarchic tendencies.
>
> MICHELS 1962, p. 368

There is one paragraph in Nowak's *Power and Civil Society*, that (though not exactly phrased in technical language) expresses the possibility of more room to manoeuvre between the determined processes in a similar way:

> People are not capable of everything in history. It is history that happens, creating certain frameworks that cannot be crossed by individuals and even by entire classes. However, it is also not true that people can do nothing, because these frameworks may be formed according to realistic aspirations. People do not create history, nor are they subordinated to it. They can do neither everything nor nothing. They can do a lot: they can shape it.
>
> NOWAK 1991, p. 161

To such an interpretation one could add the claim that Michels wrote *Political Parties* with a certain pedagogical intention, as Timm Genett (2012) suggests. He claims (Genett 2012, p. 82) that the practical consequence of Michels' dismissal of an institutional solution of the democratic problem is that the quality of democracy depends on the democratic virtue of the citizens. Indeed, the following quote shows that there are passages in *Political Parties* that would support ascribing this pedagogical intention to Michels, for example the following:

> it is, consequently, the great task of social education to raise the intellectual level of the masses, so that they may be enabled, within the limits of what is possible, to counteract the oligarchical tendencies of the working-class movement.
>
> MICHELS 1962, p. 369

The attempt of thinking these rather contrary interpretations "together" evokes the question of a possibility of changing the rather "descriptive" elitist theory of democracy into a critical tool.

THE IRON LAW OF OLIGARCHY   243

1.3   *Remarks on Michels' and Nowak's Methodological Approaches*

Writing *Political Parties* from the perspective of a member of the Social Democratic Party, Michels frequently refers to processes and struggles within the party that did not produce any sources. The distinction between the formal and informal influence of leaders that I will introduce in section 3.2 *Institutional level* (informal influence designates the influence that a leader exerts that is not reflected in his institutional position) could serve as a possible way of understanding this phenomenon. Nevertheless, in my view, the accusations levelled by Gordon Hands, namely that Michels' analyses tend to provide "proof by anecdote" (Hands 1971, p. 157), and that he conceptualized certain tendencies and then found historical examples from various areas for them, can be justified in the sense that the historical examples Michels refers to show a wide spectrum in terms of the institutional frame, time and countries. Michels not only analyses dynamics within the German Social Democratic Party of the first half of the 20th century, but also the processes within labor unions and tendencies in Social Democratic movements in Italy, France, England, Denmark, and the United States. Such a wide range to empirical examples / proofs suggests a need for setting a specific focus in the attempt to reconstruct Michels' theory. For the comparison with Nowak's theory of power, I am therefore going to focus on Michels' analysis of processes within the German Socialist Party at the beginning of the 20th century and leave out other aspects that he presents in his book.

2   Presentation of the Iron Law of Oligarchy

2.1   *Materialist Level of Power*

2.1.1   The Relation between Michels' Analysis and the Marxist
               Materialist Conception of History

Lipset writes in the introduction to the English translation of *Political Parties* from 1962:

> Michel's view of power rests basically on the assumption that the behavior of all dominant minorities, whether in society at large or in organizations, must primarily be interpreted as following a logic of self-interest, of exploiting the masses to maintain or extend their own privilege and power. In this respect, Michels explicitly accepted the Marxist materialist conception of history.
>
> LIPSET 1962, p. 35

Michels does not explicate his understanding of classes and of the relation between political parties, but his analysis (and the fact that he still uses the terms "proletariat," see for instance Michels 1962, p. 365 and "bourgeoisie," see: p. 227) indicate towards an understanding that on the one hand is not entirely disconnected from the Marxian idea of a class division between owners and producers and that on the other hand sees political parties (and the German Social Democratic Party in particular) as class organizations whose primary aim consists in striving for the interests of the class members (in this case: the democratic / socialist interests of the proletariat). This striving collides with a tendency towards oligarchy "which is inherent in all party organization" (Michels 1962, p. 50). In other words: political parties, first established as class organizations, due to their inner dynamics then develop a striving for emancipating themselves from their class. Timm Genett (2012, p. 77) phrases a consequence of such an understanding of classes in society in the context of Michels' theory, when he emphasizes that oligarchization arises from democracy, on the basis and under the conditions of an egalitarian society.

2.1.2   Economic Property

In order to understand Michels' conceptualization of economic superiority, one needs to distinguish three instances within the party: the party (the organization as such) that has an interest in restraining the leaders, who have an interest in exercising power over the rank-and-file members; and finally the rank-and-file members, among them members that could potentially become leaders, for example those who stand as a candidate for a higher political position.

Based on these assumptions, one can outline three aspects of the economic superiority of the leaders according to Michels: Firstly, the practice of paying for the services rendered to the party by its employees (Michels 1962, p. 135) has two consequences: The party (the organizational apparatus) possesses an authority over the leaders that are paid for their work, the leaders subject themselves to the party will. The financial binding becomes stronger than the ideological binding of the leaders in the sense that the leaders "fulfill their duty" no longer for reasons of personal ideology, but for financial reasons. Furthermore, the leaders of the German Social Democratic Party are able to employ methods of oppression, "such as the threat to give no aid in men or money on behalf of the electoral propaganda of a candidate from whose views they dissent, although the local comrades give this candidate their full confidence" (Michels 1962, p. 148). Additionally, party leaders have the power to declare boycott of bars/ small shops that are frequented chiefly by members of the working class, and thereby causing their absolute ruin (Michels 1962,

THE IRON LAW OF OLIGARCHY   245

p. 148). Thirdly, sections of the party that are financially superior have an easier time with sending delegates to party congresses: "In Germany, therefore, the financial superiority of the rich comrade over the poor one is often replaced by the superiority of the rich branch" (Michels 1962, p. 141).

2.2   *Institutional Level*

In Nowak's typology, the institutional dimension refers to power that manifests in institutional hierarchies and ascribed positions as opposed to the primary, actual dimension of power. I would like to present two aspects of Michels' analysis in this category: Firstly, how in Michels' view the technical need for organization leads to hierarchical bureaucratic order; and secondly the phenomenon of parliamentarism. In the chapter *Mechanical and Technical Impossibility of Direct Government by the Masses*, Michels writes: "The most formidable argument against the sovereignty of the masses is, however, derived from the mechanical and technical impossibility of its realization" (Michels 1962, p. 65). Michels describes how the practical need for delegation (since a form of government where the masses would gather every time when they need to make a new decision is made impossible by problems associated with time, distance, and the means of communication, and then direct settlement of controversies) causes the formation of a hierarchical bureaucracy that becomes an ends in itself. The fact that leaders that have acquired an institutional position within this hierarchy are officially representing the will of the masses becomes a narrative, a farce: "To represent, in this sense, comes to mean that the purely individual desire masquerades and is accepted as the will of the mass" (Michels 1962, p. 77). In more specific terms, Michels points to the "essentially parliamentary character of the modern socialist parties" (Michels 1962, p. 153). The parliamentarian, according to Michels, escapes the supervision of the rank and file of the party and the control of its executive committee, the power of the parliamentarian is derived from the electoral masses, his dependence on the party is only indirect.

2.3   *The Level of Consciousness*

2.3.1   The Relation between Party and its Program

An important line of argumentation in Michels' explanation of the oligarchization of parties is a mechanism that can be called the mechanism of goal displacement: The original goals of the member party are exchanged for goals that ensure the survival and growth of the party and its power sphere. Organization shifts from being a means for the realization of democratic goals towards being an end itself, motivating the decisions of leaders that are against the interest of the membership and in favor of their own status and power; thus, this leads to decisions that consequently can be described as corrupt. Furthermore, Michels explains that once a party is established, the mechanism of goal displacement might even become effective on the level of new members since it is not necessary to agree with the program in order to join a party: "A party is neither a social unity nor an economic unity. It is based upon its program. In theory this program may be the expression of the interest of a particular class. In practice, however, anyone may join a party, whether his interests coincide or not with the principles enunciated in the party program" (Michels 1962, p. 351). The interests or practical tendencies of the leaders might be opposed to the actual party program: a proletarian movement may have capitalist leaders (Michels 1962, p. 352).

2.3.2 Media Control

Michels clearly asserts that it is the party leaders who have control over the press as a formal mean of communication: "Speaking broadly it may be said that it is the paid leaders who decide all the political questions which have to do with the press" (Michels 1962, p. 152). The press is an important means for the leaders to exert influence over the masses since the circle of the written word is more extensive than the reach of the spoken word. Additionally, the press can be used to cultivate a "sensation" and thereby ensure the sympathy of the masses for a leader and the leaders can use the press in order to make attacks upon their adversaries (Michels 1962, p. 149). The anonymity of political journalism, which Michels sees as prevailing (especially in Germany) has two consequences. On the one hand, the voice of a single journalist "appeals to the public with the entire force of this collective authority" (Michels 1962, p. 151), the crowd thus reads political journals as coming from the totality of the leaders, which minimizes the possibility for differentiated criticism. On the other hand, it is easier to attack adversaries violently and personally: such an attack has a strong effect since the rank and file regards it as coming from the totality of the leaders, the whole editorial staff feels responsible for what has been published and thus makes common cause with the aggressor. The person attacked is not aware of the aggressor's identity; and in the event he discovers this, journalistic etiquette forbids him to conduct a personal counter attack.

2.3.3 Education as a Condition of Leadership

By attaching great importance to something he calls the "cultural" or even "intellectual" superiority of leaders, Michels claims that education is an important condition of leadership. For Michels, the character traits of the leaders are self- reinforcing in the sense that "as they (the leaders, own remark) become initiated into the details of political life (...), the leaders gain an importance

THE IRON LAW OF OLIGARCHY   247

which renders them indispensable so long as their party continues to practice a parliamentary tactic" (Michels 1962, p. 109). He acknowledges the possibility that leaders of working-class origin, once they managed to acquire a post within the party mechanism, get familiar with the mode of life of the petty bourgeois (Michels 1962, p. 108). They are thus able to acquire technical knowledge of public life and thus to increase their superiority over the rank and file.

3   Leszek Nowak's Theory of Power

3.1   *Materialist Level*

The main goal of Nowak's *Power and Civil Society* is to outline the dynamic elements of power (in this way Nowak separates his theoretical aim from static analyses of power such as those provided by Weber, see: Nowak 1991, p. 49). His theoretical starting point is that of non-Marxian historical materialism, as an approach that criticizes Marxism for reducing "the regularities of political phenomena to the laws of motion of an economic system" (Nowak 1991, p. 49) and radicalizes it in the sense that it sees class division occurring not only in the economic sphere, but also in the sphere of spiritual production and politics (Nowak 1991, p. 4). However, in *Power and Civil Society*, the main subject of interest is the mechanisms of domination that occur in the political sphere (Nowak 1991, p. 25). In order to analyze these mechanisms, Nowak makes use of the method of idealization. He starts by creating a first, highly idealized model that only considers the most important factors of interest to him. For this model, Nowak lists six idealizing assumptions. He considers a society that is isolated, only divided into two political classes, with a constant level of technology, with rulers that apply the means of coercion directly; moreover, this society lacks political institutions and social- political consciousness (Nowak 1991, p. 49–50). Nowak then undertakes a process of concretization, creating subsequent models by removal of some of the idealizing assumptions.

Nowak sees the dynamics of power as determined by the rule of political competition. In his first model Nowak presents a materialist conception of power that refers to the actual disposal of the means of coercion. The class that possesses the means of coercion is thus the class of rulers of a given society. Nowak bases his assumptions about the dynamics in the relation between power and civil society on the so-called non-Christian model of man (see Nowak 1991, pp. 11–15). This model entails two basic human attitudes: enslavement (offering goodness in return for extreme evil; in the most basic sense, enslaving a citizen thus means "breaking" him; posing an extremely high level of threat to the citizen that eliminates his hostility towards his oppressor and instead produces a tendency of kindness towards the oppressor, see Nowak 1991, p. 11) and satanization (offering evil in return for extreme goodness). Nowak's basic assumption is an asymmetric ruler- subject relationship since the ruler, as being in the possession of the means of coercion, has the possibility to enslave citizens. On the macro-social level, the rulers sum up their spheres of influence and "constitute the range of regulation, which increases as a result of competition between rulers" (Nowak 1991, p. 26) Nowak hypothetically identifies the interest of the ruling class as maximizing the sphere of regulation (Nowak 1991, p. 27). This is reached through the reproduction of enslavement. The interest of the civil society, on the contrary, is to maximize the sphere of civil autonomy. Nowak sees the dynamics of the relation of the authority and the civil society as a phenomenon that depends on the social needs that arise at a certain stage. He assumes that as time passes in the stage of enslavement, social bonds between the members of civil society revitalize and revolutionary attitudes spread (Nowak 1991, p. 37). He thus distinguishes between different stages of the relation between power and civil society (revolutionary areas, solidary areas and the area of class peace, see: Nowak 1991, p. 35). A certain range of regulation is necessary to maintain social integration and prevent a stage of anomie. Class peace is thus the state of balance between power and civil society (in relation to Michels' theory, this stage is the most relevant, since Michels conducts his analysis within a democratic system and does not consider revolutionary situations). However, Nowak's main thesis is that after a certain amount of time this state of balance transforms into a totalized system since "the entire machine of power absorbs more and more of the civil society" (Nowak 1991, p. 39, see also: Banaszak 1997, pp. 384–385, in the terms of Tomasz Banaszak democracy thus transforms into an autocratic system; Banaszak 2022, p. 242). Power thus consists of subsequent circles of enslavement, which constitute the actual order. Therefore, in the course of competition, the participants of power are differentiated and create chains of enslavement, from which the structure of enslavement originates.

3.2 *Institutional Level*

In his second idealized model, Nowak removed the idealizing assumption that ignores the fact that society S is organized into certain political institutions. He describes the interest of the rulers to institutionalize the social structure that had been constituted by the natural processes described in the materialist model. By ascribing spheres of influences to positions, the rulers secure these spheres of influences. This process might lead to a reversion of the relation between influence and institution in the sense that the position is no longer securing actual influence, but rather offering influence itself (Nowak 1991,

THE IRON LAW OF OLIGARCHY

249

pp. 71–72). These observations leads Nowak to construct the *Pyramid of Political Rule*, which describes a certain institutional structure as opposed to the actual hierarchy of power. The institutionally attached sphere of influence is highest at the top and then weakens. The constituents of the *Pyramid of Political Rule* are: the supreme ruler, the elite of power and the apparatus of power. Servants of the subsequent ranks comprise the structure of institutional positions. Apart from the possibility of the existence of a "real" ruler whose range of influence is equal to his institutional position, Nowak mentions two ways in which the relation between the range of influence and the institutional position can manifest itself: The existence of a "figurehead," whose sphere of influence is empty; and the existence of a "power behind the throne," who, to some extent, takes over the rulers sphere of influence (Nowak 1991, pp. 72–73). Nowak's distinction between a pyramid that reflects the institutional hierarchies within political rule and an actual hierarchy of power suggests a distinction between the formal and informal influence of rulers: On the one hand, the formal position of a leader within the organizational structure collides with a certain range of influence, leaders are allowed and expected to make decisions that correspond with their formal position and their access to certain extent is determined by their formal position. On the other hand, the actual influence a leader is able to exert might not correspond to his institutional position: in the everyday political reality, not every decisions relates to an explicit institutional hierarchy. The influence a leader exerts beyond his institutional position can be called informal influence.

Tomasz Banaszak points out that Nowak's materialist-institutionalist Model II "is too poor to capture the internal diversity of civil society" (Banaszak 1997, p. 386; 2022, p. 245) and lacks a concept of a political party. For his analysis of Hannah Arendt's distinction between two- party and multi- party political systems, he introduces the concept of a political party into the language of non-Marxian historical materialism (he remarks that the assumption that civil society is organized in terms of political parties remains an idealizing assumption since it omits the non-political forms of civic mass organizations, see Banaszak 1997, p. 386). Since the main subject of Michels' analysis are the internal processes within political parties, his transfer is useful in the context of this paper since it enables a comparison between Nowak and Michels on the layer of party structures. Banaszak describes a given party sub- society as consisting of the sphere of party power and party members. He creates the notion of the party pyramid analogous to the notion of the *Pyramid of Political Rule*, consisting of the party leader (equivalent of the highest ruler in the state pyramid), the party elite (equivalent of the state elite), party apparatus (equivalent of the governing body) and party members (Banaszak 1997, p. 386). The concept of the sphere of regulation on the state level is translated into the sphere of party regulation.

In relation to party members, the party authority plays a dual role: On the one hand, it subdues party members, on the other hand, it stops the increase of the scope of regulation of state power and thus enlarges the area of civil autonomy with respect to the state (Banaszak 1997, p. 387). The position of a party in society thus depends on one hand on the degree to which the party is able to maximize the civil autonomy (respectively: the degree to which the party manages to limit the control of the state over citizens) and on the other hand on the strength in the sphere of party regulation. As long as the degree to which the party is able to maximize the civil autonomy is higher than the strength in the sphere of party regulation, the support for the party by the citizens increases. When the strength in the sphere of party regulation for the society decreases, the support for party authorities decreases (Banaszak 1997, pp. 387–388; 2022, p. 246). Based on this assumption, Banaszak presents an idealized dynamic model of the party/ member state relations (Banaszak 1997, p. 389; 2022, pp. 246–247). When a new party emerges, it has a support from citizens that is higher than zero, which also causes a tendency of the state power to make certain compromises at the beginning of party activity. Thus, at the beginning of party activity, the sphere of civil autonomy is growing faster than the sphere of party regulation (the compromises of the state power according to Banaszak are related to the fact that any area of state regulation violates the applicable law recognized by the state authority, thus an official organization threatening the revelation of these fact may result in the withdrawal of the democratic state from the outlawed regulation of citizens). At some point, the degree to which the party is able to maximize the civil autonomy is no longer growing, which together with the (natural) growth of the sphere of influence of the party regulation causes the decline of "a party's social status indicator" (Banaszak 1997, p. 388; 2022, p. 248) and thus the spreading of rebellious attitudes among the party members towards party power. The form of the party rebellion is simply to leave the party, which ultimately leads to the party's collapse as it transforms into a so- called "couch party."

3.3 The Level of Consciousness

The third model Nowak created in *Power and Civil Society* is a materialist-consciousness model. It is thus a model that tries to conceptualize the formation of socio-political collective consciousness (while, again, rejecting the institutional dimension of power), assuming that collective actions are determined by different regularities than individual actions since they relate to the material interest of a group. The fact that the interest of a group is class- dependent

THE IRON LAW OF OLIGARCHY   251

(the main interest of the rulers is to increase the sphere of regulation, the main interest of the citizens is to increase the sphere of autonomy) leads Nowak to define (from the perspective of non-Marxian historical materialism) the main variety of the collective consciousness as class consciousness (Nowak 1991, p. 94). The beliefs that class consciousness includes are functional in relation to the interest of the class, which after Nowak (taken from Hochfeld 1963, see: Nowak 1991, p. 94) means that these beliefs constitute an indispensable condition for the occurrence of a state of affairs remaining in the interest of this class, and thus, as long as this state of affairs belongs to the range of contradiction of interests of both classes, constitute an indispensable condition for the lack of this same state of affairs for the antagonistic class and is thus dysfunctional for this antagonistic class. In this context, Nowak distinguishes between ideology (as a form of social thinking that expresses the interest of the authority) and utopia (as a form of social thinking that expresses the interest of the civil masses). Ideology is a system of social-political beliefs that stresses only the solidary aspects of the system of power, the consciousness interest of the class of rulers is that the masses believe in the ideology of the authority (see Nowak 1991, p. 96). On the contrary, utopia sees social resistance as the only way of solving the conflict of the contradictions between the governing and the governed and thus ignores the role of social consensus. Additionally, it links the materialist explanation of the present time with an idealist program, only offering a guarantee of the good-will of the revolutionaries, but not a guarantee that program will be realized after the social system against which utopia turns ceases to exist (Nowak 1991, p. 97).

4 Attempt at a Comparison between Michels' and Nowak's Approaches to Power

4.1 *Material Level*

4.1.1 The Structure of Society

In order to contextualize a comparison between aspects of Michels' and Nowak's theory of power, I would like to point out a major difference in the way Michels and Nowak relate to a two- class society system. Whereas Nowak's dynamic models are based on the assumption that a society is eternally separated into a class of rulers and a class of the ruled, Michels' understanding of the relation between classes and political parties (as mentioned in sub-section 2.1.1 *The relation between Michels' analysis and the Marxist materialist conception of history*) suggests an understanding of classes that is more fluid: when emancipating themselves from the social basis, parties strive towards a shift from the proletarian class to the bourgeois class. Party oligarchization is thus a phenomenon that occurs between class and representatives of class.

4.1.2 Coherence and Incoherence between in the Interests and Actions of the Masses

A significant difference between Nowak's and Michels' interpretation of the possibilities of the masses lays in their interpretation of the relation between the interests of the masses and their actions. In his chapter on the nature of power, Nowak hypothetically identifies the interest of civil society as "maximizing the sphere of civil autonomy" (Nowak 1991, p. 27). This interest corresponds with actions that have an actual influence on the relation between the authority and civil society; in this sense, Nowak ascribes coherence to the interest of the civil society and its actions. In the introduction to *Political Parties*, Michels ascribes an interest to the masses that can be interpreted as similar to what Nowak called "maximizing the sphere of civil autonomy." He writes: "In theory the principal aim of socialist and democratic parties is the struggle against oligarchy in all its forms" (Michels 1962, p. 50). There is a difference between Nowak's and Michels' assessment of the significance of the masses′ interest: Nowak sees the interest of the masses as a constitutional factor that counteracts the interest of the authority. In contrast, Michels sees the masses′ interest of struggling against oligarchy as constantly counteracted by their psychological tendencies; their incompetence on the one hand and their tendency for veneration of the leaders on the other hand. The psychological tendencies of the masses are stronger than their interests and thus render it impossible for the masses to act according to their interest.

4.2 The Institutional Level

Whereas for Nowak, the dynamics of power seem to be determined by the *Rule of Political Competition* as a principle in itself, for the explanation of Michels' *Iron Law of Oligarchy,* the dynamics set off by organization are crucial. Since Michels sees no possibility for the realization of direct government by the masses (Michels 1962, pp. 63–77), organization is a phenomenon that necessarily evokes with the realization of democracy. Organization (in Michels' analysis not always sharply separated from the phenomenon of bureaucracy) enables the rise of power and eventually corruption.

4.3 The Level of Consciousness
4.3.1 Processes of Mythologization

The relation between the interest of the masses and their actions, as explained in sub-section 4.1.2 (*Coherence and incoherence between in the interests and*

THE IRON LAW OF OLIGARCHY   253

actions of the masses) on the consciousness dimension of power at the level
of consciousness is reflected in the different processes of mythologization that
the masses have to face. What Michels describes could be phrased as "mythologization from beyond." Besides ascribing a "universal" incompetence (Michels
1962, p. 111), a lack of ability for self- organization and "a general sentiment of
indifference towards the management of its own affairs" to the masses (Michels
1962, p. 105); Michels describes a cult of veneration among the masses, a "commonly latent adoration of the led" (Michels 1962, p. 93), a reverence for individual leaders which for instance manifests in "the tone of veneration in which
the idol's name is pronounced" (Michels 1962, p. 93). Thus, there is no need for
the ideology to be imposed by the leaders on the masses. Ideology is evoked
within the masses, as a consequence of a phenomenon of mass psychology.
The adoration of the leaders interacts with their power insofar as it increases
their self-esteem of the leaders, which reflects back on the masses and even
enhances their admiration.

In contrast, Nowak initially sees the collective consciousness of a class
as functional in relation to the interest of the class, which has two consequences: On the one hand, the consciousness of the civil society is called
"utopia" and not "ideology." Utopia emphasizes the need of social resistance
and ignores the role of social consensus (Nowak 1991, p. 97). Thus, the problem with utopia is exactly the opposite problem of Michels' problem with the
ideology that is evoked within the masses: Whereas Michels does not ascribe
any attempt at social resistance to the masses, for Nowak, the masses are in the
epistemological situation of knowing "the truth about the opponent and fal-
sity about themselves" (Nowak 1991, p. 104). On the other hand, it is the interest
of the leaders, in terms of consciousness, "that the masses believe in the ideology of the authority" (Nowak 1991, p. 96); the leaders want to preoccupy "the
masses with ideas that will prevent them from recognizing the antagonistic
aspects of the existing system" (Nowak 1991, p. 96). The process of mythologization is thus initiated within the authority, "from above," and not (as for
Michels) within the masses, meaning "from beyond."

4.3.2   The Mechanism of Goal Displacement
Whereas for Nowak, pragmatical and ideological circumstances are coherent,
in the sense that actual power relations are determined by the distribution of
the means of coercion, for Michels, the impossibility of direct government by
the masses and the indispensability of a representational system causes a shift
in power relations that in the first instance is pragmatical: Since a direct government of the masses is impossible for mechanical reasons, for example due
to a lack of means of communication and difficulties with the coordination

regarding space and time (Michels 1962, p. 65), representational positions are established for the pragmatic reason of making a government of the masses possible. This pragmatical shift is interlinked with an ideological shift. Michels does not believe in the possibility of representing the complexity of a heterogeneous mass and on the other hand thinks that representation under this condition means that "the purely individual desire masquerades and is accepted as the will of the mass" (Michels 1962, p. 77). The latter aspect points towards the mechanism of goal displacement that was already mentioned in sub-section 2.3.1 (*The relation between party and its program*), once the leaders gained power, their former goals of making a contribution to the party transform into goals of maintaining and growth of power spheres. The mechanism of goal displacement has two factors: On the one hand the "psychical transformations" (Michels 1962, p. 365) the leaders undergo in the context of their political career (shifting from a sincere – and in the positive sense – ideological interest in influencing to the mere wish for gaining, maintaining and increasing power); on the other hand the principle of organization as such: the "technical necessities" (Michels 1962, p. 365) of democratic government necessarily cause a redistribution of power relations, of a "dominion of the elected over the electors" (Michels 1962, p. 365).

5   The Process of Oligarchization

The last step of the comparison aims to point out certain differences between Michels' and Banaszak's/Nowak's general vision of oligarchization. For Banaszak, the process of the oligarchization of a party begins after the party has gained power. Banaszak situates the role of the political party between the relation between civil autonomy and state power and the relation between civil autonomy and party power (Banaszak, 1997, pp. 387–388). On the one hand, the party strengthens the position of the citizens towards the state apparatus and provides them with a sense of unity; on the other hand, the party power strives to maximize its own scope of regulation over the party members. As the party members are confronted with party authorities that partly represent their interests (the increase of civil autonomy with respect to the state power) and partly act against their interests in the increase of civil autonomy by increasing the scope of party regulation, the party members for a long time are obedient towards the party authority since it strengthens their position towards the state apparatus. Only later, when the party is no longer able to provide the increase of civic autonomy, and when it increases its own scope of regulation beyond the patience threshold of the party members, the party

THE IRON LAW OF OLIGARCHY   255

members show resistance towards the party authorities. The form of showing resistance is simply to leave the party, and thereby transforming it into a
couch party.

In contrast to Banaszak, Michels situates the process of oligarchization
in the context when the party already is in power. Regarding Michels' analysis, it is possible to distinguish between primary and secondary factors of
oligarchization. The fundamental factor that determines oligarchization is
the technical indispensability of leadership, thus the assumption that the
realization of direct government by the masses is impossible, for technical
reasons. Representation is required, and representation equals leadership.
Oligarchization within democracy is thus "the outcome of organic necessity,
and consequently affects every organization" (Michels 1962, p. 366); an effective counter-tendency is inherent in democracy itself.

The secondary factors of oligarchization are of an anthropological nature.
Michels often refers to these factors as "psychological," but in the frame of this
comparison, it can be claimed that these factors are based on anthropological
assumptions that not only encompass people's consciousness or mental level,
but also treat these dimensions as belonging together with their physical abil-
ities. These factors are on the one hand the tendencies of the leaders to organize themselves, to strive for power and to consolidate their interest; and on
the other hand the passivity of the masses and their perennial incompetence.

As was mentioned in sub-section 3.1 (*Materialist level*) Michels' analysis of oligarchizational processes can be situated within Nowak's cyclical
model of stages of the relation between power and civil society (Nowak 1991,
p. 31): Michels analyzes the stage that in Nowak's model is called "area of class
peace." Nowak draws the development in this stage as a linear, thus at first
civil alienation is low, and consequently so is civil rebellion; then, the circle
of enslavement gradually grows and causes an increase in rebellious attitudes that ultimately results in a revolutionary area (Nowak 1991, pp. 31–32).
Interestingly, Michels' vision of oligarchizational processes in this stage is not
linear, but cyclical in itself. On the level of individual leaders, he summarizes
the phenomenon as an amalgamation of elites: new aspirants to power within
a party do not completely defeat old elites, which leads to "a *reunion des élites*,
an amalgam [...] of the two elements" (Michels 1962, p. 182). The process is
cyclical in the sense that the attacks by new aspirants towards the established
power elite are constantly renewed, but always, these new aspirants always
"end by fusing with the old dominant class" (Michels 1962, p. 371).

This ever-renewed process of amalgamation is reflected in a cyclical development of democracy itself. Michels concludes *Political Parties* by stating:

256 MENKE

> The democratic currents of history resemble successive waves. They break ever on the same shoal. (...) When democracies have gained a certain stage of development, they undergo a gradual transformation, adopting the aristocratic spirit, and in many cases also the aristocratic forms, against which at the outset they struggled so fiercely.
>
> MICHELS 1962, p. 371

Michels does not think it will ever be possible to break this cyclical mechanism.

References

Ansell, Ch. (2001). Oligarchy (Iron Law). In: *International Encyclopedia of the Social & Behavioral Sciences*. 2001, pp. 10853–10855. Retrieved February 6, 2018, from https://www.sciencedirect.com/science/article/pii/B0080430767011827.

Banaszak, T. (1997). Problem autokratyzacji ustroju demokratycznego. In: L. Nowak, P. Przybysz (eds.) *Marksizm, liberalism, próby wyjścia*, pp. 381–398. Poznań: Zysk i S-ka.

Banaszak, T. (2022). How Democracy Evolves into Autocracy. In: K. Brzechczyn (ed.). *New Developments in Theory of Historical Process. Polish Contributions to Non-Marxian Historical Materialism,* vol. 119, pp. 239–255. Boston/Leiden: Brill.

Bluhm, H., S. Krause (2012). Einleitung. Robert Michels' Soziologie des Parteiwesens. Oligarchien und Eliten – die Kehrseiten moderner Demokratie. In: H. Bluhm, S. Krause (eds.) *Robert Michels´ Soziologie des Parteiwesens. Oligarchien und Eliten – die Kehrseiten moderner Demokratie,* pp. 9–19. Wiesbaden: Springer VS.

Christiano, T. (2006). Democracy. In: *Stanford Encyclopedia of Democracy*, Retrieved July 7, 2018, from: https://plato.stanford.edu/entries/democracy/.

Genett, T. (2012). Demokratische Sozialpädagogik in der Krise der Aufklärung- zur Ambivalenz eines Klassikers der Elitentheorie. In: H. Bluhm, S. Krause (eds.) *Robert Michels' Soziologie des Parteiwesens. Oligarchien und Eliten – die Kehrseiten moderner Demokratie,* pp. 69–85. Wiesbaden.

Hands, G. (1971). Roberto Michels and the Study of Political Parties. *British Journal of Political Science,* 1 (2), 155–172.

Käsler, D. (2018). Michels, Robert. In: *Neue Deutsche Biographie 17* (1994), Online Version Retrieved May 18, 2018, from: https://www.deutschebiographie.de/pnd118733737.html#ndbcontent, 451–452.

Laurence, M. (2017). Democratic Theory. In: *Oxford Bibliographies* 2017, Retrieved July 7, 2018, from: http://www.oxfordbibliographies.com/view/document/obo-9780199756223/obo-9780199756223-0162.xml.

Lipset, S. M. (1962). Introduction. In: R. Michels, *Political Parties. A Sociological Study of the Oligarchical Tendencies of Modern Democracy,* transl. by Eden and Cedar Paul, pp. 15–39. New York: The Free Press.

Michels, Robert (1962). *Political Parties. A Sociological Study of the Oligarchical Tendencies of Modern Democracy.* transl. by Eden and Cedar Paul. New York: The Free Press.

Milner, M. Jr. (2015). *Elites. A General Model.* Cambridge/ Malden: Polity Press.

Nowak, L. ([1985] 2011). Od rewolucyjnej do reformistycznej teorii socjalizmu. In: L. Nowak, *Polska droga od socjalizmu. Pisma polityczne j 1980–1989,* ed. by K. Brzechczyn, pp. 590–604. Poznań: IPN.

Nowak, L. (1988). Czym był dla mnie marzec? *Czas. Pismo Społeczno-Polityczne,* 1, 37–38.

Nowak, L. (1991). *Power and Civil Society. Toward a Dynamic Theory of Real Socialism,* translated by Krzysztof Sawala. New York: Greenwood Press.

CHAPTER 12

The Social Role of the Ceremonial: Andrzej Falkiewicz's Conception of Culture and the Theory of the Spiritual Momentum in Non-Marxian Historical Materialism

Iwo Greczko

Abstract

The author of this article compares Andrzej Falkiewicz's theory of culture as a homeostatic-azimuthing system, combined with the concept of an individual horizon and valuation, with Nowak's theory of spiritual momentum (spiritual production) in non-Marxian historical materialism. Falkiewicz's theory was created in response to Nowak's model, and it contains a critical part aimed at solving the problems which Falkiewicz believes were not been solved in Nowak's model. After a summary presentation of the theory of spiritual momentum in Nowak's non-Marxian historical materialism and of Andrzej Klawiter's, Piotr Buczkowki's and Krzysztof Niedźwiadek's developments of that theory, as well as of Falkiewicz's theory of culture, the author of this article indicates that the nature of spiritual production in the latter concept, unlike in the former, is solidaristic and not antagonistic. Both approaches, though, emphasize the *stricte* material nature of spiritual production. In the summary, further possible directions of research are indicated, including the possibility of trying to synthesize the discussed approaches.

Keywords:

Ceremonial – spiritual momentum – spiritual production – homeostatic-azimuthing system – solidarism – antagonism

1 Introduction

The aim of this article is to present Andrzej Falkiewicz's[1] conception of culture and to compare it with the theory of spiritual momentum in non-Marxian historical materialism (n-Mhm). The subject matter of the comparison was chosen because of the over twenty-year-old exchange of thought between Leszek Nowak and Andrzej Falkiewicz who treated the theory of n-Mhm as a starting point for formulating his own proposals in social philosophy. Falkiewicz postulated that spiritual production should be understood more broadly than in n-Mhm.[2]

The second section presents the theory of spiritual momentum in n-Mhm, developed primarily by Nowak (Nowak, *et al* 1987; Nowak 1988; 2022) but also by Piotr Buczkowski, Andrzej Klawiter (Buczkowski, Klawiter, Nowak 1987) and Krzysztof Niedźwiadek (1985; 1989). The third section summarize Falkiewicz's (1980; 1989ab; 1991) theory of culture which consists of the concepts of social ceremonial, social utopia, culture as a homeostatic-azimuthing system, individual horizon, and valuation. In the summary, we show the scope and nature of the differences between the two approaches are shown, with the use of four comparative criteria, which are also interpretive criteria: the subject matter of (collective) belief, the status of culture, the function of culture, and the way of understanding culture.

2 The Basic Assumptions of the Spiritual Momentum in Non-Marxian Historical Materialism

Non-Marxian historical materialism can be viewed as a kind of generalization of Marxian historical materialism.[3] Nowak assumes that class divisions emerge in three domain of social life: politics, economy, and culture – and not only

---

1 Andrzej Falkiewicz (1929–2010) – literary critic, writer, and philosopher. In 1993–1995 he was a senior assistant in the Institute of Philosophy of Adam Mickiewicz University in Poznań.

2 Some of those concepts where created in the course of a discussion with Nowak and some independently of it. In this article, I quote *Teatr Społeczeństwo* (The Society Theater) written before the beginning of the argument which resulted directly in the publication of the book entitled *Jeden i liczba mnoga: o materializmie historycznym i metafizyce unitarnej Leszka Nowaka* (One and the Plural Number: on Leszek Nowak's Historical Materialism and Unitarian Metaphysics) and of Falkiewicz's later essays.

3 Most important works in English; see: Nowak 1980; 1983; 1991c, on methodological approach of Leszek Nowak and Poznań School of Methodology, see: Coniglione 2010, pp. 165–184, on Nowak – Borbone 2016; 2021.

in the economy, as is assumed in classical Marxism. The conflict in politics is between the classes of rulers and citizens, in the economy – owners and direct producers, and in the spiritual momentum – priests and the faithful.

The internal structures of those three domains are analogous, that is, consisting of three levels: material, institutional, and consciousness. This means that, for example, the momentum of spiritual production also has an institutional level (in the form of organizational units, management offices, etc.) and a consciousness one. An important element of this level is an auto-ideology which masks and justifies spiritual domination of the priests and motivates the followers to carry out the tasks ascribed to them by the class of priests. This auto-ideology is not consciously chosen but becomes widespread by the trial and error mechanism. (Nowak 1991a, p. 169).

Apart from class conflict (between direct producers and the owners of the means of production, citizens and rulers, and followers and priests), there is also a supra-class rivalry. This occurs between the dominant classes, so it depends on their continued existence. For example, the class which has productive forces at its disposal and dominates the direct producers tries to enslave them politically, in addition to the economic domination. At the same time, the class of rulers is maximizing political control, which gives rise to a supra-class rivalry between the classes of oppressors (Nowak 1991a, p. 181).

The assumption regarding the separateness of class divisions leads to the concept of their accumulation. Power can be concentrated. Apart from the three-momentum type of society, with three of classes of oppressors, each having a different kind of the "material forces of the society," there are also two-momentum societies (economic-political, economic-hierocratic, and political-hierocratic) and one-momentum societies in which one class holds all the power and is simultaneously the rulers, the owners, and the priests. The two-momentum and one-momentum societies are not called class societies but supraclass societies because of double class divisions in them (one category of people decides with regard to the use of two or three types of material forces in the society). Importantly, there are also no-momentum societies, in which class divisions have been eliminated. In a no-momentum society, everyone has the same opportunities for using the means of production, coercion, and indoctrination. In such a society, there are no classes and no inequalities with regard to access to its productive forces. In such an order, exploitation as well as political and spiritual rule are abolished (Nowak 1991a, pp. 178–180).

It is worth adding that the course and effect of a supraclass conflict depend on the form of government and on the stage of the evolution of that conflict. Krzysztof Brzechczyn distinguishes eighteen types of societies, each of which initiates a separate line of development (Brzechczyn 2004, p. 76; 2007).

THE SOCIAL ROLE OF THE CEREMONIAL   261

Although each of those societies evolves differently, not all of the class rule
configuration types fulfill the criterion of stability, and not all of them are durable enough to constitute a separate development line. In a stable system, the
structure of class rule is preserved in time; one of the conditions for that is
the preservation of the population balance (Brzechczyn 2004, pp. 79–81). For
example, if procreation is prohibited, genocide is prevalent, or ecological balance is lost, the given line of development can be closed because the systemic
causes will bring the existing model of power down, internally, as it were. In
other words, some social systems are a 'blind alley' of the evolution of the configuration types of class rule.

3   The Specificity of the Spiritual (Cultural) Momentum in Non-
         Marxian Historical Materialism

Let us take a closer look at the cultural momentum. In the spiritual sphere,
just like in any other historical-material momentum, we can distinguish three
levels: material, institutional, and consciousness. Let us now compare them.
The first one, material, is the means of spiritual production. The class division
into priests and followers is made on that level – it consists in the inequality of access to the means of indoctrination. That inequality leads to spiritual
oppression, that is, to an attempt at controlling the followers so that whenever
they face a problem in life, they turn to the greatest possible number of ideas
imposed by the priests. The oppressed (the followers), though, inevitably resist
the oppression. In that approach, the people who have at their disposal the
means of cultural transmission (that is, the means of spiritual production) also
have the power to "shape the minds," to censor and impose ideas, so the sender
of a message is the doctrinaire, and the follower is the indoctrinated. The institutional level always emerges as an adaptive measure. Productive forces – in
this case, those of spiritual production – determine production relations, which
means that the organizational systems which is preserved is the one which is
best adapted to the level of those productive forces, and that the way of the
organizing production that becomes prevalent is the one that guarantees the
highest possible "newly produced value," that is, the "living product" obtained
with the use of the tools of the given type (Buczkowski, Klawiter, Nowak 1987,
p. 271 and p. 274). In other words, that "value" is the indicator of the effectiveness of the use of the tools. Similarly, that ideology from a set of historically
existing ideologies becomes prevalent which is the most effective at legitimiz-
ing the functioning system of the organization of production. The nature of
the selection is also adaptive as well here. In short, such a social consciousness

(ideology) becomes prevalent to the extent that it guarantees effective functioning of the related material-institutional system. That actually applies to all three momentums. The method of production determines the way production is organized in a given historical period, and the organization of production, in turn, is reflected in the system of social consciousness.

The spiritual momentum has also similar internal structure. The class of priests satisfies the spiritual needs of the faithful because it has the material means of spiritual production, makes decisions about way of organizing spiritual production (churches, cultural organizations, censorship agencies, centers for supporting culture, etc.), and is motivated by an auto-ideology (which explains why that particular system of ideas is the only one that would satisfy the followers' need for meaning). Of the set of the existing systems of the organization of production, that one becomes prevalent which allows the greatest popularization of ideas which are in line with the priests' interest; and of the set of the historically existing systems of control of the tools of spiritual production, that one is chosen which allows the greatest increase of the number of faithful. As we have mentioned, the axiological level exists here as well; it justifies, at a metalevel, why the priests' doctrine is the best possible (for example, because it is scientific or because it will liberate humanity). Let us add that the terms priests and the faithful in this division – determined by unequal access to the means of spiritual production – are used in a more general sense than in everyday speech. A lay person who propagates, for example, a positivist-scientific world view can be a priest, and a transhumanist who believes that science can create meaning may be a follower.

In the spiritual momentum, priests strive to gain spiritual authority over the class of the faithful. Nowak writes that "the aim of a typical priest is to gain control over the greatest possible number of ideas used by people in their everyday lives" (Nowak 1991a, p. 171; 2022). Since the priests' interest is to "spiritually enslave" followers, they tend to expand their sphere of influence by breaking up individual faith relationships. The success of those endeavors depends on whether the priests' worldview satisfies the followers' spiritual needs. We can model[4] the dynamics of the conflict between the classes of oppressors and of the oppressed. The world view promoted by the priests is defined as a collection of myths (obtained with the use of procedures of mythologization, from the selected initial theses) which allow them to solve the followers' problems in life and to satisfy their "spiritual needs" (Nowak 1991a, p. 172). In their

---

4 A society in the spiritual momentum goes through the phases of the initial rejection, the absorption of alternatives, schisms, ecumenism, assimilation, and paganization.

THE SOCIAL ROLE OF THE CEREMONIAL

reflections on the structure of religious revolutions, Buczkowski, Klawiter, and Nowak also assume a mechanism – which is external with respect to their model – of the appearance of "prophets" who introduce new values to culture. According to those authors, that process cannot be modeled, so it must be assumed to be random (Buczkowski, Klawiter, Nowak 1987, p. 301, Nowak 2022). It follows that the concept is no longer deterministic.

In the spiritual momentum, worldviews play a different role than ideologies (on the, consciousness level in each of the three momentums). Their role is to invest the followers' lives with meaning and not to distort the actual relations between the owners and the direct producers or the subjects and the rulers.

Let us add that Nowak distinguished between an ideology and a utopia. The function of an ideology is, as has already been mentioned, to distort the actual class relations so that the "masses ... do not understand the very fact of the division of society by access to the means of coercion" (Nowak 1991b, p. 136). A utopia, on the other hand, expresses the interests of the enslaved. It emphasizes the contradictions between the interests of the rulers and the ruled, and it accentuates the role of social resistance. Interestingly, Nowak also admits the possibility of the existence of an ideological-utopian amalgam in a society, which would encompass contents expressing the interests of both the rulers and the subjects. Such a 'mixed' doctrinal system:

> rationalizes the attitude which the majority of citizens assume in the range of public order. The attitude is one of loyalty towards the authority, if it manages to maintain the sphere of regulation in the administration-minimum, and also one of readiness to restrict it, if the authority goes beyond this minimum.
>
> NOWAK 1991c, p. 101

4 Krzysztof Niedźwiadek's Development of the Theory of Spiritual Momentum

In Niedźwiadek's elaboration, just like in Nowak's theory, every historical-material momentum has a social consciousness which regulates the system of the organization of tool production and the system of the disposal of those tools. Niedźwiadek calls that consciousness an ideological consciousness system (Niedźwiadek 1985, p. 18, and 39; 1989, p. 175). In the spiritual momentum it is identical with the contents propagated by the class of priests. Ideas are created from the bottom-up, but the unequal access to the means of spiritual production prevents the propagation, in a society, of those ideas which contradict the priests' interest. However, the fact that both the followers and the priests can create ideas is a *novum* in relation to the previously discussed approach in which it is either assumed that ideas are only created by the priests or it is added that prophets may emerge randomly and contribute revolutionary values to the culture.

Niedźwiadek also introduces the function of a spiritual lessee ("leaseholders") who propagates the contents controlled by a priest but does not have access to the means of spiritual production and is subjected to the decisions of those who do have those means at their disposal. Such a lessee makes a living by "using the tools of spiritual production" (Niedźwiadek 1985, p. 34; 1989, p. 171). A spiritual lessee can be *a creator* or *a propagator*. Creators "carry out an introductory selection of ideas: they decide about what is going to be popularized (within the framework of authority granted to them by spiritual "leaders") and what is not" (Niedźwiadek 1989, p. 179), while propagators "copy and distribute the ideas selected by the creators" (Niedźwiadek 1989, p. 179). Both groups, then, are subordinated to priests, except that propagators are subjected to them through creators. Together, they form the machinery of indoctrination.

As regards the oppressed in the spiritual momentum, Niedźwiadek divides them into: 1) *a merely-faithful* and 2) *a follower*. A being a merely-faithful means to be a passive recipient of the contents of official spiritual messages. A merely-faithful consumes such contents without necessarily identifying with them. A follower, on the other hand, is "spiritually enslaved" and does not take any independent steps toward solving moral dilemmas or satisfying the abovementioned "need for meaning." Priests strive for, on the one hand, extensive rule, that is, "the popularization of the highest number of ideas compatible with the interest of the class of priests" (Niedźwiadek 1989, p. 172) and, on the other hand, intensive rule, that is, the greatest possible influence on the merely-faithful and the most effective transformation them into followers (Niedźwiadek 1989, p. 174).

Niedźwiadek also introduces the notion of a submomentum. A submomentum emerges from a previously uniform momentum when that system, as a whole field, is divided into new, relatively autonomous subsystems as a result of increasing specialization. Thus, there appear "several different systems of the organization of production, systems of controlling the tools, institutional systems, and systems of consciousness" (Niedźwiadek 1989, p. 166) and all those systems are interrelated: the material one with the institutional one, the institutional one with the system of consciousness (Niedźwiadek 1989, p. 166). Niedźwiadek calls that phenomenon a qualitative systemic change in the

THE SOCIAL ROLE OF THE CEREMONIAL

momentum of spiritual production. The systems can be isolated (limited to a level) or complex. That division can also occur by subject matter, for example, a scientific world view may emerge, and a new submomentum can be created. It competes with the 'remainder' of the momentum, that is, for example, the religious submomentum. In such a way, the complexity of the social organization of production grows, which results in the creation of the religious, artistic, and scientific submomentums (Niedźwiadek 1989, p. 178). In Niedźwiadek's opinion, it is those three competing submomentums that comprise, in principle, the spiritual (or cultural) sphere of society – however, the author does not exclude the possibility of the emergence of new submomentums.

5 The Basic Assumptions of Andrzej Falkiewicz's Conception of Culture

The basic anthropological assumption in Falkiewicz's conception is that there is no "self-existent human being" or "human soul," or "inner truth" because the nature of whatever makes us human is *stricte* social (Falkiewicz 1980, p. 9, p. 31, and p. 47). A human being is created by communal requirements and can only exist in a community which carries out the civilizing and humanizing process by way of, for example, education. An individual who would like to object to the norms imposed by the community must refer to other norms, which are also created by society, so he or she only "exchanges one 'public opinion' for another 'public opinion'" (Falkiewicz 1980, p. 34 and p. 42). Thus, total authenticity is impossible. Although society appreciates the 'degree of novelty' contributed by an individual, a human being must be socially created – that is, formatted according to the prevailing cultural patterns – before becoming a creator:

> A human being is created, modeled, and ruled from the outside. All contacts among people are contacts of objects. The necessity of ceremonial, of an external and visible gesture, is already contained in the statement above. Although a person may sometimes have the impression of fighting for freedom, the fight is only for a different kind of bonds which will 'create' – that is, restrict – that person in a different way. To be a human being always means to be outlined from the outside.
>
> FALKIEWICZ 1980, p. 106

It follows that the author of an action – that is, the acting subject – is always a community, even if it operates through individuals (objects). Similarly, the author of thinking is always a community because thinking is a "social process" (Falkiewicz 1980, p. 45 and 89). In Falkiewicz's view, an independent individual is an "unnecessary hypothesis," especially at the 20th-century stage of the development of production, because the freedom of that individual is included in the economic system, and increasingly this only means the "freedom to consume." Thus, the foundation of humanity is not freedom – as humanists would argue – but a community which, let us repeat, constitutes and makes possible the existence of human beings. At the same time, the more developed a society, the more invisible and non-invasive the operation of the system of norms collectively imposed on the individual participating in the social theater (Falkiewicz 1980, p. 54 and p. 61).

Let us take a closer look at the social theater in which an individual actor – the subject of action – functions. Falkiewicz defines the theater as a "material system of contacts" and an "organized system of reactions of a group for the purpose of transmitting those reactions to another group of people." Understood in that way, the theater is a "part of human nature" (Falkiewicz 1980, p. 35 and p. 39). By acting – that is, imitation – we learn to copy the patterns recommended from the top down. Falkiewicz also calls that phenomenon ceremonial or social staging. Social theater mediates and transmits cultural contents. In other words – in Witold Gombrowicz's terms – it constructs form. It is the 'conveyor belt' of what is collectively called the truth. That truth comes to man from the outside, in material form. Some examples of this are a gesture, a dolmen, a pyramid, a religious rite. The archetypal condition of the production of faith was the holy stone which became "the first intersubjectivity" resulting from the amazing discovery that "the object is not me," and it becomes the "truth" and a "symbol of unification" (Falkiewicz 1980, pp. 30–31). The living truth – that is, a truth which is important and inspiring for people – connects the participants of the ceremonial. It is a "way of being" (Falkiewicz 1980, p. 151) practiced en masse. In an individual representative of the species, considered separately from what has been imposed upon him by culture, we only find the basic impulse of survival. Falkiewicz writes about this as follows: "the self-preservation instinct is located in me, an individual, and metaphysical needs are located in people" (Falkiewicz 1980, p. 222). In that approach, the degree of inventiveness and the direction of social evolution will be determined by collective faith, that is, social truth transmitted through the material ceremonial. (Falkiewicz 1980, p. 73) We will return to this issue.

Let us sum it up. Falkiewicz assumes that the whole of human activity is regulated socially, that is, spiritually. For example, society controls the type of clothing or the way of consuming food. All those elements are a part of the ceremonial and have a physical foundation. One example of that could be the

THE SOCIAL ROLE OF THE CEREMONIAL 267

marking of the authority of the President of the Council of Ministers of the Republic of Poland by his suit and the flags behind his back. A priest wears a clerical collar; if the priest was wearing a tracksuit, the words "a husband and wife" would not be performative – unless we agreed on another convention. The nature of those forms, which are modeled collectively, is temporal and historical.

Thus, the ceremonial is a material condition for the existence of spiritual production, or of "materialized collective consciousness" (Falkiewicz [1989b] 2016, p. 30, p. 126). It is worth noting here that Falkiewicz is a materialist who assumes holism and not individualism at the epistemological level (Falkiewicz [1989b]2016, p. 31, p. 35, and p. 47), as was assumed by Nowak (Nowak 1991a, p. 29). Falkiewicz emphasizes the role of spiritual production when he writes that "the changes of technology can necessitate a modification of the ceremonial, but I can also imagine the reverse situation in which changes of the ceremonial entail changes ... in the relations of production and productive forces" (Falkiewicz 1980, p. 160). The latter relation would not be possible within the framework of n-Mhm.

According to Falkiewicz a human being "only exists to the degree of being felt and experienced by others;" the goal of a human being is to leave a mark on society so that "not all of that being's life is wasted" (Falkiewicz 1980, p. 37 and p. 48). At the same time, the superior system is the community, and no individual functions as an enslaver. Individuals are animated by the social organism which is created jointly by those individuals. The nature of spiritual production here, then, is solidaristic (and not antagonistic like in Nowak's theory). Nowak's model is linked with Falkiewicz's theory through ontological individualism (the only thing that exists in society are individuals) and through epistemological holism (we cannot explain the laws governing a community by referring, in a reductive manner, to a lower level, for example, to the psychological mechanisms supposedly governing individuals' choices).

6 Andrzej Falkiewicz's Discussion with Leszek Nowak

Because of his assumptions, the spiritual momentum – contrary to the remaining two (political and economic) momentums – should be treated as a crucial for Falkiewicz. The philosopher argues that before the political rule of a ruler, for example, a general who declares martial law, there is always the ceremonial, that is, the general's hat, uniform, and insignia, which are immediately recognized and considered to be significant by the members of the community. If the community saw the uniform as a funny costume, the political rule could not exist. That means that leading an army (political rule) is preceded by human ceremonial (spiritual power) which always already has a material basis, that is, for example, the said hat (Falkiewicz [1989b] 2016, p. 127). Falkiewicz also writes as follows about that issue:

> You wrongly narrow down the material means of spiritual production to the means of transmission (a medieval monk's parchment, the television network of today); the decisive mechanism here is not that of transmission but of mediation, what I call the ceremonial (a church building, a church ceremony, a banner, statues, marches, etc.).
>
> FALKIEWICZ [1989b] 2016, p. 39

It means that in Falkiewicz's approach, "the material means of spiritual production" also include demonstrations, strikes, pennons, masses for the motherland, or resistors pinned to lapels. It also means equal access to the means of spiritual production, without class division.

As regards Nowak's world view, which consists of a set of myths which satisfy the followers' need for meaning, its counterpart in Falkiewicz's conception is utopia. However, Falkiewicz's definition of that term is broader than in non-Mhm, in which it organizes the thinking of the oppressed about social matters. For Falkiewicz, utopia is the whole of the desires (aims, values) and intuitions of a community. It contains all human aspirations comprised by living culture (Falkiewicz 1989a, p. 292). Its task is to create meaning through material structures. There is room in it for an "unfulfilled remainder," that is, new, creative elements (produced in literature, philosophy, poetry) which have not yet fully become a part of social consciousness – they are still waiting to be realized, and they cannot be embraced in whole by any participant of the ceremonial. Utopia also comprises scientific concepts and is the source of new phenomena – cultural, social, and spiritual – which are "functionally identical with religions" (Falkiewicz [1989b] 2016, p. 196).

Utopia is a part of the homeostatic-azimuthing system. In Falkiewicz's writings, a homeostatis is also called an epistemon, and an azimuth – eschaton. An azimuth (eschaton) is an unconscious (or half-conscious) utopian goal of mankind. It generates an epistemon which grounds and controls the conditions of (scientific or pre-scientific) researchers' experiences. This means that our general human (sometimes not conscious) faith – in salvation, progress, or procedural rationality – comes first. Only after we have decided on a particular azimuth (eschaton), can we adjust our (research, artistic) practice accordingly. For example, for at least two hundred years we have been observing fast scientific progress because we chose the eschaton which led to that. We can admire

THE SOCIAL ROLE OF THE CEREMONIAL   269

Gothic cathedrals because they were built in accordance with an epistemon –
which encompasses the technology for constructing such temples – regulated
by the eschaton of that time, that is, by faith in salvation, which results from
the mass scope and spiritual power of Christianity. The reason why other historical societies have not achieved such technical progress is not because they
were backward but because they have set, consciously or not, other goals for
themselves. Those goals are set at the level of the community. This is a solidaristic understanding of utopia. Everyone participates in it. At the same time, no
individual can control or counter the direction of history on his or her own.

A homeostat-epistemon is a regulator which contains recommendations
about how to realize the selected values. No non-humanistic area of human
life can oppose the power of the prevailing homeostatis, to which it is imper-
ceptibly subordinated (Falkiewicz 1989a, p. 290). Falkiewicz stresses that every
homeostat-epistemon finally wears out and ceases to satisfy the human need
for meaning, especially when it begins to fulfill an ideological function. At that
point, a new eschaton must be prepared. This will, in turn, generate an appropriate homeostat-epistemon which will condition the way of experiencing
reality.

Falkiewicz also reflects on the relation between an individual and a society,
and he tries to add a rung between individual experience and the power of
collective consciousness, that is, between the individual world of inner experience and the homeostatic-azimuthing system. For that purpose, he distinguishes between internal and external individual freedom. External freedom
is freedom "from" (hunger, oppression, coercion), while internal freedom is
a disposition which enables choice even in conditions of objective, physical
enslavement (Falkiewicz 1991, p. 112). Philosophical, artistic, and scientific
creativity depends on the possession of that internal freedom which makes it
possible to modify social patterns and restrictions. A creator is only a creator
insofar as he or she can transcend what is in the world, and for a society, "the
degree of novelty, the creative contribution of every member to the common
pool is [very] important" (Falkiewicz 1980, p. 34). It is the only way in which
an individual may contribute to the prevailing eschaton. Still, an individual is
shaped by the community, and freedom – that is, finding new values – assumes
the form of "running out – toward." If I do not take into account the broader
context of my life and actions, I tend to perceive my activity as rather pointless
(Falkiewicz 1991, p. 122). Thus, an individual's horizon is never only individual,
which is why it indirectly connects with the level of collective consciousness
determined by eschaton (azimuth) and epistemon (homeostatis). It follows
that, generally speaking, humans assign values by identifying with a being
which is larger than them. Individuals accept the interests of other people – of

their families, nations, humanity – as their own. If I were 'radically' rational, I could even give my life for a being larger than I, with which I would identify. In that approach, values are r e q u i r e m e n t s imposed on us by that larger being.

In such a way, Falkiewicz adds a 'binder' which connects individual freedom and the self-existence of an individual's internal world with the suprahuman social being. The social and individual horizons clash. There is a level of individual, human experience, and another, suprahuman, intersubjective level over it, on which we communicate with other representatives of our species. On top of the latter, there is the third level, of social consciousness, of collective thinking (Falkiewicz 1989a, p. 282). It is only on that third level that the said homeostatis (azimuth, eschaton), controlled by collectively professed faith, is created. The already discussed ceremonial ensures a transition between the first and third levels.

Let us summarize the above. Falkiewicz's understanding of 'spiritual momentum' is very broad. In the azimuthing-homeostatic system he defines, which is created by a ceremonial society, there is room not only for linguistic but also for non-verbal, symbolic, and subconscious content. As we have noted, in Nowak's view, ideas are created by "prophets" and managed by the class of "priests" which indoctrinates the followers with the use of the "means of transmission" and which fights – in a Machiavellian reflex action analogous to that of the political momentum – for a broader scope of its spiritual power (Nowak 1991a, p. 171). Falkiewicz, on the other hand, assumes that the condition for practicing a faith is a material medium which fulfills, as we have mentioned, the spiritual function of 'mediating' meaning and founding culture. In this case, it is impossible to keep the economic, political, and spiritual momentums apart. Falkiewicz tries to demonstrate that the material products of man cannot be separated from the spiritual realm. From that perspective, even chair manufacturing depends on spiritual production. Both their being produced and their look result from the technology we possess which is encompassed in the epistemon-homeostat (which defines how we perceive reality and manipulate it). That epistemon-homeostatis, in turn, depends on the collective faith (azimuth-eschaton, that is, a utopia). For Nowak, on the other hand, production and politics are independent from the spiritual realm, and the ceremonial is a means for transmitting the prevailing world view which satisfies the faithfuls' need for meaning (Buczkowski, Klawiter, Nowak 1987, p. 312).

Falkiewicz emphasizes that if such an assumption were accepted, one would have to conclude that Nowak's postulate about the existence of triple rule (with the rulers having simultaneous access to the economic, political, and spiritual momentums) in the Polish People's Republic in the 1980s was

THE SOCIAL ROLE OF THE CEREMONIAL

wrong, and that there were actually "only double rulers who only aspired, ineffectually, to the triple rule" (Falkiewicz [1989b] 2016, p. 31). Although they had the means of mass indoctrination, their position was weak, permanently threatened by the ceremonial of the opposition: masses for the motherland, resistors pinned to lapels, leaflets of the opposition, or texts painted on walls (Falkiewicz [1989b] 2016, p. 129).

To sum up, Falkiewicz claims that having access to the means of public coercion is secondary with respect to the management of the spiritual momentum. That is a culturalist stand. Collectively professed faith plays, through the epistemon, a founding and regulating role in social reality. It does not only invest reality with meanings but also creates conditions for experiencing it and, thereby, for the existence of political power. As we have noted, a general's power is preceded by his hat which s y m b o l i z e s the fact that he is generally c o n s i d e r e d to be a ruler, and a people's tribune by, let us say, being carried by people. Without an advantage in the spiritual realm, it is not possible to retain the economic means, especially political power. That is why the metaphorical "hat" must be taken off the wearer, and power must be "ripped away," in Falkiewicz's words, with the use of *stricte* spiritual means: independent publishing houses and underground press, through a 'battle of ceremonials' " (Falkiewicz [1989b] 2016, p. 60, pp. 128–129). That approach implies the impossibility of complete triple rule. There is always an "unfulfilled remainder," that is, a space in which collectively unrealized values emerge, a life-giving area of unbounded spirituality which enables social evolution (Falkiewicz [1989b] 2016, pp. 164–165). Complete enslavement is impossible, and it has never happened in the history of mankind. If it did, it would stop history.[5] Let us now present a few conclusions.

7   Summary

In non-Marxian historical materialism, class conflict plays a key role in the theory of the spiritual momentum, just like in other momentums. In Falkiewicz's conception of culture, priests and their world view only constitute a fragment of the spiritual reality. None of the participants of the ceremonial has direct access to the highest level – that of utopia (or eschaton, azimuth), and culture (the homeostatic-azimuthing system) encompasses the whole of human

---

5   Let us note that in Nowak's theory, that problem is solved by adding randomness, in the form of "prophets," to the model.

desires and values, whether conscious of not. The definition of Nowak's or Niedźwiadek's world view, despite certain differences and although it satisfies the followers' needs, is closer to what Falkiewicz calls a "degraded utopia" than what he calls an "azimuthing system" or "eschaton."

In Nowak's and Niedźwiadek's approaches, the sphere of the human spirit is another field on which the class conflict takes place. In Buczkowski, Klawiter, and Nowak's approach, "prophets" – who appear randomly in history – bring new values to culture. As we have noted, within the framework of n-Mhm, one can try to predict the probability of the absorption of the new, revolutionary ideas by the prevailing system (for example, by a great, monotheist religion prevalent at the given place and time) or of their contribution to the creation of a new paradigm. For Falkiewicz, the spiritual momentum is an all-embracing sphere of man's spiritual activity which has an impact on the prevailing ways of thinking and research prayers, through a homeostat-epistemon ("good practice," habits, theoretical and material tools, painting techniques, fashions) which is supported by an azimuth-eschaton ("utopia"), that is, for the purpose we are looking for, the final value. The ideologies which serve as a battlefield for priests of various religions and world views who fight for greater power are only reflections, clichés. In the presented concepts, Falkiewicz appears to be convinced that culture has a founding role. The differences between the two approaches can be illustrated in the form of Table 12.1.

I believe that the following issues should be the subject of further research:

i. whether the concept of the means of spiritual production in n-Mhm could be expanded to encompass the "ceremonial," "utopian" cultural production defined by Falkiewicz, including non-verbal means (music, painting, etc.), and what the relations between the means of ceremonial – which contain the whole social, inter-human aspect – and the means of indoctrination should be;[6]

ii. whether Falkiewicz's concept of culture as a homeostatic-azimuthing system could be treated as an exemplification of a classless society in which everyone has equal access to both material forces and the means of production.

---

6 Nowak's and Niedźwiadek's "priests" only call upon the intellect, while Falkiewicz's ceremonial – for example, religious or patriotic – also appeals to embodied emotions.

TABLE. 12.1 A comparison of Falkiewicz's conception of culture and the theory of the spiritual momentum in Non-Marxian historical materialism

The comparative criterion	Leszek Nowak	Andrzej Falkiewicz
The subject matter of collectively practiced faith	A world view consisting of a set of myths	A utopia (also called eschaton or azimuth)
The status of culture	One of three social momentums	Basic Culturalism
The function of culture	Culture satisfies the followers'/adherents' need for meaning and allows them to solve their problems by referring to the ideas propagated by the priests.	It regulates the manner in which the participants of the community experience reality through an epistemon (the actual religious and research practices, artistic styles, etc.), and it determines the direction of social evolution through the eschaton.
The understanding of culture	In the antagonistic understanding, values are the tool of spiritual authority.	In the solidaristic understanding, they bond the human community together and set a purpose for it.

References

Borbone, G. (2016). *Questioni di Metodo. Leszek Nowak e la scienza come idealizzazione.* Roma: Acireale.

Borbone, G. (2021). *The Relevance of Models. Idealization and Concretization in Leszek Nowak.* Műnchen: Grin Verlag.

Brzechczyn, K. (2004). *O wielości linii rozwojowych w procesie historycznym. Próba interpretacji ewolucji społeczeństwa meksykańskiego* [On the Multitude of the Lines of Development in the Historical Process. An Attempt at Interpretation of

Evolution of Mexican Society]. Poznań: Wydawnictwo Naukowe Uniwersytetu im. A. Mickiewicza.

Brzechczyn, K. (2007). On the Application of Non-Marxian Historical Materialism to Development of Non-European Societies. In: J. Brzeziński, A. Klawiter, T.A.F. Kuipers, K. Łastowski, K. Paprzycka, P. Przybysz (ed.), *The Courage of Doing Philosophy. Essays Presented to Leszek Nowak*, pp. 235–254. Amsterdam – New York, NY: Rodopi.

Buczkowski, P. L. Nowak, A. Klawiter (1987). Religia jako struktura klasowa. Przyczynek do nie-Marksowskiego materializmu historycznego [Religion as a Class Structure. A Contribution to non-Marxian Historical Materialism]. *Studia Religiologica*, 20, 271–313.

Coniglione, F. (2010). *Realtà e astrazione. Scuola polacca ed epistemologia post-positivista*. Roma: Bonanno Editore.

Falkiewicz, A. (1980). *Teatr Społeczeństwo* [The Society Theatre]. Wrocław: Ossolineum.

Falkiewicz, A. (1989a). The Anatomy of Utopia. In: L. Nowak (ed.), *Dimensions of Historical Process. Poznań Studies in the Philosophy of the Sciences and the Humanities*, vol. 13, pp. 281–297. Amsterdam: Rodopi.

Falkiewicz, A. ([1989b] 2016). *Jeden i liczba mnoga: o materializmie historycznym i metafizyce unitarnej Leszka Nowaka* [One and Plural Number: on Leszek Nowak's Historical Materialism and Unitarian Metaphysics]. Wrocław: Oficyna Wydawnicza ATUT – Wrocławskie Wydawnictwo Oświatowe.

Falkiewicz, A. (1991). The Individual's Horizon and Valuation. In: P. Buczkowski (ed.), *The Social Horizon of Knowledge. Poznań Studies in the Philosophy of the Sciences and the Humanities*, vol. 22, pp. 111–128. Amsterdam/Atlanta: Rodopi.

Niedźwiadek, K. (1985). Struktura i rozwój momentu produkcji duchowej [The Structure and Development of the Momentum of Spiritual Production]. In: P. Buczkowski, A. Klawiter (eds.), *Klasy – światopogląd – idealizacja*, pp. 17–45. Poznań: PWN.

Niedźwiadek K. (1989). The Structure and Development of the Society's Mode of Spiritual Production. In: L. Nowak (ed.). *Dimensions of Historical Process*, pp. 157–181. Amsterdam: Rodopi.

Nowak, L. (1980). *The Structure of Idealization. Towards a Systematic Interpretation of the Marxian Idea of Science*. Dordrecht: Reidel.

Nowak L. (1983). *Property and Power. Towards a non-Marxian Historical Materialism* (Theory and Decision Library, t. 27). Dordrecht/Boston/Lancaster: Reidel.

Nowak, L. (1988). Spiritual Domination as a Class Oppression: A Contribution to the Theory of Culture in Non-Marxian Historical Materialism. *Philosophy of Social Sciences* 18, 231–238.

Nowak, L. (1991a). *U podstaw teorii socjalizmu* [The Foundations of the Theory of Socialism]; vol. 1: *Własność i władza. O konieczności socjalizmu* [Property and Power. On the Necessity of Socialism]. Poznań: Nakom.

Nowak, L. (1991b). *U podstaw teorii socjalizmu* [The Foundations of the Theory of Socialism]; vol. 3: *Dynamika władzy. O strukturze i konieczności zaniku socjalizmu* [The Dynamics of Power. On the Structure of Socialism and the Necessity of its Disappearance] Poznań: Nakom.

Nowak L. (1991c). *Power and Civil Society. Toward a Dynamic Theory of Real Socialism.* New York: Greenwood Press.

Nowak, L. (2022). Religion as a Class Structure: A Contribution to non-Marxian Historical Materialism. In: K. Brzechczyn (ed.) *New Developments in Theory of Historical Process. Contributions to Non-Marxian Historical Materialism. Poznań Studies in the Philosophy of the Sciences and the Humanities,* vol 119, pp. 3–51. Leiden/Boston: Brill.

Index of Names

Ahmad, Eqbal 190, 191
Ajdukiewicz, Kazimierz 17, 18, 84, 88–90, 97, 105
Althusser, Louis 19, 28, 37
Amin, Samir 20, 23
Anderson, Perry 13, 14
Ansell, Christopher 239, 256
Appelbaum, Richard E. 14
Arendt, Hannah 249
Aristotle 17, 135
Arrighi, Giovanni 20, 23

Balibar, Etienne 19
Banach, Stefan 17
Banaszak, Tomasz 85, 105, 248–250, 254–256
Barach, Peter 227, 235
Basham, Arthur Llewellyn 128, 157
Beaney, Michael 90, 105
Będkowski, Marcin 85, 88–91, 101, 105
Bell, Daniel 77, 79
Berlin, Isaiah 20, 41, 43
Bettin Lattes, Gianfranco 227, 235
Bluhm, Harald 240, 241, 256
Bobbio, Norberto 232, 235
Bocheński, Józef Maria 17
Bois, Guy 14
Bolotnikov, Ivan 10
Borbone, Giacomo xi, xii, xvi, 19, 37, 56, 59, 79, 80, 81, 163, 191, 217, 228, 235, 259, 273
Borowska, Ewa 112, 125
Boudon, Raymond 231, 235
Bratkiewicz, Jarosław 112, 125
Braudel, Fernand 23
Bręgiel-Benedyk, Marta ix, xii
Bręgiel-Pant, Marta xi
Brien, Kevin M. 14
Brown, Norman W. 140, 157
Brożek, Anna 85, 89, 91, 101, 105
Brzechczyn, Krzysztof viii, ix, xi–xiii, xiv, xvi, 3, 18, 19, 22, 26, 37, 46, 55–60, 80–83, 90, 106, 119, 120, 125, 131, 133, 158–160, 163, 180, 182, 183, 188, 190–192, 207, 208, 210–214, 217, 222, 225, 226, 235–237, 256, 257, 260, 261, 273–275
Brzeziński, Jerzy xiii, 39, 54, 83, 125, 158, 159, 194, 214, 274

Buchanan, James 47, 54
Buczkowski, Piotr 59, 73, 80, 81, 159, 192, 222, 235, 259, 261, 263, 270, 272, 274
Burawoy, Michael 175, 192
Burbelka, Jolanta 34, 37, 38
Busino, Giovanni 227, 235, 237

Cardoso, Fernando 23
Chavance, Bernard xiii
Chmielewski, Piotr 112, 125
Chodak, Jarosław 190, 192
Christiano, Tom 239, 256
Chwalisz, Piotr 77, 80
Chybińska, Alicja 85, 89, 91, 101, 105
Ciesielski, Mieszko vii, ix, xii, 58, 80, 85, 92, 98, 106, 131, 158, 160, 180, 192, 237
Cohen, Gerald Allan 20, 38, 42
Coniglione, Francesco 17, 38, 59, 80, 83, 163, 192, 217, 236, 259, 274
Czajkowski, Waldemar x, 21, 27, 31, 38
Czerwińska-Schupp, Ewa 80, 191

Daly, Chris 89, 106
Davies, Matthew I. J. 112, 125
Deneen, Patrick 53, 55
Derrida, Jacques 13
Dunn, Stephen P. 112, 125

Egiert, Robert 82, 159, 163, 192
Elster, Jon 42
Etzioni-Halevy, Eva 195–197, 199–214, 227

Falkiewicz, Andrzej xii, 85, 92, 105, 106, 258, 259, 265–274
Frank, Andre Gunder x, 20, 23–25
Frege, Gottlob 17, 20
Freud, Sigmund 6
Fukuyama, Francis 5, 14, 43, 44, 53, 55
Furtado, Celso 23

Gadamer, Hans-Georg 14
Gangānātha, Jhā 128, 158
Garcia de la Sierra, Adolfo 18, 38
Gellner, Ernest 77, 81
Genett, Timm 242, 244, 256
Gerratana, Valentino 236

278 INDEX OF NAMES

Giedymin, Jerzy 18, 105
Godelier, Maurice 19
Goedel, Kurt 17
Goldfrank, Walter L. 190, 192
Gombrowicz, Witold 31, 84, 85, 92–93, 95,
    97–100, 104–106, 163, 266
Gomułczak, Aleksandra xi, xvi
Gottlieb, Roger S. 14
Graca, Laura da 112, 125
Gramsci, Antonio 228, 236
Greczko, Iwo xii, xvi
Gregor, Mary 236
Gronov, Jukka 14, 15
Guala, Francesco 229, 236
Guggenheim, Scott E. 194

Habermas, Jurgen 14, 19, 20, 38
Halas, Juraj 19, 38
Hands, Gordon 243, 256
Harsanyi, John 47
Hegel, Georg Wilhelm Friedrich 18, 21, 87, 201
Heller, Włodzimierz 82
Hirst, Paul 14, 15
Hochfeld, Jerzy 251
Huxley. Aldous 32

Isaak, Jeffrey C. 14, 15
Ivanyk, Stepan 105

Jadacki, Jacek 85, 87, 90, 107
Janiszewski, Zygmunt 17
Jay, Martin 14, 15

Kant, Immanuel 232, 233, 236
Karczyńska, Eliza ix, xii, xiii, 80, 106, 160,
    192, 237
Käsler, Dirk 240, 256
Keddie, Nikki Ragozin 190, 192
Keller, Suzanne 227, 236
Khmelnytsky, Bohdan 10
Kiedrowski, Krzysztof 75, 77, 78, 79, 81
Kieniewicz, Jan 157, 158
Klawiter, Andrzej xiii, 16, 38, 39, 54, 59, 73,
    80–83, 125, 158, 159, 192, 214, 222, 235,
    258, 259, 261, 263, 270, 272, 274
Klerk de, Frederik Willem 25
Kołakowski, Leszek 43
Kościelniak, Cezary 136, 158
Kostka-Napierski, Aleksander 10
Kotarbińska, Janina 18

Kotarbiński, Tadeusz 17, 18
Krause, Skadi 240, 241, 256
Krygier, Martin 236
Kudelska, Marta 140, 158
Kuipers, Theo A.F. xiii, 39, 54, 83, 125, 158,
    214, 274
Kymlicka, Will 53, 55

Lange, Oskar 18, 221
Łastowski, Krzysztof xiii, 16, 39, 54, 85, 106,
    107, 125, 158, 163, 192, 194, 214, 235, 274
Laurence, Michael 239, 256
Le Bon, Gustave 232, 236
Leśmian, Bolesław 19
Leśniewski, Stanisław 18, 97
Lindenbaum, Alfred 18
Lipset, Seymour Martin 240, 241, 243, 257
Lombardini, Siro 237
Łukasiewicz, Jan 18
Lukes, Steven 14, 15
Lunn, Eugene 14, 15
Luxemburg, Rosa 23
Lyotard, Jean-Francois 20

Mączak, Antoni 14, 15
Malewski, Andrzej 18
Mandela, Nelson 25
Mann, Michael 28, 29, 38
Marx, Karl vii, 6, 8, 14, 25, 27, 31, 33–35, 42,
    43, 45, 46, 73, 78, 102–104, 112, 163, 164,
    217, 218, 221–224, 226, 232, 233
Menke, Regina xii, 229, 236
Michalski, Franciszek S. 158
Michels, Robert 216, 217, 227, 229, 236,
    238–257
Mikołajec, Jarosław 38
Milner, Murray, Jr. 239, 257
Modzelewski, Karol 10, 15
Moore, George Edward 20
Morgan, Ruth A. 112, 125
Morishima, Michio 42
Mosca, Gaetano 195, 216, 217, 227–229, 236, 241
Mussolini, Benito 240

Nichols, Elizabeth 175, 190, 192
Niedźwiadek, Krzysztof 192, 258, 259, 263–
    265, 270, 272, 274
Nietzsche, Friedrich 13
Niewiadomski, Marek 58, 81, 181, 193
Norkus, Zenonas 186, 193

INDEX OF NAMES

Nowak, Andrzej 191
Nowak, Leszek vii–xiv, 3–22, 26–28, 30–34, 38, 40–47, 52–55, 58–79, 81–107, 111, 119, 125, 129–133, 136, 143, 158–161, 163, 178, 180, 181, 185, 186, 192, 193, 195, 205–208, 210, 211, 213–229, 233–243, 245, 247–254, 256–263, 267, 268, 270–275
Nowak, Marek 191
Nowakowa, Izabela 58, 59, 63, 75, 77, 83, 86, 87, 90, 107, 130, 163, 193
Nozick, Robert x, 40, 41, 44, 46–55

Olson, Mancur 8, 15
Orlik, Piotr 158
Ossowski, Stanisław 17

Pakszys, Elżbieta 193
Paprzycka, Katarzyna xiii, 21, 38, 39, 54, 82, 85, 106, 107, 125, 158, 159, 214, 235, 274
Paprzycki, Marcin xii, 38, 213, 215, 235
Pareto, Vilfredo xi, xii, 195, 216, 217, 227–235, 237, 241
Parry, Geraint 227, 237
Paul, Cedar 257
Paul, Eden 257
Paul, G.A. 107
Popper, Karl Raimund 20, 22, 41, 43, 56, 226, 237
Porshnev, Boris 6
Post, Emil 18
Poulantzas, Nikos 19
Price, David H. 112, 126, 171
Przybysz, Piotr x, xiii, 39, 47, 54–56, 82, 93, 107, 158, 159, 213, 214, 256, 274
Pugachev, Yemelyan 10
Putnam, Hilary 12

Quine, Willard Van Orman 86, 89, 97, 105, 107

Raffini, Luca 1
Rawls, John 47, 54, 56
Rorty, Richard 5, 14
Roemer, John 13, 15
Rogacz, Dawid vii, ix, xiv
Rostow, Walt W. 162, 194
Russell, Bertrand 89, 90, 97, 105, 107
Rutkowska, Karolina xi, 227, 237
Ryan, Michael 13, 15
Ryle, Gilbert 90, 91, 105, 107

Salamucha, Jan 18
Sandel, Michael 53, 56
Sawala, Krzysztof 257
Sawer, Marian 112, 126
Schumpeter, Joseph 241
Siegel, Achim 58, 83
Sierpiński, Wacław 17
Silski, Jerzy 191
Skocpol, Theda xi, 161–180, 183–190, 194
Słuszkiewicz, Eugeniusz 128, 159
Sobieraj, Iwona 38
Sorel, Georges Eugene 241
Strawson, Peter 90, 107
Such, Jan 193

Tarski, Alfred 17, 18
Taylor, Michael 175, 194
Thapar, Romila 128, 156, 157, 159
Tomczak, Grzegorz 58, 83, 187, 194
Topolski, Jerzy x, 18, 19, 38, 39, 59, 83
Torpey, John 176, 194
Traczykowski, Dominik 105
Trimberger, Ellen Kay 194
Tullock, Gordon 54
Twardowski, Kazimierz 16, 18, 19

Ulmen, G. L. 112, 126

Wallerstein, Immanuel x, 20, 23–28, 39, 162
Weber, Max 6, 165, 229, 241, 247
Weller, Robert P. 194
Wesołowski, Włodzimierz 191
Wiegner, Adam 18
Wiśniewski, Jan 193
Wittfogel, Carl August 111–119, 122, 124, 126
Wittgenstein, Ludwig 13
Wnuk-Lipiński, Edmund 28, 39
Woleński, Jan 17, 39, 85, 88, 89, 90, 101, 105–107
Wood, Allen 42

Zamiara, Krystyna 55
Zarębski, Tomasz ix, xi, xiv, xvii, 131, 159, 160
Zeidler, Paweł xiii
Zeidler-Janiszewska, Anna 193
Zielińska, Renata 75, 83
Zingarelli, Andrea 125
Żyromski, Marek 196, 214, 215

Subject Index

absorption
  of elites   xi, 195, 196, 203, 204, 205, 208, 209, 210, 211, 212
    progressive   195, 212
    regressive   195, 212
abstraction   xi, 46, 57, 58, 75–79
agrarian despotism   111, 117
analytical Marxism   3, 20, 42
antagonicity   vii–ix

ceremonial   258, 259, 265, 266, 267, 268, 270, 271, 272
civil society   68, 69, 176, 207, 209, 247–249, 252, 253, 255
class structure   26, 111, 114, 119, 121, 124, 128, 165, 167, 172
comparative historical sociology   163, 190
concretization   xi, 12, 21, 32, 36, 54, 57–59, 61, 63, 65–67, 70, 71, 74–76, 78, 79, 216, 229, 230, 241, 247

de-abstraction   57, 58, 75–79
democracy   xii, 5, 42, 43, 44, 173, 178, 195–205, 208, 209, 227, 232, 238, 239, 240–242, 244, 252, 255
destabilization   xi, 57, 58, 77, 79

elite theory   195, 196, 209, 213, 216, 238, 239, 240, 241

feudalism   3, 4, 10, 14, 46, 63, 64, 65, 185

historiosophy   ix, x, 16, 17, 20–22, 29, 30, 32, 34, 35–37, 40–47, 52–54, 102
holism   vii, 61, 267
homeostatic-azimuthing system   258, 259, 268, 269, 271, 272
hydraulic society
  in general   111, 114, 116, 117, 118, 122, 124
  semicomplex   xi, 115, 118
  complex   115, 116, 118, 123, 124
  theocratic   xi, 117, 118, 122, 123
  quasi-hierocratic   118

idealization   xi, 19, 20, 21, 23, 25, 27, 41, 45, 46, 57, 58, 59, 61, 74–76, 78, 79, 84, 95, 97, 98, 130, 131, 163, 212, 216, 217, 220, 221, 224, 230, 231, 234, 238, 247
Indian society   127, 128, 136, 155
interpretation   xi, 7, 8, 11, 13, 16, 19, 20, 22, 23, 25, 45, 60, 61, 74, 84, 85, 90–95, 98, 100, 127, 129, 130, 140, 157, 163, 220, 221, 241, 242, 252

liberal historiosophy   x, 40–47, 52, 53, 54

Marxism   vii, 4, 7, 9, 11, 13, 17, 19, 20, 26, 40–43, 45, 53, 104, 162, 221, 240, 247, 260
Methodology   x, 19, 25, 43, 44, 57–79, 84, 163, 216, 217, 219, 222, 229
modernization   161, 162, 163, 164, 165, 166, 172, 177, 178, 188, 189

non-Christian model of man   60, 68, 69, 84, 94, 95, 247

paraphrase   x, xi, 84, 85–92, 94, 95, 97–101, 105, 111, 119, 122, 124, 161, 163, 167, 177–179, 180, 185–190, 209, 212
philosophy of history   vii, 3, 16, 17, 21, 43
Poznań School of Methodology   xvi, 16, 59, 163, 259

rationality   20, 42, 84, 92, 101, 104, 175, 181, 182
  irrationality   68, 102
  counter-rationality   101
real socialism   viii

social revolution   161, 164, 165, 172, 173, 174, 186, 190, 218, 219
social structure   vii, 27, 29, 31, 123, 127, 129, 133, 135, 138, 153, 162, 168, 184, 197, 248
solidarism   46, 53, 258
spiritual momentum   78, 258–272
spiritual production   57, 72–78, 103, 141, 206, 228, 247–262, 264, 265, 267, 268, 270, 272
stabilization   x, 57, 58, 77–79

theory of power   xii, 41, 57, 58, 59, 60, 65, 67, 68, 69, 71, 74, 76, 77, 179, 180, 195, 209, 210, 213, 238, 243, 247–254
theory of property   57, 58, 60–66, 68, 73, 76

Printed in the United States
by Baker & Taylor Publisher Services